Darwin:
A Photographic History

Matthew Stephen

First Published in 2018

GPO Box 4766, Darwin, Northern Territory, 0801.

ISBN: 978-0-646-99230-3

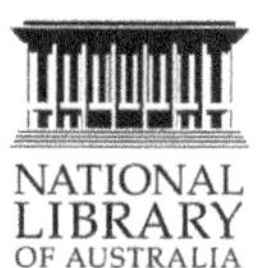

A catalogue record for this book is available from the National Library of Australia

Front Cover:

Top: Darwin 2017. Image courtesy of the Darwin Waterfront Corporation. (Unknown, DWC, Image Collection, DJI_0123.)

Bottom: Darwin, arial view, c1930. (Unknown, NTAS, Charles Wilson Collection, NTRS 3335 Item 284.)

Layout and design by UniPrint, Charles Darwin University, Darwin NT 0909, Australia

Printed in 2018

Author's Note

I have always had a fascination with historic photographs. One of my family's prized possessions is the *Official History of Australia in the War of 1914-1918*, edited by C.E.W. Bean. Before I could read any of the 12 volumes I could look through volume XII, *Photographic Record of the War*. I am forever grateful to my parents that our house was full of history books. Fast forward to my career as a historian in the Northern Territory where I quickly realised that many of our shared histories are documented in photographs as often as in text. When viewing photographs with others I am always surprised by how the discussion will reveal so many stories and characters beyond the images we are looking at. As my obsession with photographs deepened so did my desire share this experience with a wider audience; *Darwin: A Photographic History* is the result.

One of Darwin's charms is that it remains a small town in many respects. The history, heritage, library and archives community is a small but dedicated group. My thanks to all of the staff at the Northern Territory Library, Archives Service, Place Names Register, Heritage Branch, and Darwin City Council Records Office who have assisted me in the development of this book. Thanks also to Regis Martin for his fine photographs which have brought this history up to date; and to Norm Cramp, Director of the Darwin Military Museum and Bob Shewring, President of the Returned Serviceman's League Darwin Sub-Branch, for assisting with my many queries regarding World War II sites around Darwin. Finally a special thanks to Georga and Tess for keeping me grounded and my partner Robyn Aitken for her editing and steadfast and patient support in all my endeavours.

Dr. Matthew Stephen

Caution

This book includes images and names of deceased people that may cause distress to Aboriginal and Torres Strait Islander peoples.

Contents

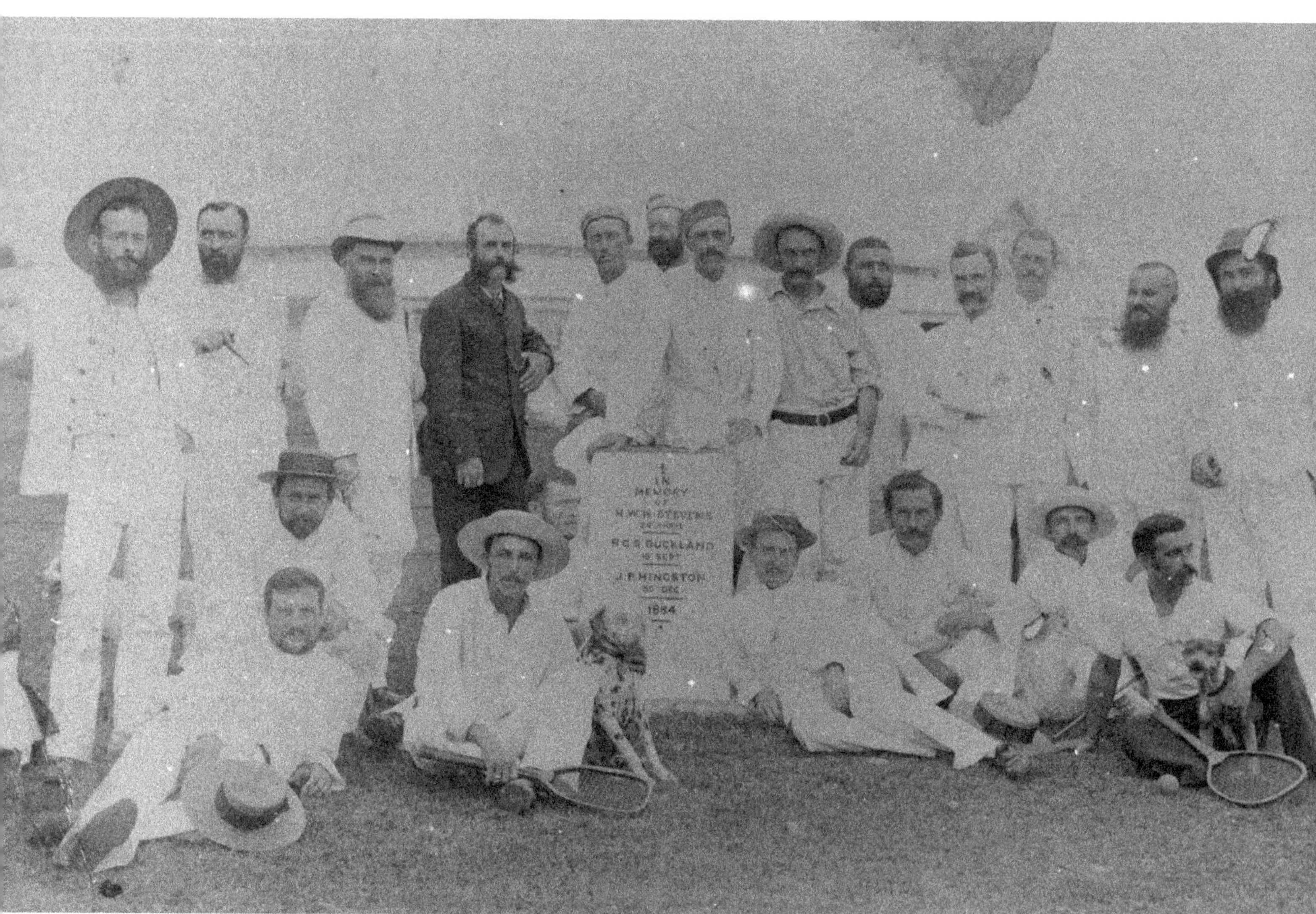

Group of men, possibly customs, BAT or Overland Telegraph staff, near a memorial erected in 1884 to H.W.H. Stevens, R.C.S. Buckland and J.R. Hingston. This is a 'mock' memorial because all of the men mentioned on it are alive at the time. It is perhaps a special 'gift' to the group or to mark a special occasion from their Palmerston gentlemen friends. (unknown, SLSA, Searcy Collection, PRG 280/1/2/232.)

Darwin ~ *Garrmalang*

Introduction

Darwin is Australia's northern most capital city located at 12° 25' South latitude and 130° 50' East longitude. It is Australia's only capital city situated in the tropics. The climate is defined by a 'Wet' season (October to April) with an average rainfall of 1660 millimetres and a 'Dry' (May to September) with almost no rain. The average daytime maximum temperature is 32 degrees Celsius and the average daytime minimum temperature 23 degrees Celsius. At night, the temperature rarely falls below 20 degrees Celsius.

Compared to other Australian state capitals Darwin's European history from 1869 is short but eventful. Despite this relatively short history very little of Darwin's built heritage remains. Consequently, it is difficult for locals and visitors to get a sense of the city's past or how it has evolved. The purpose of this book is to provide a glimpse of the physical and social evolution of Darwin. It is a fascinating and colourful history that explores Darwin's colonial origins as South Australia's Northern Territory, the Commonwealth's Northern Territory from 1911 to 1978 when it gained Self-Government, Darwin's role in World War I and II, and the city's resilience in the face of cyclones that threatened to destroy the city in 1897, 1937 and 1974.

Darwin or *Garrmalang* is situated upon Larrakia land. The Larrakia are the traditional owners of the land and waters of the greater Darwin region. They have always maintained their connections to the region and continue to do so. The Kenbi Land claim, commenced in 1979 and settled in 2016, was the longest running Aboriginal land claim in Australian history. It is testament to the patience and resolve of the Larrakia people. Although Darwin is built upon Larrakia land its Aboriginal history is significant to Aboriginal people from across the Northern Territory. While this history touches upon the Aboriginal history of Darwin it cannot do justice to its full depth and breadth. Where possible the Larrakia name for locations is included to acknowledge the Larrakia people and their continuous connection to the land.[1] For those wanting to gain a fuller understanding of this history the bibliography provides a starting point.

Darwin has always been a cosmopolitan city. Until 1911 when the Commonwealth Government took control, the European population was outnumbered by the Aboriginal and Chinese communities. Census figures at this time indicate that the town of only 1380 people was one of Australia's most cosmopolitan. Represented in this number were: '442 Chinese, 374 Europeans, 247 Aborigines, 81 Japanese, 60 Filipinos, 49 Javanese, 24 Malays, 4 Siamese, 5 Cingalese, 5 South sea Islanders'.[2] This was completely contrary to the Commonwealth's 'White Australia' immigration policy of the time.

---

1 After consultation the advice I received on Larrakia place names is that there is no clear, authoritive list and they tend to change over time. Consequently the sources cited were considered appropriate. Cooper, Robert, Larrakia Nation Aboriginal Corporation, CEO, Personal communication, email, 3 October 2018, & Lee, Bilawara, Larrakia Elder, Personal communication, email, 16 October 2018.

2 Donovan, *At the Other End of Australia*, 4.

Throughout its history Darwin has been perceived by southern Australia as the frontier. Isolation from a distant 'Southern' Government has been both a blessing and a curse. It was easy for Governments from all eras to ignore North Australia and deny it the resources and infrastructure to develop to its full potential. Darwin has responded with a pride in being different to the rest of Australia and defying convention by going its own way. One blessing is that it has always been a vibrant multicultural place despite Government policies and is even more cosmopolitan today than it was in earlier times. To many it is these qualities that give the city its character and dynamism.

Darwin is fortunate that its European history has been documented in photographs. This book largely draws upon public photographic collections. Thousands of photographs were considered but ultimately only a small number were selected to illustrate the social and physical history of the sites chosen. A brief history of each site is provided but for those who would like to know more they should consider the bibliography as a starting point.

When Darwin was first settled in 1869 it was named Palmerston. By the 1900s the town was often referred to as Port Darwin. In 1911, when the Australian Commonwealth Government assumed control of the Northern Territory, the town was formally renamed Darwin. Generally I refer to Darwin in the context of its history but also use Palmerston or Port Darwin in the context of the colonial period. In broad terms Darwin's history can be broken into 5 periods.

1869 – 1911: The Colonial period

The colonial period includes the initial European settlement in 1869 and the events that shaped the early development of the Northern Territory under the South Australian Government. These events include the Overland Telegraph, gold discoveries, the

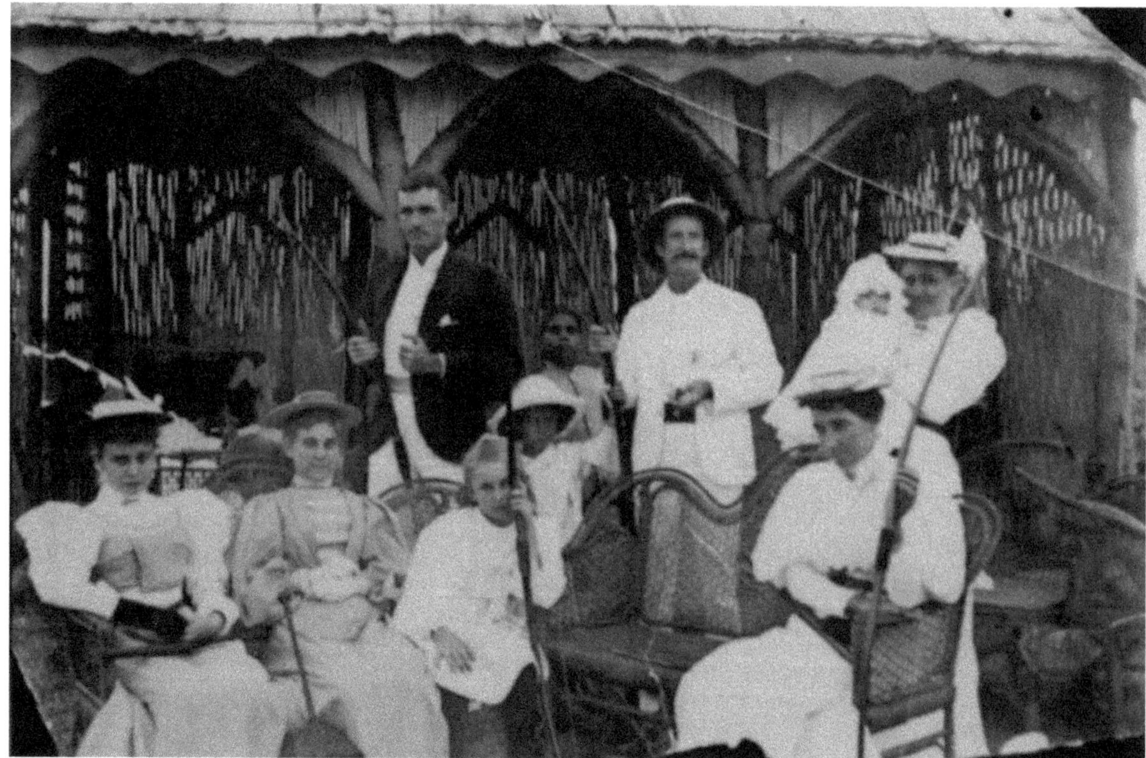

Palmerston Archery Club on The Esplanade Oval, c1887. (Unknown, NTL, Peter Spillett Collection, PH0238-2104.) See also photo B24245 on page 90 which appears to be a formal photo of the same group.

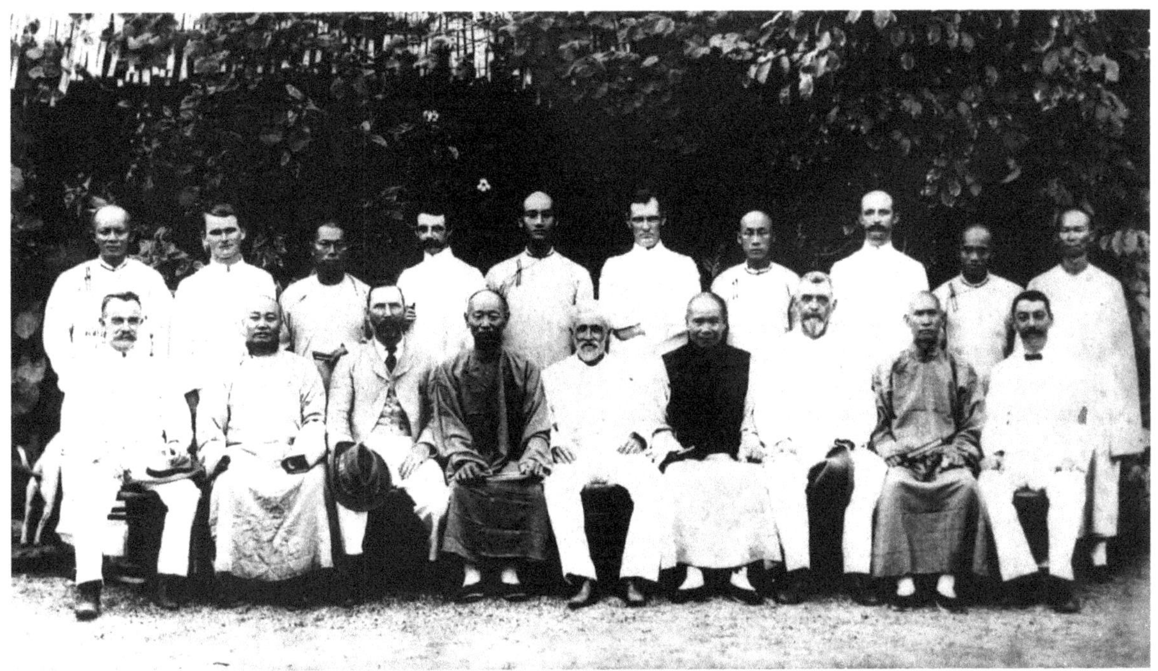

Darwin Businessmen, c1908. The European and Chinese business communities were not always united. This photo is one of the occasions they came together. Top Row (L-R): C. Hang Kim, P. Kelsey, Cheong Wo, J.M. Corr, Chin Pack Sue, W.C.P. Bell, Yen NgKan, F.E. Nicholl, Ah Sang, Chin Toy.
Bottom Row (L-R): G. McKeddie, Wing Wah Loong, A. Cameron, Chin Yam Yan, V.V. Brown, Yet Loong, E. Luxton, Wing Cheong Sing, Unknown, P.L. Brown. (Unknown, NTAS, Tamblyn Collection, NTRS 927 Item Applic.)

Northern Railway and the handover of the Territory to the Commonwealth Government.

Economic development of Palmerston and the Northern Territory during this period was erratic and modest at best. Gold mining bought some prosperity in the 1870s and 1880s and was the catalyst for building the Northern Railway. Misplaced optimism in the pastoral and farming industries foundered on a lack of understanding of the climate and soils and distant markets. The pearling industry gave a boost to the economy in the late 19th century but scattered pearl beds, dramatic tides and muddy waters meant that few profited. Mining, the railway, and the pearling industry all attracted immigrants to Palmerston from across south-east Asia. Chinese immigrants did the majority of labouring work while many others established businesses in Palmerston. Thursday Islanders, Malays, Filipinos, Indonesians and Japanese provided specialised labour to the pearling industry and made Palmerston one of the most diverse populations in North Australia. The minority European community were concentrated mainly in the government public service and staff of the postal and communications services. They also formed a small but influential business community. Despite their relatively small numbers the European community, like all British colonial outposts, dominated the political, economic and social life of Palmerston at a time when the 'White Australia' policy was developed in the run up to the Federation of Australia in 1901.

In 1897 Palmerston was hit by the first of three severe cyclones that would devastate the town over the next 100 years. It destroyed many buildings while Chinatown was almost totally wrecked. Eighteen pearling luggers were lost or severely damaged and 28 residents were killed. After the Federation of Australia when South Australia joined the newly federated nation of Australia it was clear that it did not have the financial resources to successfully develop its Territory. Instead, eleven years after Federation, South Australia saw the opportunity to hand the Territory over to the Commonwealth Government, which took control in 1911.

1911-1939: The Inter-war period

At the time of the Commonwealth takeover of the Northern Territory its population totalled 3,272 made up of 2,673 Males and 598 females. The Northern Territory *1911 Administrators Report* proudly stated 'It is worthy of note that this is the first year in the history of Northern Territory settlement in which the population has been predominated by the European race.'[3] The pride was somewhat misplaced. Although the European component of the population was counted at just over 50% of the total, Aboriginal people were excluded from census statistics. The Chinese community remained a large minority while there were also smaller Japanese, Malay and Filipino communities. The Commonwealth began its regime in the Northern Territory with great optimism and commissioned numerous reports into its potential. However, little had been achieved before the outbreak of World War I in 1914.

Darwin was transformed by World War I and the development of the Vesteys Meatworks and Freezing Works. The British Vesteys company bought industrialisation to the Northern Territory for the first time. Although only short lived, Vesteys changed the social and physical landscape of Darwin. Another major development after 1919 was the rapid development of air travel. When Ross and Keith Smith, Jim Bennett and Wally Sheirs landed their Vickers Vimy heavy bomber at Darwin's newly created airfield in December 1919 they won The Great Air Race from England to Australia and made Darwin Australia's international aviation gateway.

Post World War I was a period of economic depression for Darwin and the Northern Territory. Darwin's fortunes were further eroded between 1927 and 1931 when the Commonwealth divided the Northern Territory into two territories with Alice Springs as its southern capital. Like so many Territory innovations this too was short lived.

The economic doldrums did not change until Darwin was recognised as an important defence base for Australia's north. The construction of defence infrastructure during the 1930s slowly bought the town back to life. Darwin's population grew from 1500 in June 1932 to 3653 in June 1939.[4] The development around the Civilian Airfield resulted in the growth of the suburbs of Parap and Fannie Bay. Darwin was again severely damaged by a cyclone in 1937 but this time only one life was lost.

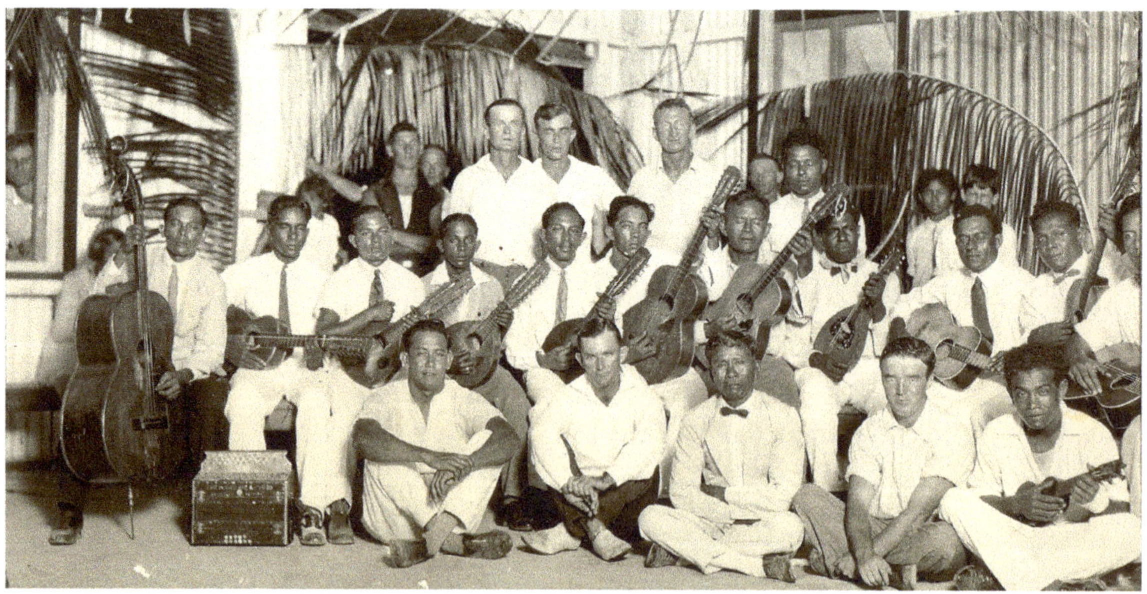

Darwin String Band, c1930. (Unknown, NTAS, Charles Wilson Collection, NTRS 335 Item 330.)

3 Northern Territory, *Report of the Acting Administrator*, 1911, 15.
4 Carment, David., *Australia's Northern Capital*, 12.

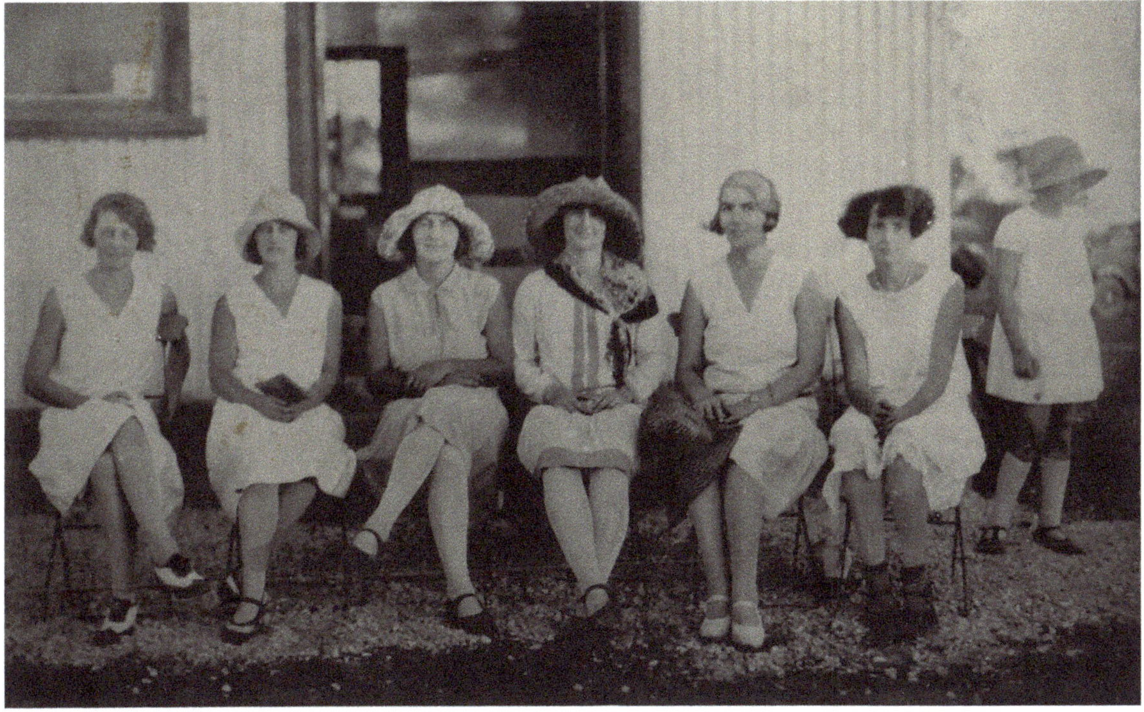

Darwin Golf Club ladies, Fannie Bay, c1935. (Unknown, NTAS, HSNT Collection, NTRS1854 Item 845.)

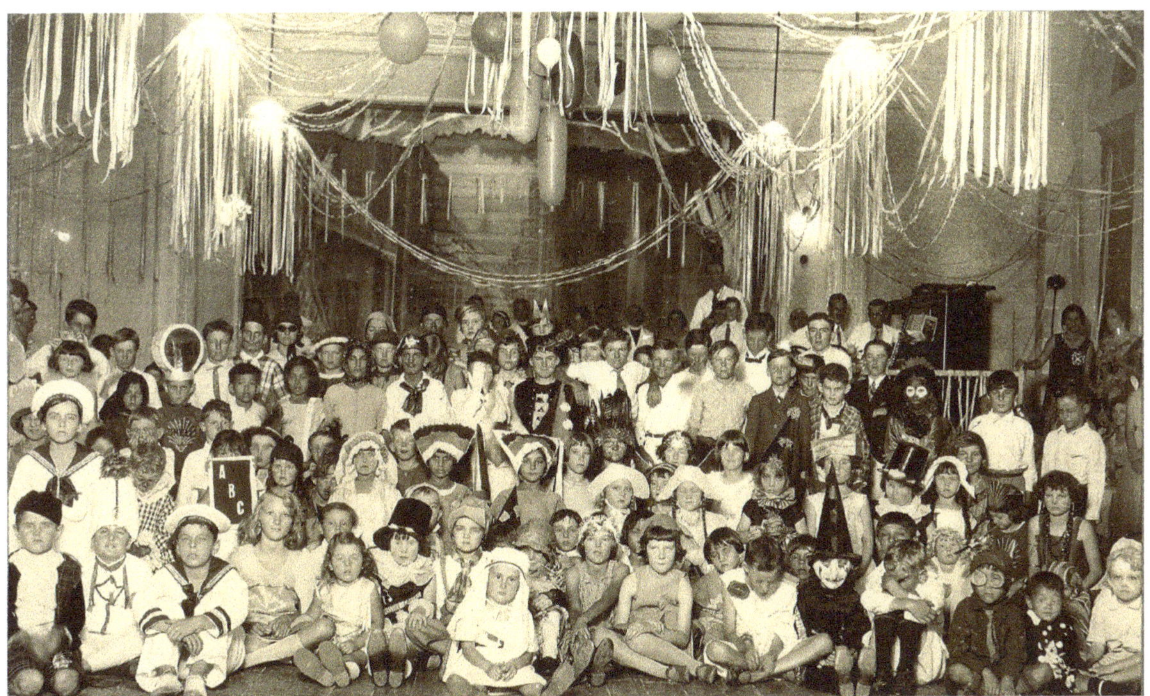

Children's Ball, c1930. (Unknown, NTAS, Charles Wilson Collection, NTRS 335 Item 388.)

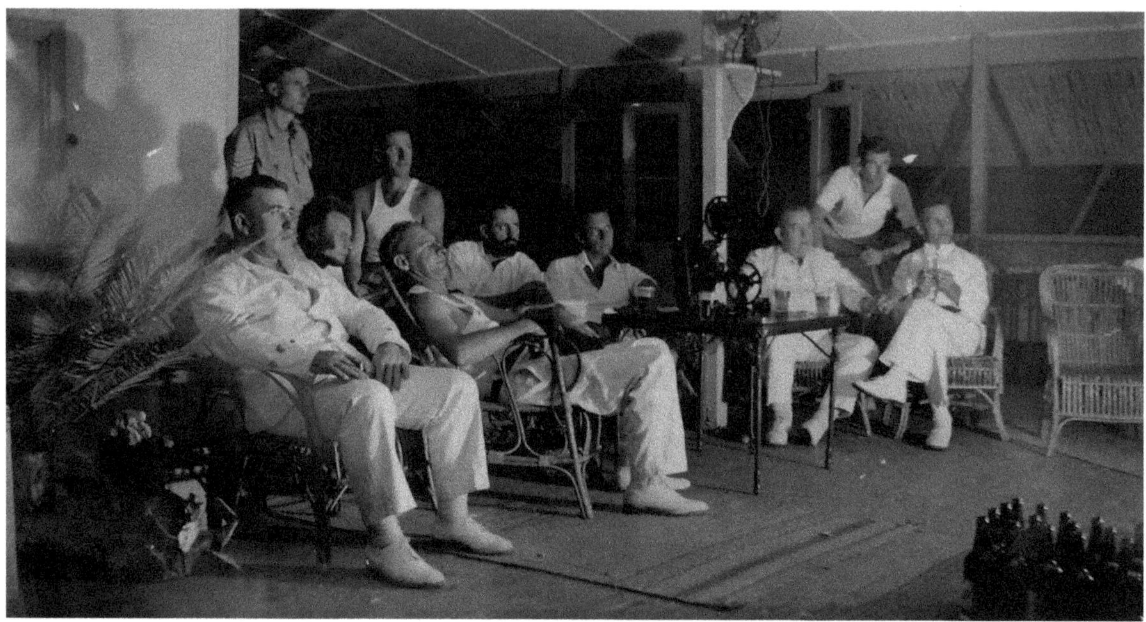

Film night at the Officers Mess, Larrakeyah Barracks, c1938. (Unknown, Angus Bird, Personal Collection, 104.)

1939-1945: World War II

World War II impacted the Northern Territory like no other part of Australia. After Japan entered the war in 1941 and began to advance towards Australia the majority of the civilian population was evacuated from the town between December and January 1942. They would not return for the duration of the war. The bombing of Darwin, on 19 February 1942 and the resultant 263 deaths, remains the deadliest military attack on Australia. Much of Darwin was destroyed or severely damaged by the air raids. The civilian administration of the Territory was transferred to Alice Springs. The air raids on northern Australia and Darwin continued until November 1943. At its height, in February 1944, the military population of the Northern Territory reached 63 690.[5] In many respects the war bought Darwin and the Northern Territory into the Australian consciousness for the first time. It also saw the population soar briefly and the development of much needed infrastructure. By the war's end this included the sealing of the Stuart Highway to Alice Springs, greatly enhanced wharf facilities, a new hospital and vastly improved water and power supplies.

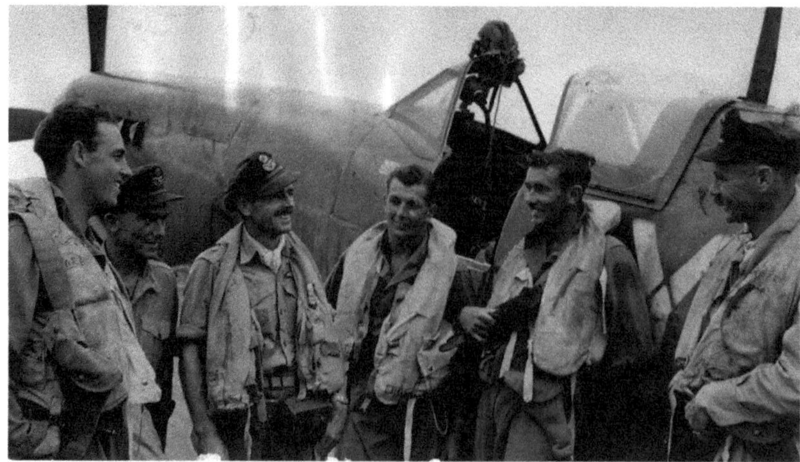

R.A.A.F. and R.A.F. Spitfire pilots based in Darwin, c1943. L-R: F/O. J. A. Pretty (Melbourne, Vic.), F/Lt. R. N. Carmichael (Mildura, Vic.), F/O. R. W. Watson (Lismore, N.S.W.), Warrant Officer C. L. Swift (Melbourne, Vic.), F/Sgt. B. F. Gurbey (Sydney, N.S.W.) and F/O. J. Weger (Brisbane, QLD.) (Argus (Melbourne, Victoria.), SLV, Argus Newspaper Collection of Photographs, H98.104/3816.)

5 Powell, Alan, *The Shadow's Edge*, 188.

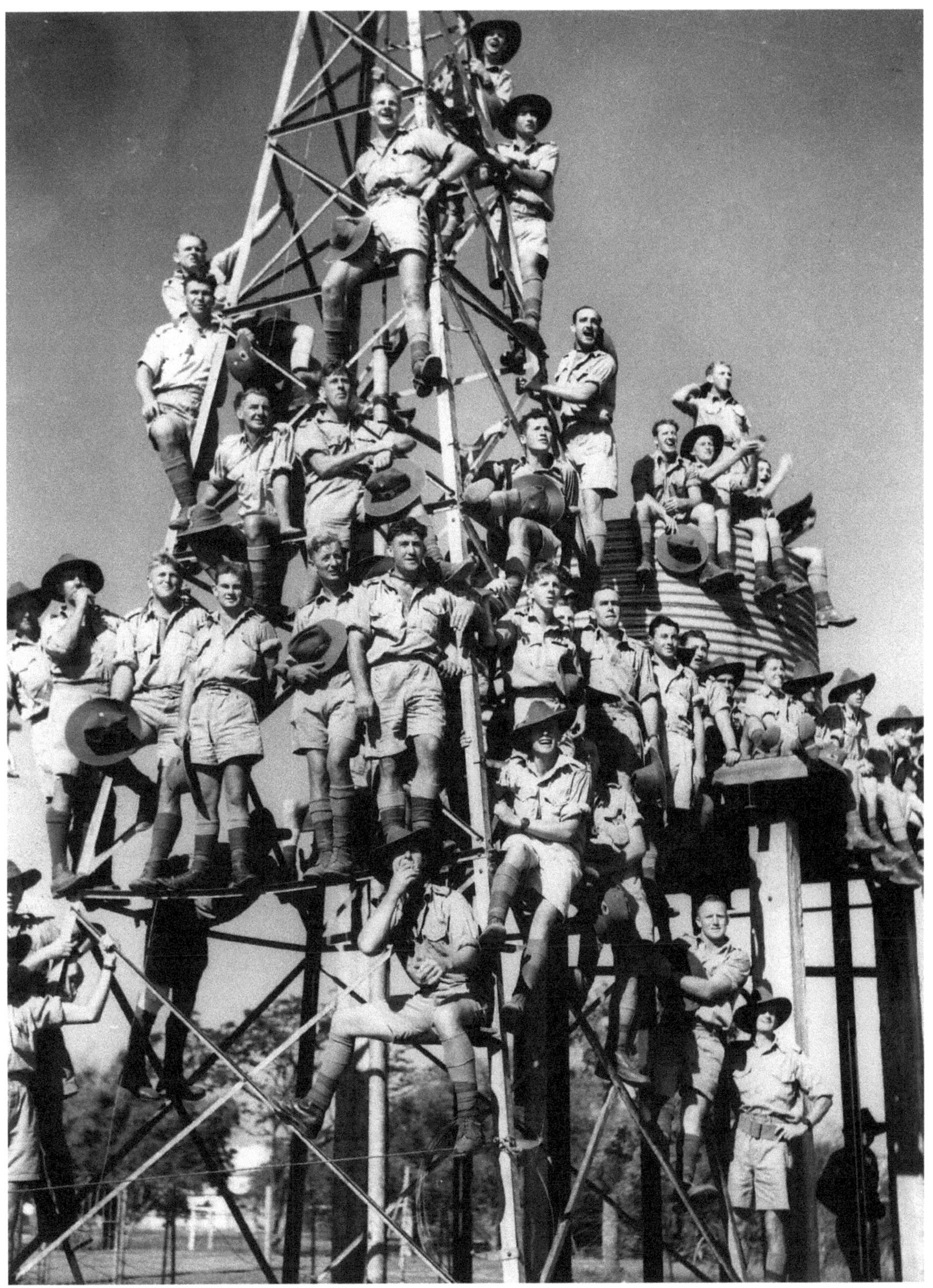

Spectators at Darwin football game, c1943. (Argus (Melbourne, Victoria.), SLV, Argus Newspaper Collection of Photographs, H99.201/5124.)

1945-1974: Post World War II reconstruction to Cyclone Tracy

Civilians began to return to Darwin in large numbers in 1946. What confronted them was a severely damaged town that had to be rebuilt. This process took many years during which time the civilian population had to make do with temporary accommodation. This time had its hardships but it also created a strong sense of community that has underpinned and defined Darwin's character since.

In 1948 the Northern Territory's Legislative Council met for the first time with 13 members, 7 appointed by the Administrator and 6 elected. So began many years of impassioned advocacy by Northern Territorians to control their own affairs. Change came slowly as the ratio of appointed to elected Legislative Council members shifted to favour the elected representatives. Finally a fully elected Northern Territory Assembly was established with limited authority in 1974.

During this period Darwin's population grew as never before and pushed development beyond the confines of the CBD, Fannie Bay and Parap to new suburbs on its northern beaches. By 1974 Darwin's population numbered 46,656.[6] This development continued steadily until it was stopped in its tracks by Cyclone Tracy on Christmas Eve 1974.

Cyclone Tracy devastated Darwin. It was a small but intense tropical cyclone with wind speeds estimated up to 150 km/h.[7] Those who survived it will never forget their experience or the complete and utter devastation it wreaked on their home. Thirteen died at sea and 53 died on land, 70 percent of the city was destroyed or severely damaged and approximately 30,000 people were evacuated south in its aftermath. Although many returned many did not. To many Darwin's history can be defined as 'before Tracy' or 'after Tracy'.

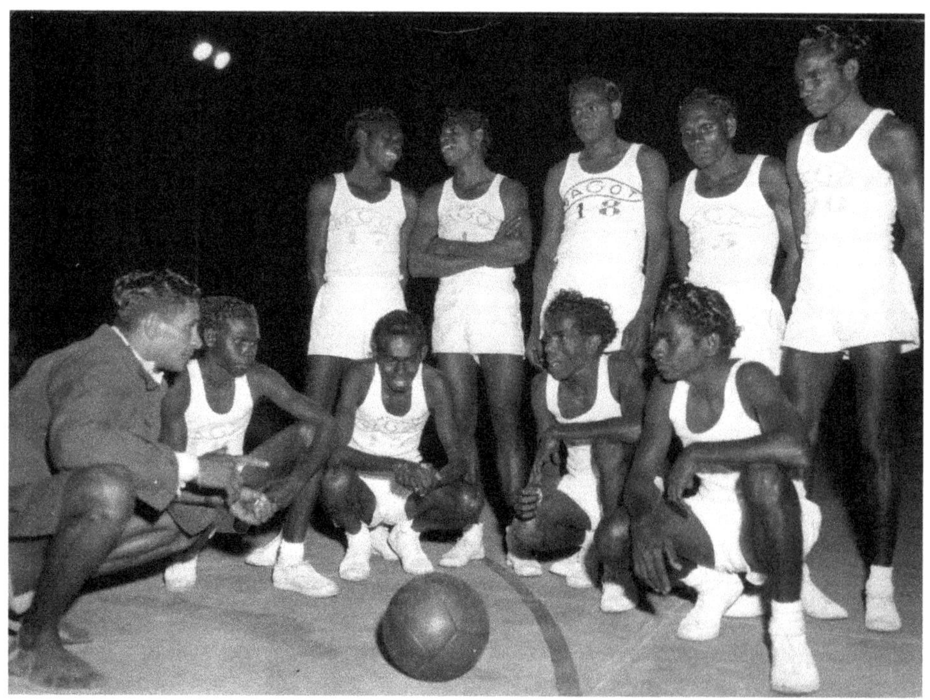

Bagot basketball team, c1953. Front row, squatting, left to right, Steve Abala, Albert Marego, John White, Peter Australia, Teddy (Ted) Cooper. Standing, left to right, Gilbert Ross, Bruce Pott, Jack White, Wilfred Wilson, David Guy. (Unknown, NTL, Harney McCaffery Collection, PH0510/0232.)

6 Carment, David., *Australia's Northern Capital*, 26.
7 *Report on Cyclone Tracy December 1974*, 45.

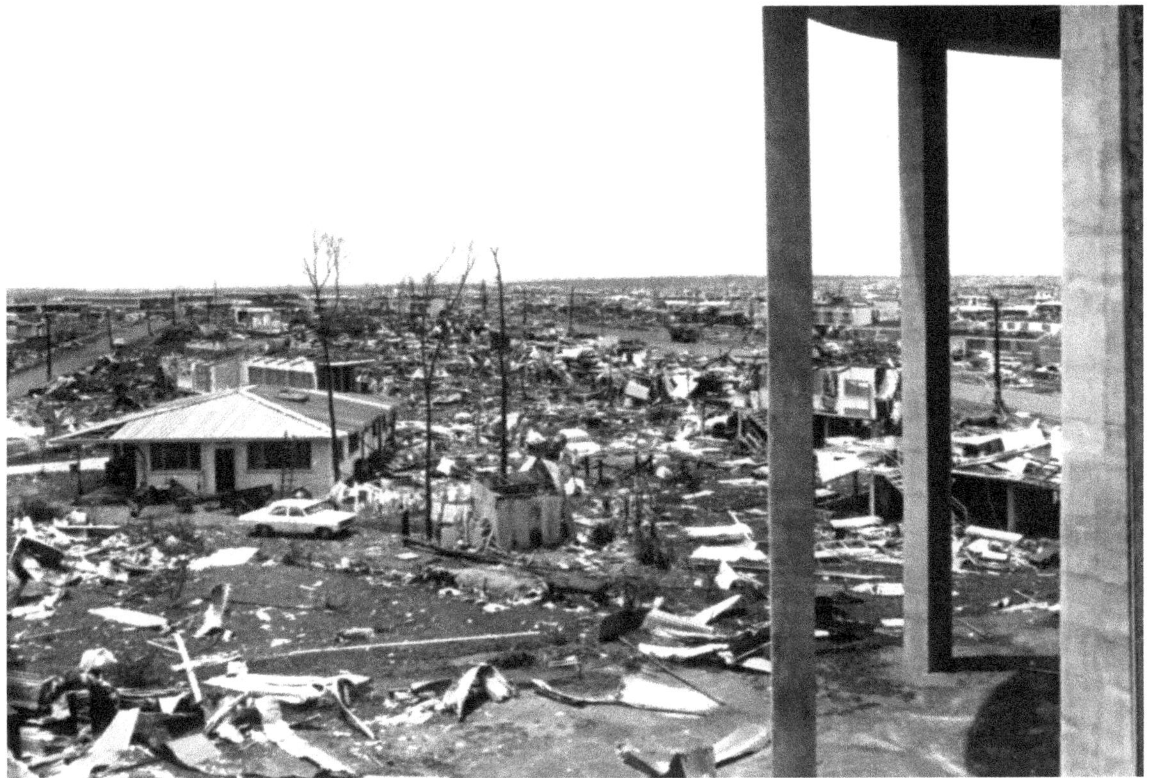

The suburb of Moil after Cyclone Tracy between Yeadon Circuit and Parer Drive, with Casuarina High School in distance, 1975. (Karlhuber, J., NTL, Northern Territory Dept. of the Housing & Construction Collection, PH0026/0022.)

1974-Current: Post Cyclone Tracy

The reconstruction of Darwin after Cyclone Tracy resulted in the city of today. The population grew rapidly and the suburbs took their current form. Growth and continuing development up to 1980 resulted in the establishment of Palmerston, a satellite city, 19 kilometres south of Darwin. The Territory economy, while still very dependent on a large government sector, has evolved into a relative successful diversified economy. Important industries include cattle, horticulture, agriculture, construction, tourism and hospitality, fishing, mining and gas.

In the political sphere the Northern Territory was finally granted Self-Government and the power to control most of its own affairs in 1978. However, the Commonwealth retains the right to overturn Territory legislation if it desires. The most noteable example of this being in March 1997 when the Federal Parliament overturned the first legislation in the world to allow voluntary euthanasia. In 1998 a referendum was held on the question whether the Northern Territory should become a state. 51 % voted no.

The 21st Century has seen enormous change to Darwin largely due to the development of the North Australian gas industry. Darwin has become the production and transportation hub of Australia's northern off shore gas fields. The first major project was ConocoPhillip's Bayu-Undan project in the Timor Sea between Timor Leste and the Northern Territory; a joint project between Australia and the newly independent Timor Leste Government. Construction of the onshore plant began in 2003 with the first shipment of liquefied natural gas to Japan in 2006.[8]

8 ConocoPhillips, www.

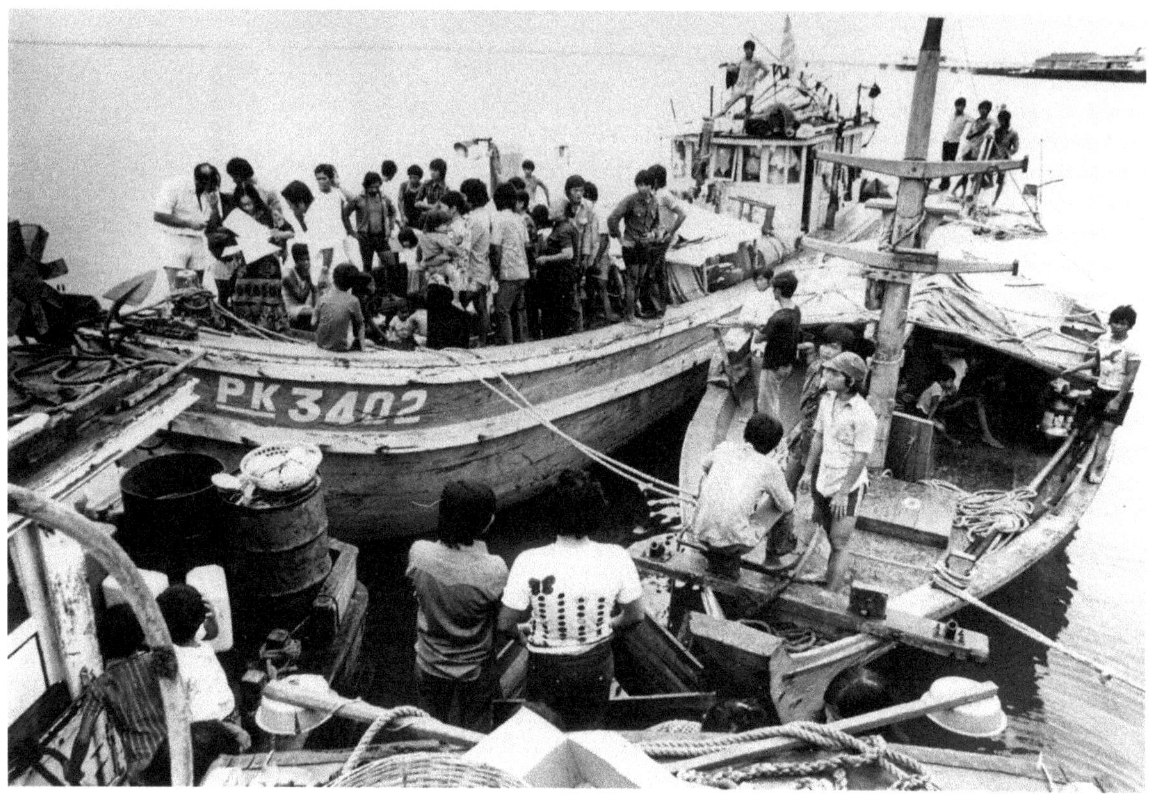

Vietnamese refugees upon arrival in Darwin Harbour, c1976. (Unknown, NTAS, John England Collection, NTRS 1637 Item 60.)

This was followed by the INPEX LNG project in September 2008 which plans to commence production in 2018.[9]

The gas industry has not only been an economic boost to the Territory it has resulted in new port facilities in Darwin Harbour and transformed the Darwin CBD. In 2000 almost none of the many high rise buildings seen today to accommodate the workforce required for these major projects existed. To some locals this is a sign that 'Old Darwin' has disappeared while others see it as a pointer to Darwin's future.

As Australia's northern most capital Darwin is an important social and economic hub situated close to south East Asia. Those that live here look north as often as they look south. Darwin's character and diversity is its strength. Forged in adversity Darwin's people know that when challenged, whether it by cyclone, war or depression they have a history of strength and resilience that enables them to hang on, rebuild and thrive.

9 Inpex, www.

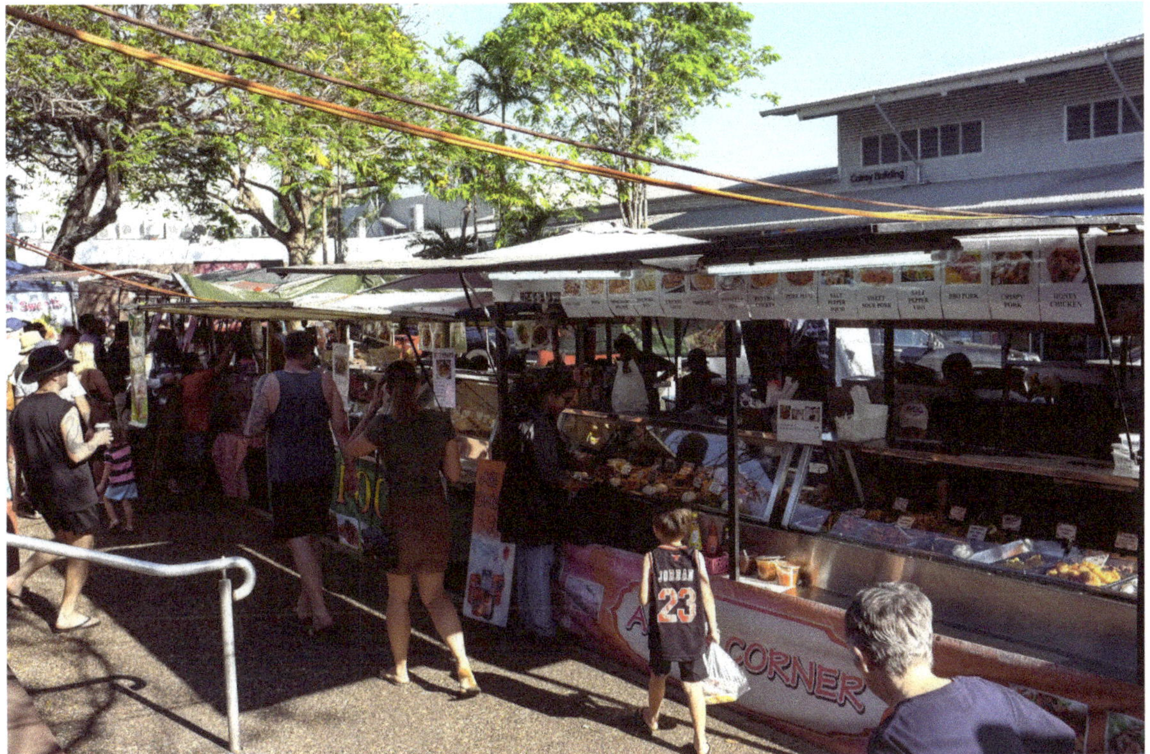

Parap Markets, 2017. (Martin, R., Matthew Stephen, Personal Collection, ParapMarket_05.)

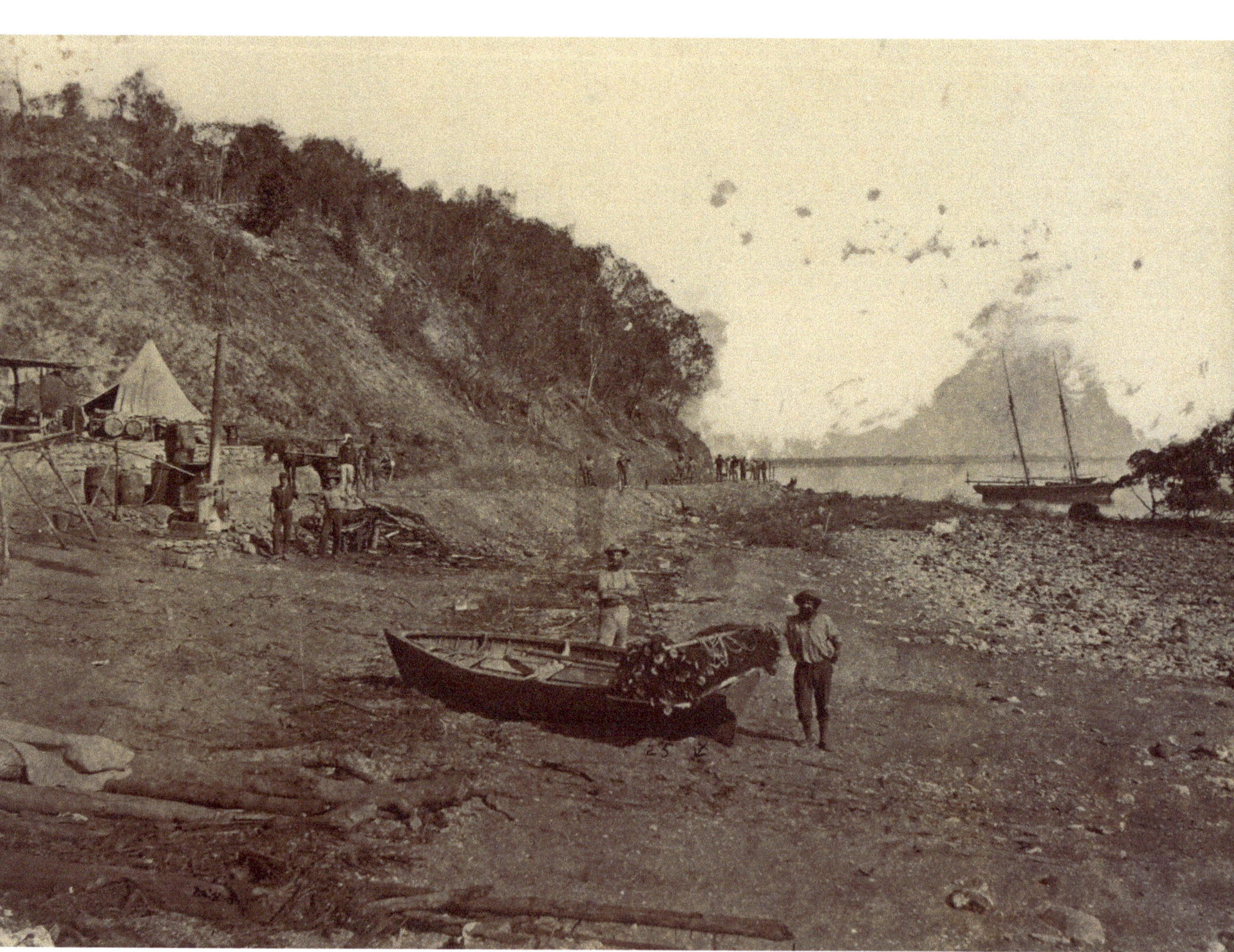

Fort Hill, 1869. (Sweet, S.W., SLV, Views of Darwin and Roper River, N.T. [picture], H141659.)

Chapter 1

Fort Hill ~ *Mayrere*

It is generally accepted that the first Europeans to enter Darwin Harbour in September 1839 were aboard *HMS Beagle* commanded by Captain J.C Wickham. One of the officers, Lieutenant John Lort Stokes, took a whaler and entered the harbour and named it Port Darwin after Charles Darwin who had previously sailed on the *Beagle*.

South Australia annexed the Northern Territory in July 1863. Its first attempt at colonisation was at Escape Cliffs, at the mouth of the Adelaide River, 50 kilometres northeast of Darwin. This was abandoned after just two years due to poor site selection that offered no suitable port, and little arable land for settlement.[1] The selection of a new site for South Australia's northern capital was entrusted to George Woodroffe Goyder, South Australian Surveyor General. His task was to identify a suitable site, and to survey a town and as much as the hinterland as possible. Based on Stokes writings he selected Port Darwin for settlement. Goyder arrived at Port Darwin in February 1869 with a party of 150 men and established a base camp below Fort Hill. Goyder, nicknamed 'Little Energy' for his work ethic and efficiency, completed the survey by the end of September. His expedition surveyed 269,467 hectares which included the town of Palmerston, as it would be known, and its hinterland. His legacy is Darwin's Central Business District's grid pattern layout, similar to that of Adelaide, the Capital of South Australia. Most of Darwin's streets are named after members of Goyder's survey party.

The first of many physical changes to Fort Hill occurred soon after Goyder's departure. A causeway known as Cook's Jetty was constructed as a landing point for freight, but proved to be unfit and was abandoned. It would be the first of many wharfs built at Fort Hill.

From late 1869 European settlers began to arrive in Port Darwin but 'The Camp' at Fort Hill remained as the only settlement for some time. A pathway to Fort Point was constructed during this period.[2] The top of Fort Hill was also the site of the graves of Surveyor J.W.O. Bennett and cook, Richard Hazard, who died in 1869. Bennet was speared by Aboriginals at Fred's Pass to the south of Darwin on 24 May and died some days later. Hazard died of illness in the Surveyors Camp. In 1965 the remains of both men were relocated from Fort Hill to McMillians Road cemetery in Darwin's northern suburbs.

The Overland Telegraph transformed Palmerston into an international communications hub and secured its future. The Overland Telegraph construction workers began to arrive at Port Darwin in September 1870. The overseas cable came ashore at a point below the Government Residence (Government House) on 7 November 1871.

In 1874 the Gulnare Jetty was constructed on the eastern side of Fort Hill using the sunken hulk of the *Gulnare* as its foundation. It was in use until 1892. During the 1870s and 1880s residences and offices for the Harbour Master,

1 Powell, A. *Far Country*, 82.
2 Daly. *Digging, Squatting, and Pioneering Life in the Northern Territory of South Australia*, 53.

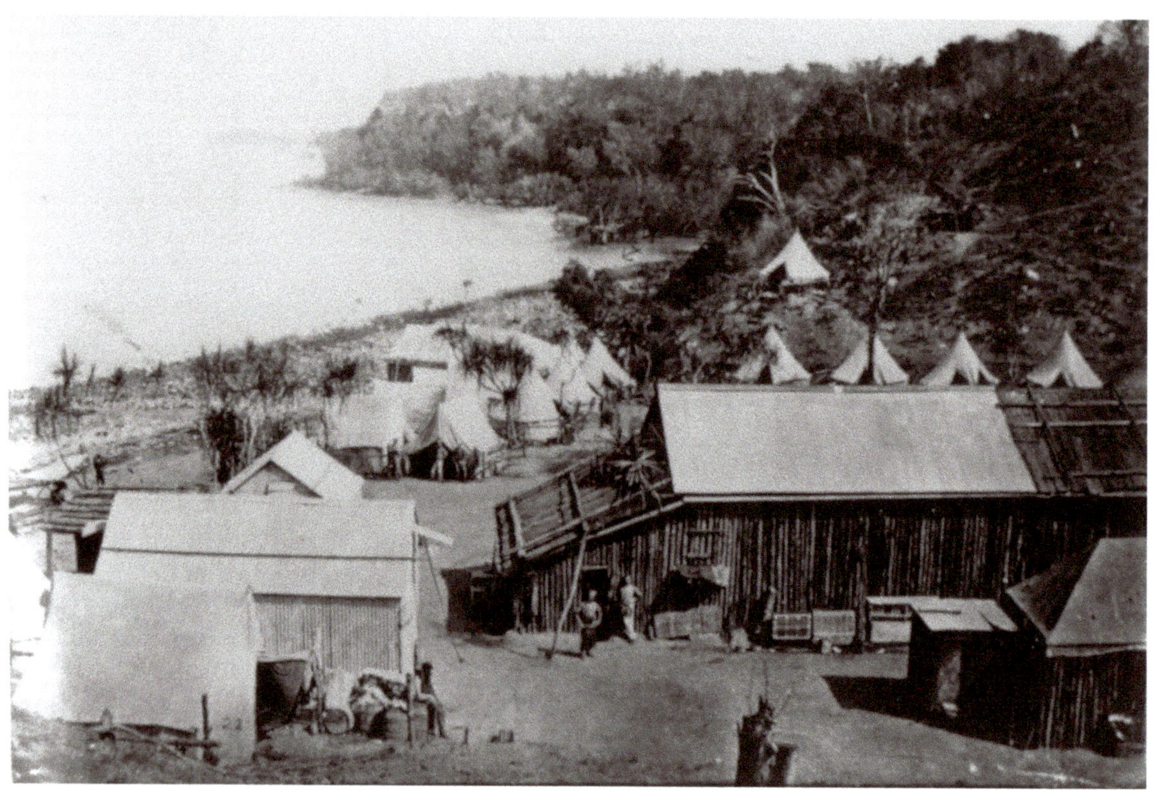

Surveyors' Camp, c1870, (Unknown, NTL, Roger Nott Collection, PH0002/0161.)

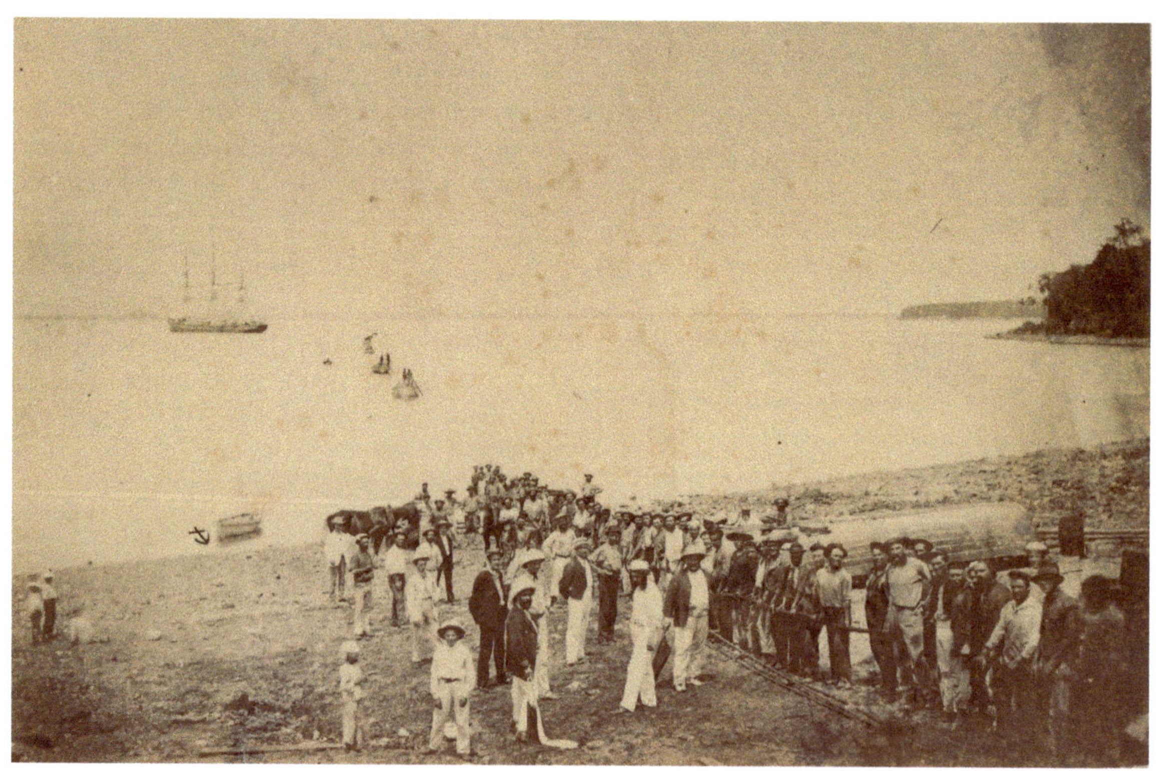

Bringing the overseas cable onshore, near the current site of the Deckchair Cinema, 7 November 1871. (Sweet, S.W., SLV, Views of Darwin and Roper River, N.T. [picture], H141666.)

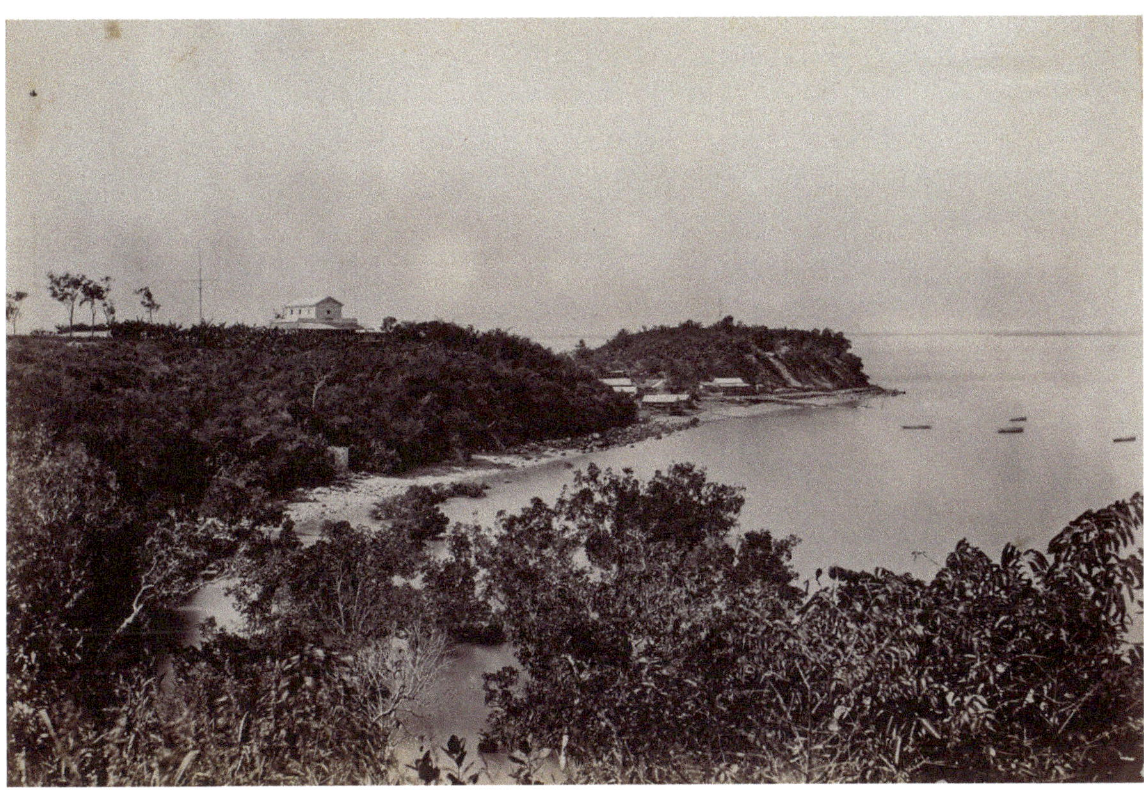

Government Residence and Surveyors' Camp at Fort Hill, 1874. (Foelsche, P., NTL, Foelsche Photograph Album, PH0111/0074.)

Medical Officer and some other government officials were located in the area of the Surveyors Camp.

In 1880 Palmerston's first public swimming baths were erected at Fort Hill for 'the health of the community [due to] the direct good derived from sea-bathing.' The baths were built close to the outer point of Fort Hill. The enclosure was built into the harbour some distance to allow for the large rise and fall of the tide. It was made from wooden posts and railings. A dressing shed was also constructed for the use of female bathers.[3] The Fort Hill baths remained in use until 1919 when they were 'swept away' by a cyclone.[4]

In 1937 rising global tensions saw Darwin identified as a potential harbour for Britain's Eastern Fleet. The plans included anchorages for 28 ships, 17 small craft and the construction of anti submarine defences. The six kilometre submarine boom net constructed to protect Darwin harbour between late 1940 and late 1942 was the longest in the world. The net stretched between Dudley Point and West Point. A depot and wharf were constructed on Fort Hill to service the anti submarine boom. The work, which included the construction of a railway branch line, was completed by the end of 1941. It required a significant portion of Fort Hill to be demolished to make way for a new concrete Jetty. The Boom was dismantled after the cessation of World War II and was stored at the Boom Depot in case it may be needed in the future.[5]

Fort Hill was also the site of one of six oil storage tunnels constructed in the Darwin wharf precinct to replace the above ground Stokes Hill oil storage tanks during the bombing of Darwin in February 1942.

In 1965, despite protest from the Larrakia people, what was left of Fort Hill was removed, to make way for an iron ore loading facility.

3 *NTTG*, 2 October 1880.
4 *NTTG*, 29 June 1919.
5 Navy: *Serving Australia with Pride*, www.

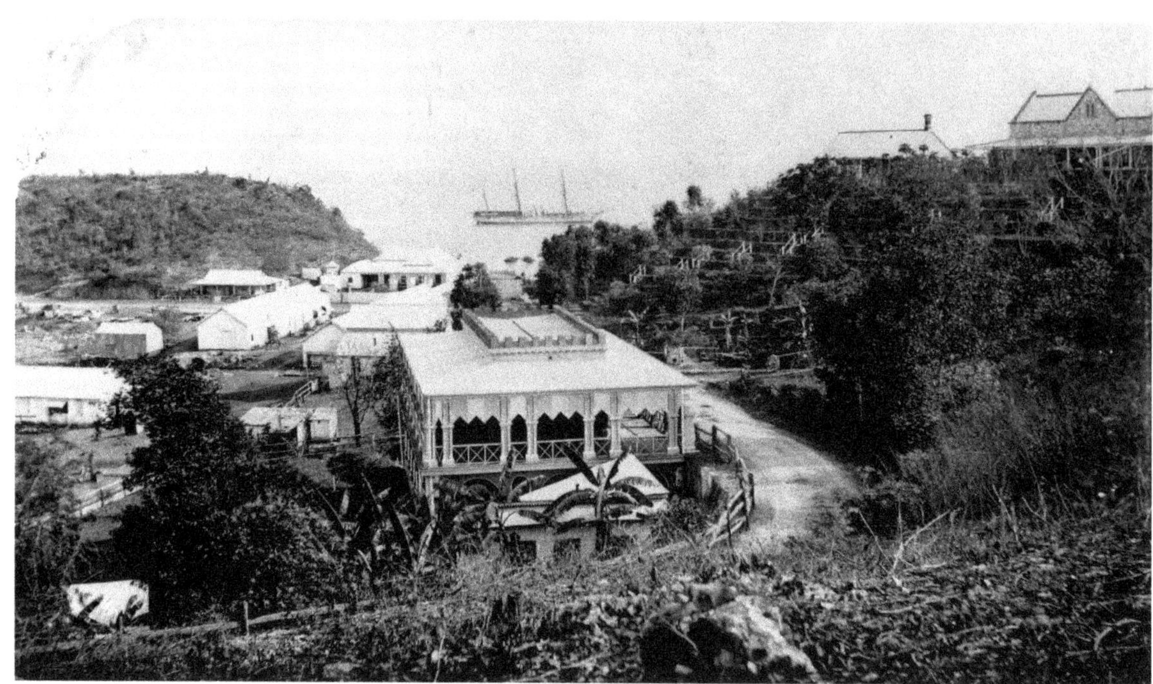

Knights Folly, overlooking Fort Hill, Government Residence to right, 1885. (Foelsche, P., NTL, Foelsche Collection, PH0111/0112.)

This loading facility was completed in 1967.[6] It remained in service until the early 1970s when the iron ore suppliers failed. Cyclone Tracy also severely damaged the facility.[7]

In 2003 the Darwin Deckchair Cinema relocated from its site near Stokes Hill to its current location in *Damoe-Ra* Park on the foreshore below the Northern Territory Legislative Assembly. The 'Deckchair' continues a long tradition of outdoor cinemas that goes back to World War I and the Don Cinema in Cavenagh Street.

2003 also saw the commencement of plans to redevelop the Darwin waterfront as a residential, commercial and entertainment precinct. The Waterfront lies on the area that was once the foreshore of Frances Bay. The Darwin Cruise Ship Terminal at Fort Hill Wharf opened in 2008. It is the first landfall for many visitors to Darwin. Goyder Park can be found at the North West corner of the Waterfront development and acknowledges the European history of Fort Hill by honouring George Goyder's 1869 survey party and marking the spot of Darwin's first European settlement. Linking the northern end of the Fort Hill area and the Esplanade is *Damoe-Ra* Park. *Damoe-Ra* is the Larrakia name for the freshwater spring above Lameroo Beach which used to run down the cliff face.[8]

The Darwin Waterfront development remains a work in progress. From the 1869 Surveyor's Camp to today's cruise ship wharf, Fort Hill has always been at the heart of Darwin's wharves and the landing point for those coming to Darwin by sea.

6 Bauman, *Aboriginal Darwin*, 17 & 24.
7 Bureau of Transport Economics, *Provision of General Cargo Facilities at the Port of Darwin*. 56-57.
8 Bauman, *Aboriginal Darwin*, 37.

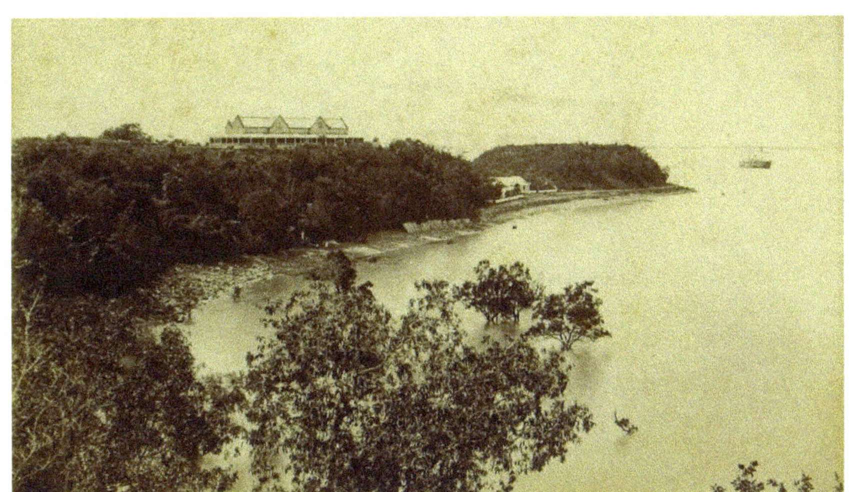

Residency and Fort Hill, c1880s. (Foelsche, P., NTAS, Foelsche Collection, NTRS 3420/P1/2.)

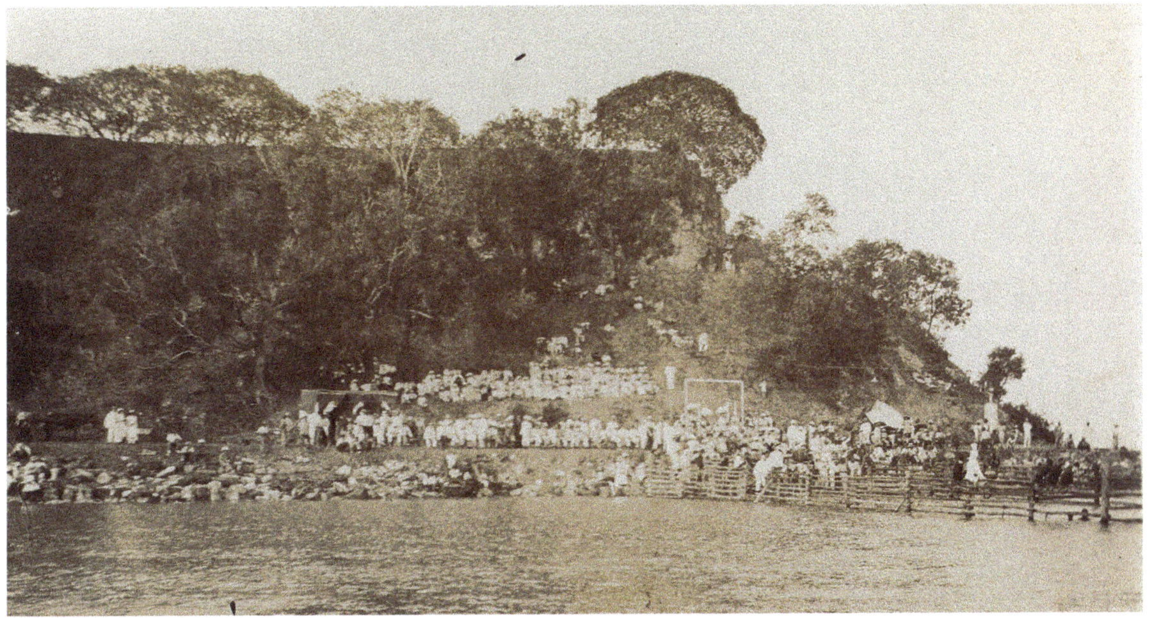

Swimming carnival, Fort Hill Baths, Darwin, October 1915. (Unknown, LNSW, E.D.W.S Donnison Collection, ML MSS 890/3/0205.)

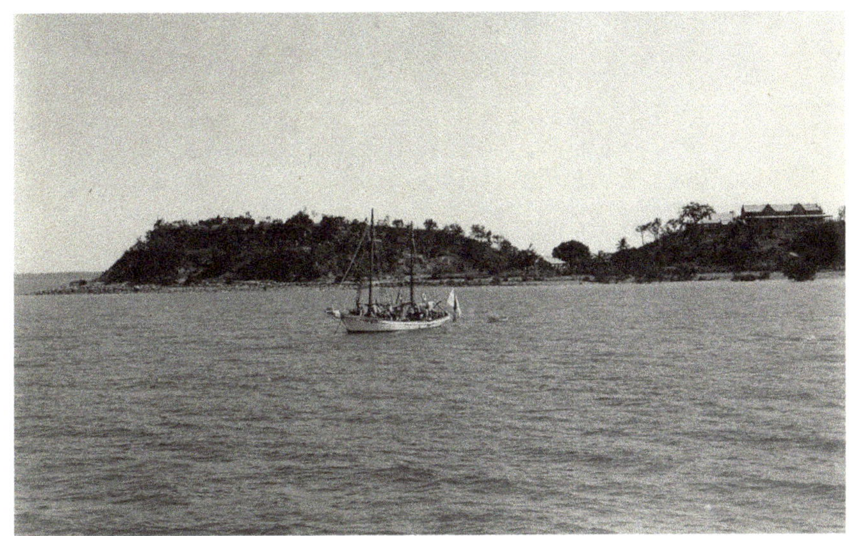

Fort Hill, c1938. (Unknown, NTAS, Garrad Collection, NTRS 1204 Item 2.)

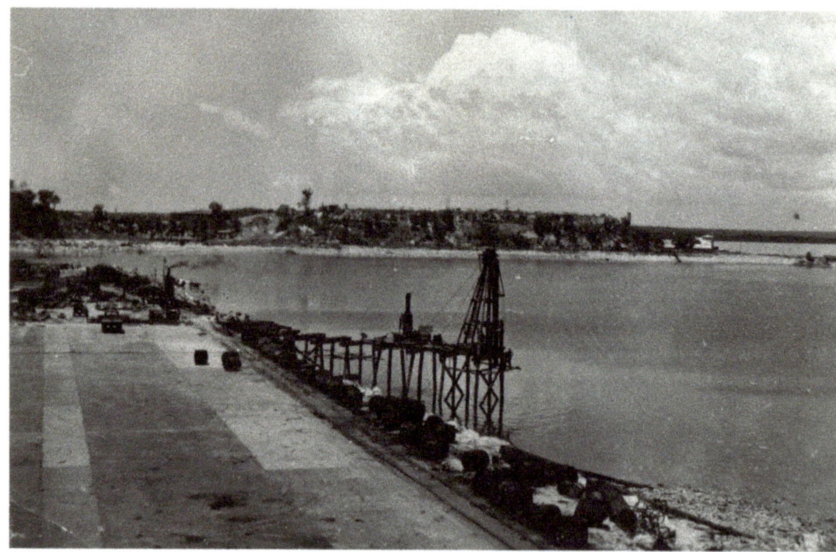

Boom Wharf, Fort Hill, c1942. (Unknown, NTAS, Beverly Collection, NTRS 2012 Item 8.)

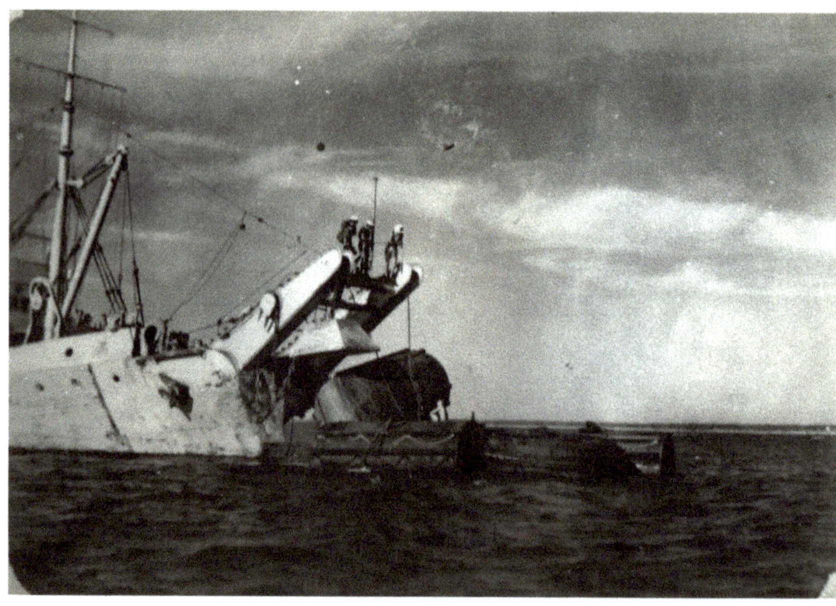

Anti submarine boom tender, 1942-1945. (Unknown, NTAS, Beverly Collection, NTRS 2012 Item 54.)

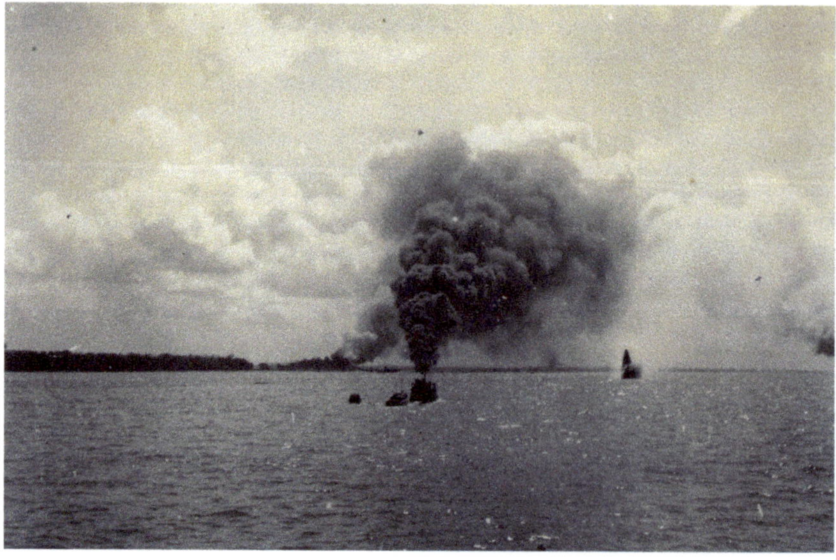

Bombed ships, Darwin Harbour, February 19 1942, US destroyer *Peary* sinking. (Unknown, NTAS, Victor Levitt Collection, NTRS 3433 Item 5.)

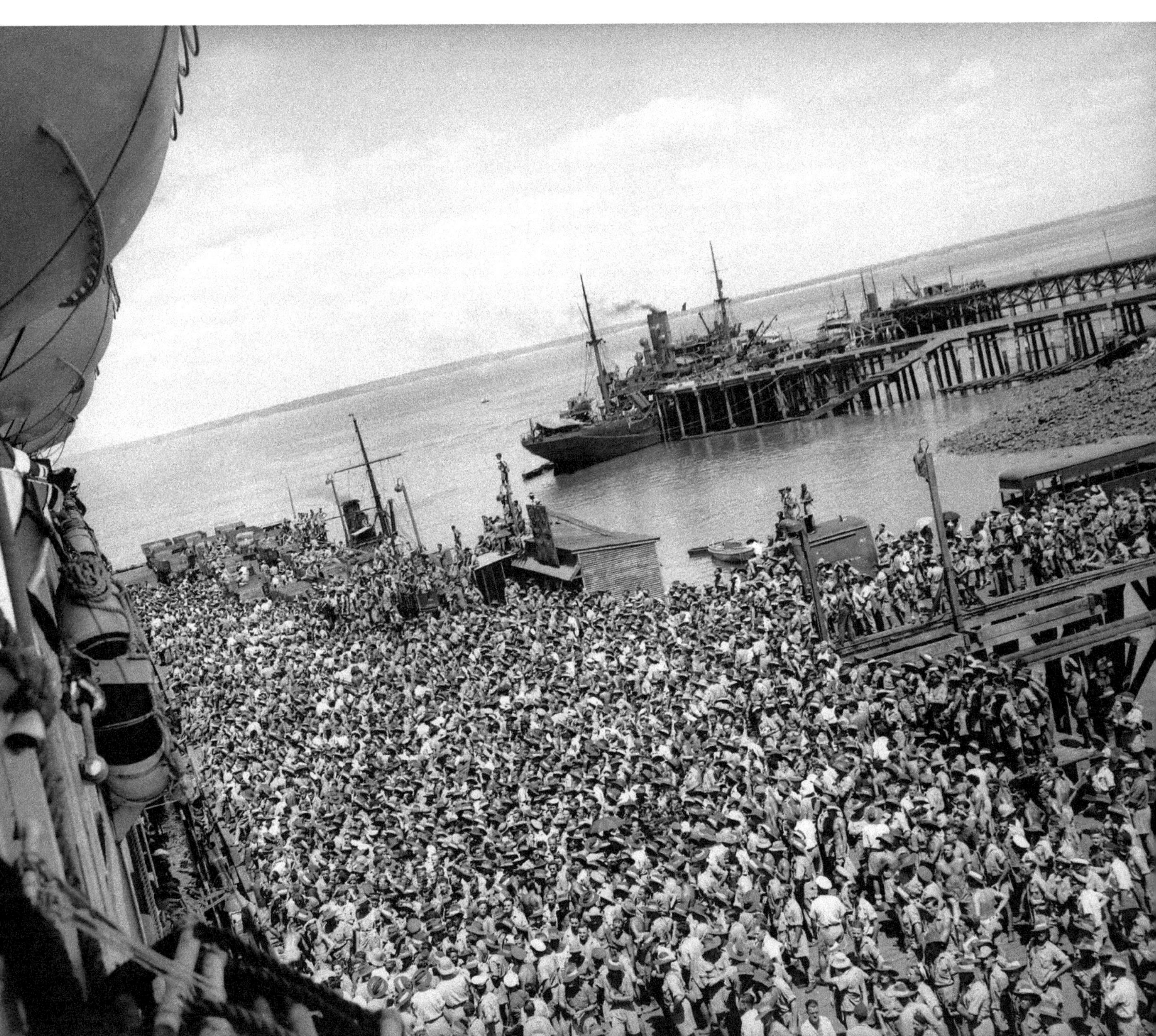

Darwin, Fort Hill Wharf, 21 September 1945. Service personnel gathered on the wharf to welcome home 760 stretcher cases and walking wounded on the hospital ship *Oranje*. The injured had been held in Japanese prisoner of war camps for three and a half years. (Unknown, AWM, Photograph, NWA0973.)

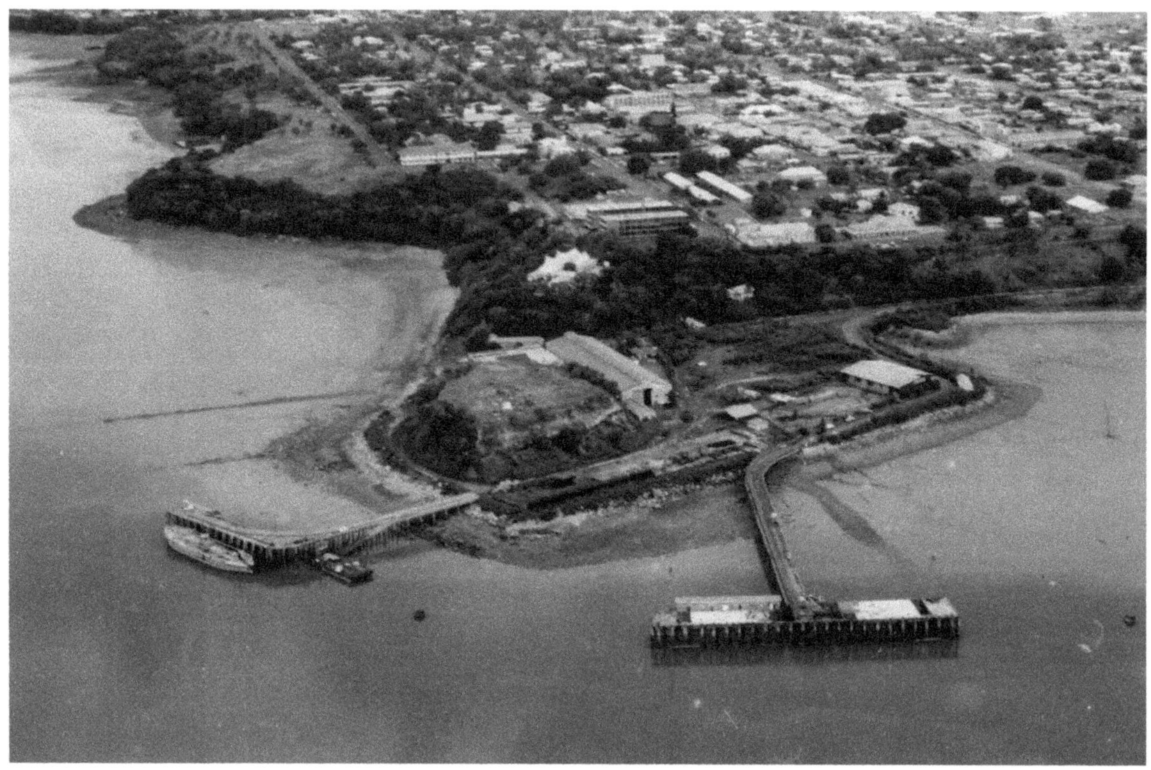

Fort Hill wharves, 1962. (Lorman, S., NTL, NT Dept. of Lands Collection, PH0139/0386.)

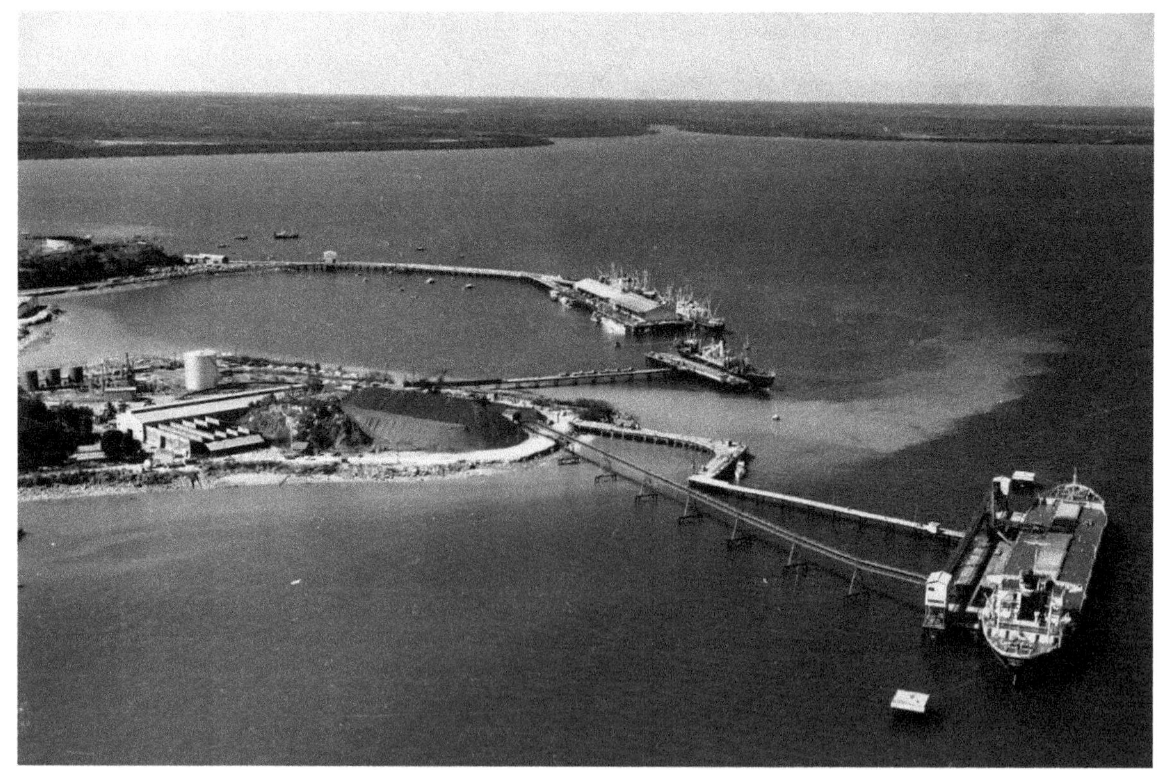

Iron Ore Wharf, Fort Hill, c1980s. (Unknown, NTAS, GPC, NTRS 3822-P1 Folder 8 Japanese bulk ore carrier.)

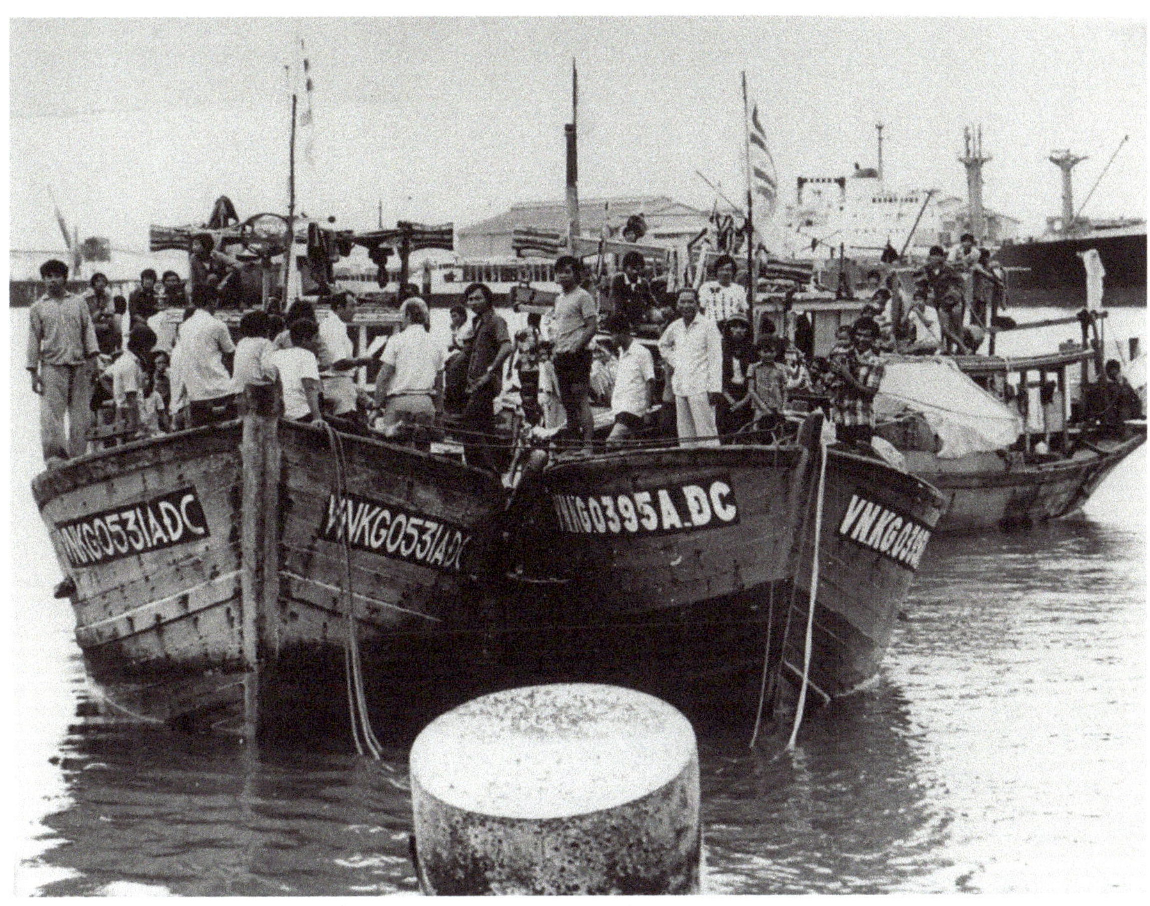

Vietnamese boat people moored near Fort Hill, c1976. (Unknown, NTAS, John England, NTRS 1637 Item 61.)

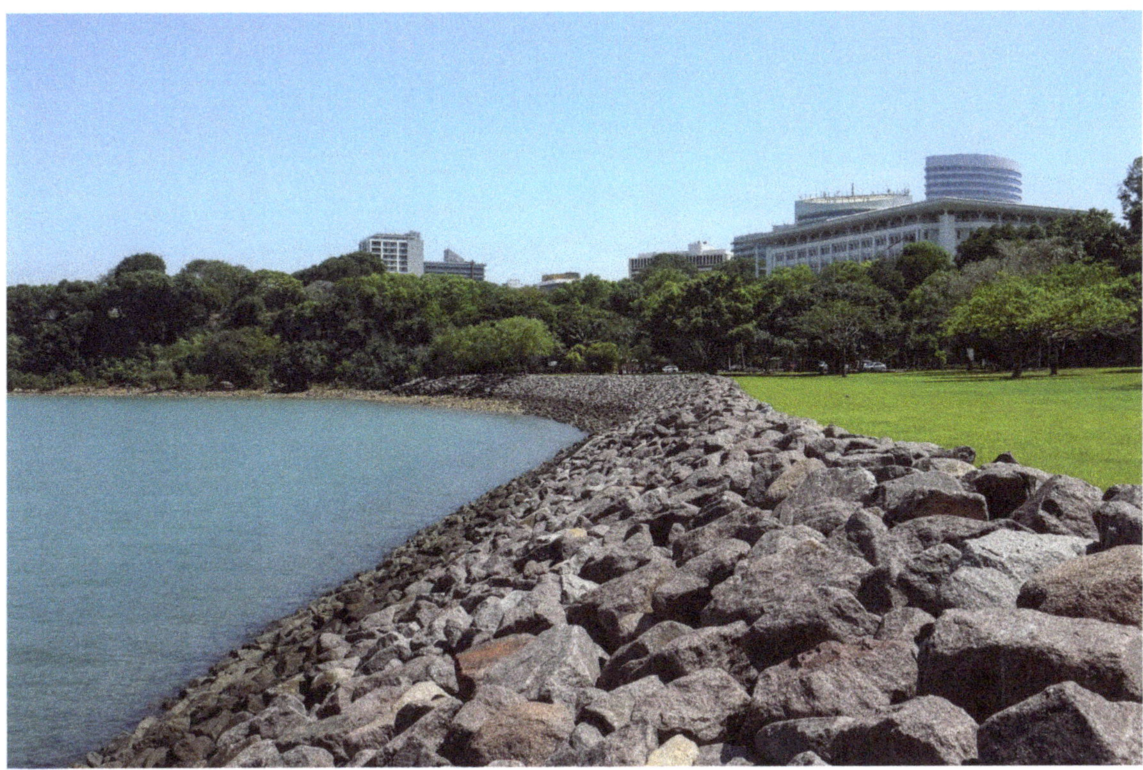

Legislative Assembly from Fort Hill shore, 2017. (Martin, R., Matthew Stephen, Personal Collection, Fort Hill Foreshore_09.)

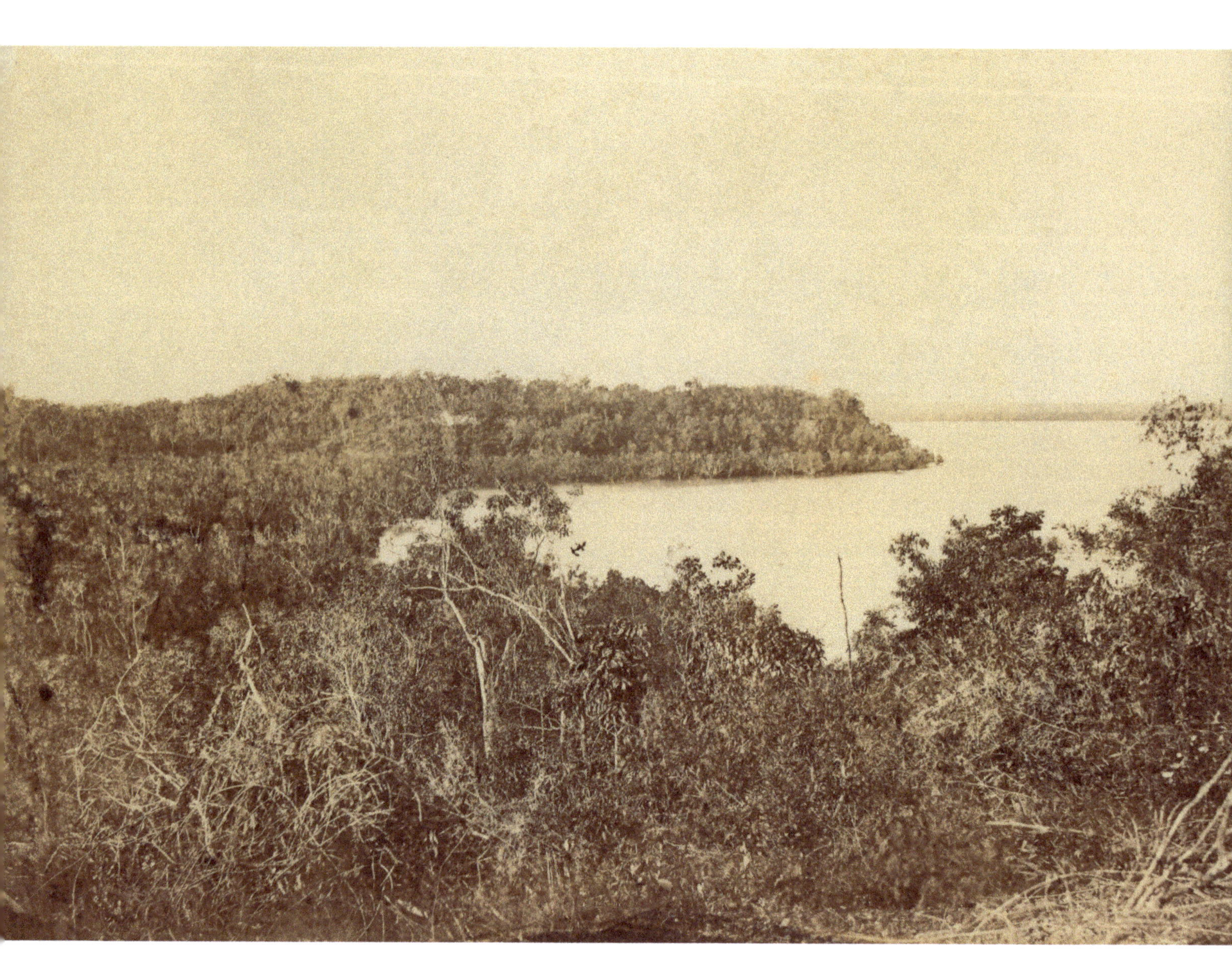

Stokes Hill, c1869. (Sweet, S.W., SLV, Views of Darwin and Roper River, N.T. [picture], H141667.)

Chapter 2

Stokes Hill Wharf ~ *Delila*

Stokes Hill contains within it a Larrakia sacred site for a spiritual ancestor known as *Chinute Chinute,* which sometimes manifests itself as a Tawny Mouthed Owl.[1]

Stokes Hill Wharf was Darwin's main shipping wharf for almost a century since its construction in 1885-86. Until the early 1950's it was known as the 'Railway Wharf' or the 'Town Wharf'. It was originally constructed as the northern terminus of the 'Transcontinental Railway' planned to link Palmerston to Adelaide. The Transcontinental Railway became known as 'The Never-Never Line' and it would not reach Darwin until 2004.

The Railway Wharf was an arced timber structure in the same position as today's Stokes Hill Wharf. Completed in 1887 it enabled the transhipment of railway construction materials for the first section of the northern railway to Pine Creek, which was opened in 1889.

The Palmerston Station and railway yards were situated to the north north-east of Stokes Hill bound to the east south east by the mangroves of Frances Bay and the high ground of the town to the north-west. The long and narrow railway yards comprised of a bond store, where ships cargos were unloaded, sorted and stored; a general store; a number of carriage sheds; a goods shed, crane and weighbridge. The passenger station was at the north eastern end of the railway yards. [2] Passengers from the Railway Wharf or station made their way to the town above via road on Knuckey Street or by foot on a path that was known both as Chinaman's or Travellers Walk. The path of Travellers Walk zig zagged from the entrance of the railway yards up to Cavenagh Street.

The Railway Wharf was weakened by the 1897 cyclone and the ravages of the Toredo mollusc that lead to its replacement. Construction took many years but was finally completed in 1904 and became known as the New Town Wharf. The right angled wharf had limited access for railway wagons but continued in service up to 1942.[3]

Darwin's strategic importance to Australia grew in the 1920s when the Imperial Conference of 1923 developed the 'Singapore Strategy', making Singapore the pivot of the British Empire's Asian defence. Darwin was identified as Australia's northern refuelling base. Construction of four oil refuelling tanks at Stokes Hill began in 1924. In 1928 a pump house was constructed on the wharf to house two refuelling pumps. Five more tanks were completed in 1932 and two more were completed in December 1941, just days before the outbreak of war with Japan.[4] Stokes Hill was Darwin's main wharf in the years leading up to World War II and as such was a hive of activity in Darwin's defence build up during the 1930s and the early years of the war.

On the 19th of February 1942 the *SS Barossa* and the *SS Neptuna* were berthed at the Town Wharf. Five gangs of labourers were working there at 10am when Japanese bombers

1 Barnes, *Heritage and Cultural Trail,* Darwin Waterfront, www.
2 Harvey, *The Never Never Line,* 305.
3 Harvey, *The Never Never Line,* 305.
4 NAA, *Preparing for War*, Research Guide, www.

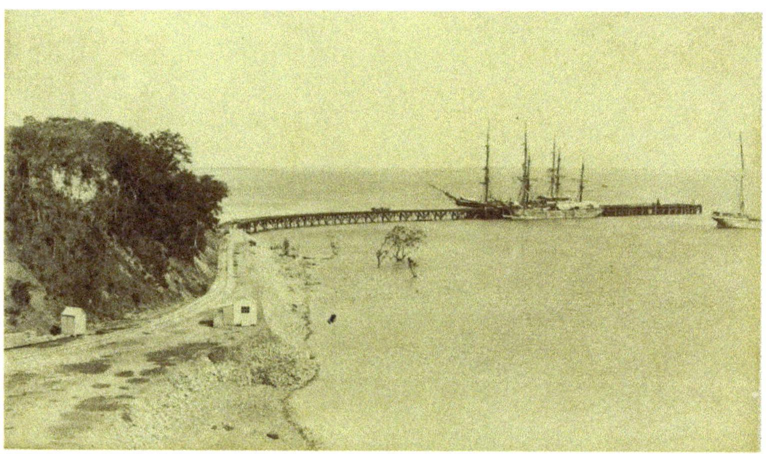

Railway Wharf, 1887. (Foelsche, P., NTAS, Foelsche Collection, NTRS 3420/P1/9.)

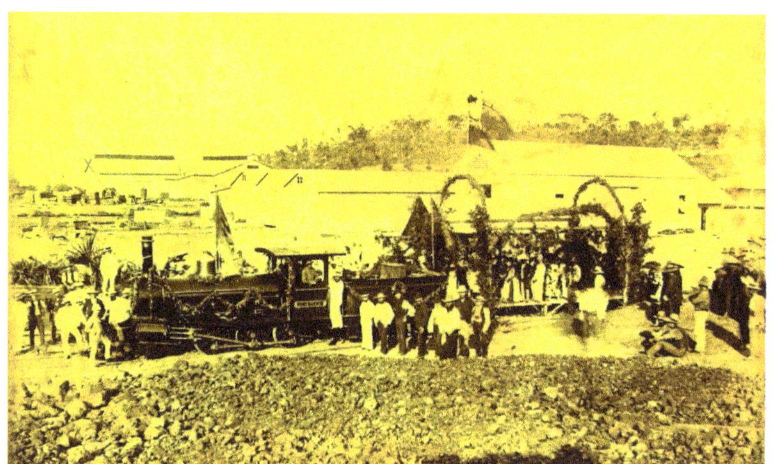

Christening of the first engine on the Palmerston & Pine Creek Railway, Palmerston railway terminus, 1887. (Foelsche, P., NTAS, Foelsche Collection, NTRS 3420/P1/47.)

attacked. The first bombs fell on the right angle in the wharf blowing a locomotive, railway trucks and workers into the sea. Twenty two wharf workers died in the first raid. Both the *Barrosa* and *Neptuna* were hit by bombs. The *Neptuna's* cargo of depth charges and anti aircraft shells exploded killing 50 of the ship's crew. Amidst the chaos following the bombing many men, most notably Jack Barclay and Johnnie Wilkshire, showed great courage to row small boats through the burning oil and debris to rescue injured men in the water.[5]

After the two Japanese air raids on the 19th of February nine ships were sunk in Darwin harbour and two outside the harbour. Parts of Darwin's central business district and Darwin's two airfields were severely damaged, 235 people died and approximately 400 were wounded. The loss of 22 local wharf and railway labourers, many of whom were members of the North Australia Workers Union, is commemorated annually on the 19th of February in a memorial service on Stokes Hill Wharf. Although the Town Wharf

5 Darwin Waterfront, *Bombing of Darwin*, www.

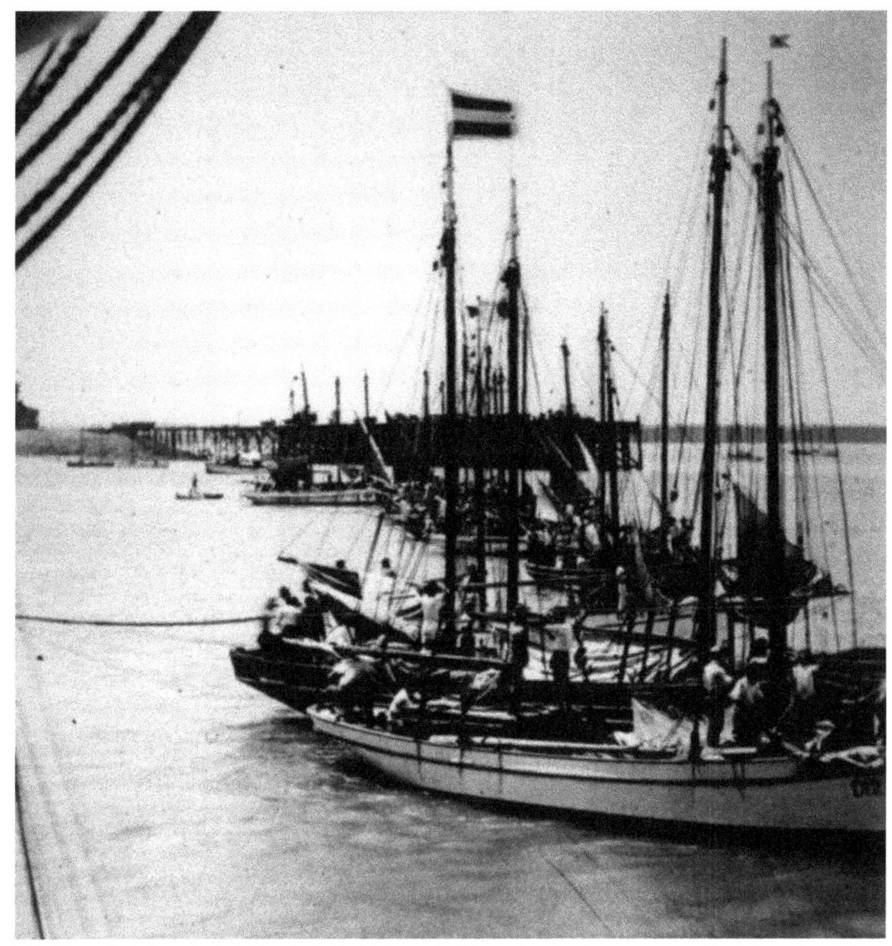

Port Darwin regatta, lugger race, c1898. (Foelsche, P., NTL, Marie & Lindsay Perry Collection, PH0560/0060.)

was returned to service during World War II the sunken wrecks remained a reminder of the devastation of the Bombing of Darwin for many years.

Stokes Hill Wharf, as we know it today, was commenced in 1953 and completed in 1956. In 1958 Stokes Hill was also selected as the site for a new power station to supply Darwin with Electricity. Stokes Hill Power Station came into service in 1962 and remained Darwin's main power station until its closure in 1987.[6]

The World War II ship wrecks were finally removed from the harbour by the Fujita Salvage Company of Japan between 1959 and 1961. The story of the Fujita Company salvage operation in Darwin is one of the Northern Territory's many fascinating histories that would become an unlikely story of peace and reconciliation.[7] The salvage operation of 120 workers led by Mr Ryugo Fujita removed 70,000 tons of iron from Darwin Harbour. In a gesture of personal reparation for the damage caused by the Japanese bombing raids on Darwin during World War II Mr Fujita commissioned 77 bronze crosses cast from metalwork recovered from the *SS Zealandia*. He donated the crosses to the newly reconstructed Darwin United Church in Smith Street, completed in July 1960. Most of the crosses were fixed on the pews. The Fujita family has maintained a connection with Darwin since.[8] The Senichiro

6 Phelts, B., *Switching On*, 51-69.
7 NAA, *Administration of the Northern Territory during the war*, Research Guide, www.
8 Navy: *Serving Australia with Pride*.www.

Fujita photograph collection which illustrates this story is held by Northern Territory Library.

Stokes Hill Wharf remained Darwin's main general cargo wharf until 1981 when a new Fort Hill Wharf was commissioned. Although the wharf is still used by commercial ships Darwin's main port and transcontinental rail terminus was transferred to East Arm in 2000.

Stokes Hill Wharf continues as a commercial wharf but it is perhaps better known now as recreation and tourist destination. There are few better places in Darwin to watch spectacular 'Build Up' and 'Wet Season' storms. A former passenger terminal on the wharf has now been converted to an interactive museum to commemorate the Bombing of Darwin and the history of the Royal Flying Doctor Service. The former warehouses at the end of Stokes Hill Wharf have been converted to restaurants and shops that are a popular destination for locals and tourists alike. Stokes Hill Wharf is also a great place to look back at the Darwin skyline and ponder just how much has changed since 1869.

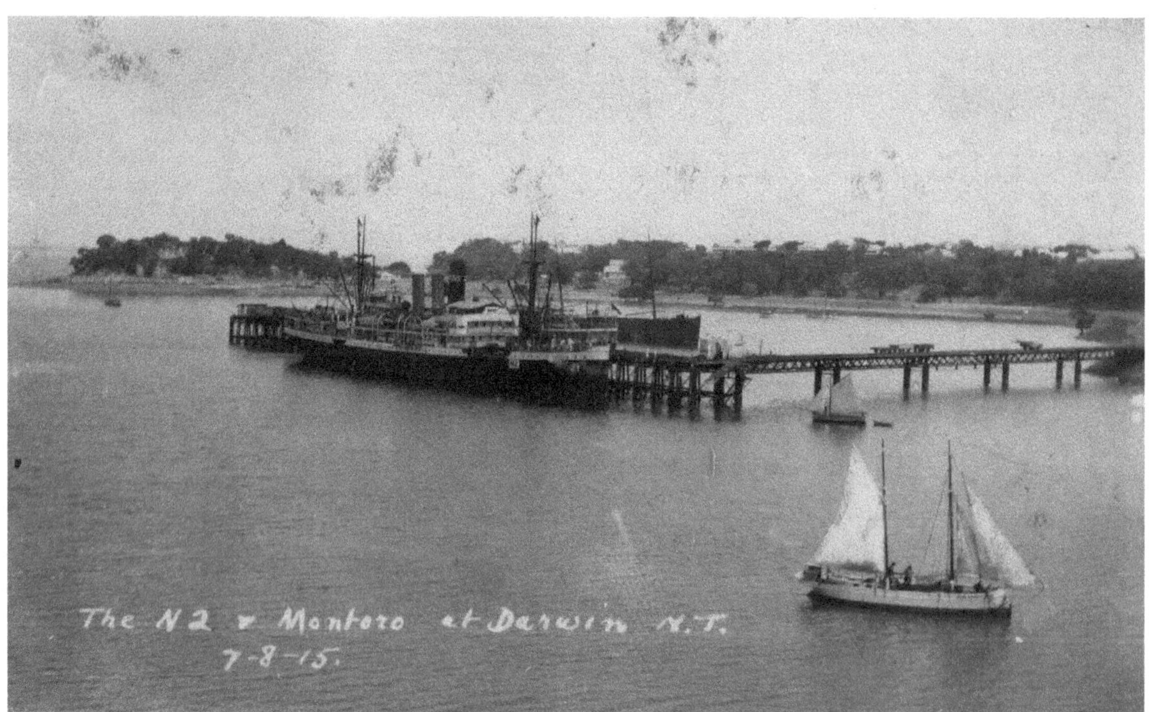

The *S.S. N2* (later *S.S. Bambra*), Western Australian Government mail service & *S.S. Montoro*, Burns Phillip Line from Singapore, Stokes Hill Wharf, 1915. (Unknown, Maxwell, Personal Collection, N/A.)

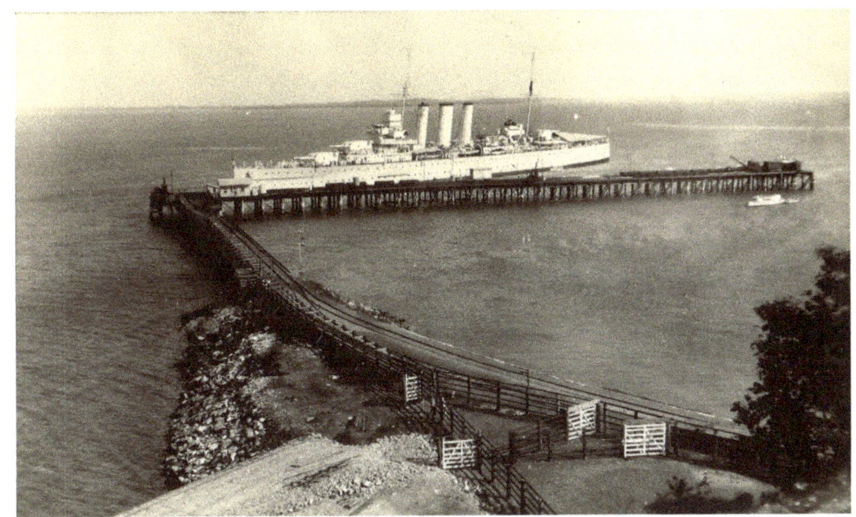

HMAS Canberra, Stokes Hill Wharf, 1929. (Unknown, NTAS, Charles Wilson Collection, NTRS 3335 Item 363.)

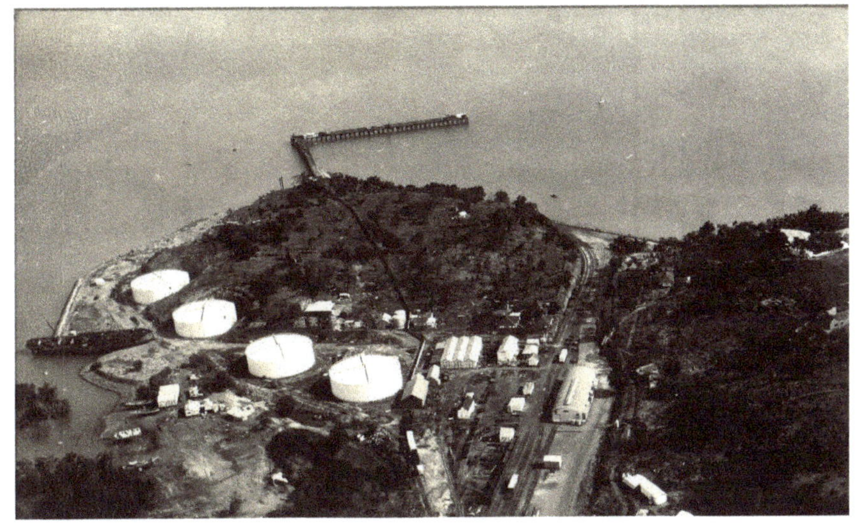

Stokes Hill Wharf, Darwin Railway Station & oil tanks, c1930. (Unknown, NTAS, Charles Wilson Collection, NTRS 3335 Item 289.)

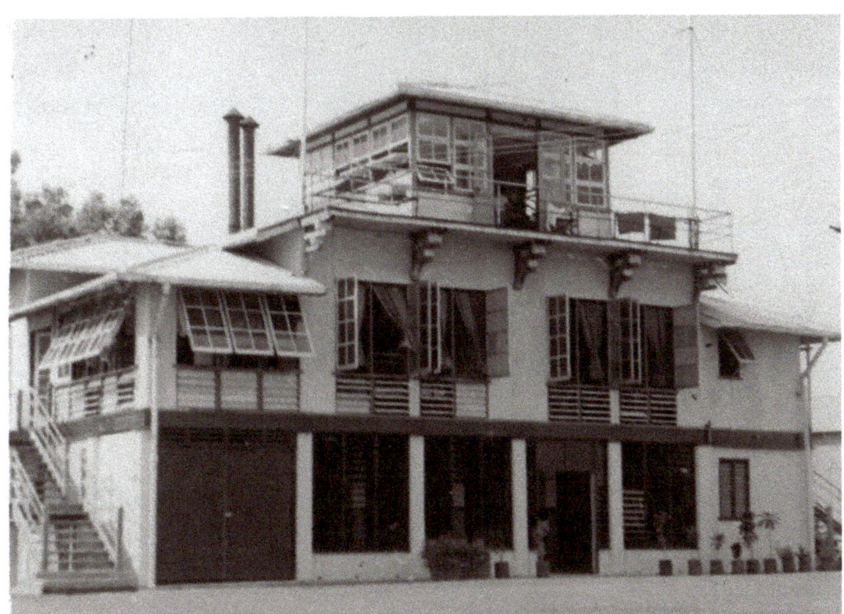

QANTAS Empire flying boat base, c1939. (Unknown, QHC, Darwin Collection, N/A.)

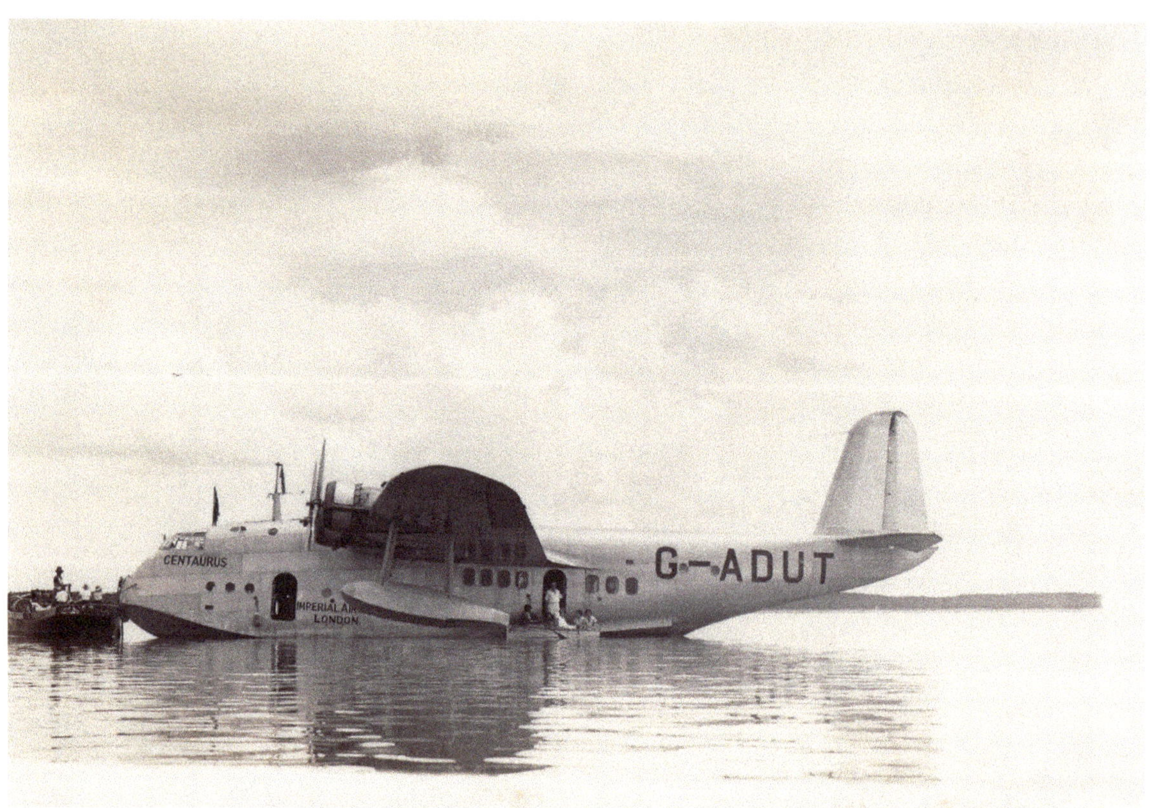

Centaurus, Short S23 C Class Empire flying boat, c1936. Refuelling tender and passengers disembarking by boat. (Unknown, Angus Bird, Personal Collection, 68.)

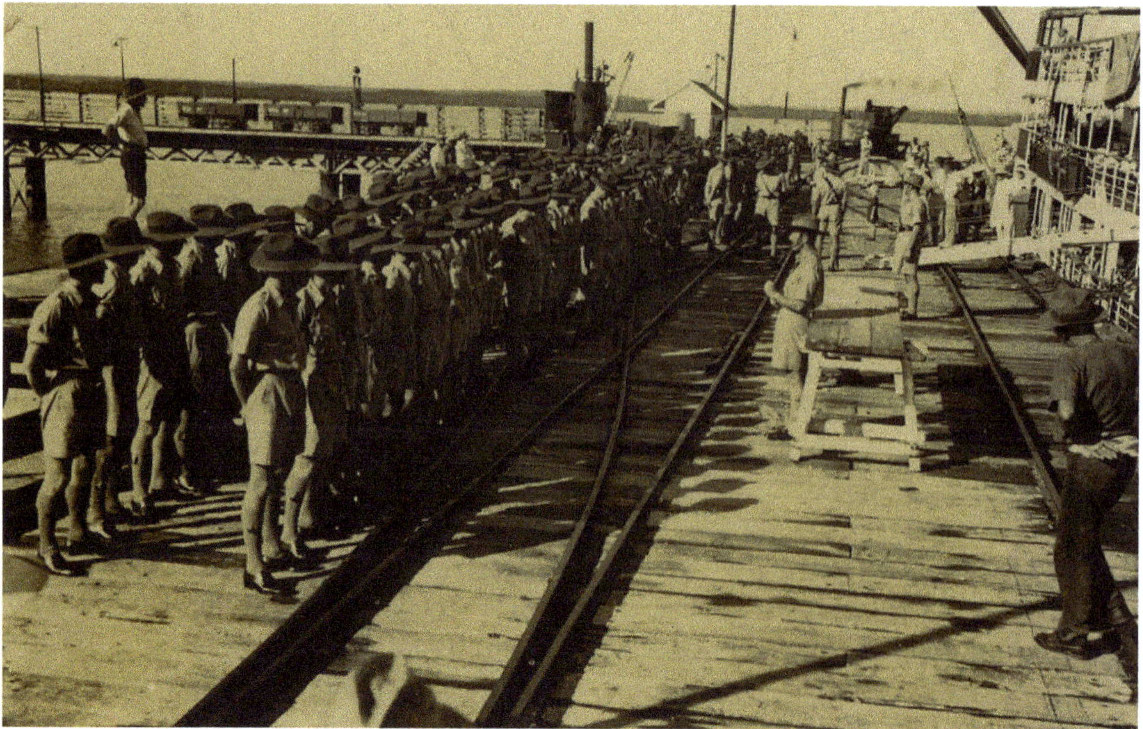

Arrival of the Darwin Mobile Force, Stokes Hill Wharf, 1938. (Unknown, NTAS, B. Humble Collection, NTRS 1168 Item 43.)

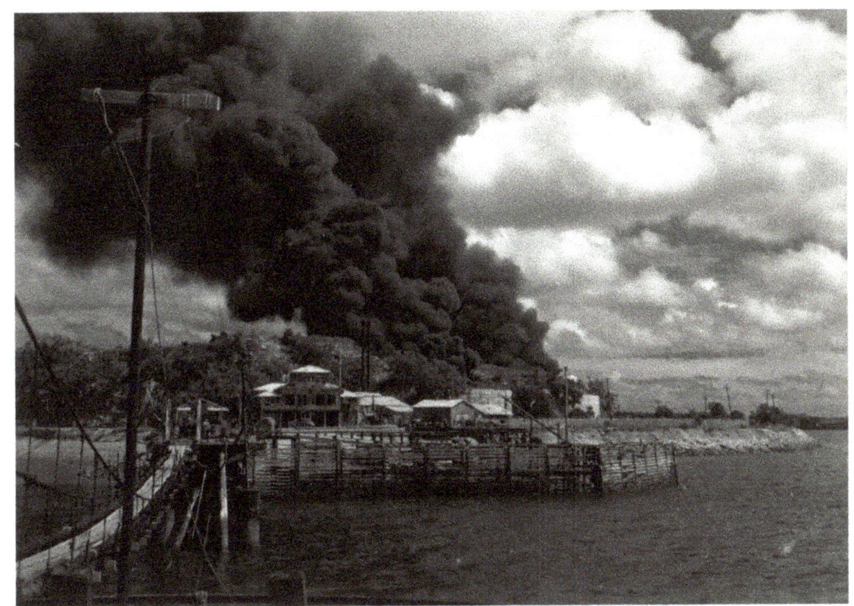

Stokes Hill Wharf, flying boat control tower with burning oil tanks in background, 19 February 1942 (Unknown, NTAS, Urquhart Collection, NTRS 258 Item 46.)

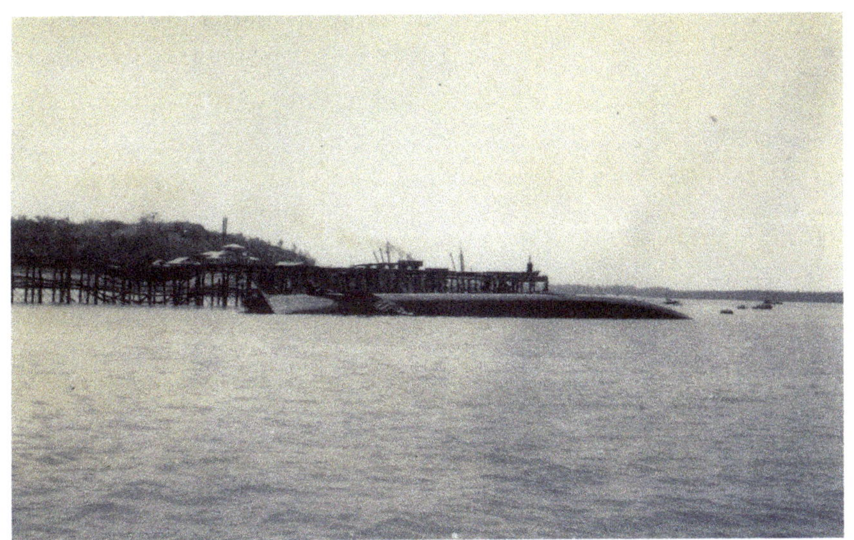

The *Neptuna* at Stokes Hill Wharf, post 19 February 1942. (Unknown, NTAS, Victor Levitt Collection, NTRS 3433 Item 19.)

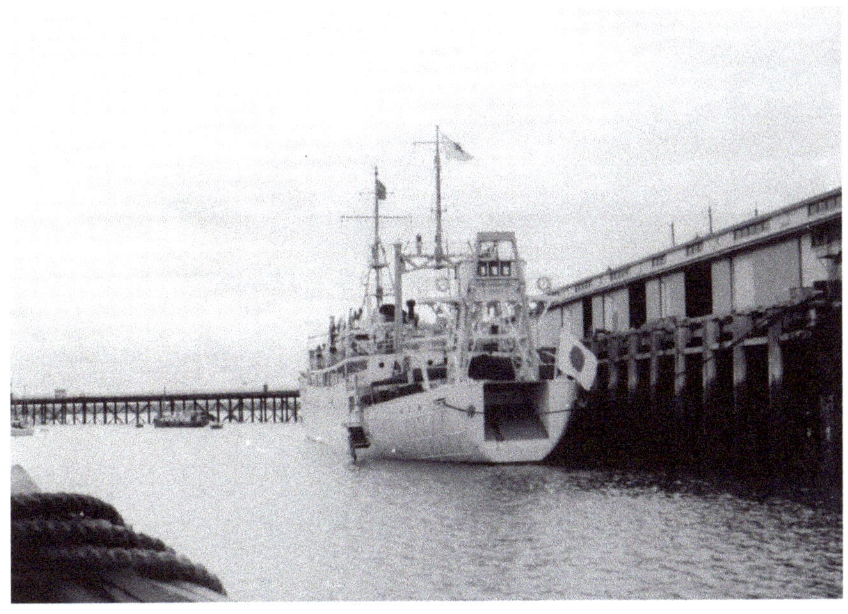

Japanese vessel, *Umtakamaru*, at Stokes Hill Wharf, 1960. Fujita Salvaging Company salvage operation, 1959-1960. (Unknown, NTL, Senichiro Fujita Collection, PH0874/0098.)

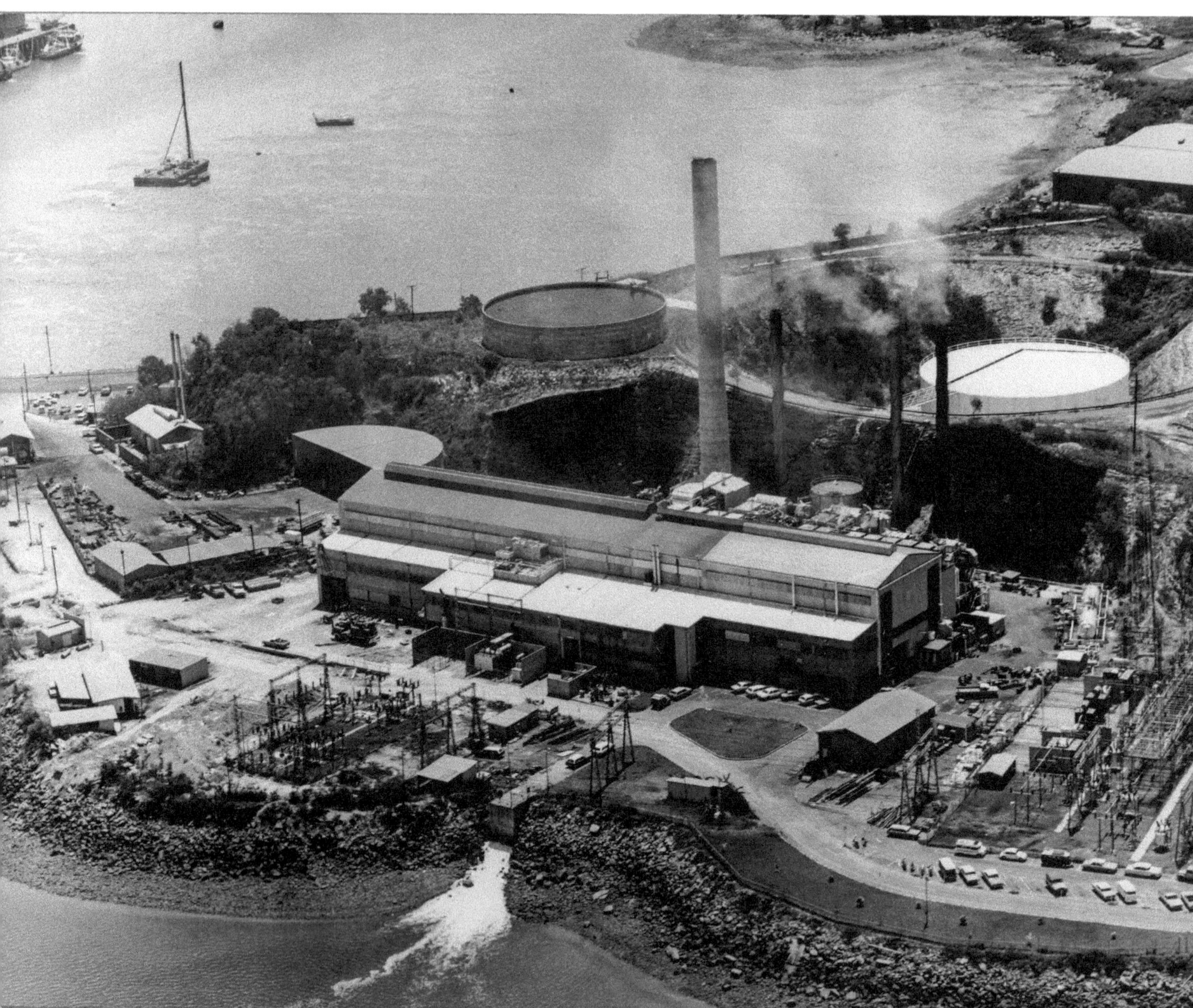

Stokes Hill Power Station, c1970s. (Unknown, NTL, ABC T.V. Collection, PH0416/0191.)

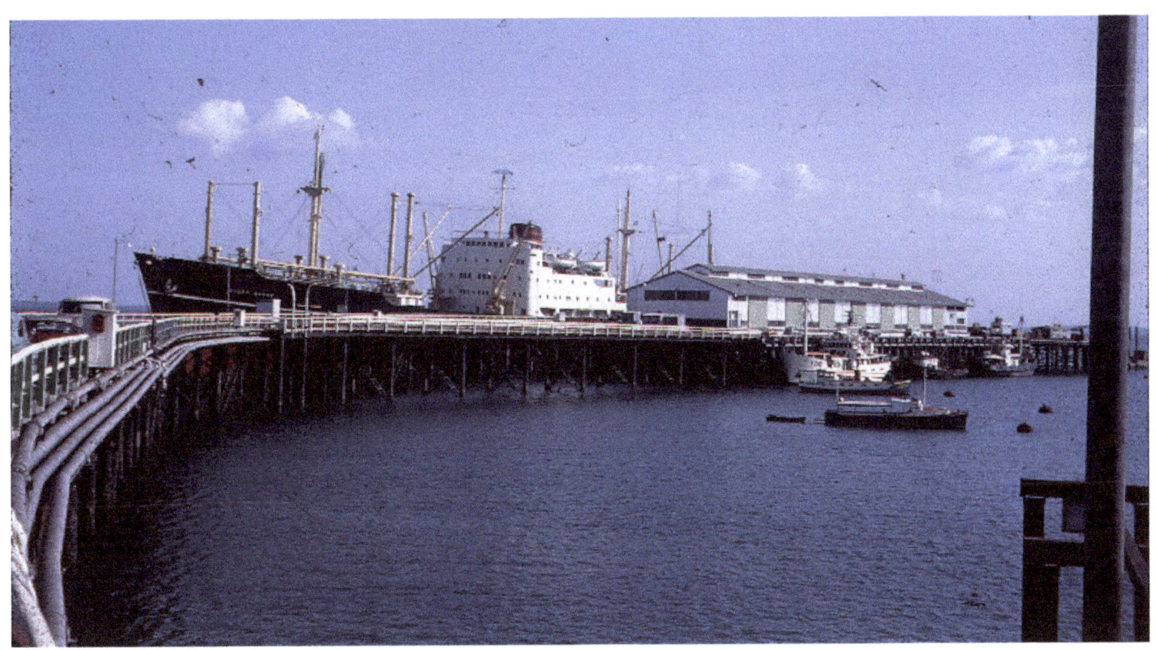

Stokes Hill Wharf, 1964. (Unknown, NTAS, Heather Graham Collection, NTRS 3406/P1/2.)

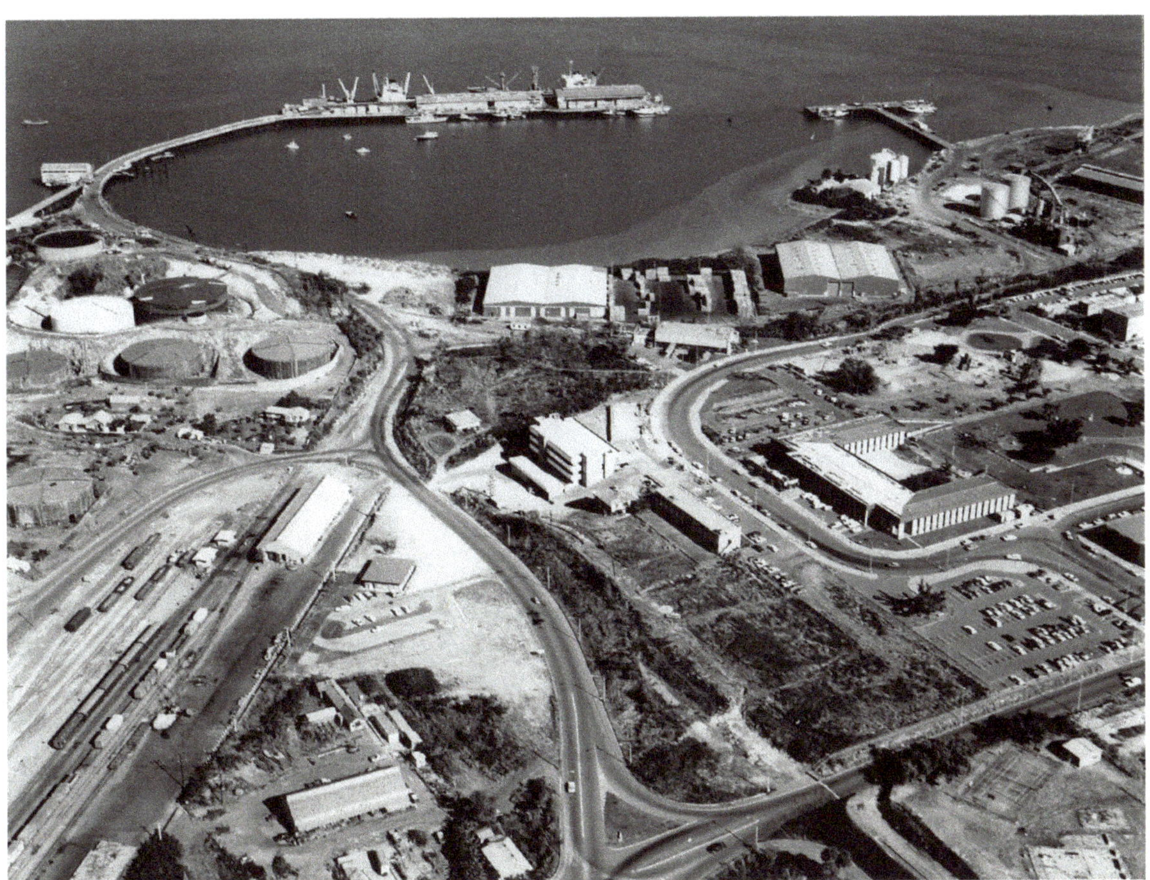

Darwin wharves, Darwin Railway Station, oil tanks & CBD east, c1970s. (Unknown, NTAS, GPC, NTRS 3822-P1 Folder 8 Aerial view of wharves, oil tanks, railway.)

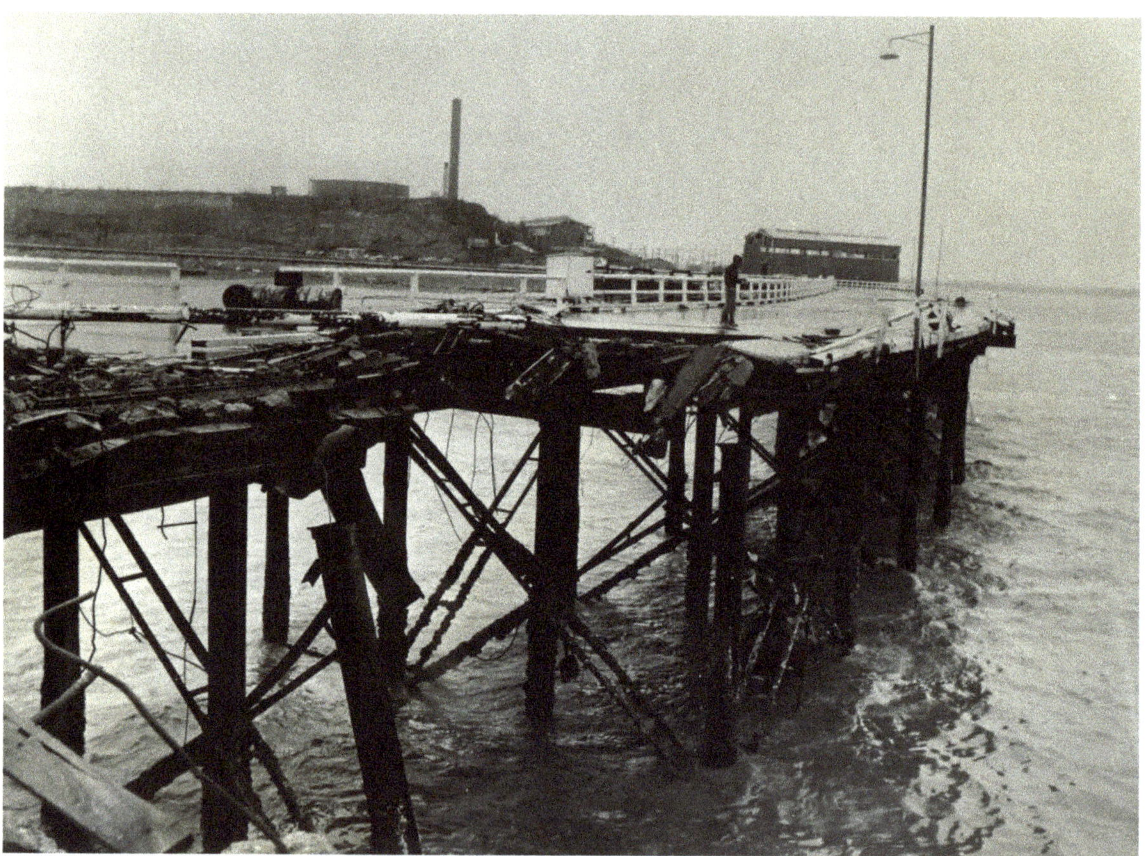

Stokes Hill Wharf, damaged by collision with *HMAS Arrow* during Cyclone Tracy, December 1974. (Unknown, NTAS, GPC, NTRS 3822-P1 Folder 66 Cyclone - Stokes Hill Wharf.)

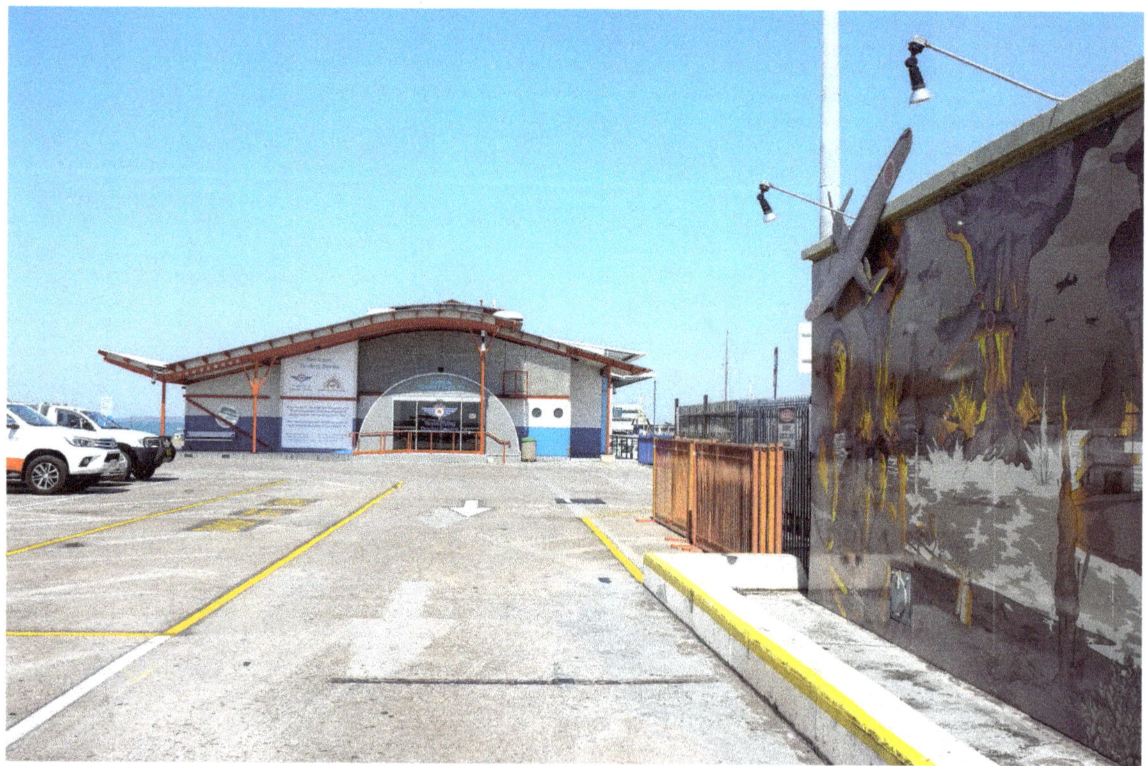

Stokes Hill Wharf, Bombing of Darwin mural and Royal Flying Doctor Service and tourist facility, 2017. (Martin, R., Matthew Stephen, Personal Collection, Wharf 07.)

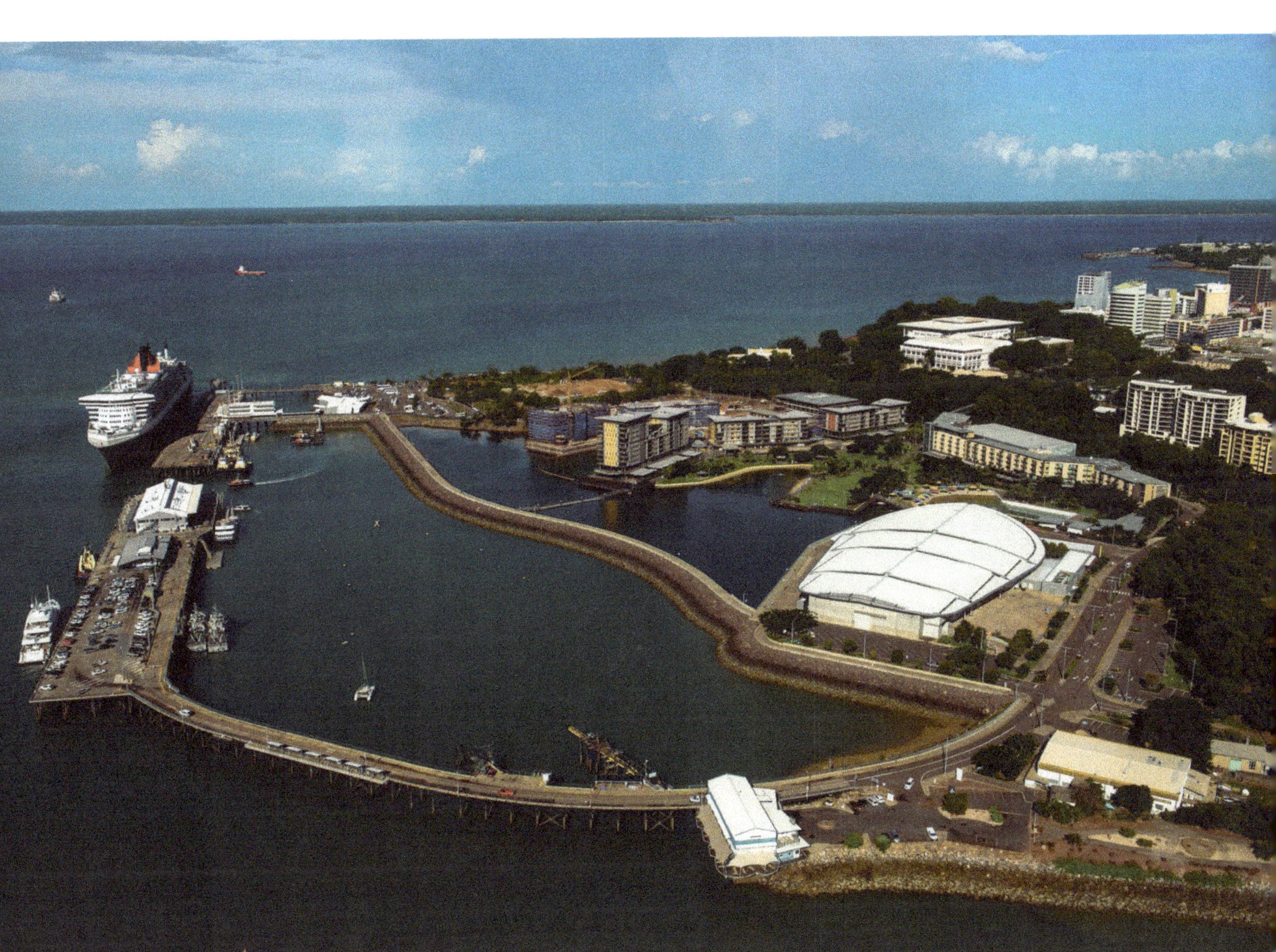

Darwin wharves and Waterfront, c2016. (Minogue, T., NT Government, Tourism NT Collection, 122099-2.)

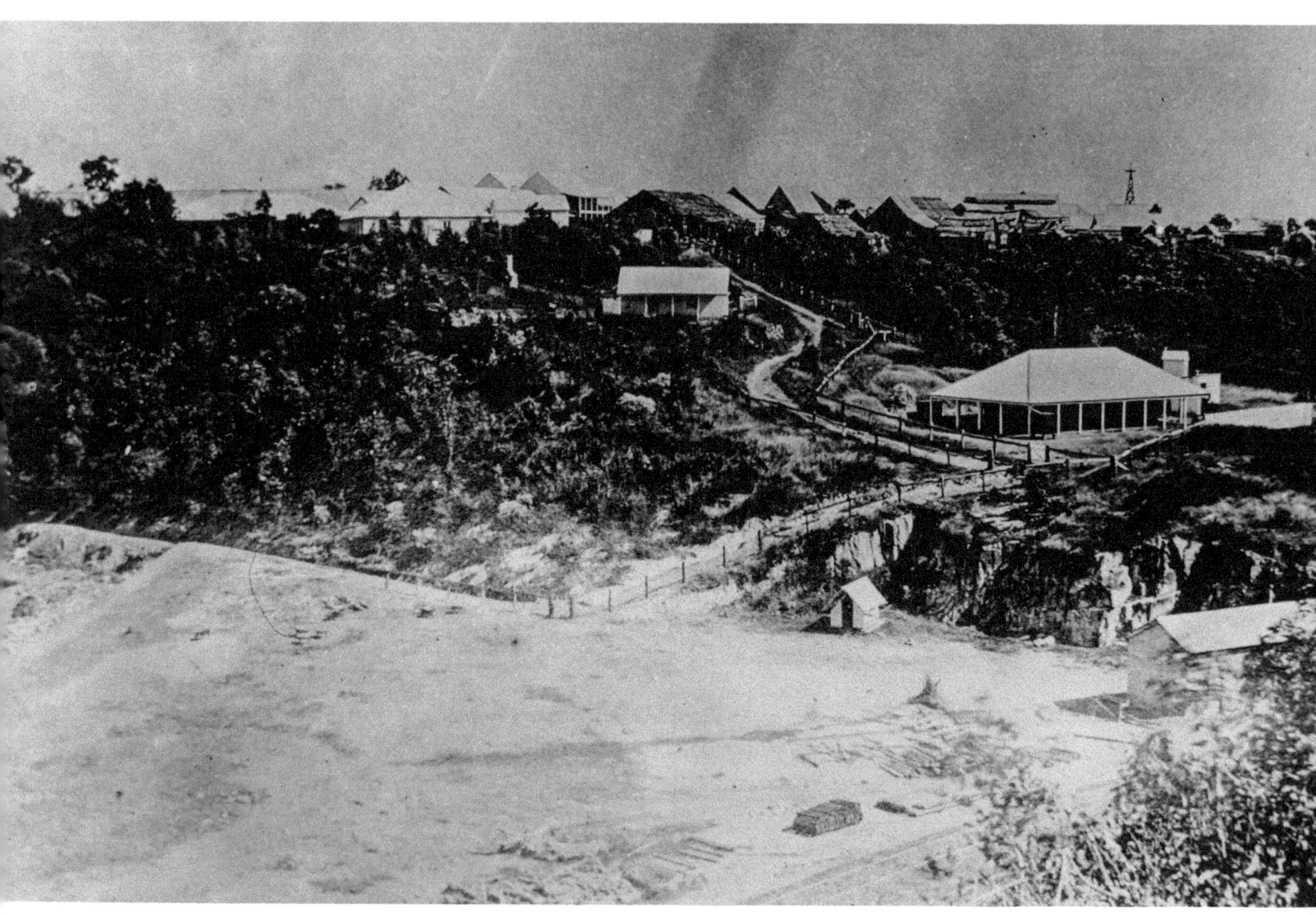

View to Cavenagh Street and Chinatown up Travellers Walk from Stokes Hill, c1888. (Foelsche, P., NTL, Foelsche Collection, PH0111/0062.)

Chapter 3

Cavenagh Street: Darwin's Chinatown

Cavenagh Street was named after Hon Wentworth Cavenagh-Mainwaring, the South Australian Commissioner of Crown Lands during Goyder's original survey of Palmerston.[1] Located at the Eastern End of the town closest to the wharf it was a prime location for businesses in the town centre.

From European settlement to World War II Cavenagh Street was Darwin's Chinatown. Darwin and the Northern Territory's reputation as a diverse multicultural community has at its foundation its Chinese and Aboriginal populations. For so many travellers visiting Darwin it was this diversity that gave the town its character. Elsie Masson, Governess to the children of the Commonwealth's first Administrator, Dr. Gilruth wrote in 1912,

> Life in Darwin is made up of many little worlds, each continuing in its own way, impinging on, but never mingling with the others. There is the life of white officialdom, the Eastern life of Chinatown, the life of the pearling fleets and, under all, the life of the native camps. A visitor may spend a week there, and the existence of these separate worlds may never dawn upon him. Or, again, in strolling along the beach, he may, in the space of a few moments, alight upon their outward signs. First he may walk into a party of blacks crooning soft corroboree songs to themselves; then he may suddenly come upon a small joss-house guarded by chipped stone dragons, with its gaudy gilt fretwork, waxen images, and pewter bowls, glimmering through the incense-thickened air; and, looking out to sea, his eye may light on a fleet of pearling luggers, sailing lazily home like a flock of tired birds against a sunset sky.[2]

Although some Chinese immigrants arrived in Palmerston soon after European settlement their numbers increased greatly after the discovery of gold during the construction of the Overland Telegraph in 1870. The gold rush in the Northern Territory was small by Australian standards and was hindered by the lack of cheap labour. Similar to all British colonies in the tropics it was believed that Europeans were unsuited to manual labour and the solution was Chinese labour.

In 1874 the South Australian Government became the first in Australia to indenture Chinese labour to work in a gold province.[3] The first group of 186 'Coolies' arrived from Singapore in 1874. Chinese people soon developed their own businesses which worried some of Palmerston's European community as evident in this newspaper report: 'The Chinese seem to be doing a considerable business in Cavenagh Street. Europeans will have to look out.'[4] By 1880 the eastern end of Cavenagh Street was known as Chinatown.[5] In 1881 the Chinese population in Palmerston had grown to 4000 while the European population was 660.[6] Like all migrants, the Chinese people bought their culture and traditions with them. Chinese temples were constructed in various parts of the town. The current Chung Wah

1 NTG, Place Names Register, www.
2 Masson, *An Untamed Territory*, 51-52.
3 Jones, *The Chinese in the Northern Territory*, 106.
4 *NTTG*, 14 September 1878.
5 *NTTG*, 26 June 1880.
6 Yee, *Through Chinese Eyes*, 4

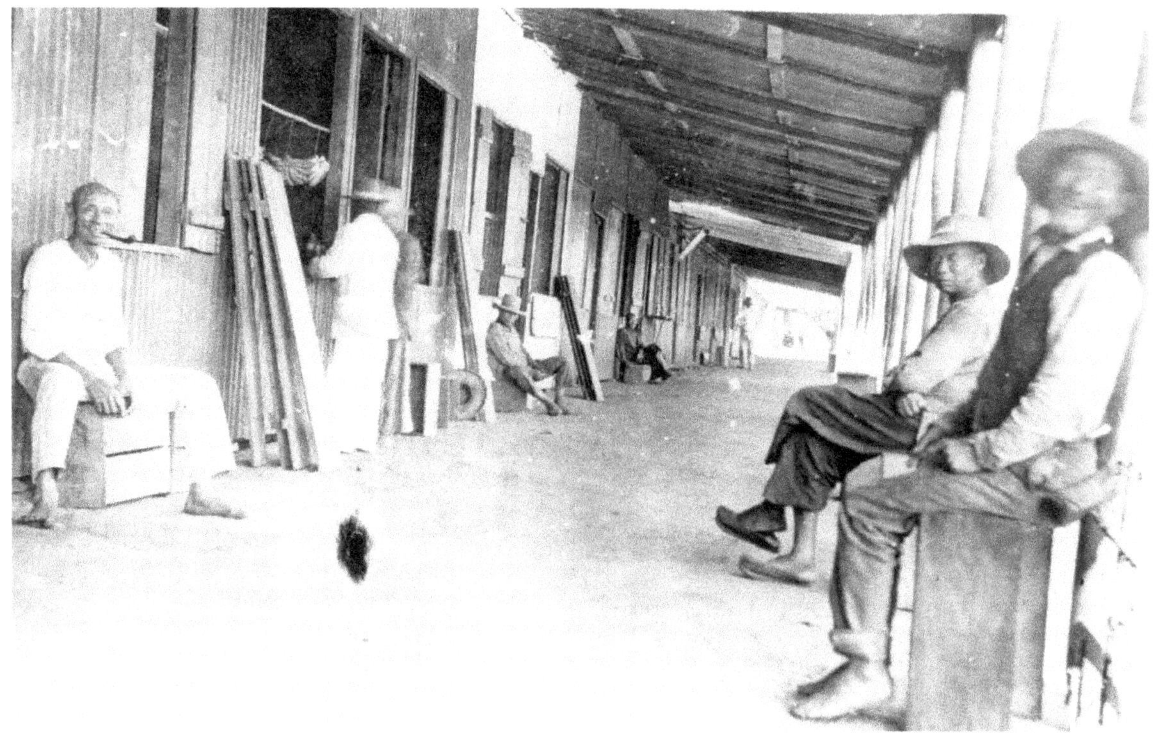

Cavenagh Street, Chinatown, c1890s. (Unknown, NTAS, HSNT Collection, NTRS 1854 Item 756.)

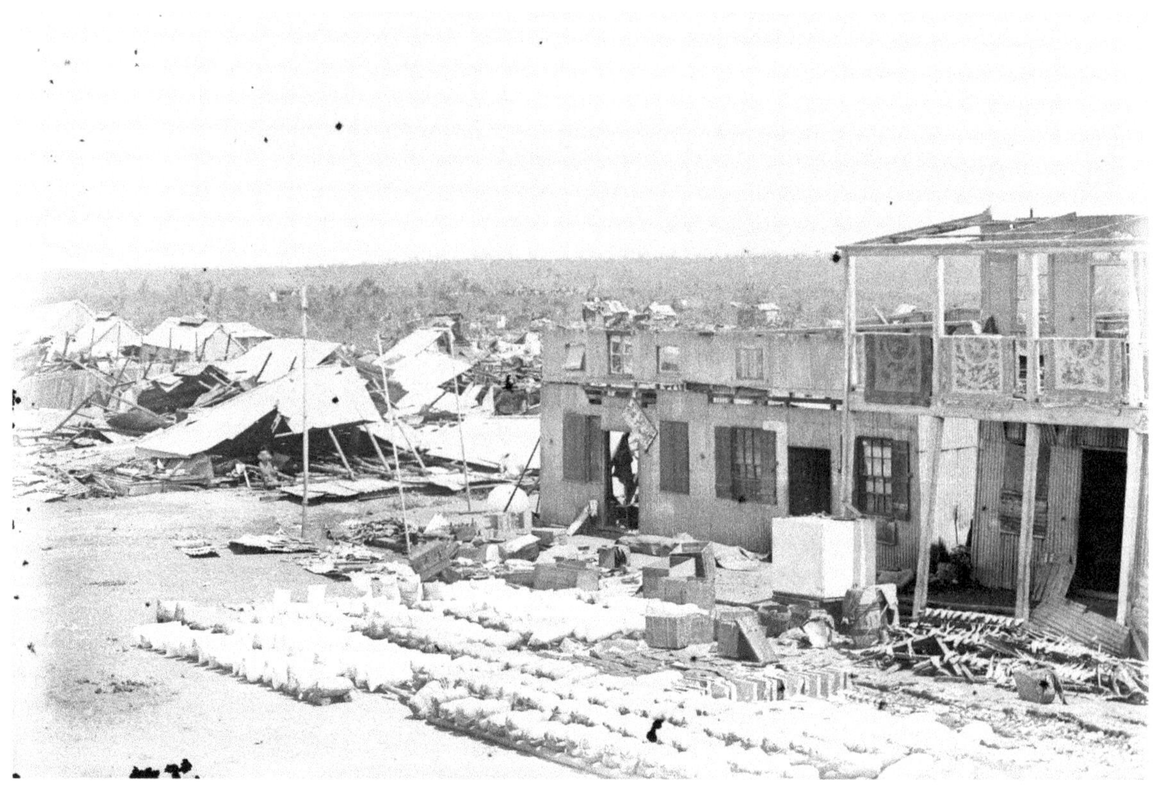

Chinese store damaged by 1897 cyclone. Drying goods on Cavenagh Street. (Bleeser, F., NLA, Florenz Bleeser Collection, PIC/9981/109.)

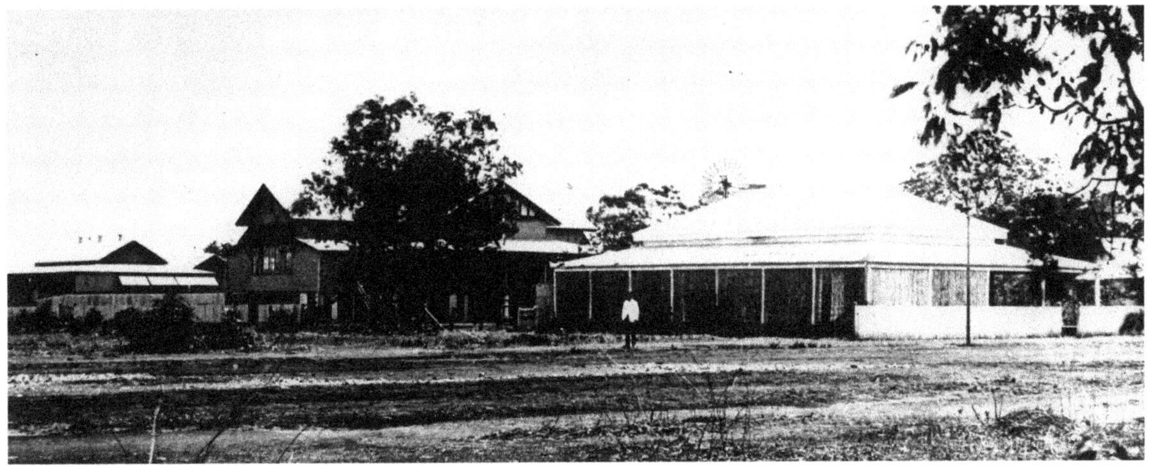

Palmerston Primary School, Cavenagh Street, c1911. (Unknown, NTAS, GPC, NTRS 3822/P1/Box 6/GPC/Fldr 99, Historic Sites, Dwn Area.)

Society temple in Woods Street was first constructed in 1887. At this time the Chinese community in Palmerston increased rapidly due to the construction of the northern section of the Transcontinental Railway, from Palmerston to Pine Creek between 1886 and 1889. The Chinese labourforce working on the railway during this period resulted in the Chinese population growing to 6,122, outnumbering Europeans 6 to 1.[7]

The 1897 Cyclone which devastated much of Palmerston almost destroyed Chinatown. 'It is impossible to describe the total state of devastation that exists in the city of Palmerston.'[8] The Terminus Hotel, the Chinese Josshouse and almost all of Chinatown, which was built of wood and corrugated iron was severely damaged. The Chinese community was largely left to their own enterprise and resources to rebuild.

From 1878 to 1910 the Northern Territory Chinese population outnumbered Europeans. Attitudes towards Chinese people amongst the Northern Territory European community in the 19th century were often contradictory. Due to the lack of European labour, most households and businesses in Darwin, as well as the mining industry, were reliant on Chinese and/or Aboriginal labour. Yet in the decades prior to Australia's federation in 1901, and the implementation of the 'White Australia' policy, Chinese and other 'aliens' were seen as a threat.

When the Commonwealth took over control of the Northern Territory in 1911 the Chinese population had fallen to approximately 1000 and by 1931 this had fallen further to 659.[9] The Commonwealth regime, guided by the 'White Australia' policy resulted in the Chinese and Aboriginal communities of Darwin experiencing discrimination in many ways. Chinatown was the subject of special attention under the guise of 'public health'. In 1912 the Commonwealth Administrator recommended that Chinatown be destroyed and rebuilt under strict regulations.[10]

The decreasing Chinese population in the early 20th century meant the Chinese were no longer seen as a 'threat'. In the 1920s Chinese people began to enter Darwin's social mainstream. Chinese sportsmen embraced Australian football and soccer and became involved in sports previously dominated by the European community. In 1923 the Darwin Chinese

7 Donovan, *A Land Full of Possibilities*, 173.
8 *SAR*, 11 January 1897.
9 Jones, *The Chinese in the Northern Territory, 91.*
10 Jones, *The Chinese in the Northern Territory*, 89.

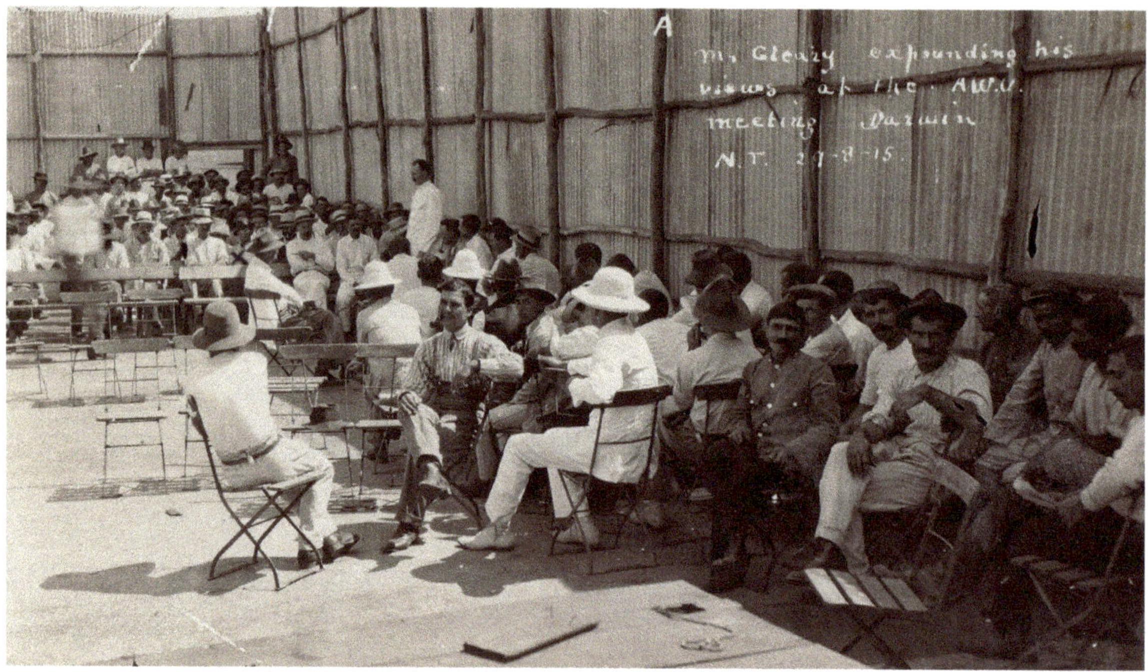

Don 'Stadium', 1915. [On reverse of the postcard.] Electing officers & settling Waterside workers strike, each member fined 2/6 for disobeying Union, when they were ordered back to work, a few days before. Don Picture Theatre. [Larry Donnison is marked with an x on the photo. Larry is the son of Elizabeth Donnison under whose name the photograph collection is donated to the Mitchell Library.] (Unknown, LNSW, E.D.W.S Donnison Collection, ML MSS 890/3/0217.)

Recreation Club (DCRC), opened its premises in Cavenagh Street.[11] The DCRC was Darwin's first non-European sports club and became a driving force in sport, particularly after World War II.

The depression hit Darwin hard and it did not begin to recover until the mid to late 1930s when the military build up stimulated the economy. Established Chinese families retained their business interests in Cavenagh Street but the next generation were beginning to branch out due to their educational attainments and took up positions in the Northern Territory Commonwealth public service.[12]

There are few reminders of Chinatown today. The Sue Wah Chin Building or the 'Stone House', as it is also known, was built in 1880. It is some distance from Chinatown proper, but is the only example remaining of Cavenagh Street shops from the 19th century. Its story reflects the experiences of many Chinese families who established Darwin's Chinatown and remain in Darwin to this day. The building was constructed as five separate shops by Sun Mow Loong, also known as Kwong Sue Duk, who retained one and sold the others. In 1895 Sun Mow Loong sold his shop to Lauritz Helleman who by 1920 had acquired the entire building. In the 1920s the property, now known as the 'Stone Houses' was transferred to Chin Toy. During World War II the Stone Houses's 'outhouses' were destroyed during Japanese air raids, but the main building escaped unscathed. The Royal Australian Navy rented the building from 1943. In 1946 the Commonwealth compulsorily acquired the property but it returned to the hands of the Chin family in 1952 after they settled an acquisition and war damage claim in 1951. The ownership of the property transferred to Mrs Sue Wah Chin, after whom the building takes its name. The Chin family retained an interest in the property until approximately 2008.[13]

---

11 *NTTG*, 11 December 1923.

12 Jones, *The Chinese in the Northern Territory*, 89-98.

13 Heritage Branch, *Sue Wah Chin Building*, 2-7. Chin, D, Personal communication, 27 July 2018.

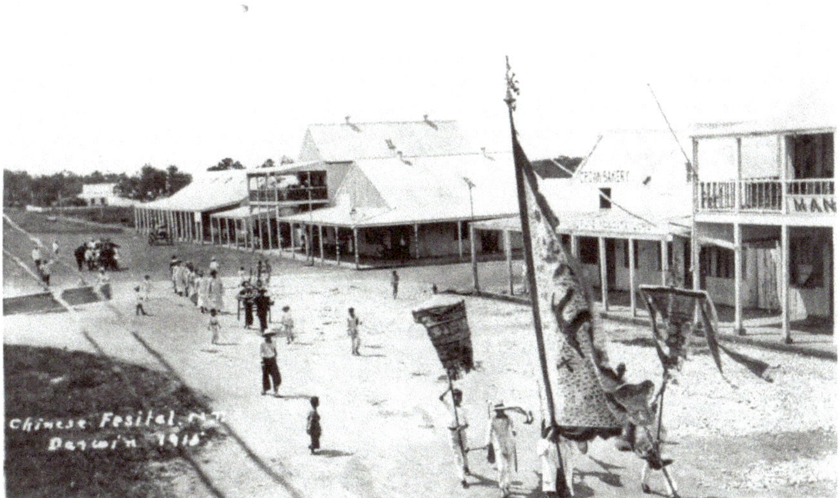

Cavenagh Street, Chinatown, Chinese parade, 1916. (Unknown, NTAS, HSNT Collection, NTRS 1854 Item 891.)

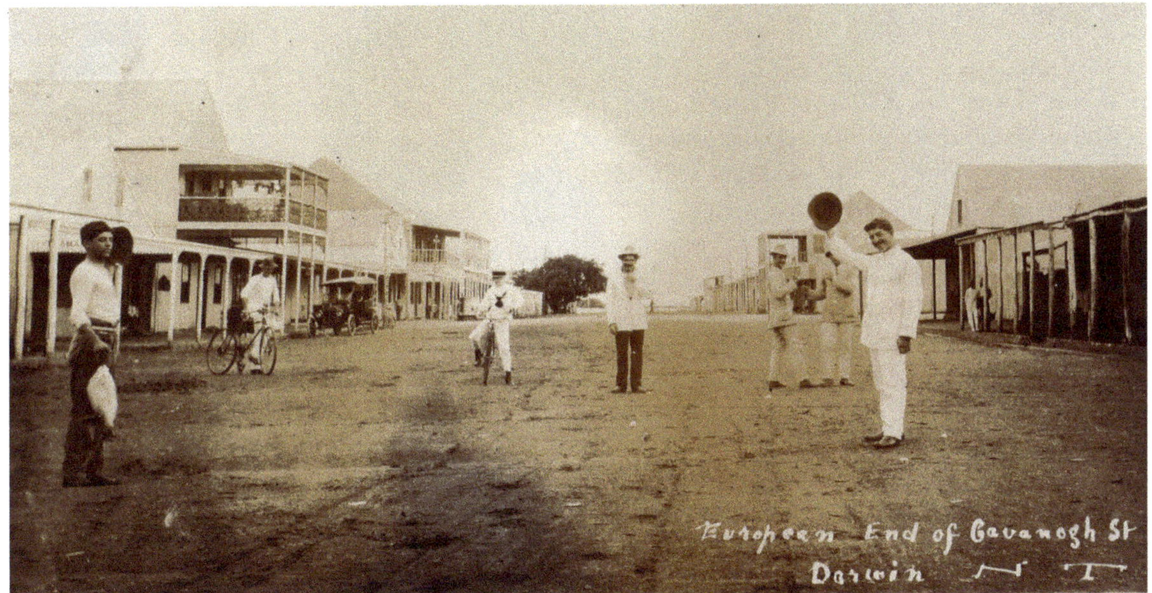

The European end of Cavenagh Street, c1916. (Unknown, LNSW, E.D.W.S Donnison Collection, ML MSS 890/3/0175.)

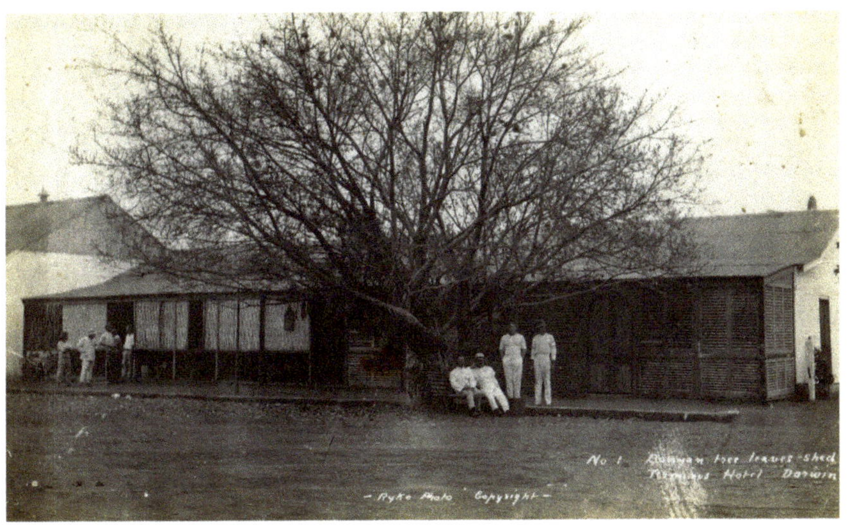

Terminus Hotel, c1916. (Reichenbach, E.F., NTL, Peter Spillett Collection, PH0413/0079.)

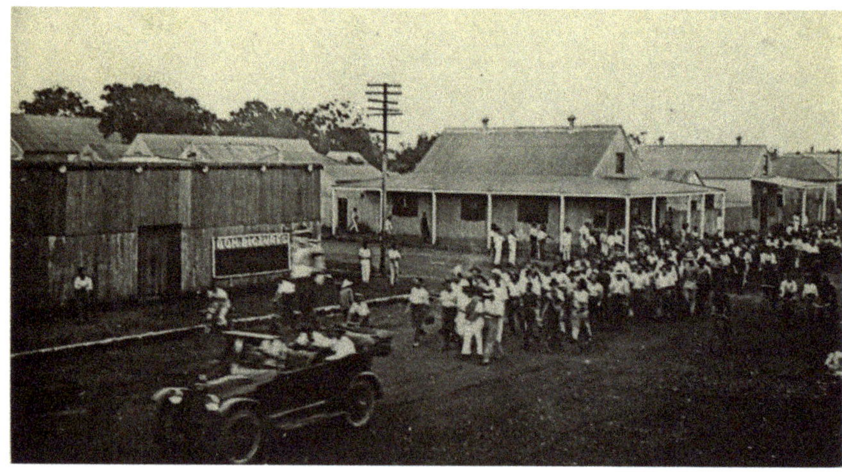

Procession following an effigy of Dr Gilruth in car at the corner of Cavenagh & Bennett Street, c1918. Don Pictures on left. (Unknown, NTAS, Rhodes Collection, NTRS 2885 Item 23.)

World War II saw the end of Chinatown in Cavenagh Street. Most of the Chinese civilian population was evacuated from Darwin in late 1941. Chinatown was severely damaged by bombing during the war. After the war many of Darwin's Chinese community returned to their homes. However, the authorities and changes in land tenure laws meant they could not rebuild in Cavenagh Street and were instead dispersed throughout Darwin. In 1946 the Chung Wah Society was formed to 'promote harmony and goodwill between the Chinese residents in the NT and people of other nationalities.'[14]

Although Cavenagh Street's development up to World War II is dominated by its Chinese history there are other important stories to tell.

In 1876 the South Australian Government established its first state school in temporary accommodation. In 1880 the new school room on Cavenagh Street was opened.[15] Palmerston Primary School and later Darwin Higher Primary School (1922) were originally located on this site. Generations of Darwin residents have fond memories of the school. Darwin Primary School and Darwin Higher Primary School relocated in stages from Cavenagh Street to Frogs Hollow on Woods street from 1951.[16] Darwin High School relocated from Frogs Hollow to its current site on Bullocky Point in 1963. Darwin Primary School at Frogs Hollow closed in 1984. Today it is a community arts precinct. The only reminder of the original Cavengh Street school is the heritage listed *Adansonia Gregorii* or Boab Tree, which was once in the school yard.[17]

Darwin has a long history of outdoor picture theatres. Don Pictures were first established in the Darwin Town Hall in 1913.[18] In 1913 they leased a site on the corner of Cavenagh and Bennett Street.[19] The Don Picture Show, an open air venue, began screening movies in Cavenagh Street in 1914.[20] Star Pictures in Smith Street opened for business in September 1929.[21] Star Pictures was purchased by Christina Gordon and her sons in 1932. Christina Gordon also ran the Victoria Hotel in Smith Street. Although both theatres operated for two years the Don Picture Theatre closed in 1932 when it was also sold to Mrs Gordon.[22] Construction of Gordon's Don Hotel began in April 1935 and opened for business in January

14 Chung Wah Society, www.
15 *NTTG* 20 November 1880, see also *NT Government Resident Report,* 17 August 1881, 3.
16 Forrest, *Memories of Frog Hollow*, 2.
17 NTG, Heritage Register, Boab Tree, Cavenagh Street.
18 *NTTG*, 20 February 1913.
19 *NTTG*, 29 May 1913.
20 *NTTG,* 1 January 1914.
21 *NTTG,* 13 September 1929.
22 *NS,* 29 April 1932.

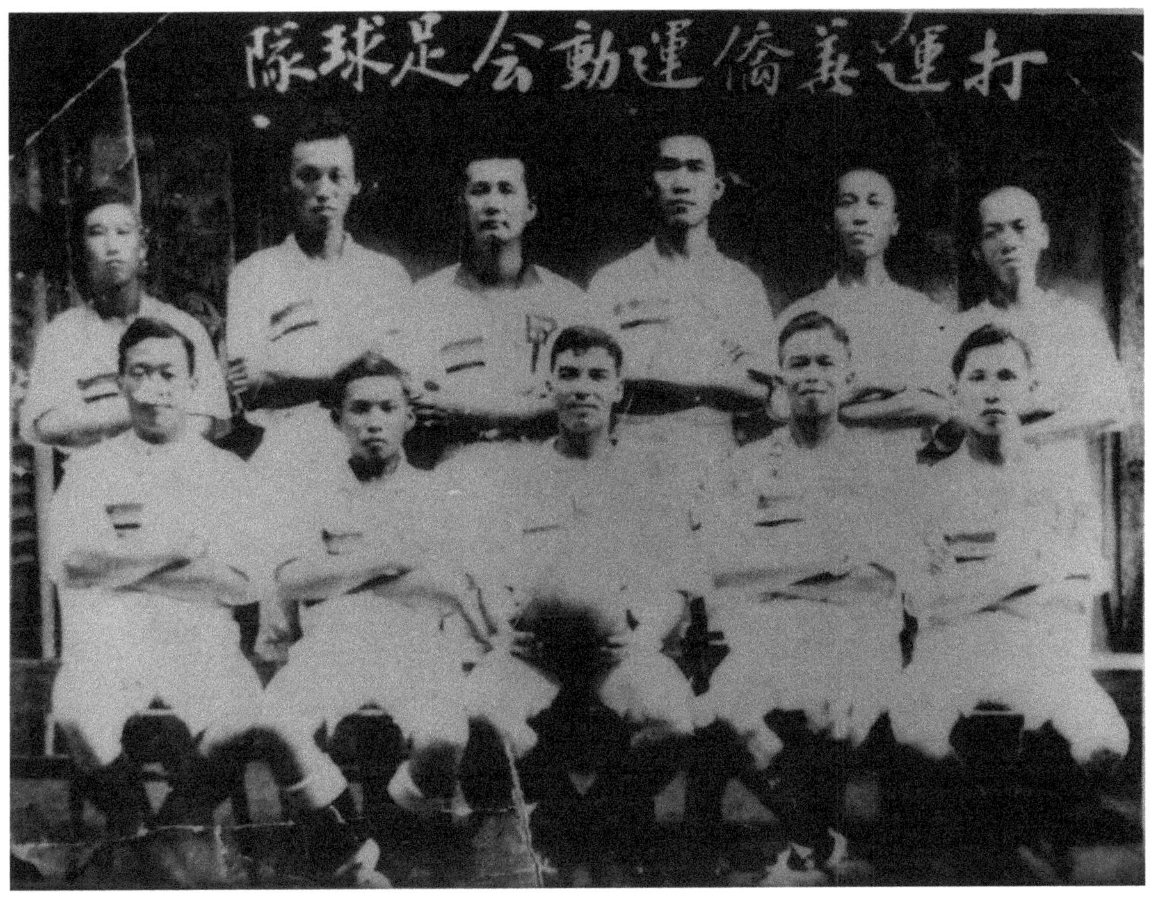

The Darwin Chinese Recreation Club, soccer team, c1920s. Back row L-R: Charles Hee, Gee Hang Yet, David Sang, Lee Ying, Tommy Ming Ket, Willy Moo. Front row L-R: Billy Quong, Henry Jan, Arthur Lee, Jack Lee, Willy Jan. (Unknown, NTL, Peter Spillett Collection, PH0238/0485.)

1936.[23] The hotel developed quite a reputation prior to World War II when it became known as 'The Blood House.' Damaged by bombing in World War II the Don Hotel did not open immediately after the war but became a government women's hostel, named Abbott's House in 1951.[24]

By the late 1940s The 'Don' Hotel was back in business in a new location on the north side of Cavenagh Street. In the 1950s the Bamboo Lounge was added to these premises. For a brief time between 1979 and 1983 The Don Hotel was reincarnated as the 'Don Casino' as an early initiative of Northern Territory Self Government to stimulate the economy. It was the first casino in Darwin and the second in Australia and was operated by Federal Hotels while their Mindil Beach Casino was under construction. After a brief but glittering episode in Darwin's history the Don Casino closed in 1983, but the Cavenagh Hotel remains on the site today.

The Terminus Hotel opened in March 1885, close to the Palmerston railway station at the wharf end of Cavenagh Street.[25] It was one of the few European establishments in Chinatown. During World War I the Terminus was one of three 'State' hotels in Darwin taken over by the Commonwealth Government. This takeover became a sore point with the public and the continuous complaints and resentment was a factor in the 'Darwin Rebellion' and attempts to force the Commonwealth Administrator Gilruth

23 *NS*, 30 April 1935 & *NS*, 28 January 1936.
24 *NS* 12 January 1951. See also NAA:F1, 1952/851.
25 *NA*, 13 March 1885.

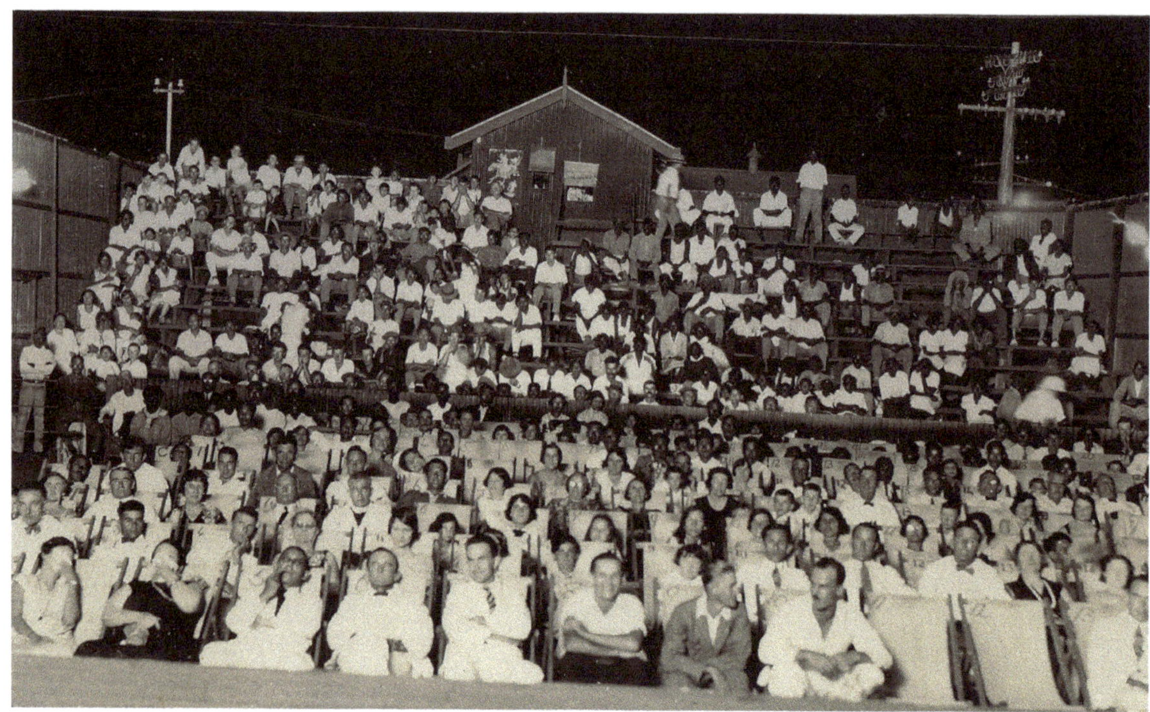

Don Pictures, Cavenagh Street, c1930. (Unknown, NTAS, Charles Wilson Collection, NTRS 335 Item 387.)

out of office. The Terminus Hotel's most notable feature was the 'Tree of Knowledge', a Banyan tree (*Ficus Virens*) that marked its location on Cavenagh Street. 'Galamarrma' to the Larrakia, the Tree of Knowledge was popular meeting place for the community. Although the Terminus Hotel was demolished after its closure in November 1931 the 'Tree of Knowledge' remained. The hotel's demise was noted in the *Northern Territory Times*. 'Many an old stager has sighed at the demolition of the Terminus Hotel, so long the rendezvous of old Territorian battlers. If walls have ears, what tales those old timbers have heard. The gap in Cavenagh Street is another reminder of how many changes life can show.'[26]

'Galamarrma' is a reminder of Cavenagh Street's early history when it extended to intersect with the Esplanade. In the mid 1960s Cavenagh Street was altered to end at Bennett Street to allow for the construction of the Darwin City Council Civic Centre. Nichols Place is now home to the Australia Broadcasting Commission (ABC) which has operated on its current site since 1967 and the Northern Territory Magistrates Court, which was opened in 1986.

The ABC played a vital role during Cyclone Tracy. In the days leading up to the Cyclone it broadcast weather updates that went largely unheeded by the community. On Christmas Eve the ABC broadcast until 2am, the height of the cyclone. It returned to the air some thirty four hours later on Boxing Day afternoon, providing vital information to the community. ABC journalist Dick Muddimer was one of the first to get word of the devastation of Cyclone Tracy to the outside world. The message was simple: 'Town Destroyed, help needed.'[27]

The history of Cavenagh Street and its past life as Chinatown provides a fascinating glimpse into Darwin's past. In the age of 'revitalising' and 'activating' the city centre today's urban planners could only dream to rekindle the vibrant and colourful scenes of pre-World War II Chinatown which was the very heart and soul of Darwin.

26 *NTTG*, 29 January 1932.
27 Roussos, & Purtill. *Cyclone Tracy*, Also Parker, Personal communication, 18 May 2018.

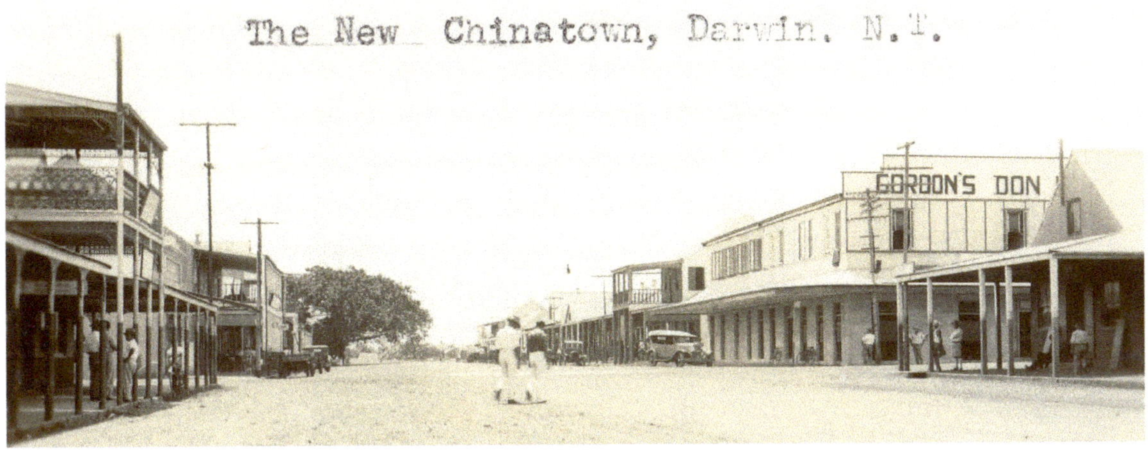

Cavenagh Street, Chinatown, c1938. (Unknown, NTAS, HSNT Collection, NTRS 1854 Item 376.)

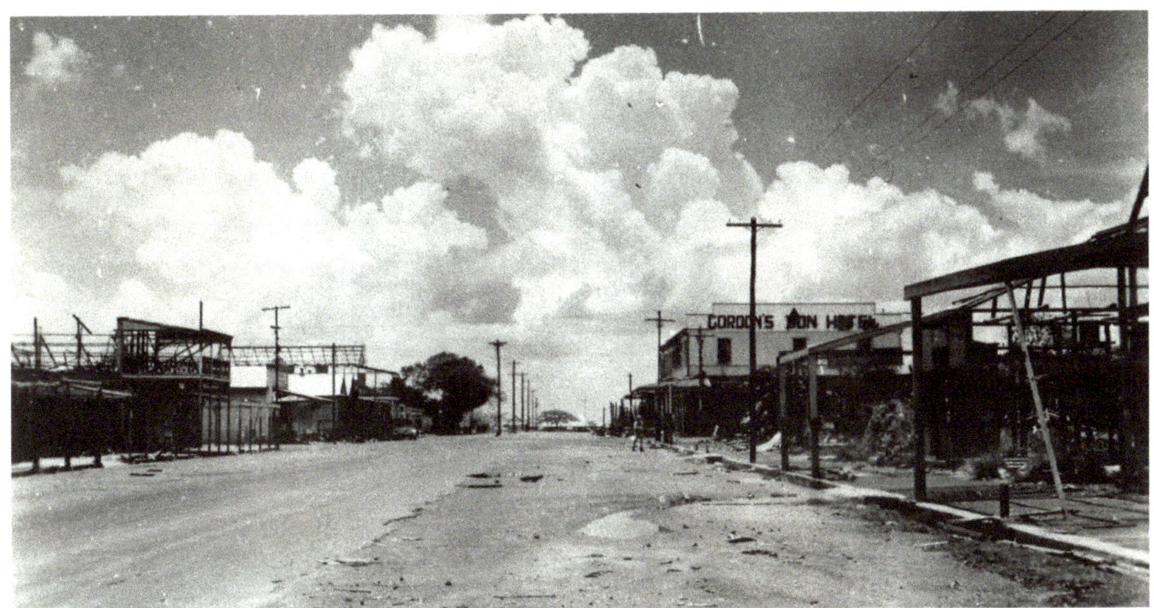

Cavenagh Street, bomb damage, looking south east towards the Tree of Knowledge, 1942. (Unknown, NTAS, J. Beverly Collection, NTRS 2012 Item 21.)

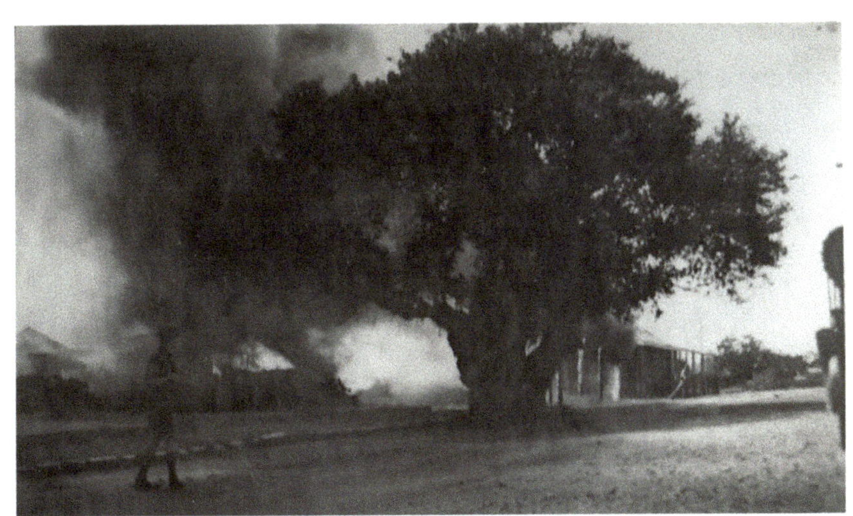

Cavenagh Street, Tree of Knowledge, after bombing raid, 1943. (Unknown, NTAS, J. Beverly Collection, NTRS 2012 Item 47.)

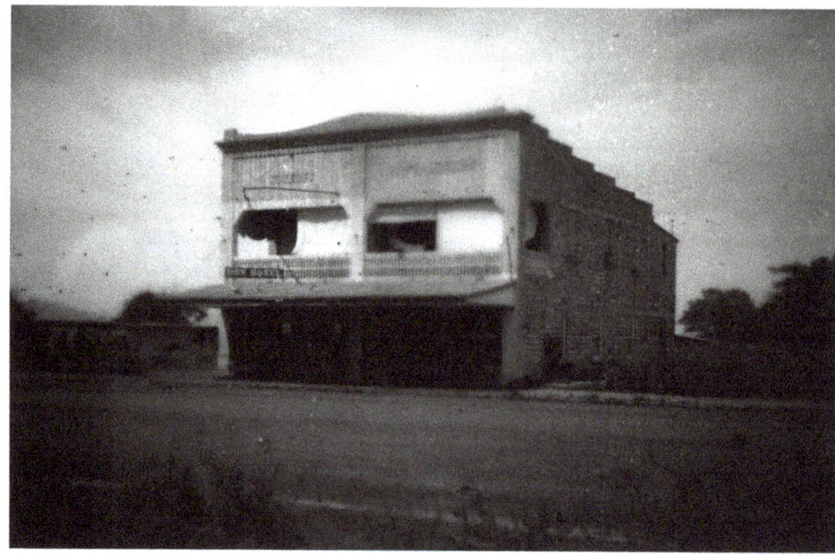

2nd Don Hotel, Cavenagh Street, c1949. (Harford, B.P., NTAS, B.P. Harford Collection, NTRS 1299 Item 220.)

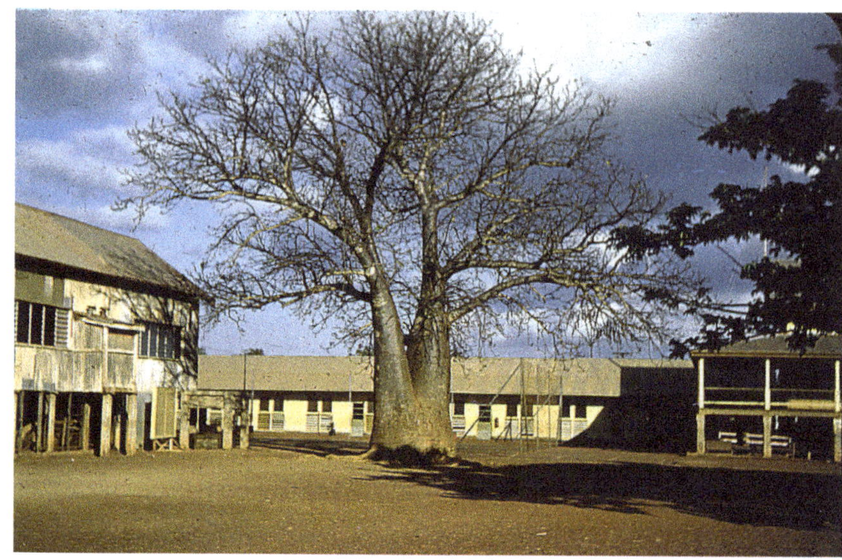

Darwin Primary School, Cavenagh Street, c1957. (Unknown, NTAS, W.C. Laidlaw Collection, NTRS 317 Item 9.)

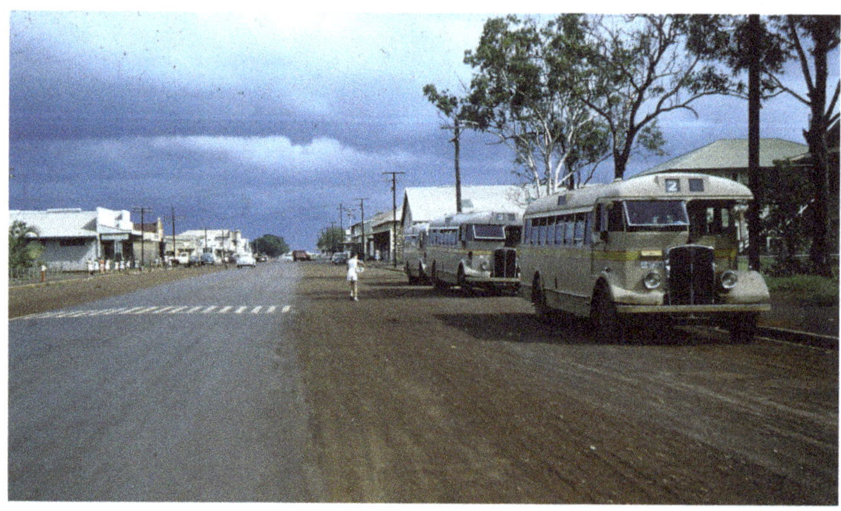

Buses waiting at Darwin Primary School, Cavenagh Street, c1957. (Unknown, NTAS, W.C. Laidlaw Collection, NTRS 317 Item 10.)

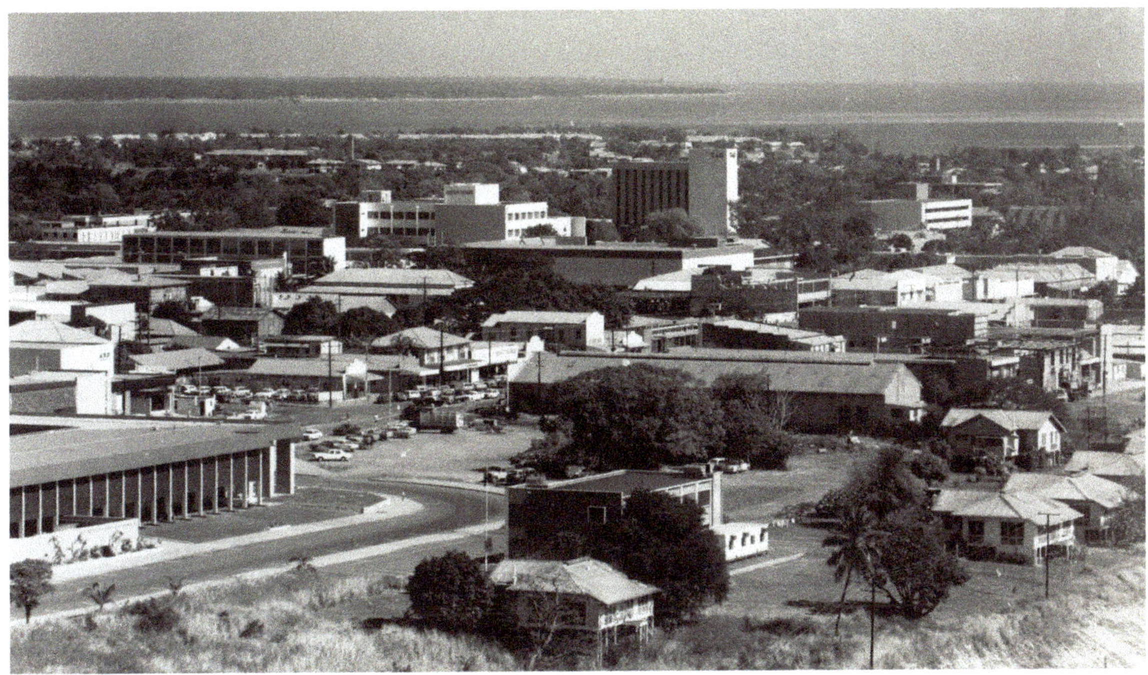

View of Darwin showing Civic Centre and Cavenagh Street. ABD 6 behind Civic Centre, T & G building in Smith Street is the only high building in the centre of photograph, 1973. (Unknown, NTL, Peter Spillett Collection, PH0238-0550.)

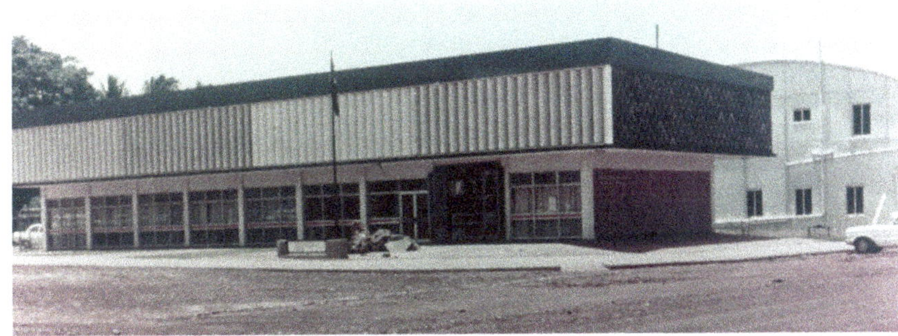

ABC & Housing Commission building, corner of Cavenagh Street and Harry Chan Avenue, 1973. (Helyar, L & G., NTL, Lois & Geoff Helyar Collection, PH0092/0189.)

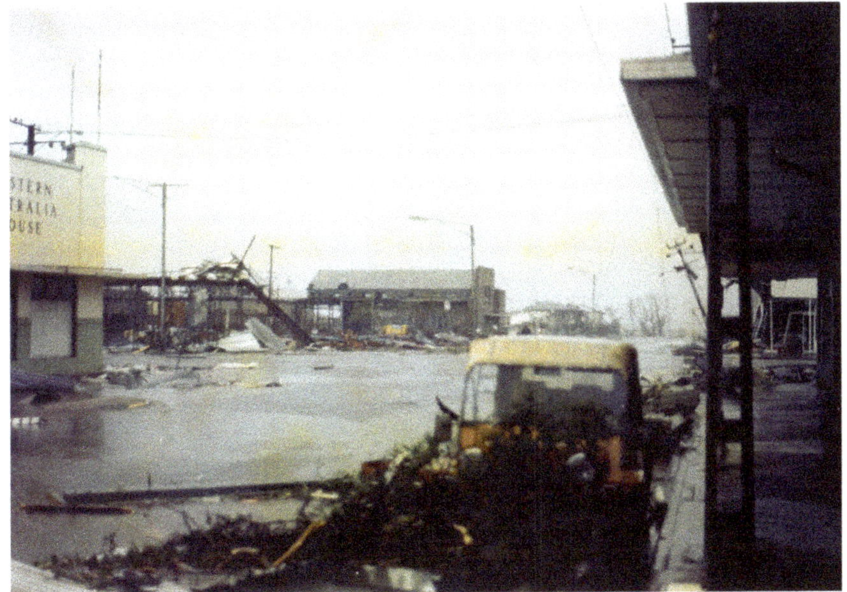

The corner of Knuckey and Cavenagh Streets, Damage after Cyclone Tracy, 1974. (Wesley-Smith, R., NTL, Rob Wesley-Smith Collection, PH0244/0023.)

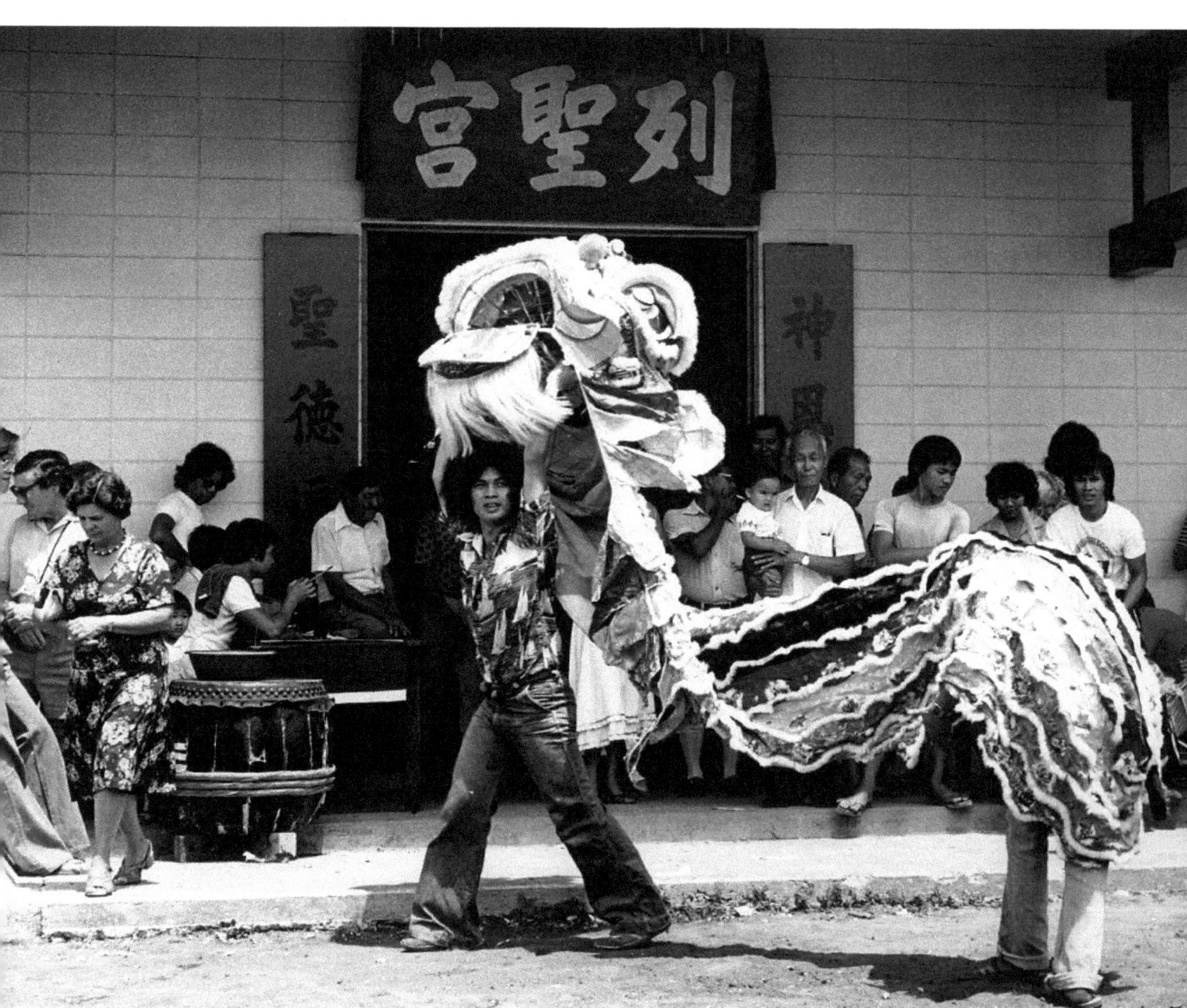

Lion dance during opening of the Chinese Temple, Litchfield Street, 1977. (Unknown, NTAS, GPC, NTRS 3822-P1 Folder 50 Lion dance, Chinese Temple opening.)

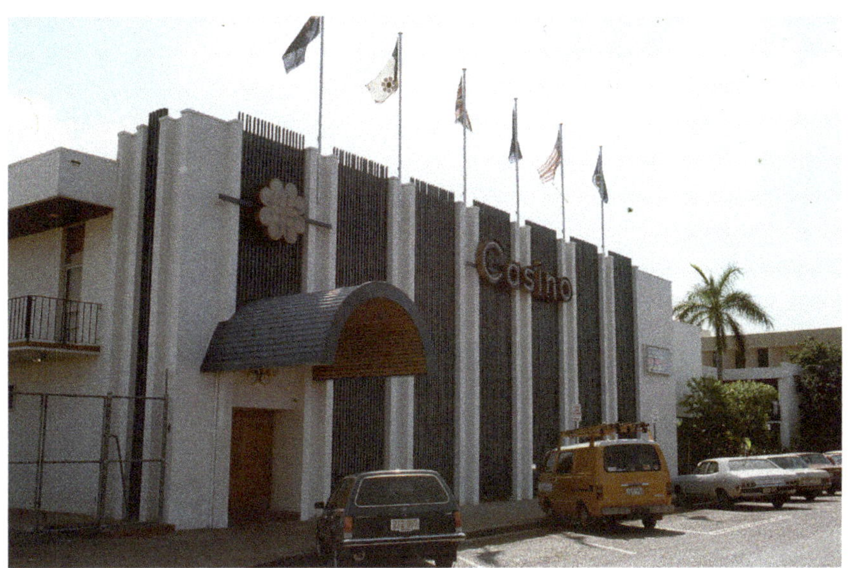

Don Casino, c1980. (Unknown, NTAS, GPC, 021_NTRS 3822-P3 Darwin Buildings Slide 18 - Don Casino.)

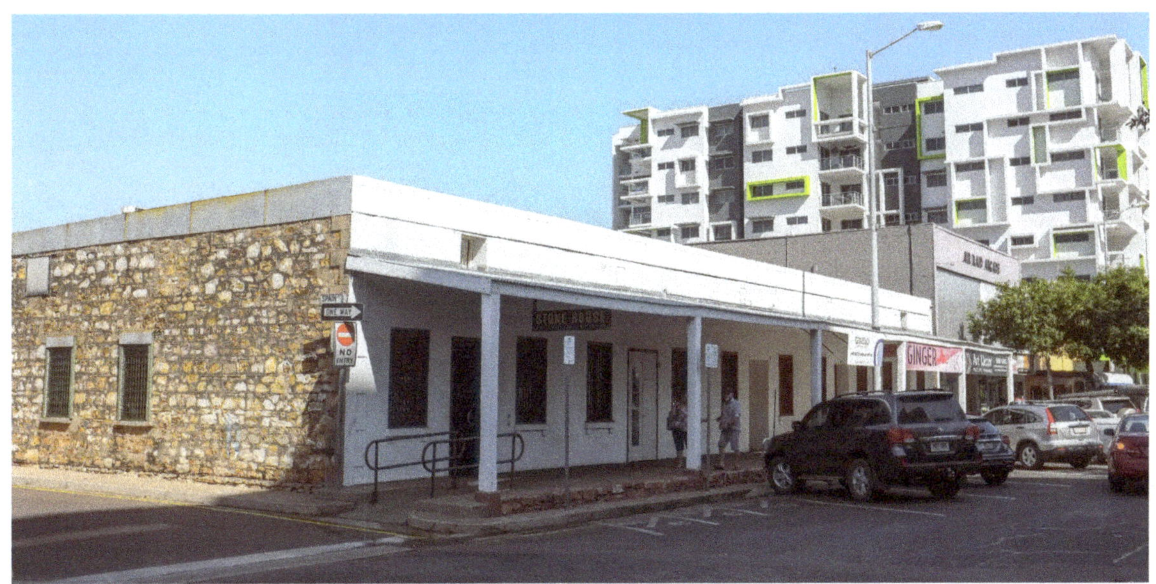

Stone House, Cavanagh Street, 2017. (Martin, R., Matthew Stephen, Personal Collection, CavanaghStr_17.)

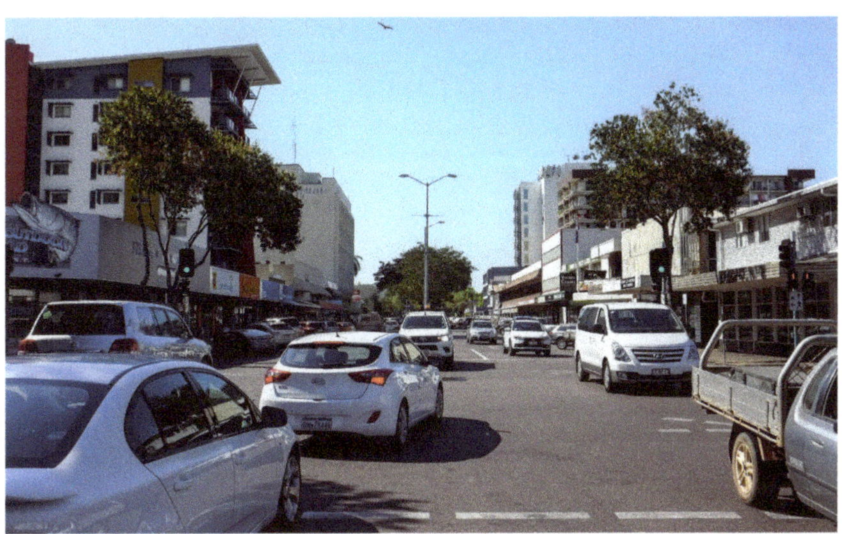

Cavanagh Street, 2017. (Martin, R., Matthew Stephen, Personal Collection, CavanaghStr_15.)

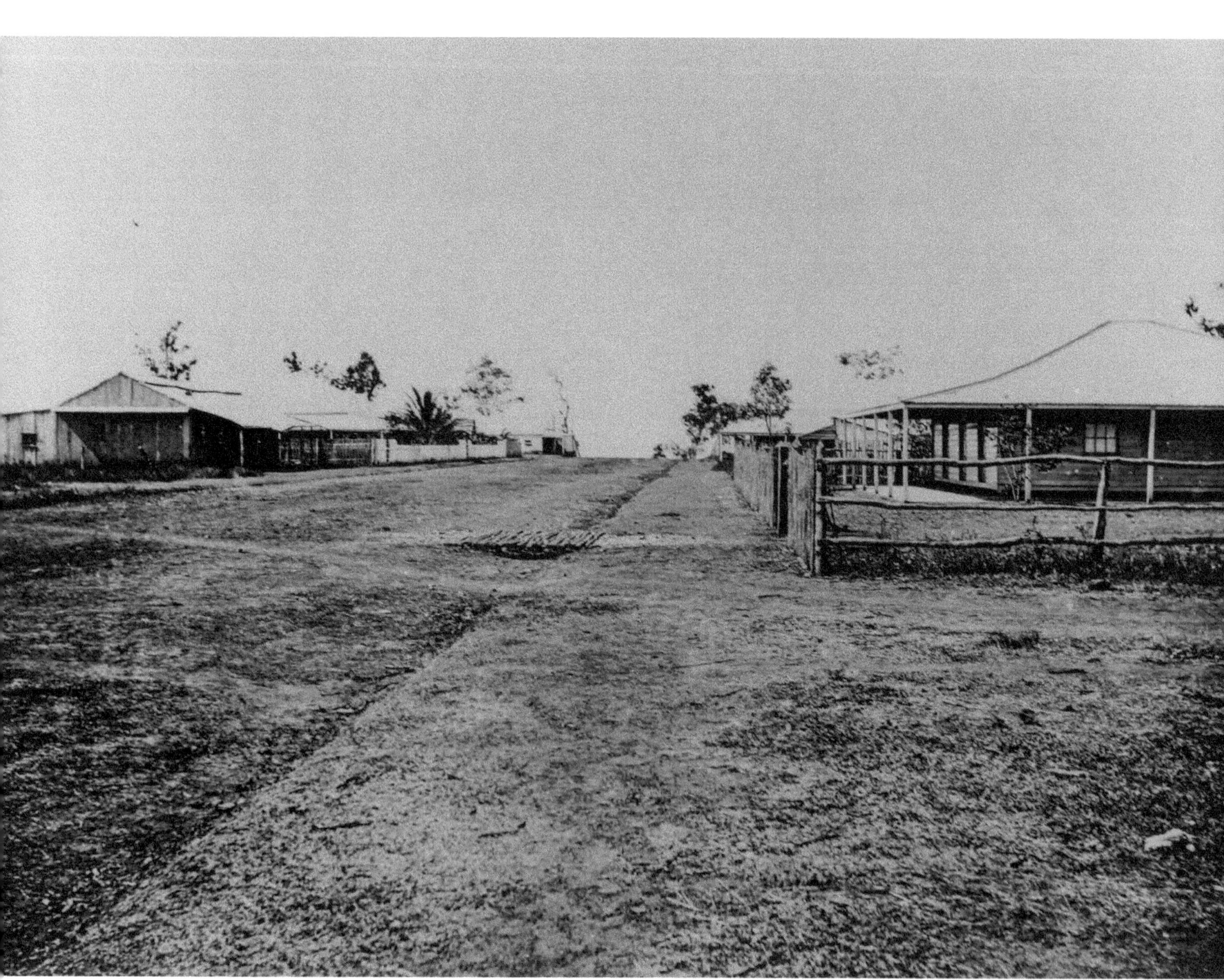

Smith Street, Palmerston, looking south east, 1879. (Foelsche, P., NTL, Foelsche Collection, PH0111/0090.)

Chapter 4

Smith Street: The Heart of Darwin's CBD

Smith Street, named after A.H. Smith, 1st Class Surveyor, in Goyder's 1869 survey party, has always been a focal point of Darwin.[1] Today it is the heart of the city's Central Business District. Running parallel to Cavenagh Street's Chinatown in the period up to World War II Smith Street developed into the 'European' business area.

Prior to World War II the corner of Smith Street and Bennett Street became known as 'Bank Corner.' The first bank established at this intersection, the facade of which can still be seen, was the Town and Country Bank completed in 1884.[2] Later the Commercial Bank took over the premises and remained there for many years. Bank Corner really took shape with the construction of the Bank of New South Wales (now Westpac) and The Commonwealth Bank (now Rourkes) in 1940.

Up to World War II, Bank Corner included a Darwin shopping institution, A.E. Jolly and Co's store. It was located across the road from the Commercial Bank. Alfred Edward Jolly established a store on the site in 1882 under the name of Jolly and Luxton, 'Importers and General Storekeepers.' Although the name changed it remained at this location until it was destroyed in the Bombing of Darwin, February 1942. A classic general store it stocked an amazing array of goods. Bank Corner was complete in 1966/67 with the construction of the Reserve Bank of Australia on the former site of Jolly's store. It operated until 1997. In 1999 the United Nations used the building as the base for its operations in Timor-Leste during its transition to an independent nation. Today the building is home to the Darwin Tourism Centre. While the name 'Bank Corner' is still used today only the Westpac Bank remains.

The Victoria Hotel was Palmerston's grandest when it opened on Smith Street in 1890. It was initially known as the Royal, but renamed the North Australian when it was opened by its owner, Mrs Ellen Ryan. The *Northern Territory Times & Gazette* reported that Mrs Ryan exhibited 'more pluck than wisdom' in the venture but the hotel was 'a credit to her enterprise and an estimable token of city improvement.'[3] The hotel was renamed the Victoria Hotel, after Queen Victoria in 1896 and is still known as 'The Vic' today. Not only did The Vic offer accommodation, food and drinks it hosted many of Palmerston and Darwin's most important social and sporting organisations which rarely had their own venues. Legend has it that Australian Rules Football, Darwin's most popular sport, was first organised over a few beers in the front bar of The Vic in 1916.[4]

The 1920s saw the development of shops and businesses into Smith Street between Bennett and Knuckey Street. On 20 October 1922 the Returned Serviceman's League (RSL) Clubrooms were opened on the corner of Knuckey and Smith Street (Now the site of the Centrepoint building). The block was donated to the RSL by Earnest Edward Jolly, son of Alfred Earnest Jolly of Jolly's Store and

1 NTG, Place Names Register, www.
2 *NTTG*, 30 August 1884.
3 *NTTG*, 12 September 1891.
4 *NTTG*, 10 February 1916.

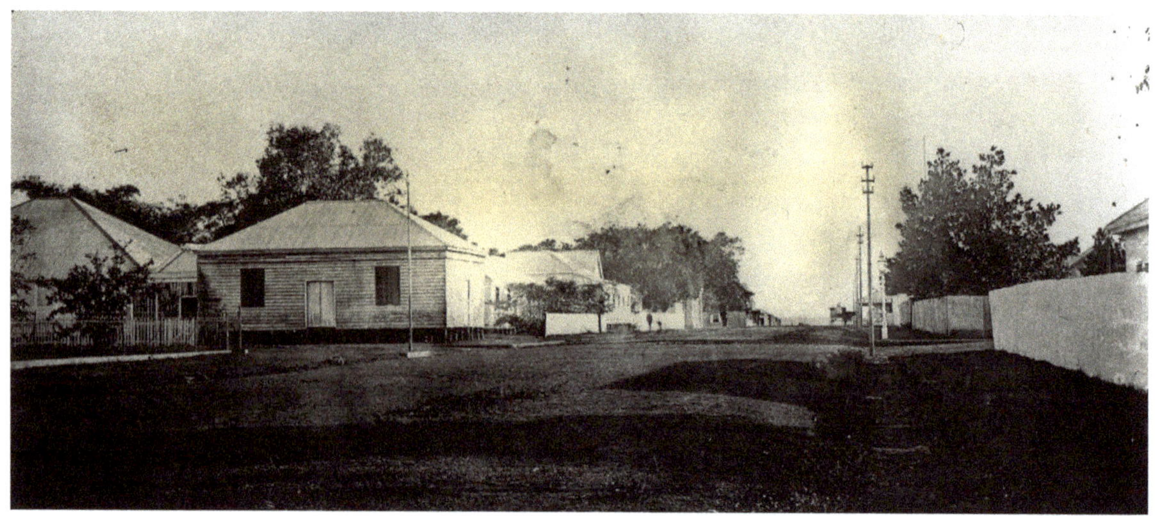

Bells Corner, corner of Bennett Street & West Lane, c1890s. (Unknown, NTAS, GPC, NTRS 3822-P1 Folder 1 Bells Corner.)

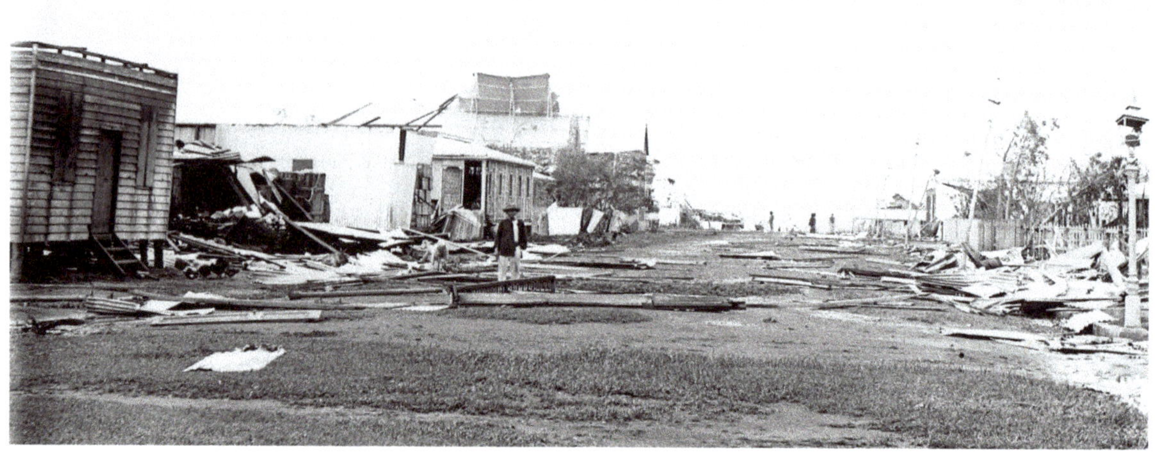

Smith Street, Victoria Hotel in background, damage after the 1897 Cyclone. (Bleeser, F., NLA, Florenz Bleeser Collection, PIC/9981/65.)

was the constructed by Harold Snell. The elevated timber building with corrugated iron roof and broad verandahs became a landmark and popular social venue. The RSL remained on the site until 1970 when it moved to new premises on Cavenagh Street.[5]

Darwin has a tradition of open air cinemas. The first was established in Cavenagh Street at The Don but it was Star Pictures that became a Darwin institution. Another Harold Snell construction, Star Pictures was completed in 1929, seating 860 people on two levels. The upper level and the back of the theatre were covered but the majority of seating was under the stars on deckchairs and benches. As Darwin's only cinema for many years' generations of Darwin residents share a Star Pictures experience. Some of the most memorable nights at The Star were the Wednesday night 'Cowboy Nights' when many of the Aboriginal community would attend the pictures. Although not strictly segregated, Aboriginal people most often sat in the 'cheap seats' at the front of the cinema while those who could afford it would pay extra for deck chairs or the luxury of the upstairs section.

5 Geddes, *Darwin Returned Services League (RSL)*, 19 & 112.

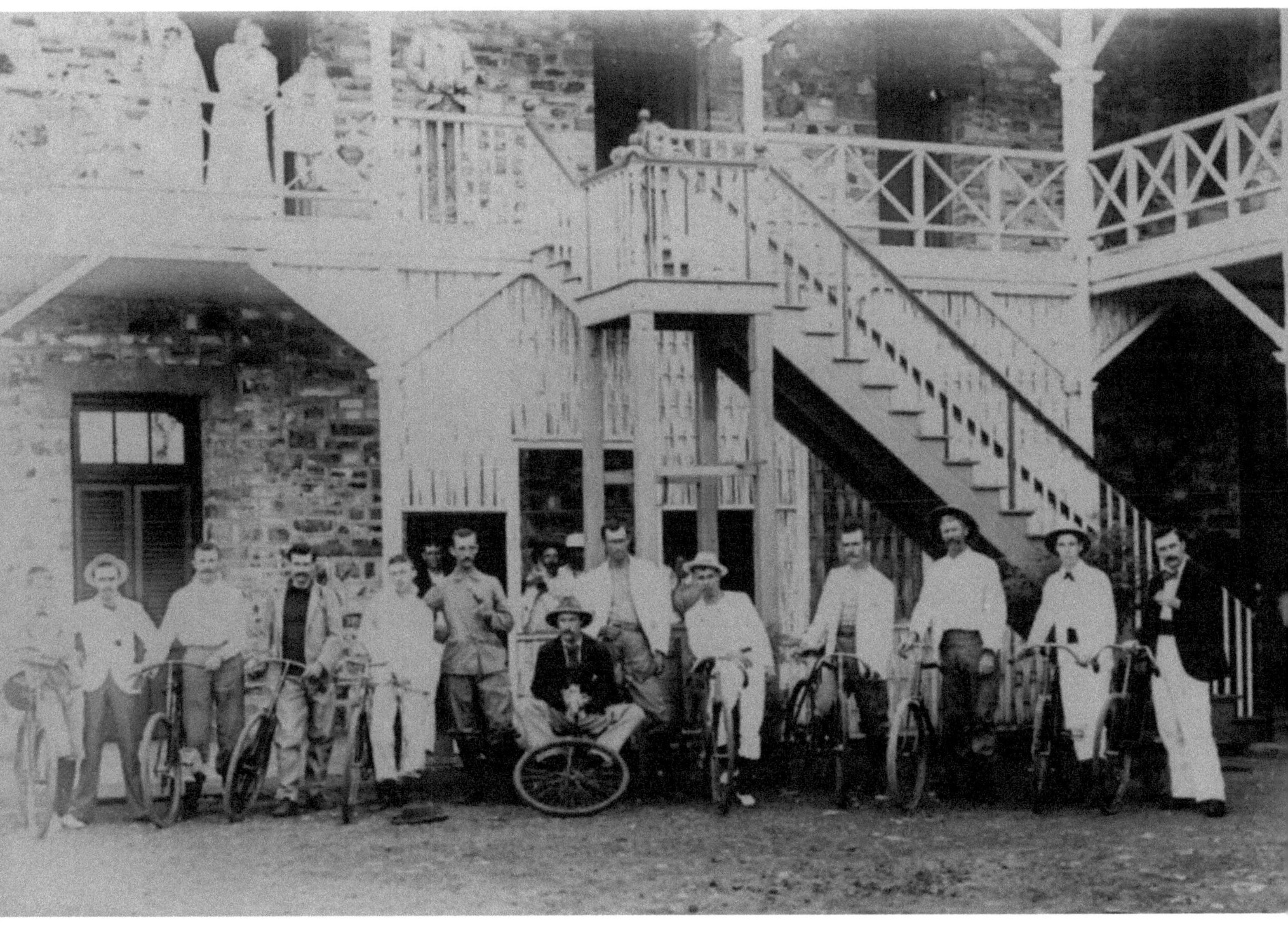

Cyclists at the Victoria Hotel, c1900. (Unknown, NTL, Peter Spillett Collection, PH0238/0650.)

The Star hosted many gala occasions but perhaps one of the most famous was in 1955 for 'Jedda', Australia's first colour feature film. Jedda was set in the Northern Territory and its two Aboriginal stars, Ngarla Kunoth and Robert Tudawali were both from the Northern Territory. Cashman's newsagency, adjacent to Star Pictures was another well known landmark in Smith Street. Its curved facade was a distinctive part of the streetscape for many years.

Cyclone Tracy severely damaged Smith Street. Star Pictures was a major casualty not reopening as a cinema after 1974. Today it is a shopping arcade through to Austin Lane. The Victoria Hotel was also badly damaged and not reconstructed until 1978. Smith Street was transformed in November 1979 when it was reconfigured as a pedestrian mall.

Darwin's CBD has been transformed in recent years with the construction of many high rise buildings. Bank Corner is now dominated by the Charles Darwin Centre built by the Paspaley Pearls Properties Group. Completed in 2015 it has retained the facade of the Commercial Bank to give some sense of Bank Corner as it was in earlier eras.

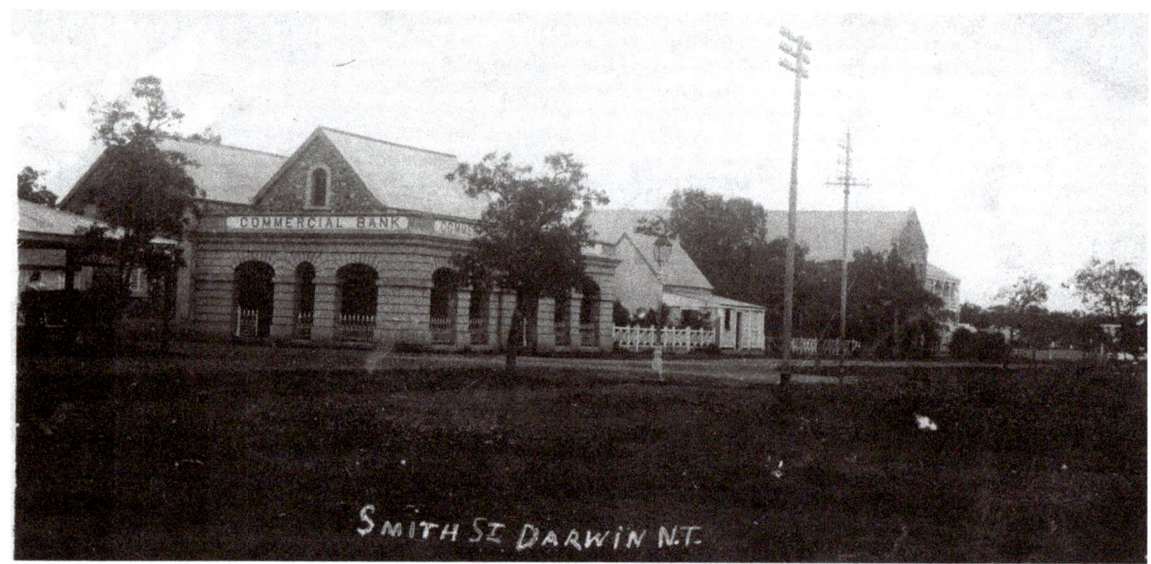

Corner of Smith & Bennett Streets, c1900s. (Unknown, Maxwell, Personal Collection, N/A.)

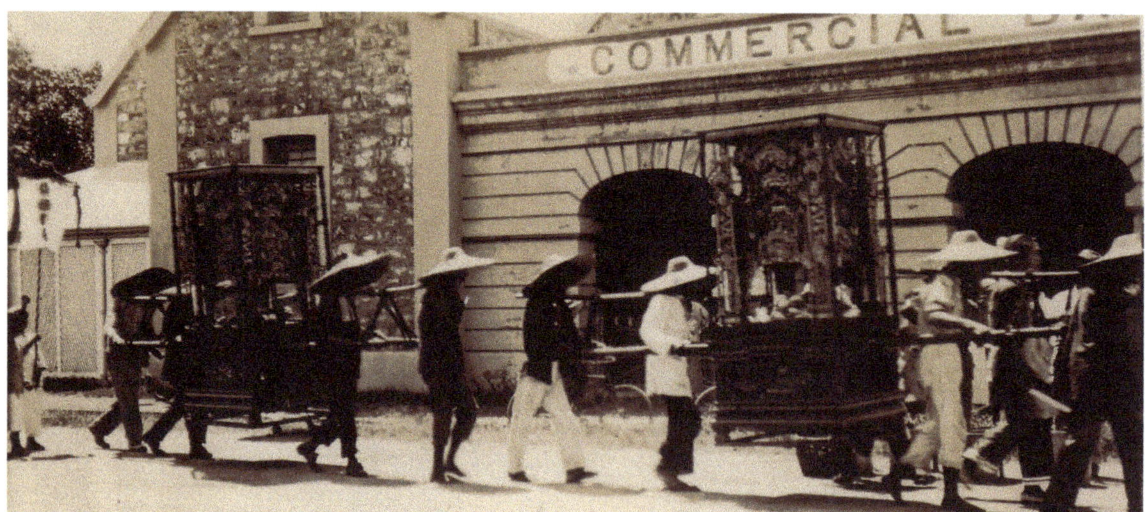

Chinese procession on Bank Corner, c1920s. (Monteith, R., MAGNT, Orr Collection, PIC521/049.)

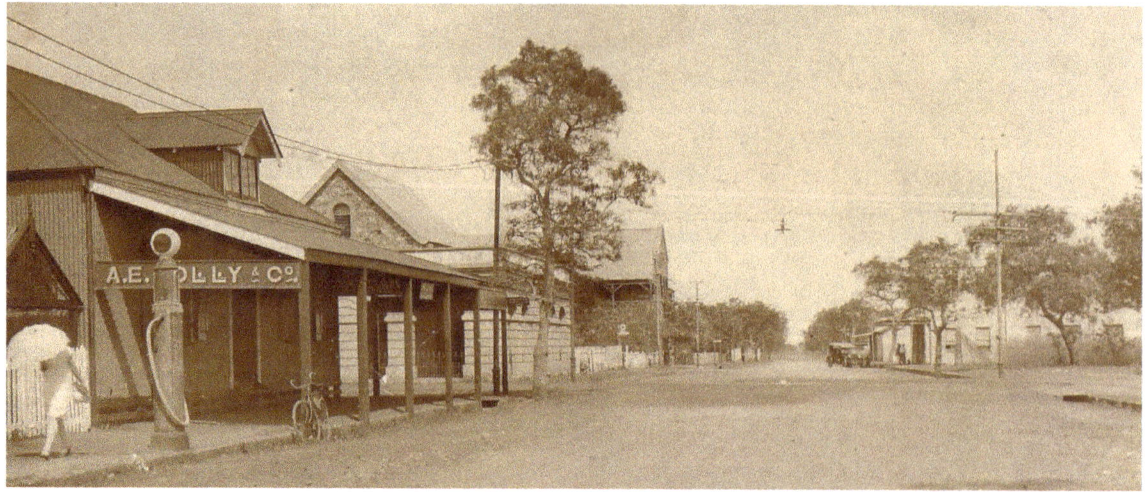

Corner of Smith & Bennett Streets, c1930s. (Unknown, MAGNT, Gwyneth Ellenden (nee Davies) Collection, PIC520/002.)

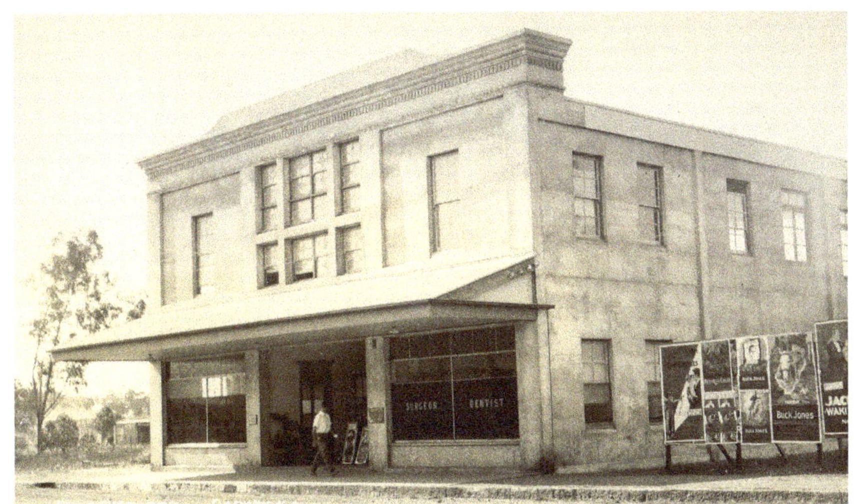

Star Pictures, c1930. (Unknown, NTAS, Charles Wilson Collection, NTRS 3335 Item 304.)

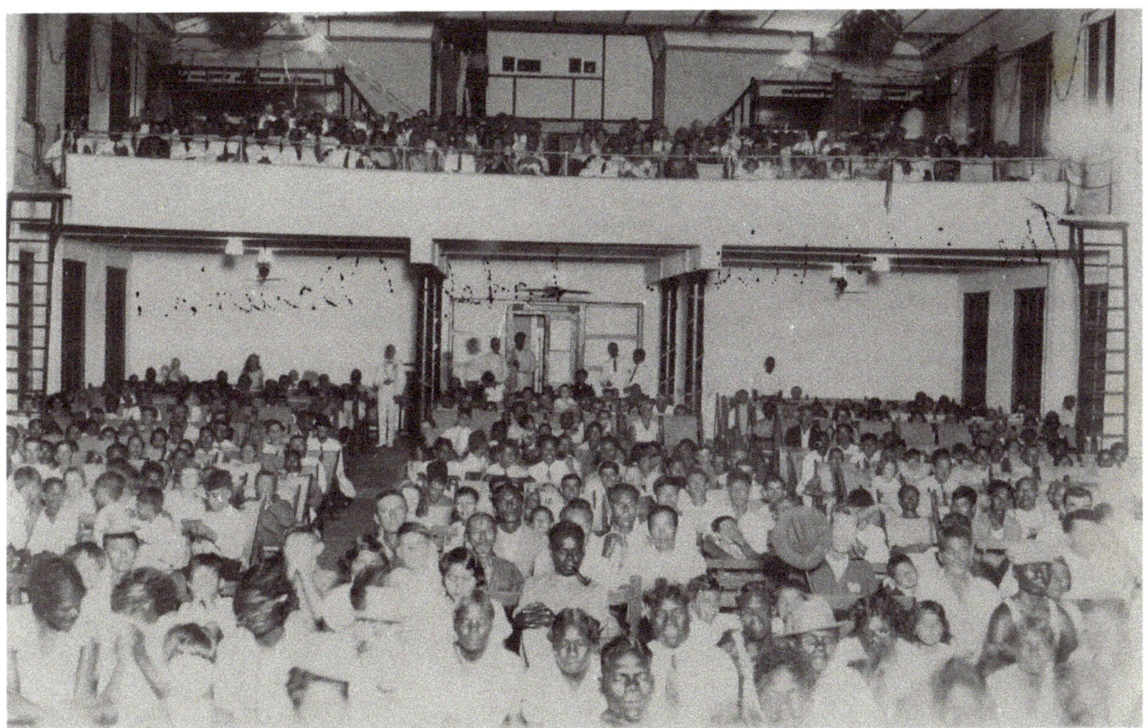

Star Pictures interior, c1930s. The cheaper seats were towards the screen. Note the man in the fourth row from the front with his hat hanging on his rifle. (Unknown, NTAS, HSNT Collection, NTRS 1854 Item 2024.)

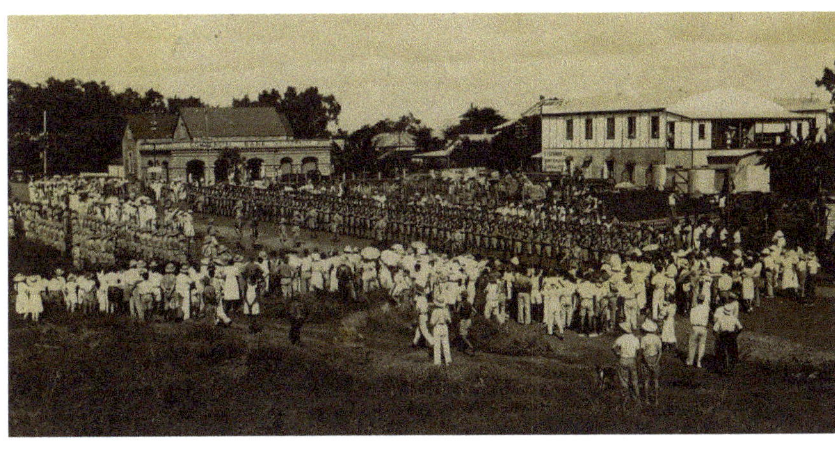

Darwin Mobile Force, welcome to Darwin by Administrator in Bennett Street. Note the Bank of New South Wales under construction, c1940. (Unknown, NTAS, B. Humble Collection, NTRS 1168 Item 49.)

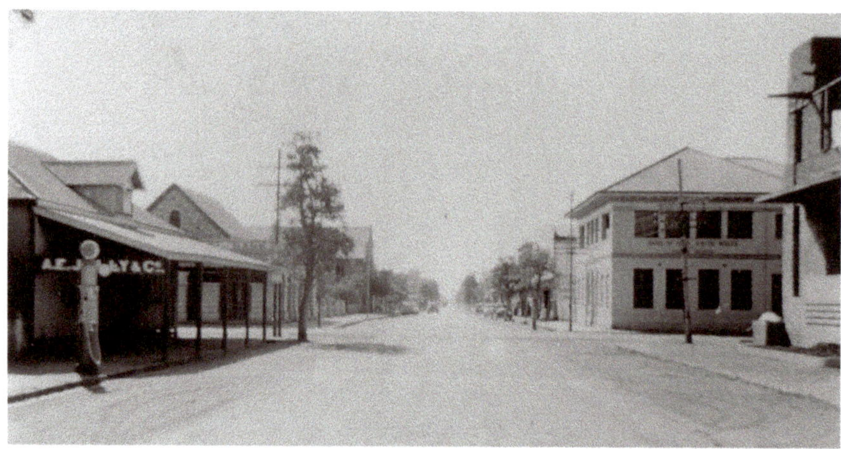

Bank Corner, c1940. The Commonwealth Bank is under construction. (Unknown, QANTAS, Heritage Collection, N/A.)

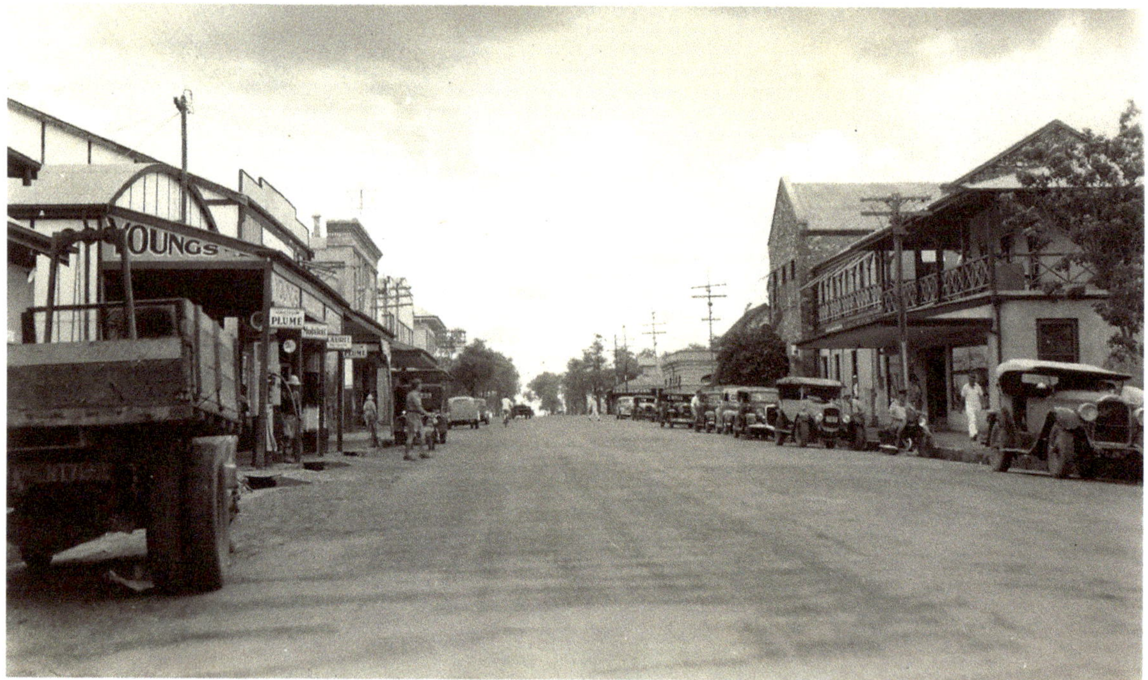

Smith Street, c1940. (Unknown, NTAS, B. Humble Collection, NTRS 1168 Item 28.)

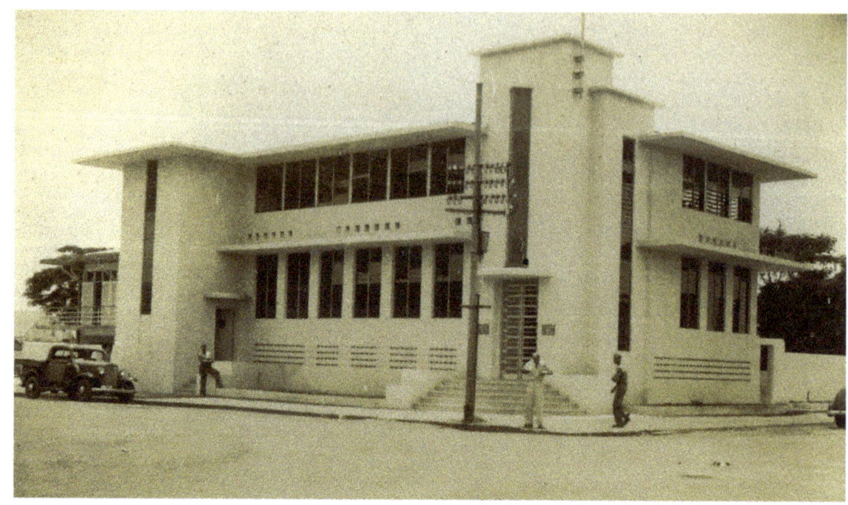

Commonwealth Bank, c1940. (Unknown, NTAS, V. Levitt Collection, NTRS 3433 Item 32.)

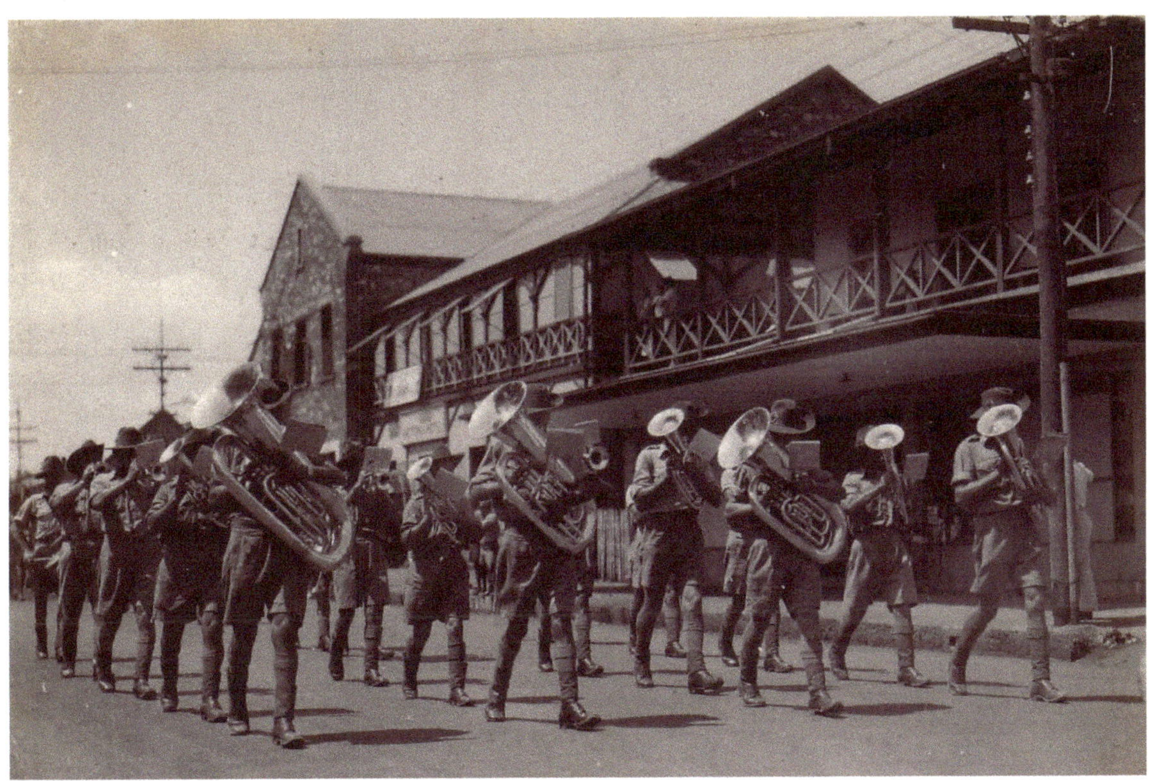

Military band, Smith Street, c1940. (Unknown, MAGNT, E.M. Wier Collection, PIC001/061.)

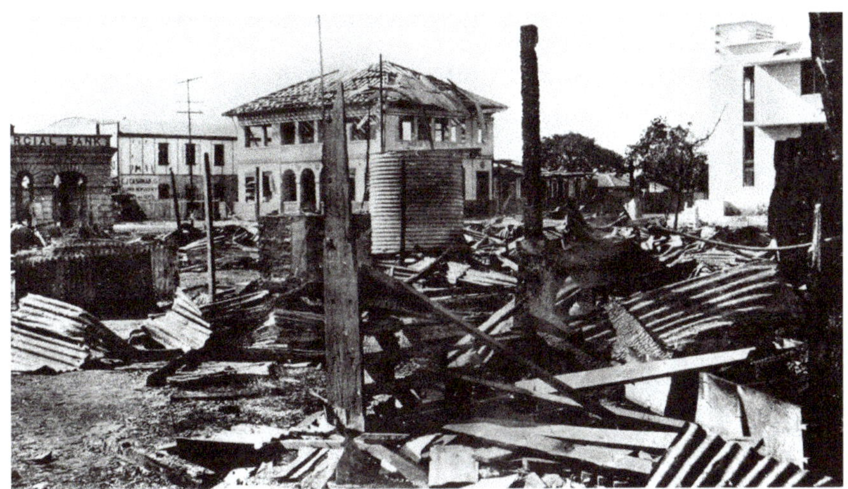

Bank Corner, 19th February 1942. Jolly's store is completely destroyed. (Unknown, AWM, Photograph, P02759.009.)

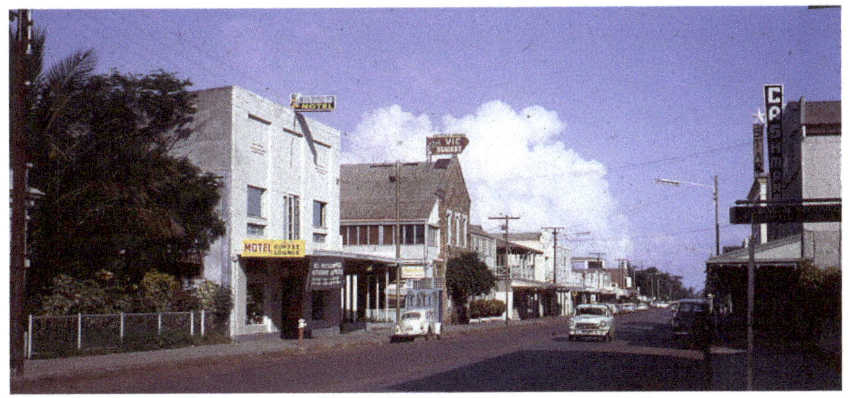

Smith Street, c1966. (Unknown, NTAS, Heather Graham Collection, NTRS 3406 Item 19.)

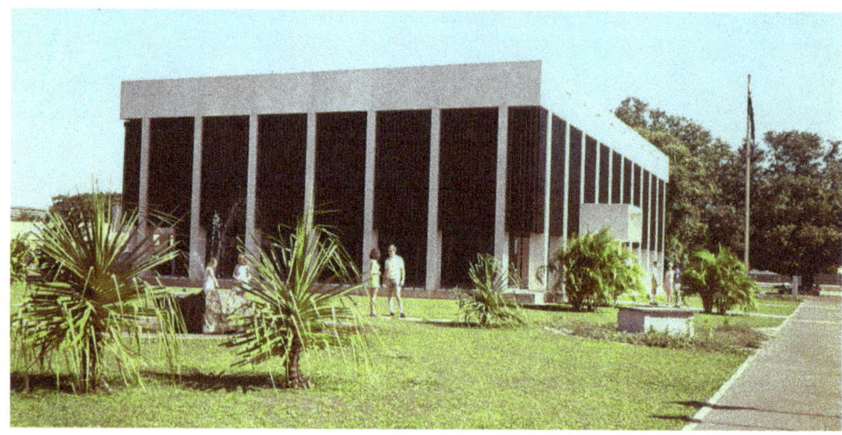

Reserve Bank building, c1970s. (Unknown, NTAS, GPC, NTRS 3822-P2 Darwin Streets Buildings.)

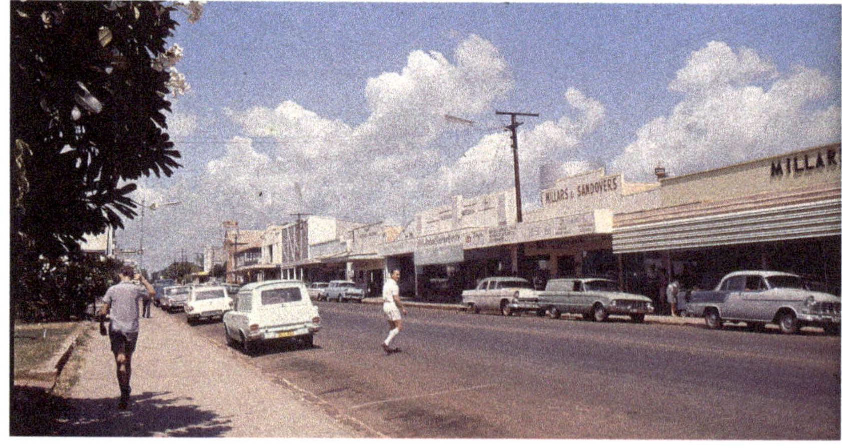

Smith Street, c1970s. (Unknown, NTAS, GPC, NTRS 3822-P2 Darwin Streets Buildings.)

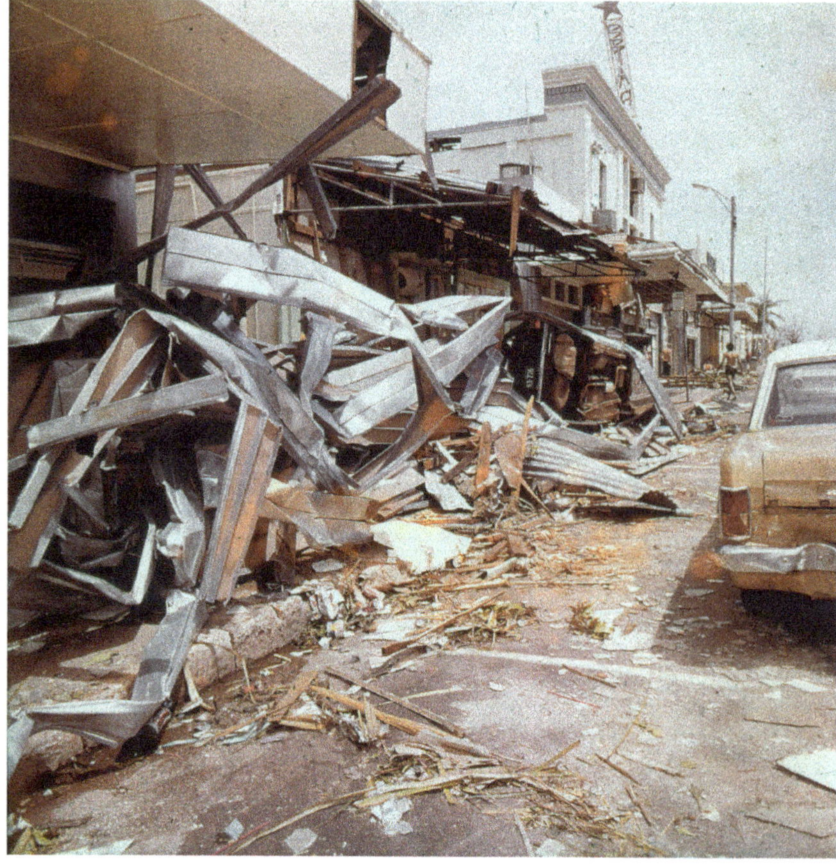

Star Pictures, Smith Street, after Cyclone Tracy, 1974. Unknown, NTAS, GPC, NTRS 3822-P2 Cyclone slide 2.)

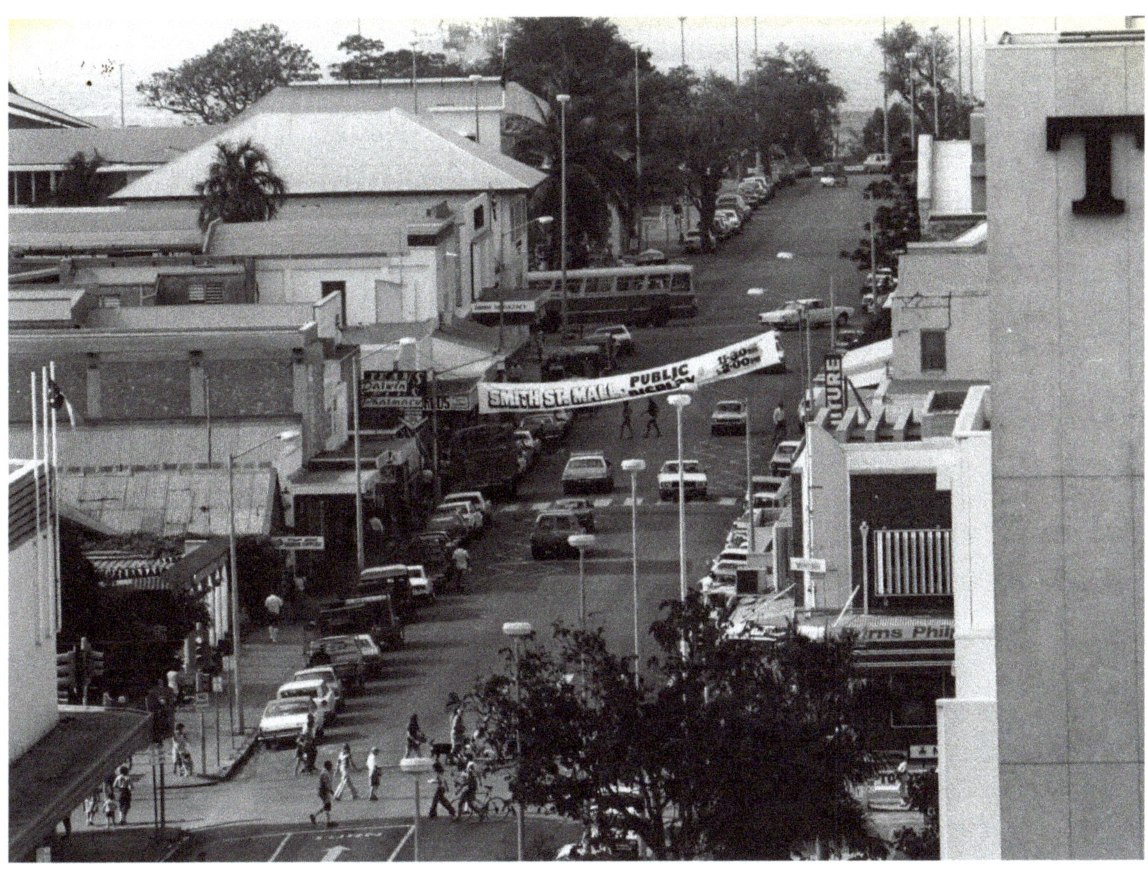

Smith Street, just prior to the construction of the Smith Street Mall, c1978. (Unknown, NTAS, GPC, NTRS 3822-P1 Folder 72 Smith Street c1978.)

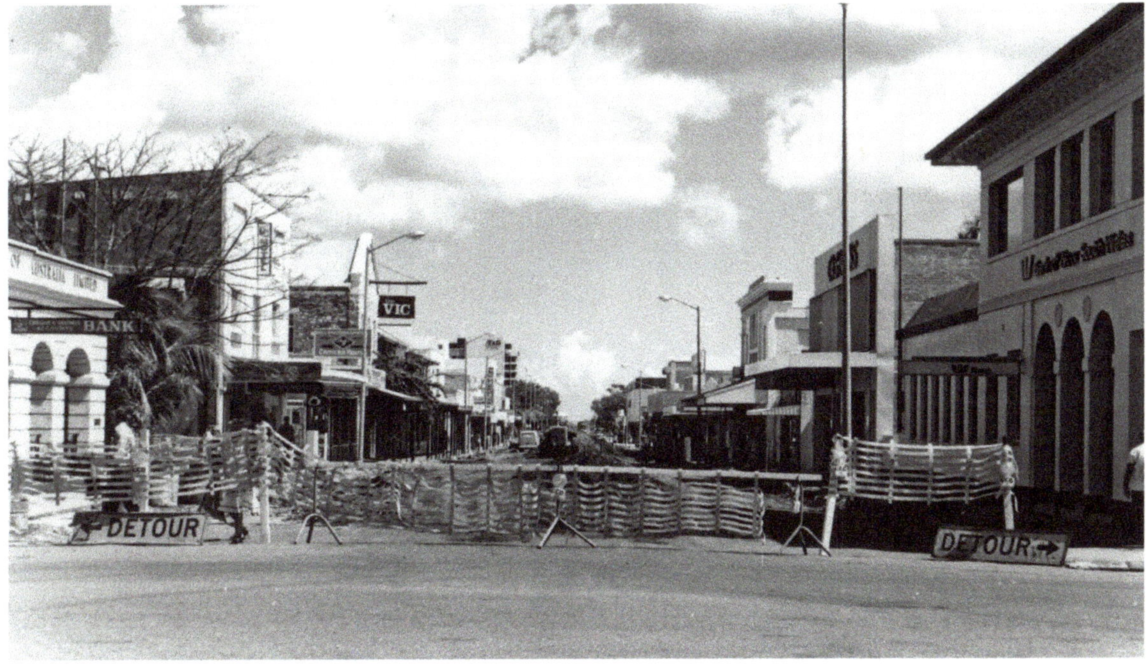

Smith Street Mall under construction, c1979. (Unknown, NTL, Northern Territory Government Photographer Collection, PH0095/0160.)

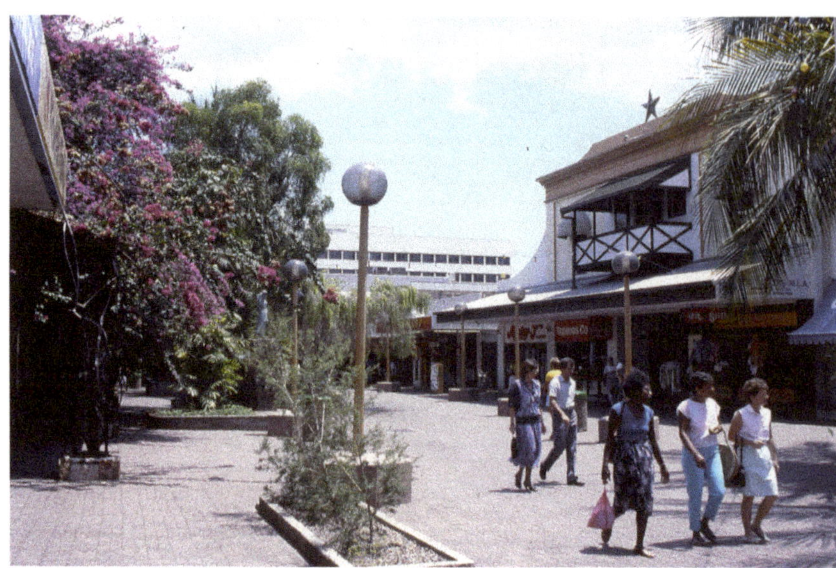

Smith Street Mall, c1981. (Wiedemann, B., NTL, Northern Territory Government Photographer Slide Collection, PH0730/0775.)

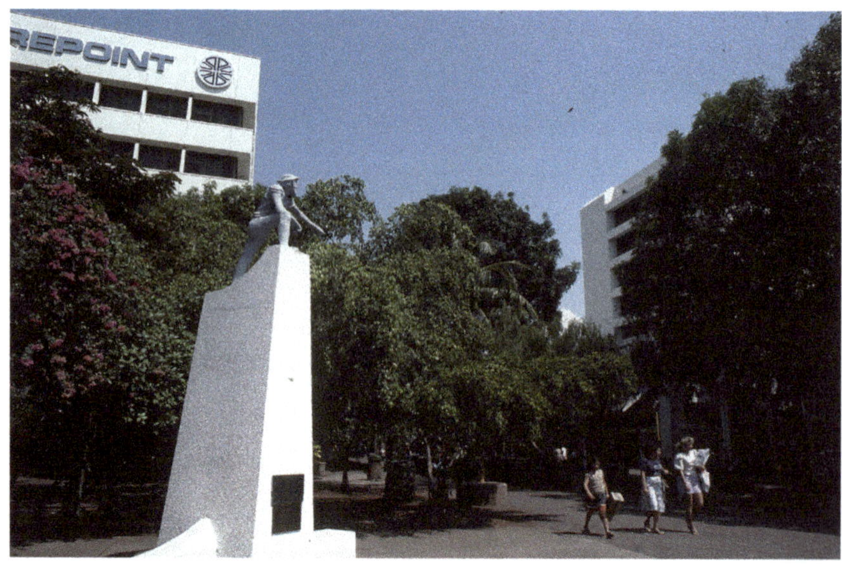

Smith Street Mall, 1985. (Unknown, NTAS, GPC, 023_NTRS 3822-P3 Darwin Streets Slide 207.)

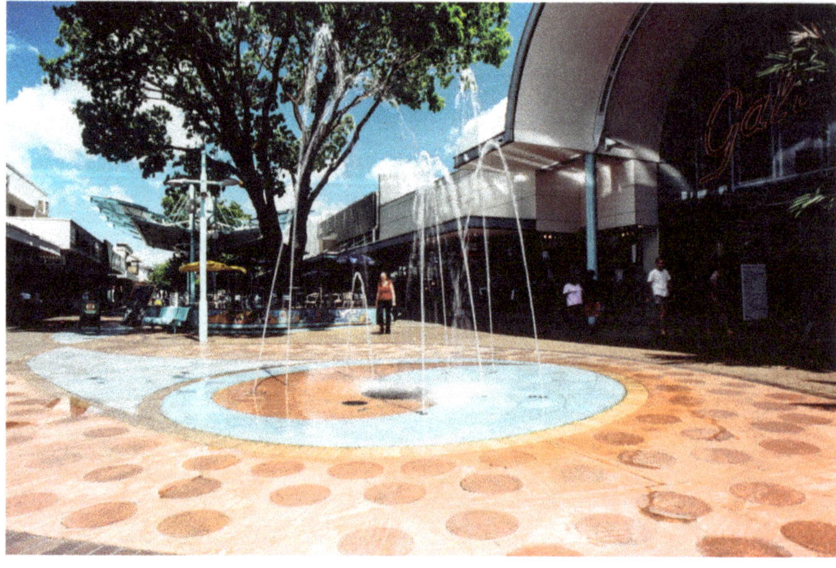

Smith Street Mall, 2002. (Carrington, S., NTL, Darwin 2002 Collection, PH0757/0027.)

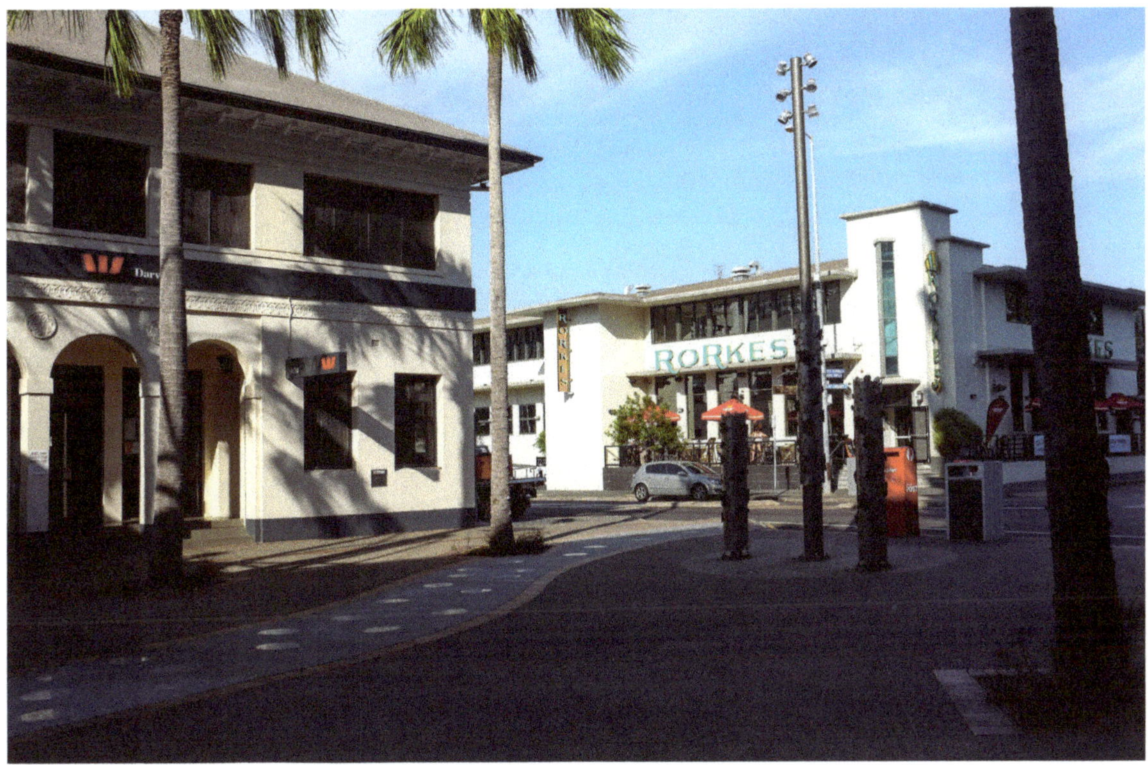

Bank Corner, 2017. (Martin, R., Matthew Stephen, Personal Collection, BankCorner_05.)

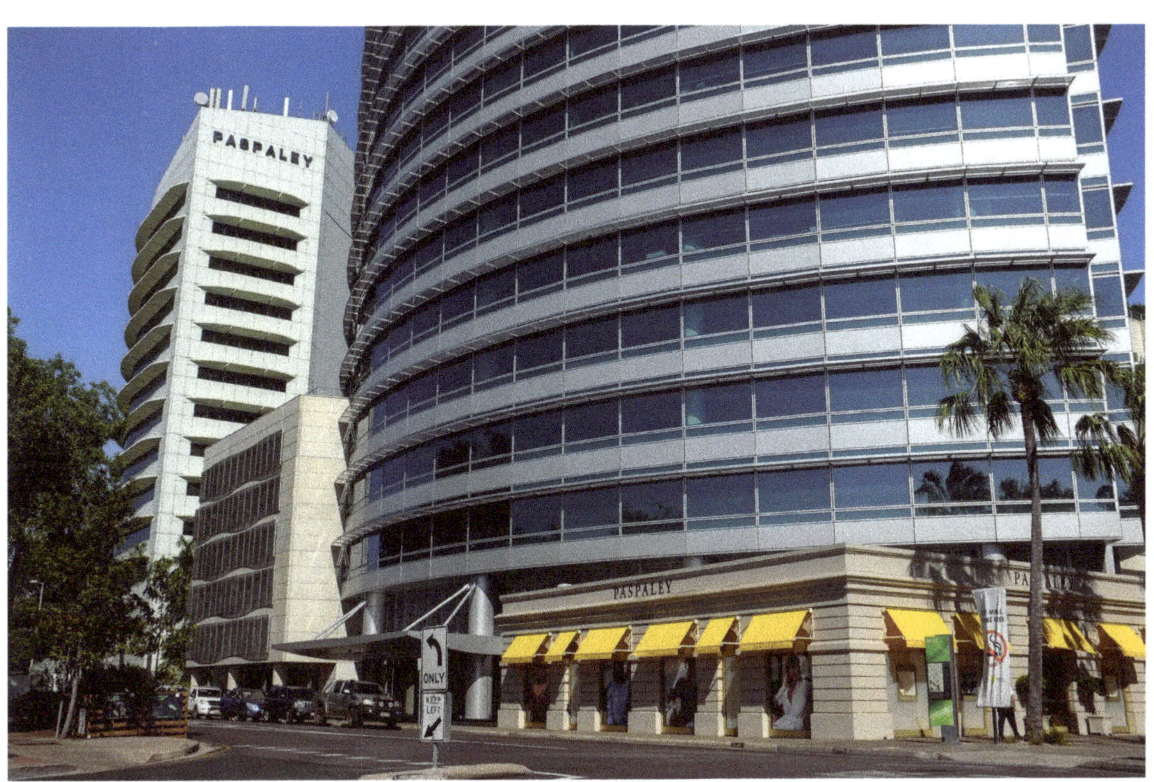

Bank Corner, 2017. (Martin, R., Matthew Stephen, Personal Collection, BankCorner_09.)

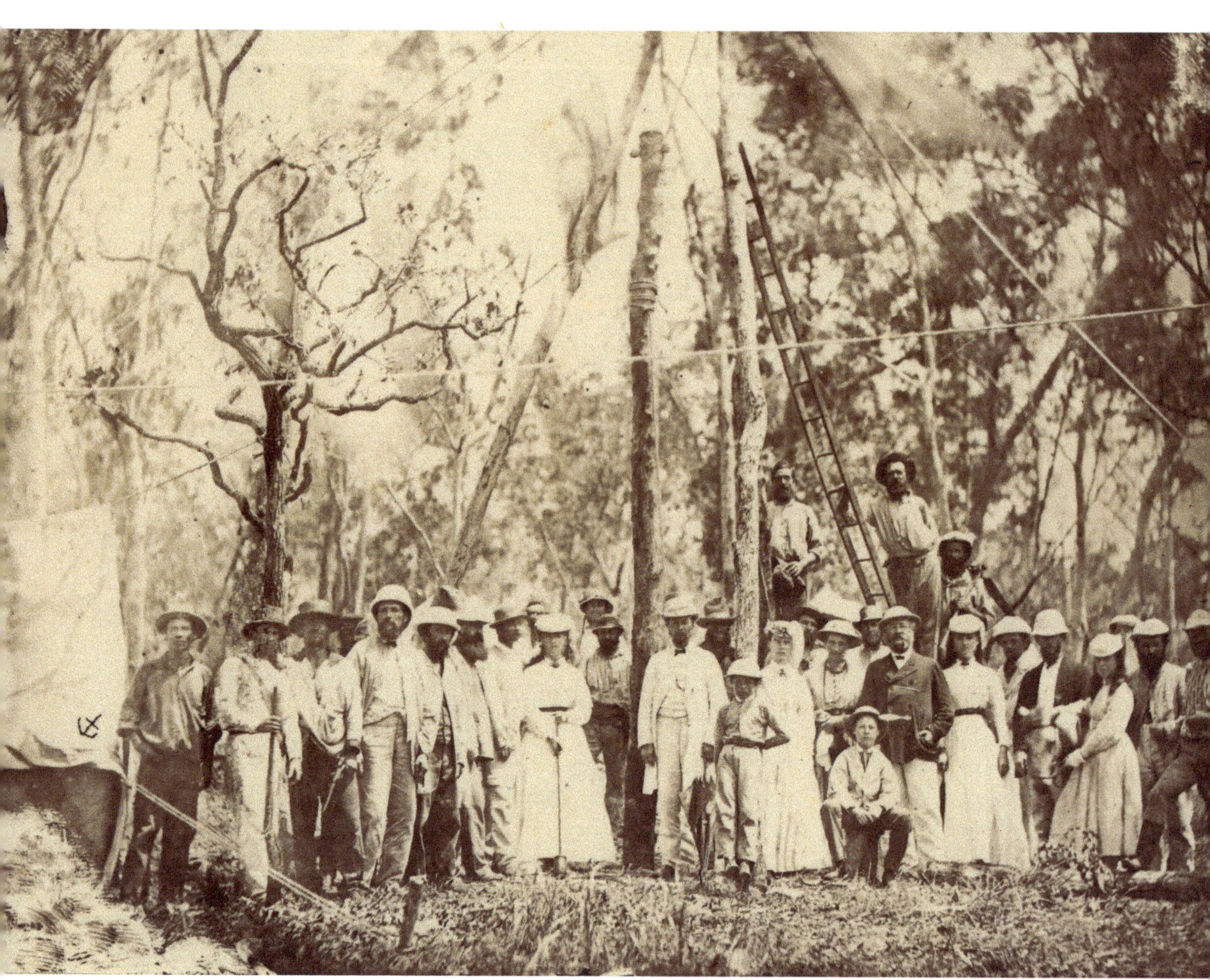

'Planting' of the first Overland Telegraph pole, 1870. (Sweet, S.W., SLV, Views of Darwin and Roper River, N.T. [picture], H10704.)

Chapter 5

Smith Street East and The Eastern Esplanade

The Esplanade overlooking Port Darwin was established as the government administrative centre soon after European Settlement. Like most British settlements the development occurred close to the port and business centre.

Initially in 1869 European settlement was concentrated at the Surveyors Camp at Fort Hill but more permanent building was soon under way on the Darwin Plateau. Selection of town lots occurred in July 1870. The accommodation for the South Australian Government Resident, the most senior public servant, was the first public building constructed. Completed in June 1871, the Government Residence, now known as the Administrator's Residence is the oldest continuously occupied residence in the Northern Territory.

On the 15th of September 1870, at the same time the Government Residence was under construction, a ceremony was held to commemorate the 'planting' of the first Overland Telegraph Pole on the corner of Cavenagh Street and the Esplanade.[1] The Overland Telegraph was the catalyst for the early development of Darwin and the opening up of the Northern Territory in general.

The Overland Telegraph had another unexpected consequence. In December 1870 Overland Telegraph northern construction parties discovered gold while sinking telegraph poles in the Yam Creek area, 140 kilometres south east of Darwin. However, the gold rush to the Northern Goldfields between 1870 and January 1873 was small and brief compared to other Australian gold rushes. The gold was too sparse and the conditions too harsh to support the independent miners who were the mainstay of Australian gold rushes in Victoria and elsewhere. The Northern Goldfields required more capital and infrastructure. Gold has been mined continuously in the region south of Darwin to Pine Creek since the 1870s but it never yielded the wealth of other Australian gold fields. Nevertheless, gold mining acted as catalyst to kick-starting the economy and an important part of the Northern Territory economy today.

The late 1870s and 1880s saw the construction of a number of stone buildings in the eastern Smith Street and Esplanade area. White ants ravaged most timber constructions and soon it became clear that more substantial buildings were required. Many of the stone buildings can be attributed to John George Knight, who amongst his many public positions was the Government Architect. Knight was the son of a stone and marble merchant and his remaining buildings such as the police station, court house, Brown's Mart and the Palmerston Town Hall were all constructed of the distinctive local Porcellanite stone.[2] The former police station and court house on the Esplanade first constructed in 1879 are now used as the offices of the Northern Territory Administrator. Also constructed in the early 1880s were The Commercial Bank, known as the 'Stone Bank' on Bank Corner and the English, Scottish and Australian Chartered Bank's 'Tin Bank' in Smith Street adjacent to Brown's Mart.

1 De La Rue, *The Evolution of Darwin*, 28. A replica telegraph pole is situated at the corner of Smith Street and the Esplanade.
2 Carment, Knight, John George, *Northern Territory Dictionary of Biography*, 324.

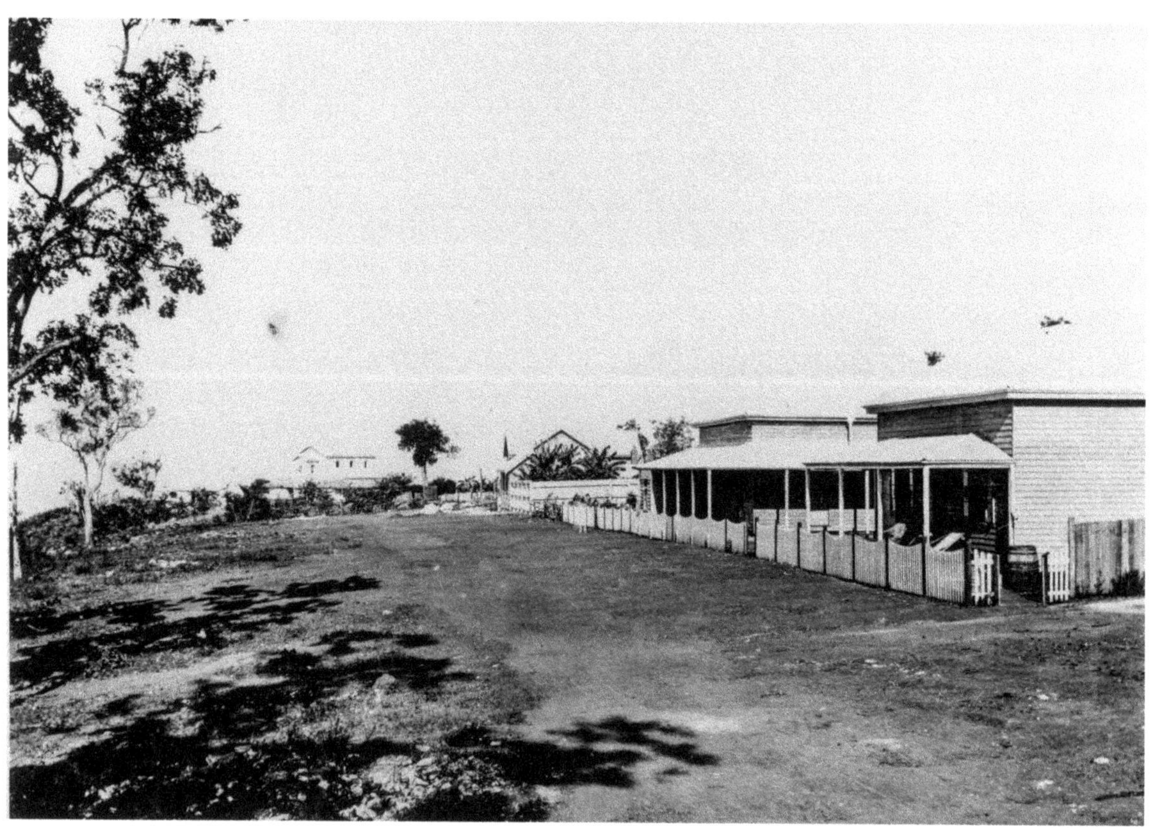

Government buildings on The Esplanade with the two storey Residency in the background, 10 June 1875. (Foelsche, P., NTL, Foelsche Collection, PH0111/0004.)

Brown's Mart is typical of the buildings built during this period that all have a varied and colourful history. Built in 1885 for V.L. Solomon and Co it was known as the Mining Exchange, 1887-1910. Like so many of Darwin's buildings it was ravaged by Cyclones in 1897, 1937 and Cyclone Tracy in 1974. Unlike other buildings, however, it has stood the test of time, and as a result has been repurposed numerous times. In 1937 the building was leased by the Bank of New South Wales as temporary premises while its own building was constructed. During World War II the building was used as a torpedo workshop. After the war until 1952 it was part of the naval headquarters and there after it was variously used by Northern Territory police, Crown Law Office and Motor Vehicle Registry. After its reconstruction following Cyclone Tracy in 1975 the building has been used as a theatre and home for Darwin's community arts.[3]

Although now in ruins the Palmerston Town Hall is another example of J.G. Knights 1880s architecture and construction. Opened in 1883 the Town Hall was initially used by the Palmerston District Council, Palmerston Institute Reading Room and Library. It also hosted innumerable town functions and social events. In 1937 the Darwin Town Council was dissolved and the Commonwealth Bank used the building as temporary premises until its own building was completed in 1940. During World War II the Town Hall became part of *HMAS Melville* shore base and remained in Navy hands until 1959. In 1954 a new town hall was built on the Corner of Mitchell and McLachlan Streets so the old town hall served as motor vehicle registry and later a museum until 1974 when it was destroyed by Cyclone Tracy.[4]

Until the completion of Christ Church in 1902 Anglican services had been held in the town

3 NTG Heritage Branch, *Brown's Mart, Fact Sheet*, 2011.

4 NTG Heritage Branch, *Town Hall Ruins, Fact Sheet*, 2011.

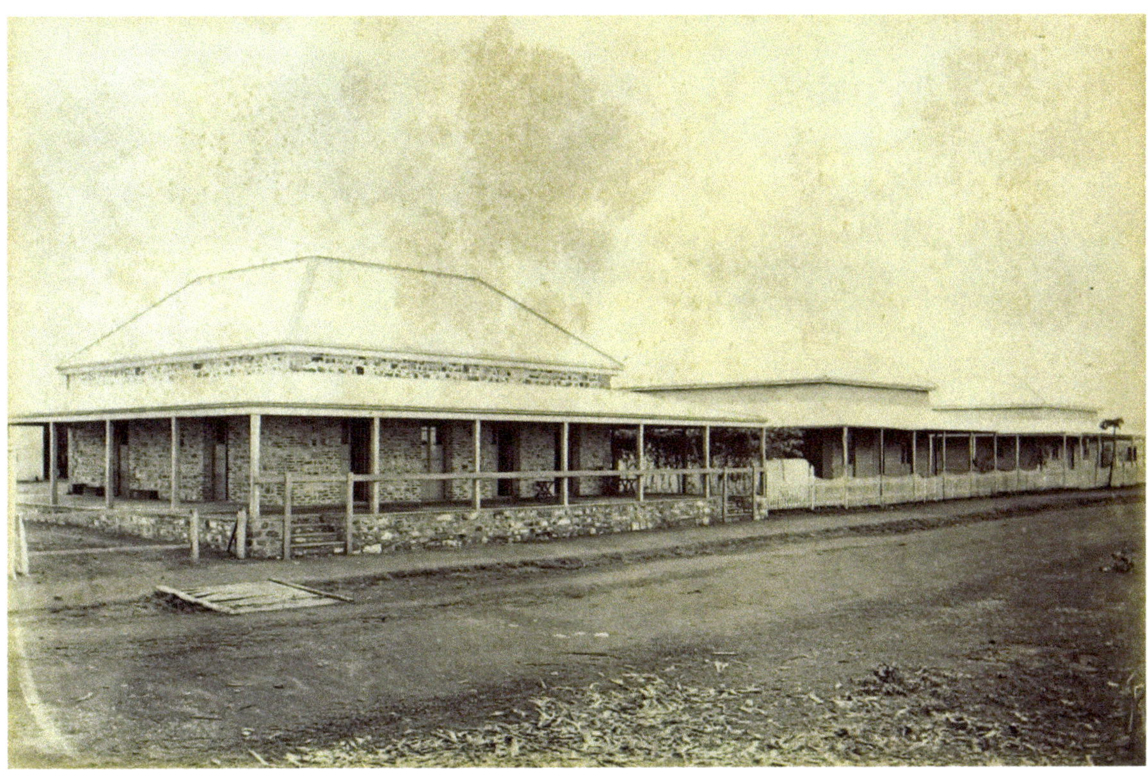

Police Station, Court House and Medical Officer's quarters, c1879. (Foelsche, P., NTAS, Foelsche Collection, NTRS 3420/P1/ Item 63.)

hall and the court house. The Church was damaged during the bombing of Darwin on 19th February, 1942. Later in the war the Navy made repairs to the church and used it as a sickbay. In 1944 the Navy also added the porch to the church and the Army added the entrance gate to commemorate those who had died while on active service in the Northern Territory. The Church became a Cathedral in 1968 when the Diocese of the Northern Territory was established. On Christmas Eve 1974 the Cathedral was almost totally destroyed by Cyclone Tracy about an hour after the Midnight service. A new Cathedral, incorporating the old porch was consecrated on Sunday 13 March 1977.[5]

The south eastern end of Smith Street was transformed when the Darwin City Council Civic Centre was constructed in the late 1960s. The site was reserved for municipal purposes in 1964. The reserve included what formerly would have been the Esplanade end of Cavenagh Street which came to an end at today's Nichols place. It included the site of the former Terminus Hotel and 'Galamarrma', the Tree of Knowledge, a site of significance to the Larrakia people and a local landmark for well over a century. The original plans for the Darwin Council Civic Centre had to be altered by three metres to retain the tree due to public protests. The Civic Centre was opened 18th August 1969 and Council Chambers officially opened 23 July 1970.[6]

Today Civic Park provides a green haven in the centre of Darwin and comes to life in August when it is transformed into Darwin's Festival Park featuring the open air Starlight theatre during the annual Darwin Festival.

5 *Christ Church Cathedral*, www.

6 Howison, Personal communication, 12 January 2018.

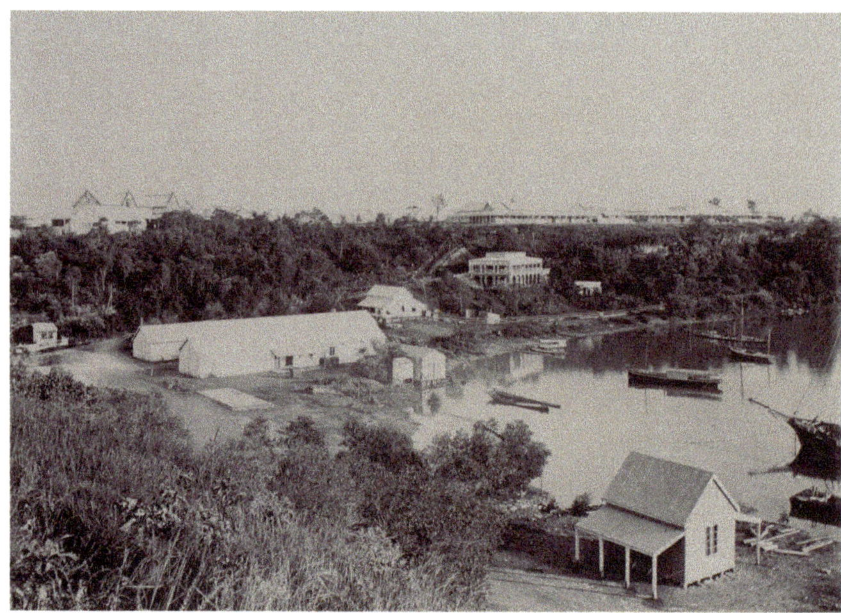

View of Government administration offices and Surveyors' Camp from Fort Hill, c1887. (Foelsche, P., NTL, Foelsche Collection, PH0111/0009.)

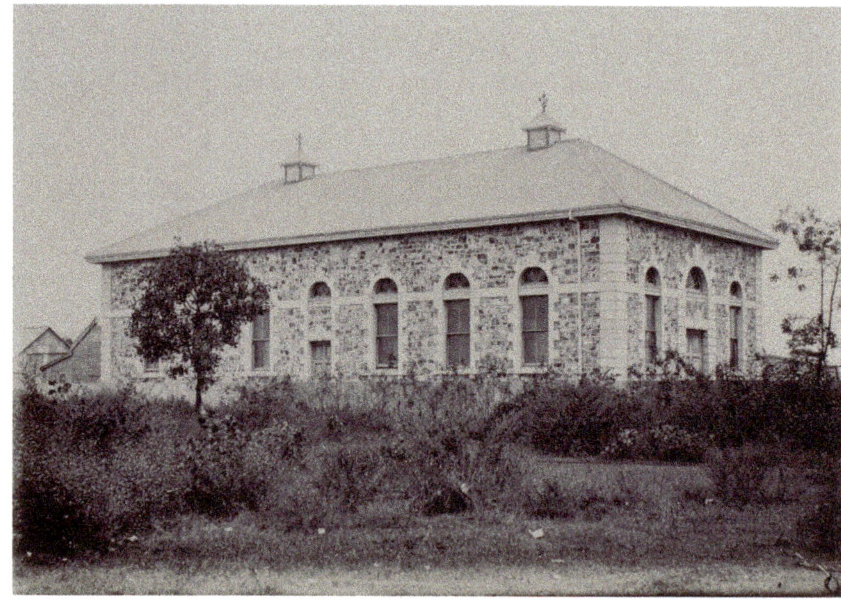

Palmerston Town Hall, 1887. (Foelsche, P., NTL, Foelsche Collection, PH0754/0023.)

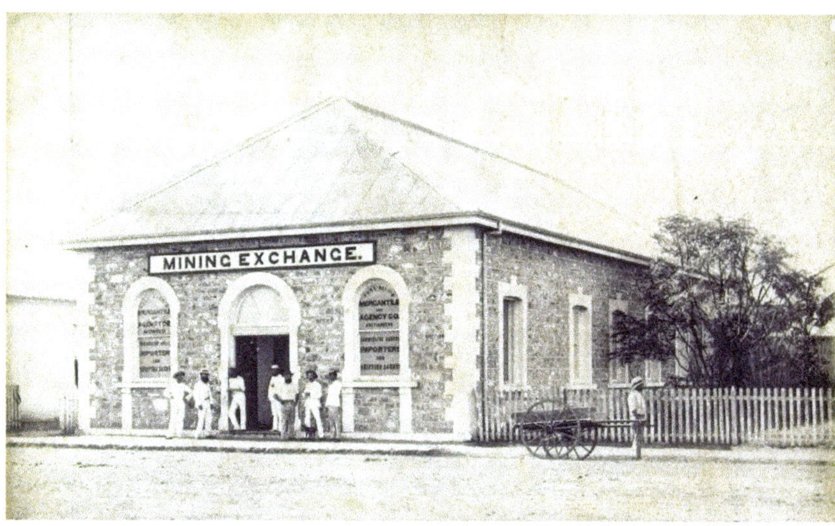

Mining Exchange, Smith Street, 1888. Later Brown's Mart. (Foelsche, P., NTAS, Foelsche Collection, NTRS 3420/P1 Item 68.)

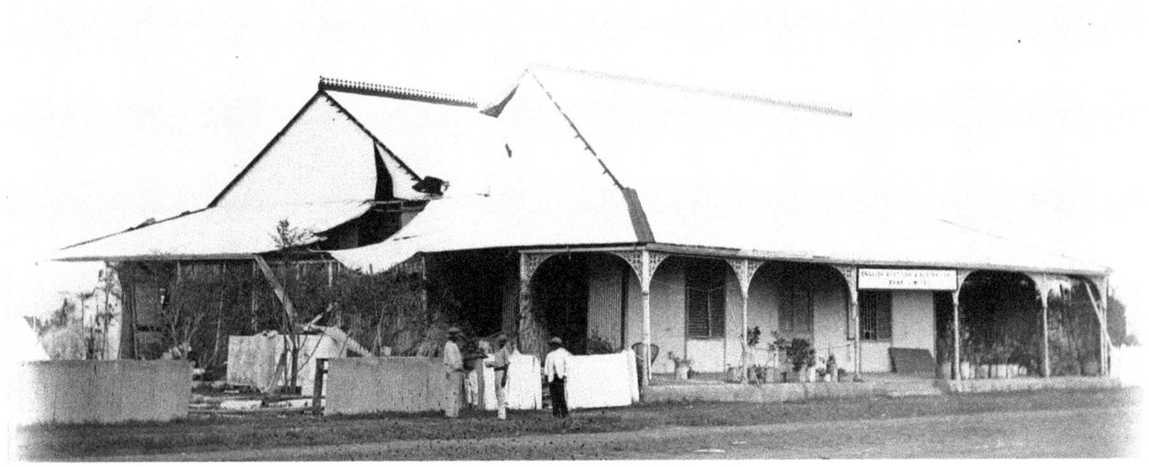

English Scottish & Australian Bank [The Tin Bank], Smith Street. Damage after the 1897 Cyclone. (Bleeser, F., NLA, Florenz Bleeser Collection, PIC/9981/75.)

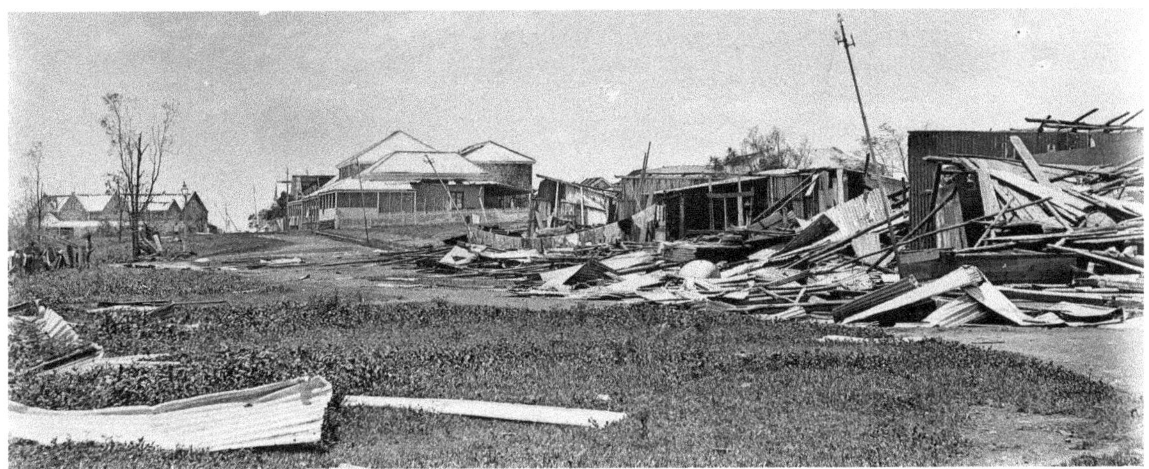

Looking towards the Government Residence past the Government offices from the corner of Cavenagh Street and The Esplanade. Damage after the 1897 Cyclone. (Bleeser, F., NLA, Florenz Bleeser Collection, PIC/9981/62.)

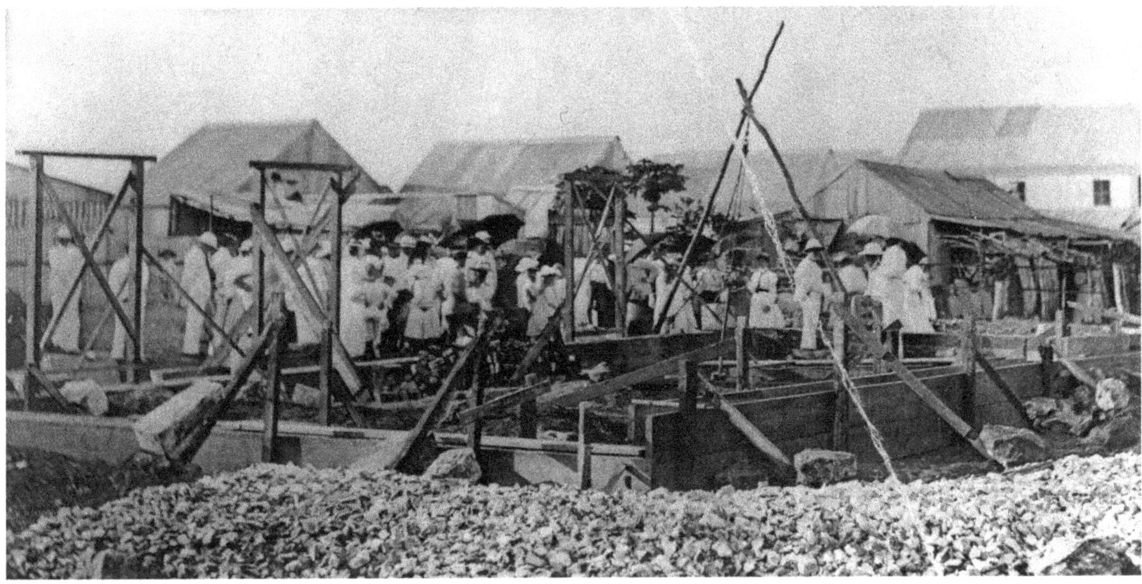

Laying the foundations, Christ Church, Smith Street, c1902. (Unknown, NTAS, GPC, NTRS 3822/P1 Folder 94.)

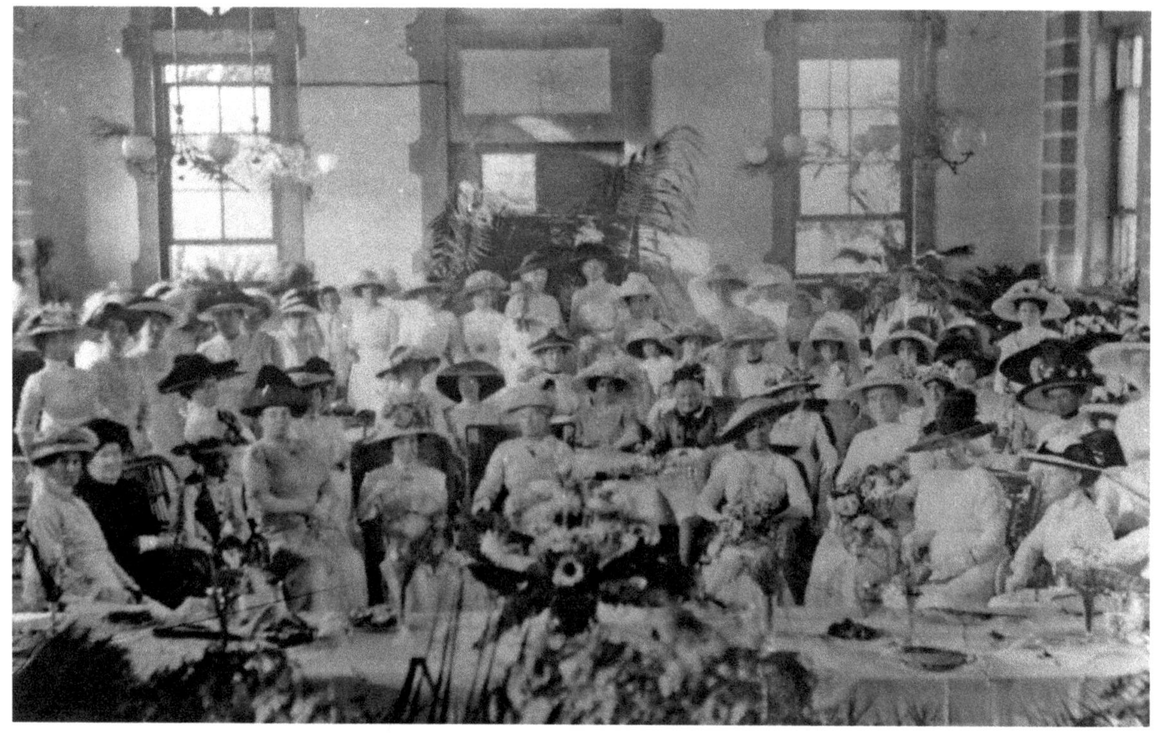

Farewell to Doctor Strangman, Town Hall, 1913. (Unknown, NTL, J.A. Austin Collection, PH0412/0038.)

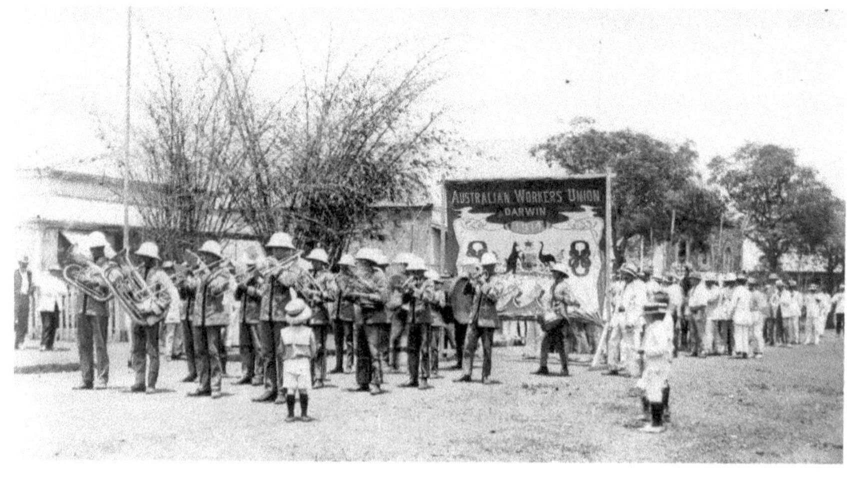

Darwin Brass Band and AWU members preparing for a parade, 1915. (Unknown, NTAS, HSNT Collection, NTRS 1854 Item 1321.)

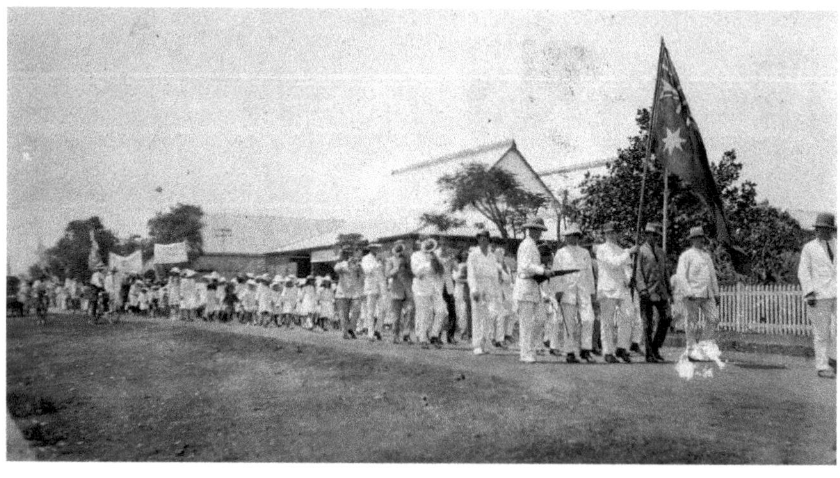

Empire Day march, passing the Tin Bank, 24 May 1918. (Unknown, NTAS, V. Dunn Collection, NTRS 2011 Item 5.)

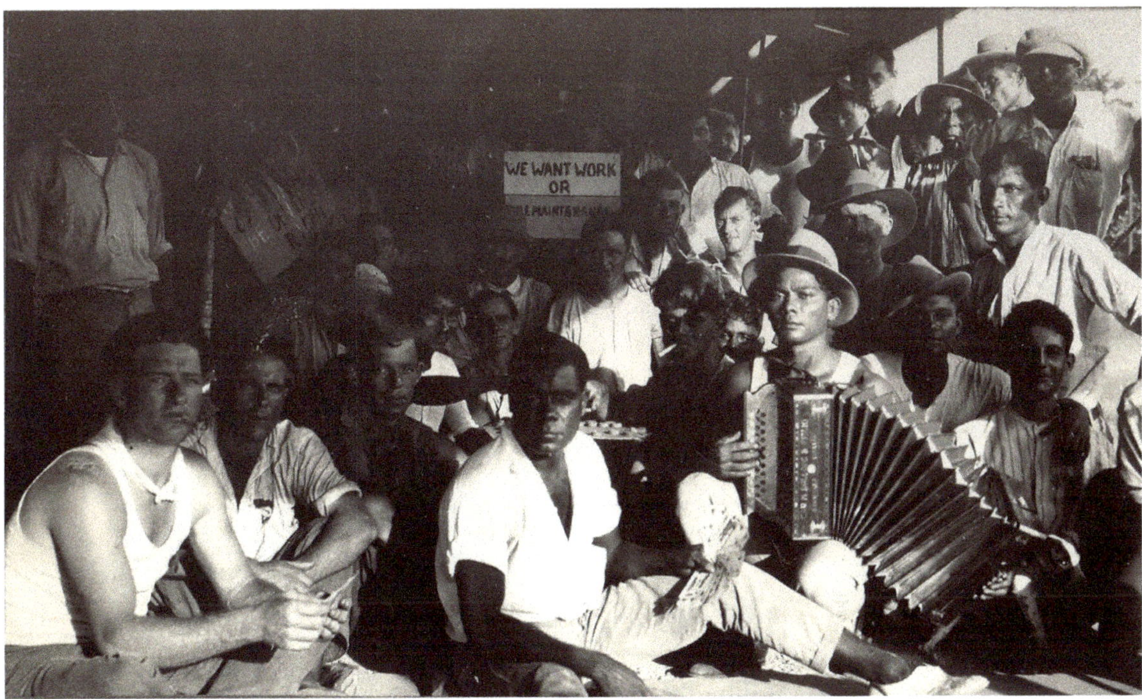

Unemployed workers protesting on the verandah of the Government offices, c 1930. (Unknown, NTAS, Charles Wilson Collection, NTRS 3335 Item 327.)

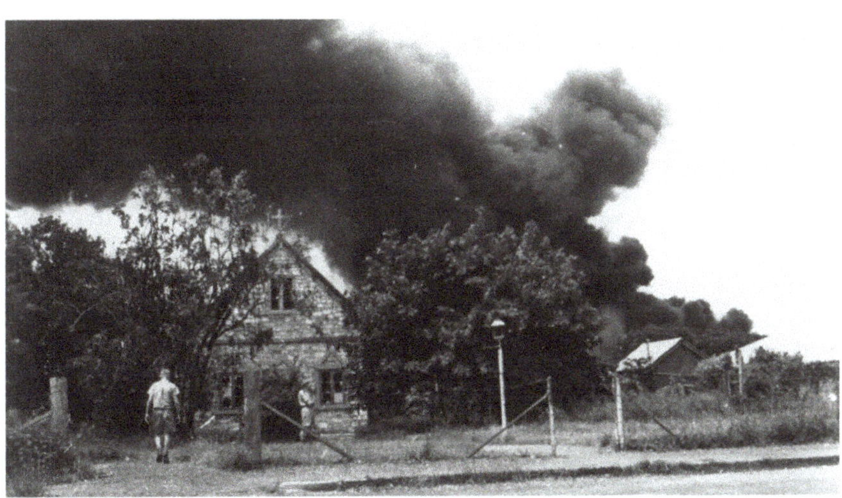

Christ Church, Smith Street, smoke from fires after air raids on Stokes Hill Wharf or oil tanks, c1942. (Unknown, NTAS, GPC, NTRS 3822-P1 Folder 99.)

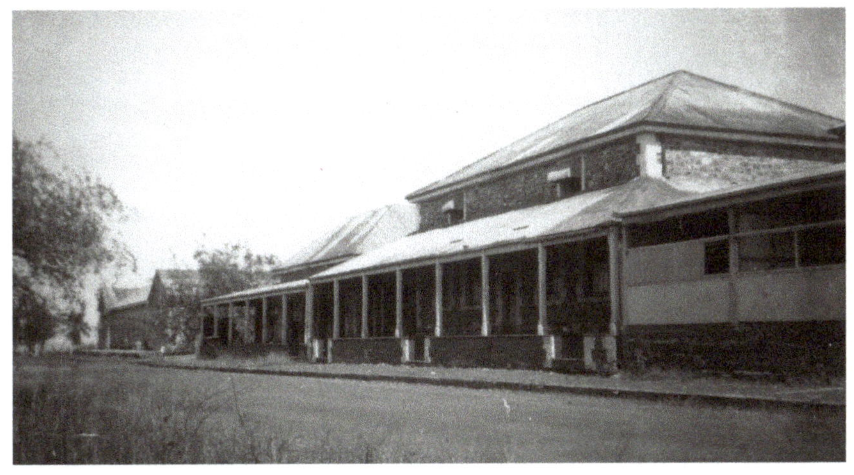

Naval HQ [Old Courthouse & Police Barracks], c1949-1951. (Harford, B., NTAS, B. Harford Collection, NTRS 1299 Item 83.)

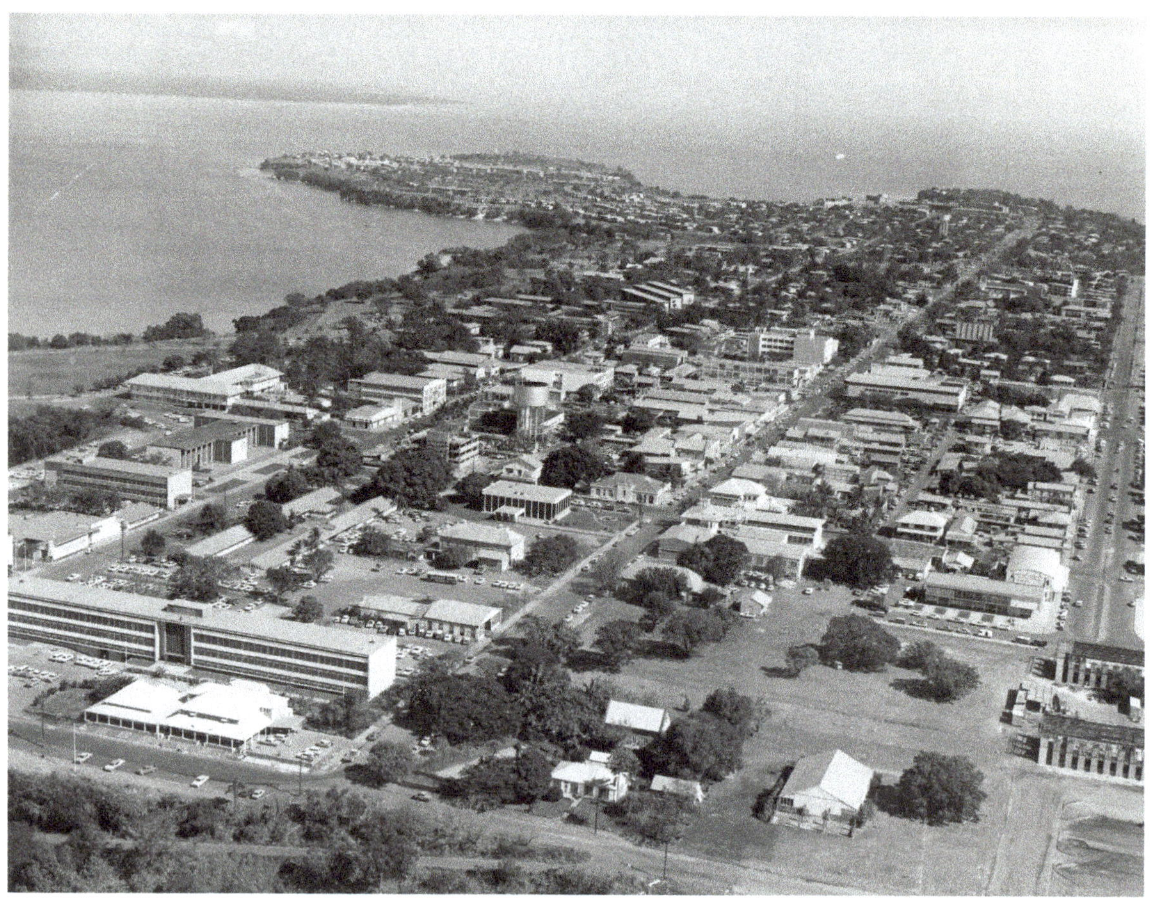

Darwin CBD, 1969. Note the Darwin Civic Centre near completion in lower right hand corner of image. (Unknown, NTAS, GPC, NTRS 3822-P1 Folder 92.)

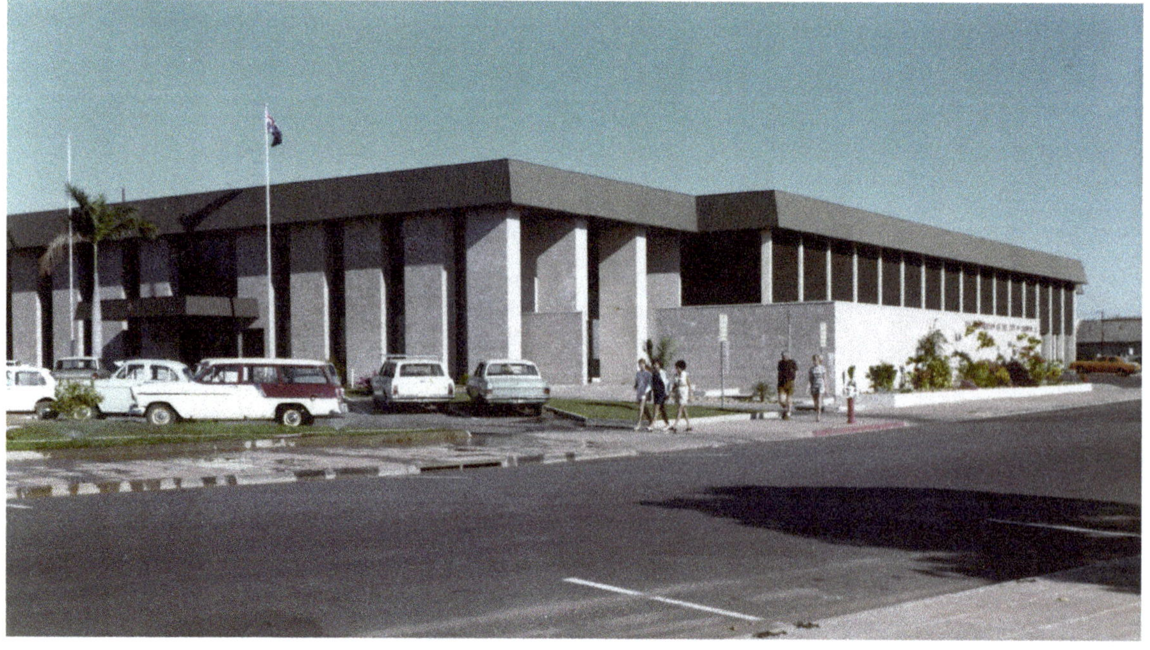

The Darwin Civic Centre soon after completion, 1972. (Unknown, NTAS, GPC, NTRS 3822-P1 Folder 70 Darwin Civic Centre 1972.)

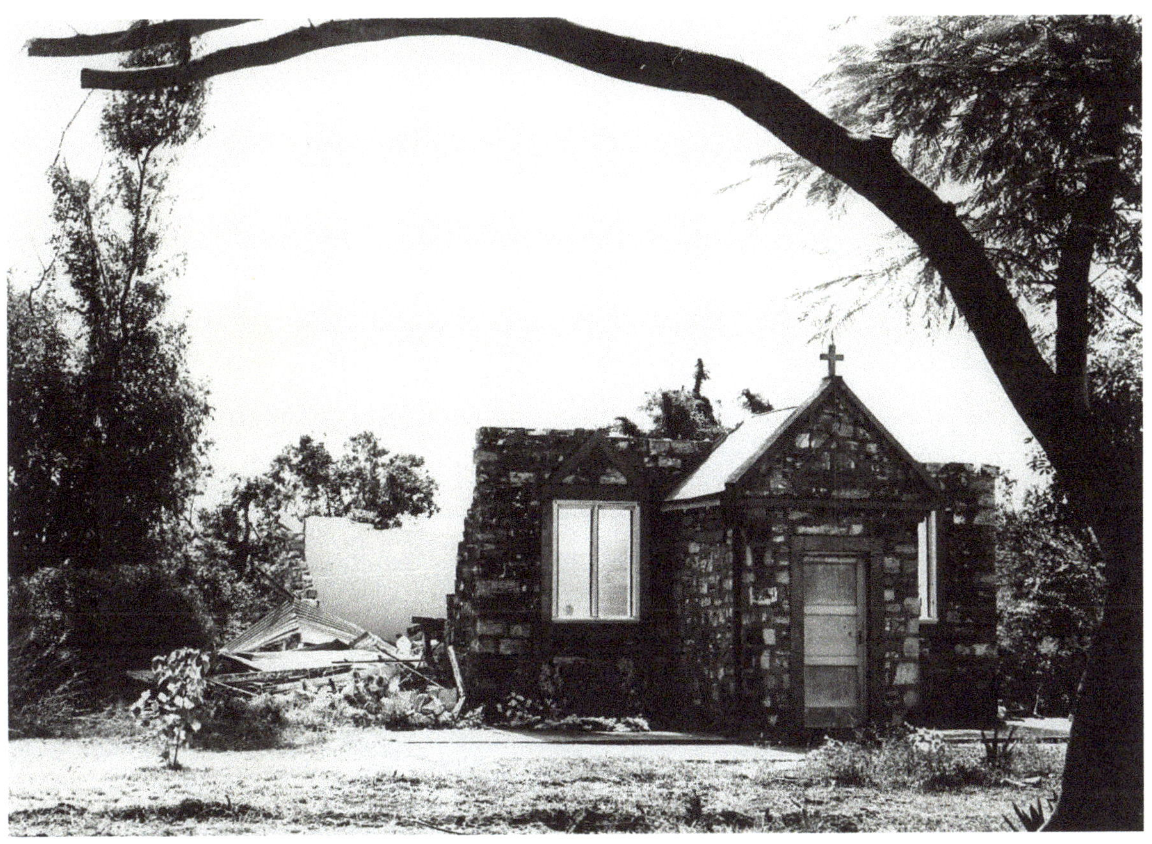

Christ Church, after Cyclone Tracy, 1974. (Unknown, NTAS, GPC, NTRS 3822-P1 Folder 52.)

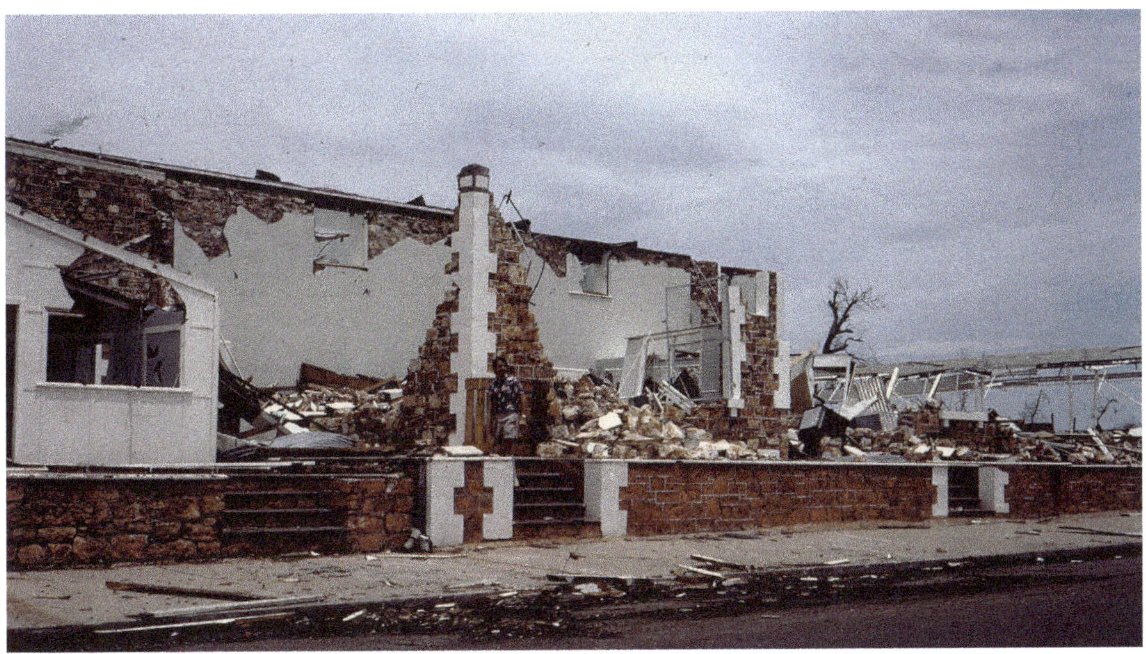

Naval Headquarters, corner of Smith Street and The Esplanade, after Cyclone Tracy, 1974. (Adams, L., NTAS, Leo Adams Collection, NTRS 3128/P1 Item 18, Smith St Administrator's offices.)

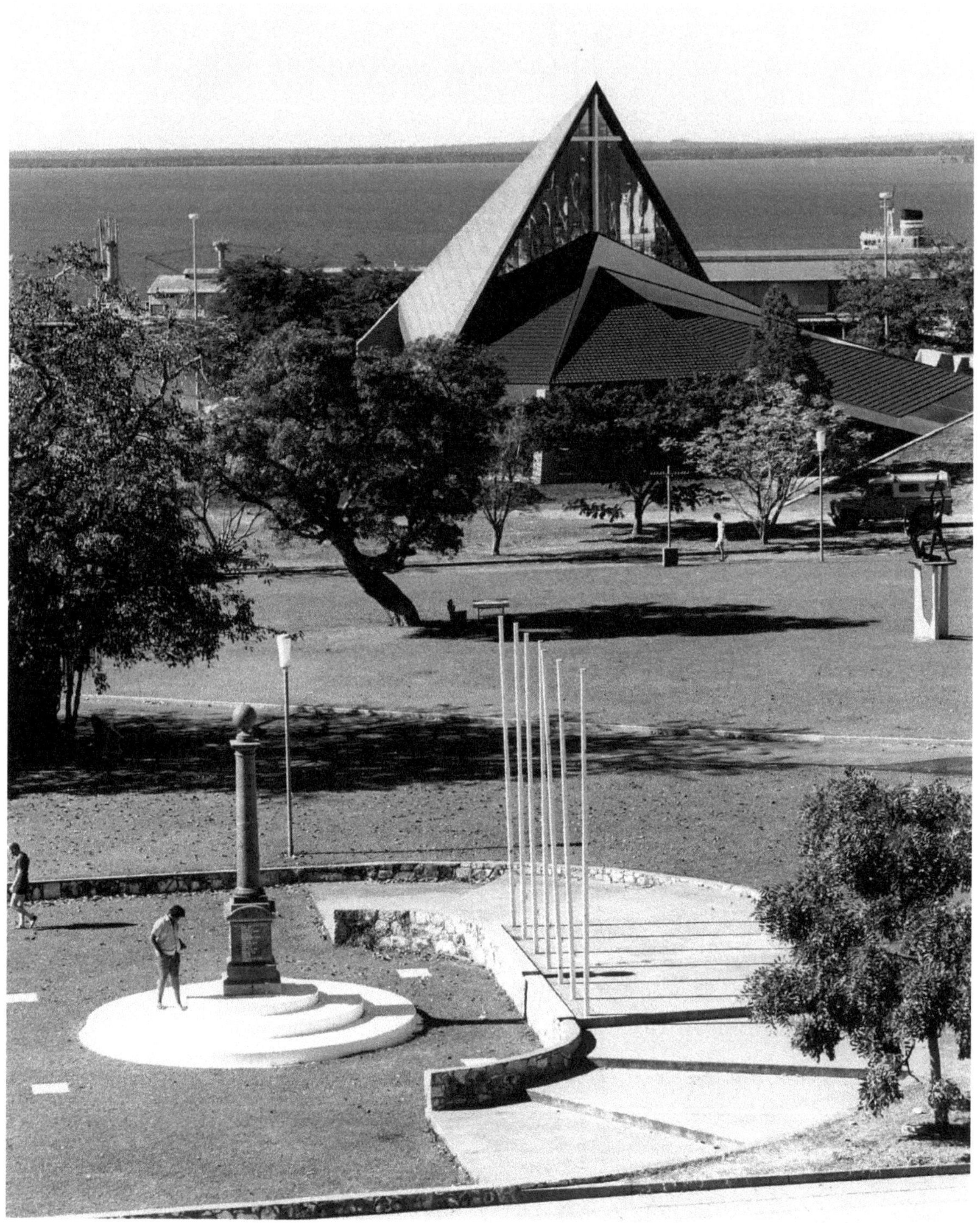

Christ Church, Civic Park & Cenotaph, c1980s. (Unknown, NTAS, GPC, NTRS 3822-P1 Folder 52 Christ Church, Civic Park and Cenotaph.)

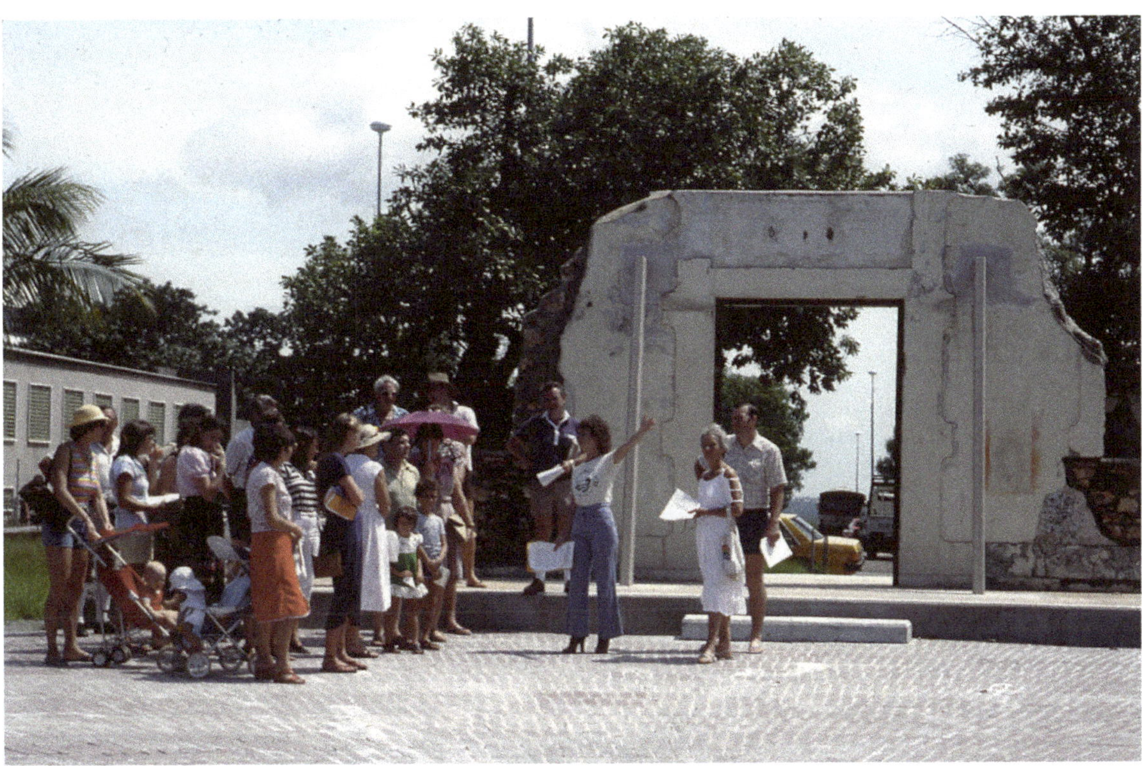

The Old Town Hall ruins, 1981. Since Cyclone Tracy the Old Town Hall Ruins have been used for a variety of purposes. (Skipsey, B.A., NTAS, GPC, NTRS 3822-P3 Darwin Historic Slide 2.)

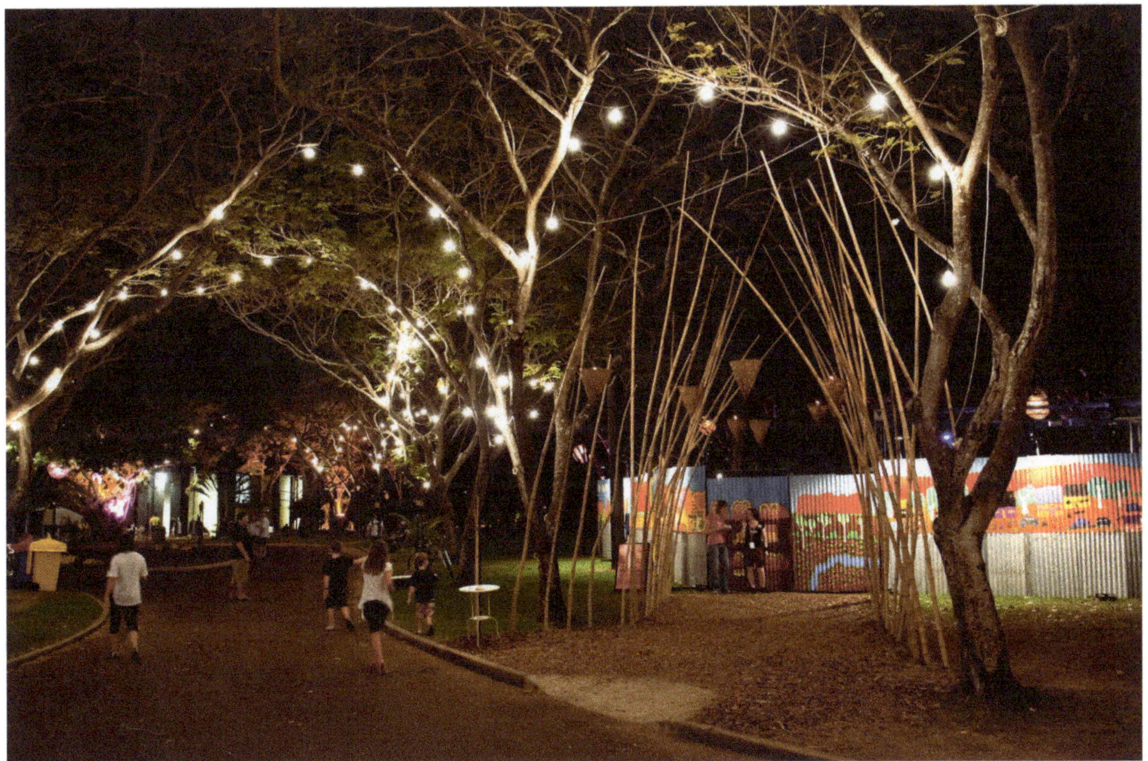

Darwin Festival Park, 2011. (Clark, D., NTL, Darren Clark Collection, PH0875/0074.)

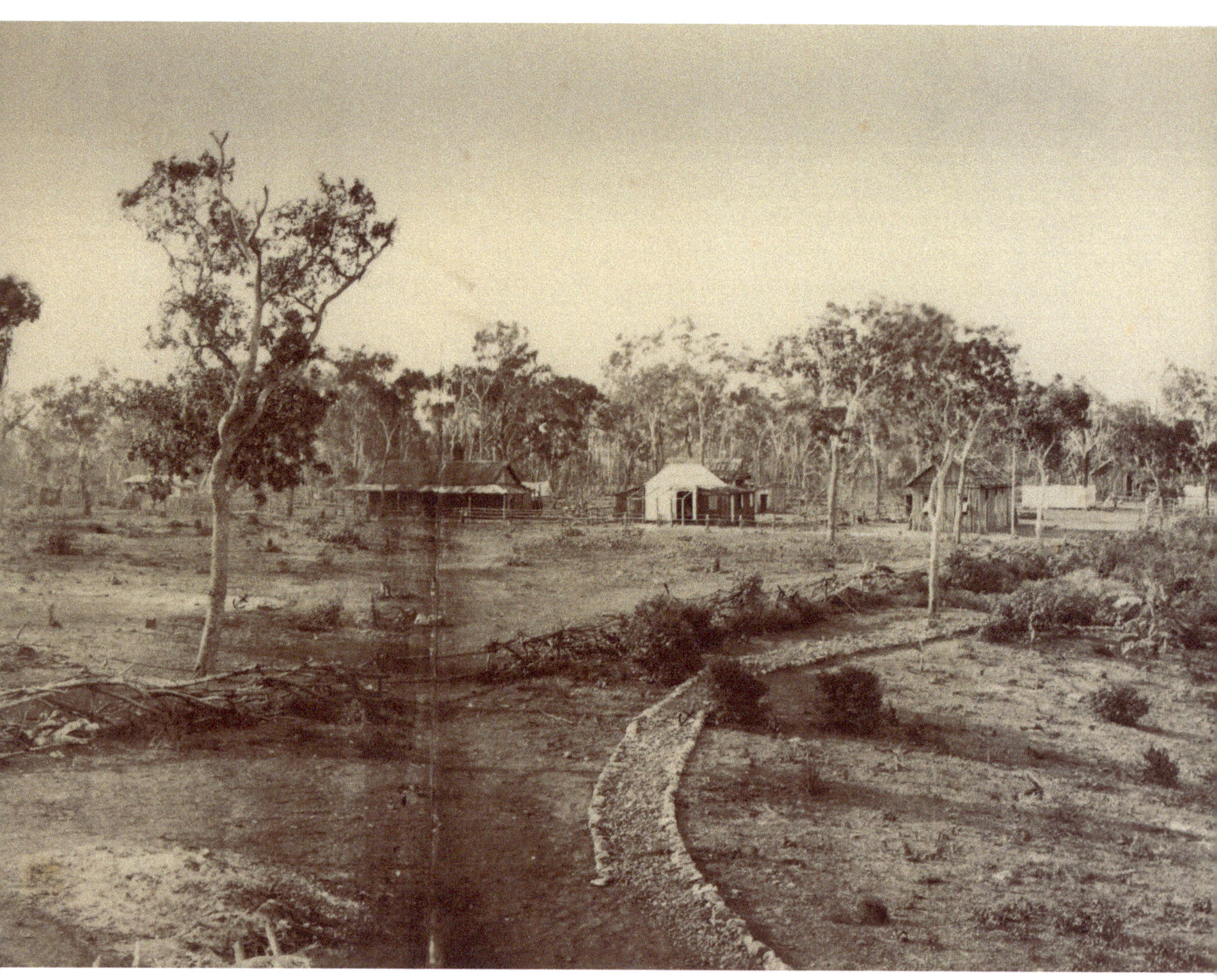

Corner of Mitchell Street and The Esplanade taken from the Residency, c1870. (Sweet, S.W., SLV, Views of Darwin and Roper River, N.T. [picture], H141681.)

Chapter 6

The Administrator's Residence and Liberty Square

The site of the Government Residence with its commanding view of Darwin harbour was selected in 1870 by the first South Australian Government Resident, Bloomfield Douglas. The 'Residency', as it was known, began life as a single story dwelling completed in 1871. The second Government Resident added a second storey but it was devoured by termites and was removed when major renovations were undertaken in 1879, giving it the current appearance. Sometimes known as the 'House of 7 Gables,'[1] The Residency has retained its colonial character despite a number of makeovers to keep it up to date.

The first undersea telegraph cable to Australia was a revolution in global communications previously reliant on mail by sea. There was fierce inter-colonial rivalry to construct the Overland Telegraph Line and thereby securing the international telecommunications terminus in Australia. South Australia secured the rights by agreeing to build the line by December 1871. An incredibly ambitious undertaking given that the route chosen had only been traversed by John McDouall Stuart's expeditions between 1858 and 1862. The first Overland Telegraph construction party arrived at Port Darwin on the *Omeo* on 9 September 1870 and work began immediately. In a remarkable feat of engineering in the face of the Northern Territory's 'Wet' season and the harshest of Australia's outback conditions, the Overland Telegraph Line was completed on the 22 August 1872. Telecommunications and those who kept the lines open would play a central role in Darwin's and the Northern Territory's economic and social life up to World War II.

The Palmerston staff of the British and Australian Telegraph Company (BAT) and the South Australian Overland Telegraph arrived in September 1871. Their stone offices and accommodation built on The Esplanade across from the Residency were the most substantial in Palmerston when they were completed in June 1872. The BAT staff liked to think of themselves as upper class English gentlemen and quickly established themselves in Palmerston 'society'. Alfred Searcy, sub-collector of customs based in Palmerston 1882-1896 describes his experience of the BAT.[2]

> During my time there is no mistake the officers were a grand lot of fellows, hospitable to a fault; in fact, they were in a great measure responsible for the good name Port Darwin received from visitors. At the quarters there was a tennis-court, billiard-room, and reading room, and all those accessories which make lives of officers stationed at a tropical outpost pleasant. ... What grand 'buck sprees' we used to have there, to be sure; a lot of men together, pure fun and frolic.

Their quarters were certainly more luxurious than experienced by most of Palmerston's citizens for many years. By comparison

1 *NTTG*, 17 May 1879.
2 Searcy, *In Australian Tropics*, 366.

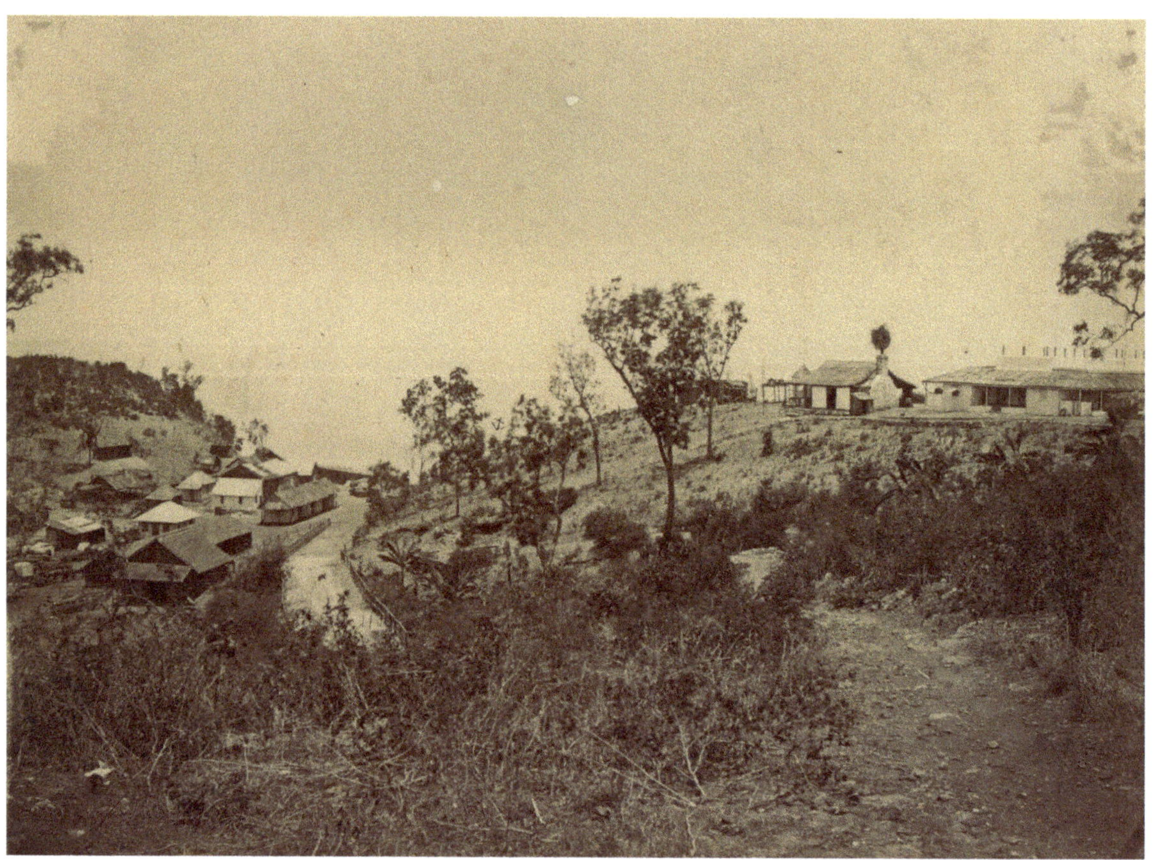

Government Residence, overlooking The Camp, Fort Hill, 1871. (Sweet, S.W., SLV, Views of Darwin and Roper River, N.T. [picture], H141687.)

Government buildings at the time consisted of a police station of two log huts, a two cell gaol and an iron house for the police Sub-Inspector Paul Foelsche.

By the 1880s the area of land bound by the Residency, The BAT, Overland Telegraph and Post Office and the Government offices on the corner of The Esplanade and Mitchell Street had become an important social and administrative hub for the growing town.

In 1919 this triangle of land was named 'Liberty Square' after the tumultuous events of the 'Darwin Rebellion' which shook the town as World War I was coming to an end.[3] The Darwin Rebellion is arguably the Northern Territory's most controversial political upheaval. A prolonged public campaign against the authoritarian rule of the Commonwealth Administrator, John Anderson Gilruth resulted in a public protest at this location. The 'Rebellion' ended with the burning of an effigy of Gilruth and a riot at Government House that ultimately led to his removal from the Territory.

World War I bought great economic and social change to Darwin. The construction and operation of Vesteys meatworks, from 1914 to 1919, resulted in a transformation of the social, political and economic landscape of Darwin. The industrialisation of the Darwin workforce also saw the rise of a significant working class and a militant local union movement, and provides the backdrop to the Darwin Rebellion.

Tensions grew throughout 1918. The union movement, under the leadership of the Australian Workers Union's, Harold Nelson, agitated against Gilruth's administration for many months. Nelson targeted Gilruth as the cause of the Territory's maladministration

3 *NTTG*, 21 June 1919.

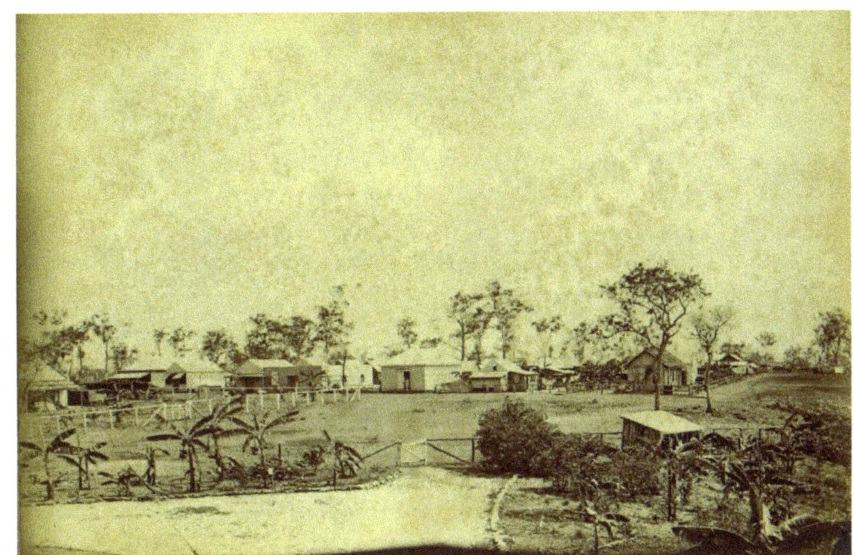

Corner of The Esplanade & Mitchell Street taken from the Residency, 1873. (Foelsche, P., NTAS, Foelsche Collection, NTRS 3420/P1/Item 38.)

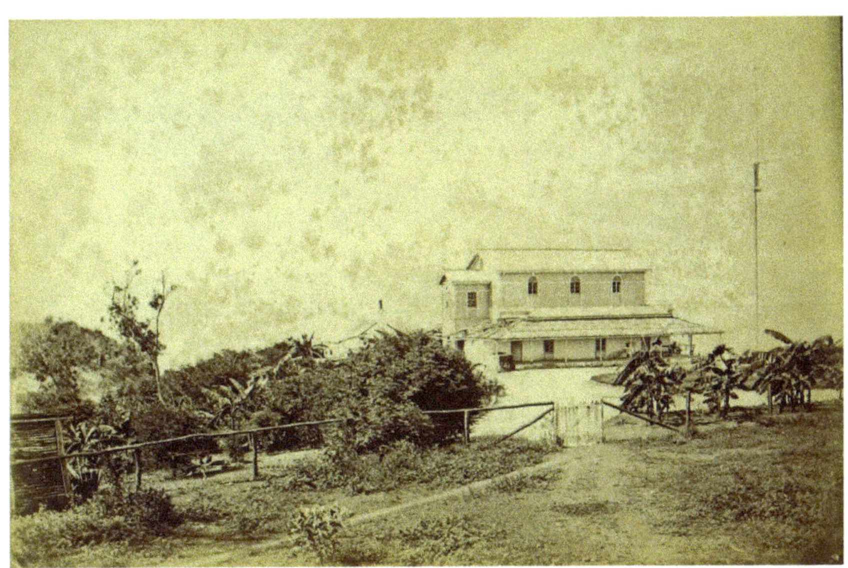

The Residency from the corner of The Esplanade & Mitchell Street, 1874. (Foelsche, P., NTAS, Foelsche Collection, NTRS 3420/P1/Item 37.)

with the catch cry 'no taxation without representation.'[4] The lack of political representation in the Australian parliament was not the only issue; wages at Vesteys, the conscription debate, and even a beer boycott of Darwin hotels all combined to increase tensions to boiling point. After a series of public meetings, union members finally confronted Gilruth at Government House on 17 December, where they demanded he leave the Territory and that an investigation into his administration be held. An effigy of Gilruth was burnt in front of Government House and a mob rushed the building resulting in a breach in the fence and some damage to the tennis court. Gilruth however, stood firm despite being manhandled by the mob. Nevertheless Nelson and the unions got their way. In February 1919 Gilruth left Darwin, never to return, and a Royal Commission on the Northern Territory Administration was conducted by Judge Norman Ewing. Harold Nelson was elected as the Northern Territory's first Federal parliamentarian in 1921 and served until 1934. Somewhat ironically, given Nelson's vociferous campaign to oust Gilruth, the Northern Territory Federal parliamentarian had no voting rights during his time in

4 NAA, *Civil Unrest & the Darwin Rebellion*, Research Guide, www.

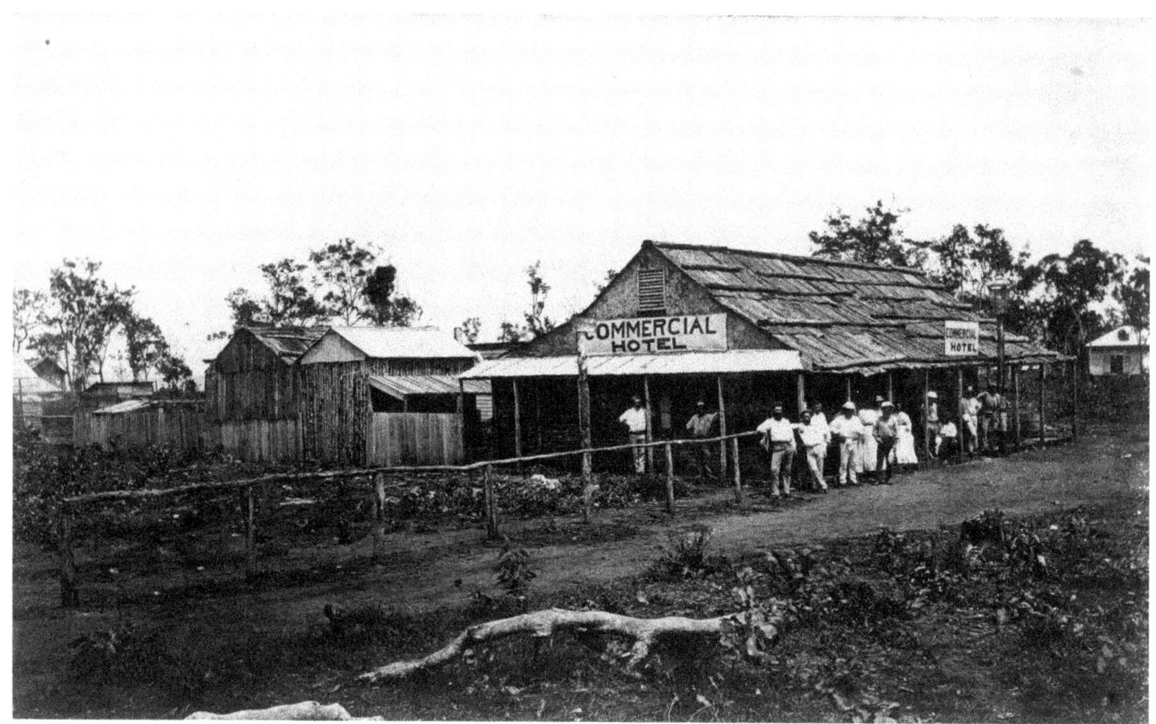

The Commercial Hotel, Mitchell Street, 1873. (Foelsche, P., SLSA , Searcy Collection, PRG280/1/43/347.)

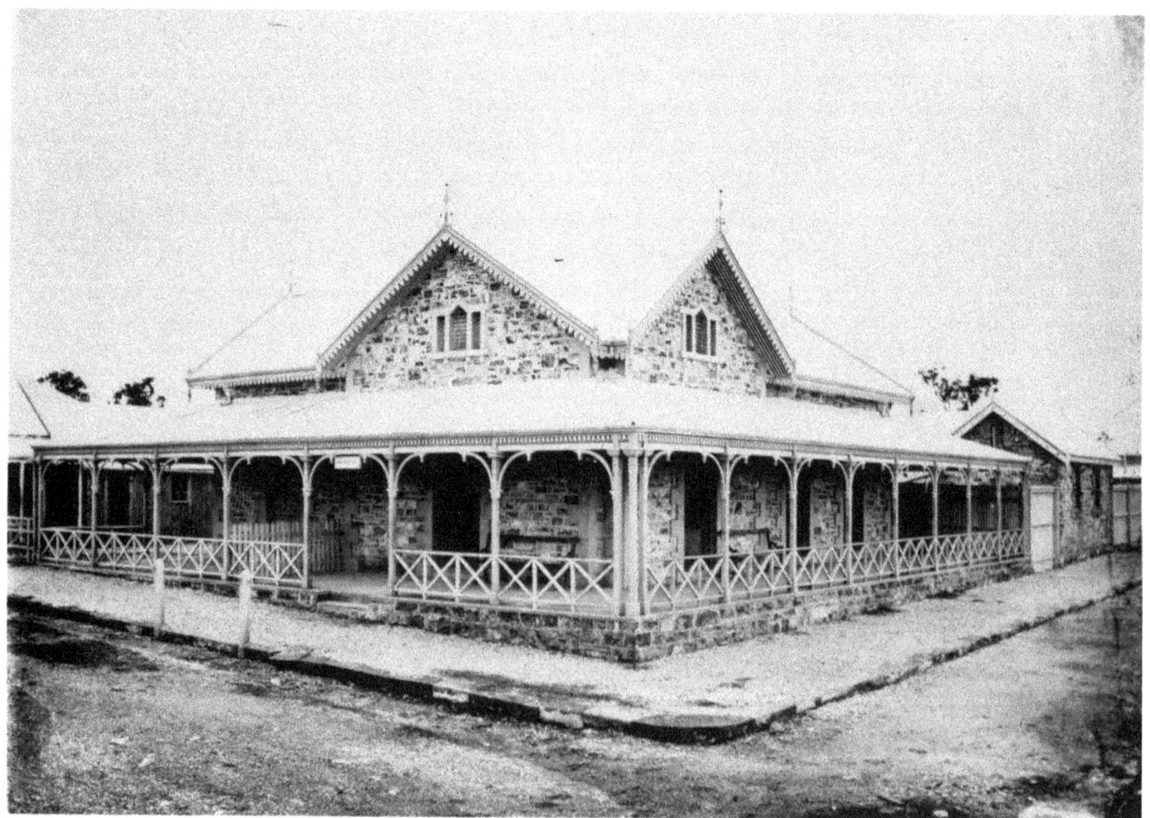

The new Police Station, corner of Mitchell Street and The Esplanade, Palmerston, 1878. (Foelsche, P., NTL, P., Foelsche Collection, PH0111-0096.)

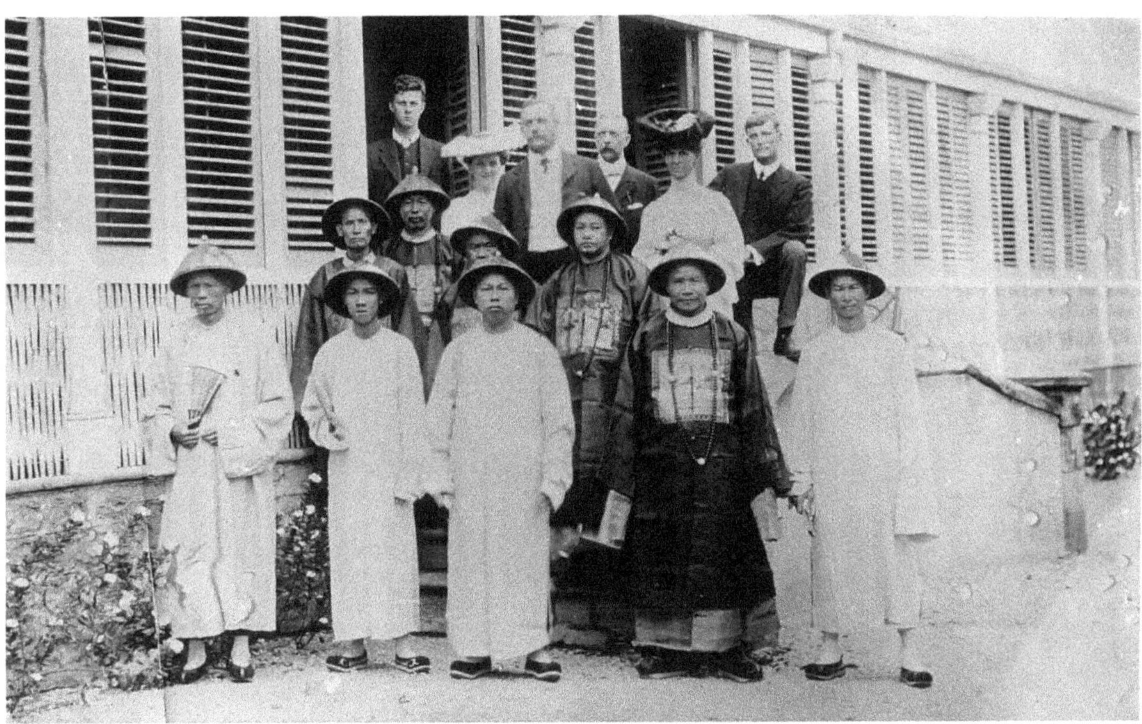

Vice regal visit to the Northern Territory, c1905. Gathering of Chinese merchants at the Residency. Back row L-R: Lloyd Herbert, Mrs Herbert, Sir George Le Hunte, Aide de Camp, Lady Le Hunte, Mr Justice Herbert. Middle row L-R: CHIN MEE LEUNG of Wing Cheong Sing, CHIN PAT MOW of Yam Yan, ? (obscured), FING HOW of Wing Wah Loong. Front row L-R: CHIN KIM KEE of Chin Leong Hen, CHARLIE YEE of Kwong Lee Cheong, BANG BEN of Cheong Woo, YUEN YET HING of Yet Loong, CHIN TOY of Fang Cheong Loong. (Unknown, NTAS, Unknown, NTRS1425 Item 6.)

parliament. It was not until 1959 that the Northern Territory Federal Parliamentarian received 'limited' voting rights on matters relating to the Territory, and 1968 for full voting rights.[5]

Liberty Square was chosen as the site for the Northern Territory's first official memorial. A cenotaph to commemorate Northern Territory's fallen World War 1 soldiers was unveiled on 24th April 1921. It was the location of Darwin's ANZAC day and other military commemorations for many years until it was moved in 1971.

Darwin's relative isolation and lack of a local economy exacerbated the effects of the Great Depression in the 1930s. The number of unemployed people reliant on Government rations in the town grew. In April 1930 growing tensions resulted in unemployed workers taking over the verandah of the Commonwealth Administrator's office demanding work or maintenance at full union rates. Administrator Wedell was locked in his office and although police soon freed him the unemployed workers occupation, supported by local communists, lasted another five days. A tent was set up in 'Liberty Square' and a red flag hoisted aloft. On 1 May 1930 the union organised the Northern Territory's first May Day parade.[6] Although tensions dissipated for a time, conditions worsened as relief work was reduced to a day a week. In early 1931 the unemployed workers again occupied the Administrator's office verandah and police were called to clear the protesters resulting in some casualties on both sides. The government solution to the unrest was

5 NAA, *Electoral Franchise and Territorians*, Research Guide, www.

6 Brian, *One Big Union*, 121. May Day parades are held annually in Darwin on the May Day public holiday.

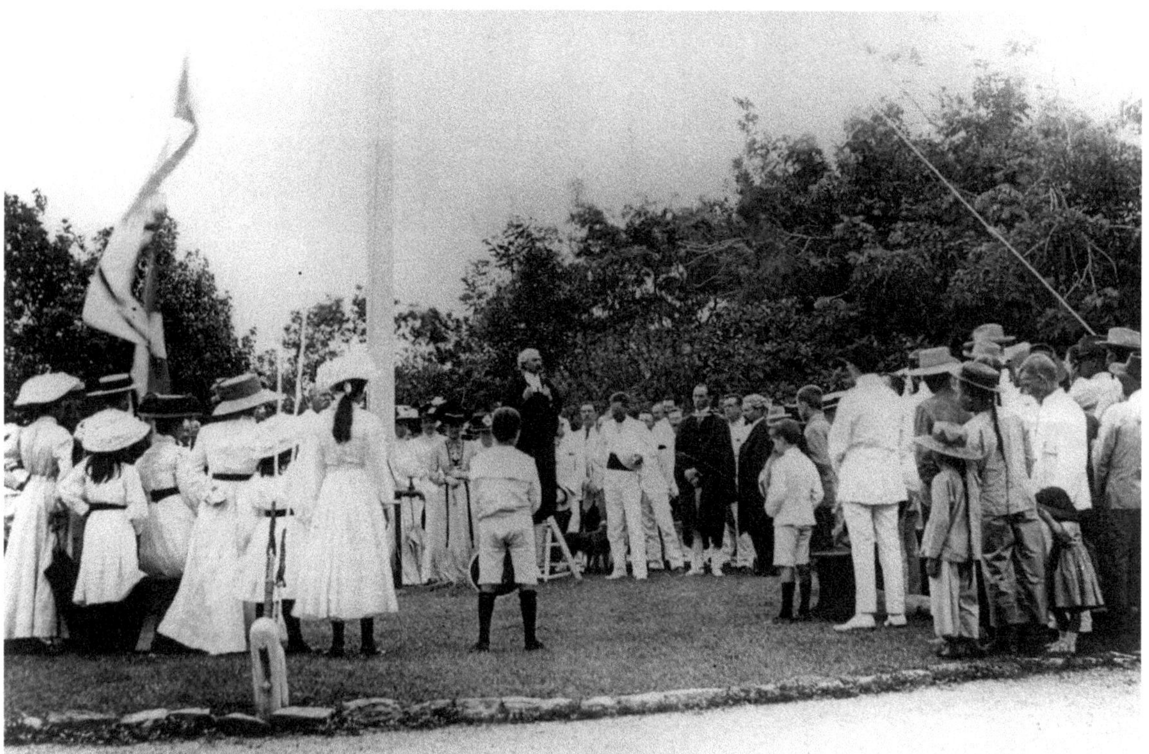

Transferring the Northern Territory to the Commonwealth from South Australia. Mr Justice Mitchell reading the proclamation and the raising the Commonwealth flag outside The Residency, 1911. (Unknown, NTL, Peter Spillett Collection, PH0238/0077.)

to provide free passage south for some and restricting unemployment relief to others. The tensions died down but it reinforced Darwin's reputation for rebellion, radicals and communists.[7]

On the 19th of February 1942 the buildings around Liberty Square were targeted by the first Japanese air raid on Darwin. The Administrator's office, located in front of Government House was destroyed as was the Crown Law Officer's office to the rear. Government House itself escaped major damage. Somewhat miraculously, given the damaged caused by the bombing, only Daisy Martin, one of the Administrator's domestic staff was killed. Greater tragedy was to occur at the nearby Overland Telegraph and Post Office buildings which were severely damaged in the first Japanese air raids when ten bombs landed within and nearby the complex. The Postmaster, Hurtle Bald, his wife Alice and their daughter Iris and six other post office staff were all killed when the slit trench they were sheltering in took a direct hit. The destruction of the post office buildings was the end of an era. The reconstruction resulted in Post Office and Telegraph infrastructure being established in other locations around Darwin. In 1954 the Post Office site was cleared to build the Legislative Council Building, which opened in March 1955. A section of the bombed Post Office was incorporated into the Legislative Council building and this was later incorporated into the lobby of the Legislative Assembly building. Although severely damaged by Cyclone Tracy the Legislative Assembly building remained in use until 1990. The section of the bombed Post Office was again reconstructed in the foyer of the Northern Territory Library within the Legislative Assembly building opened in 1994.

During the 1960s the Liberty Square area was hemmed in by the Commonwealth Centre of the Northern Territory administration. By the 1970s this consisted

7 Powell, *Far Country*, 165-167.

of eight office blocks between Smith and Mitchell Street to The Esplanade. They were required to accommodate the multitude of Commonwealth departments and their staff. The Chan building, the eighth and final building completed, is the only building remaining from this era.

The Commonwealth Centre also included an impressive modernist Supreme Court building completed in 1965. Although no longer in existence at the eastern end of Mitchell Street it was the home of the Northern Territory Supreme Court until 1991 when it was demolished to make way for the State Square development.

Liberty Square is now incorporated into the State Square as a park between the Supreme Court of the Northern Territory and the Northern Territory Legislative Assembly (Parliament House). State Square was first proposed in 1988 with construction commencing in 1990. The Supreme Court was opened in 1991. Parliament House, the seat of the Northern Territory's single chamber Legislative assembly, opened in 1994.

Today there are few reminders of the tumultuous history of Liberty Square. A small stone monument and plaque near the south east corner of the Legislative Assembly building acknowledges the 'Darwin Rebellion' but there is nothing to hint at the other important events that occurred in Liberty Square or of the many ANZAC and other military ceremonies held there for most of the 20th Century.

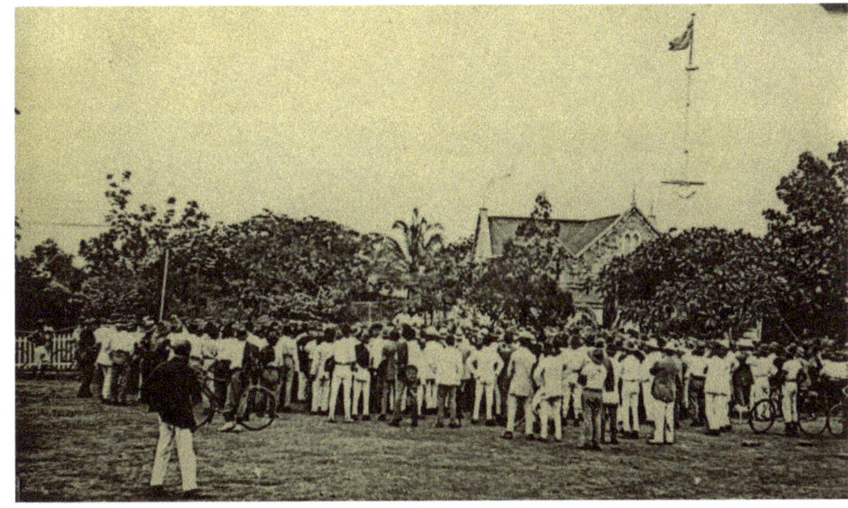

Darwin Rebellion, burning an effigy of Administrator Gilruth, in front of The Residency, 1918. (Unknown, NTAS, Rhodes Collection, NTRS 2885 Item 24.)

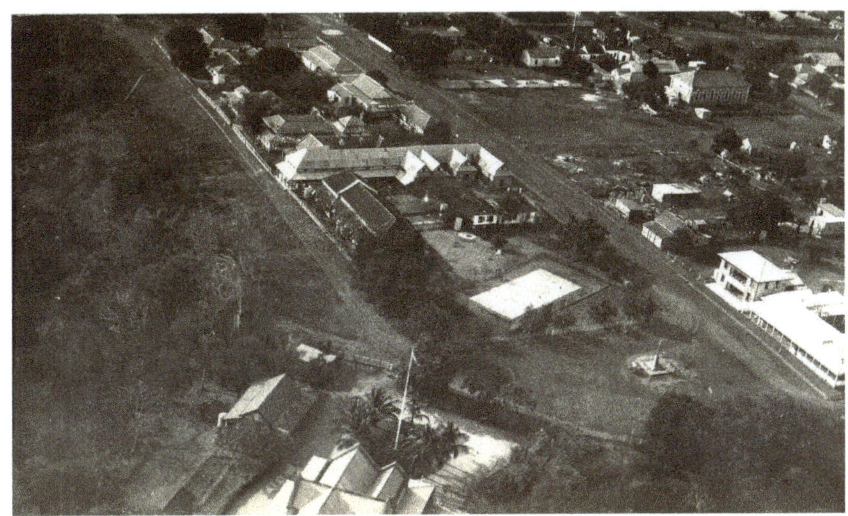

Liberty Square, Administrator's Residence, BAT and Post Office, Cenotaph and Government offices, c1930. (Unknown, NTAS, Charles Wilson Collection, NTRS 3335 Item 285.)

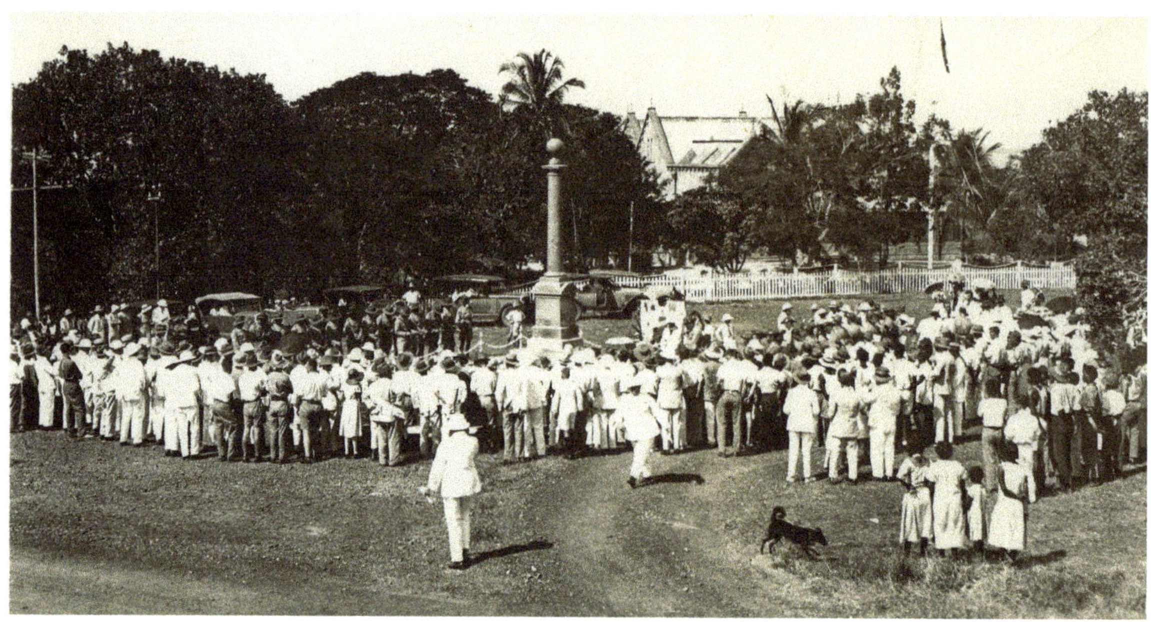

ANZAC Day, Liberty Square, 1933. (Unknown, NTAS, G. Birt Collection, NTRS 270 Item 13.)

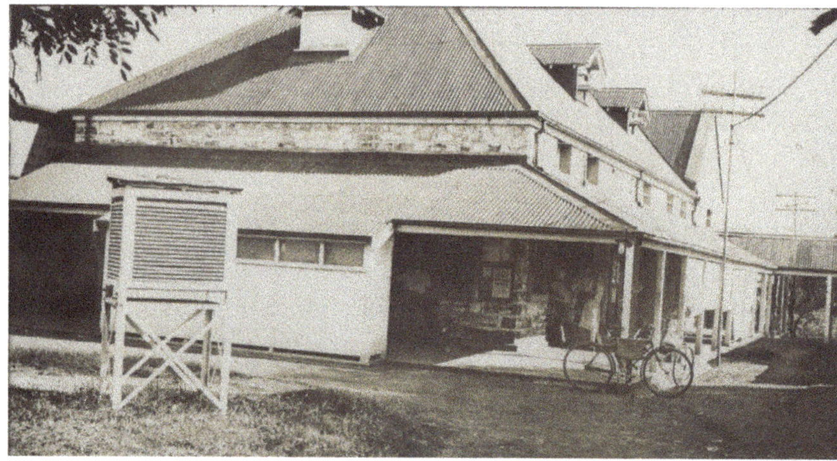

Darwin Post Office, c1930. (Unknown, NTAS, Charles Wilson Collection, NTRS 3335 Item 8.)

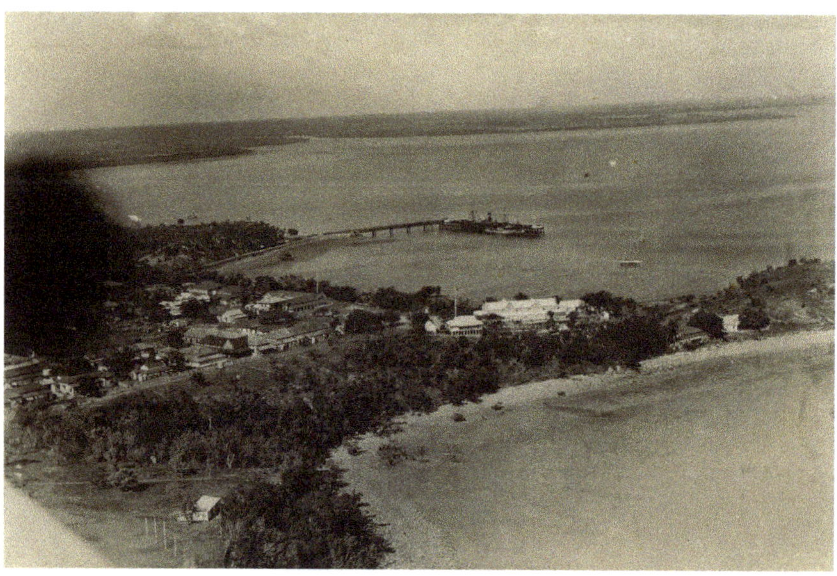

Aerial view of The Esplanade, Administrator's Residence and Darwin wharves, 1939. (Unknown, NTAS, B. Humble Collection, NTRS 1168 Item 34.)

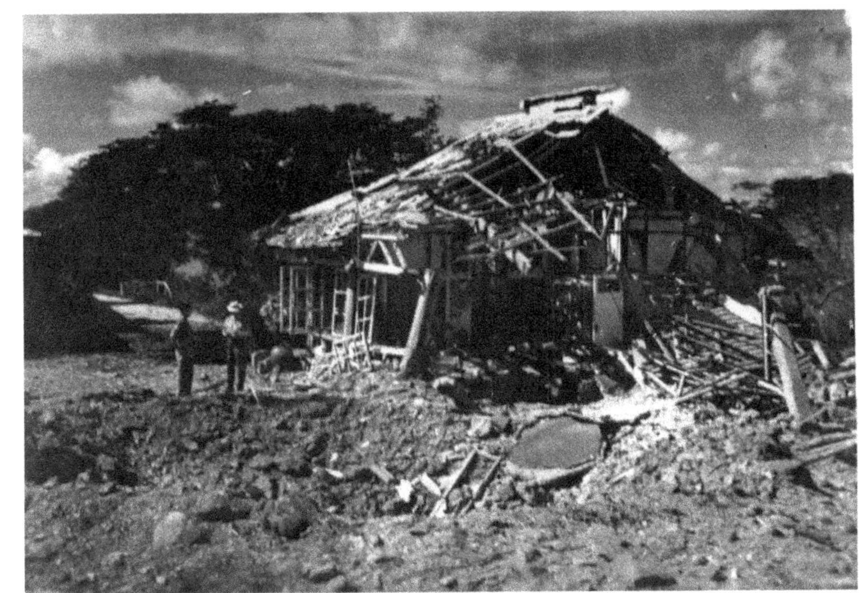

Bomb damage, Administrator's administration offices adjacent to The Residency, 19 February 1942. (Unknown, NTAS, J. Beverly Collection, NTRS 2012 Item 9.)

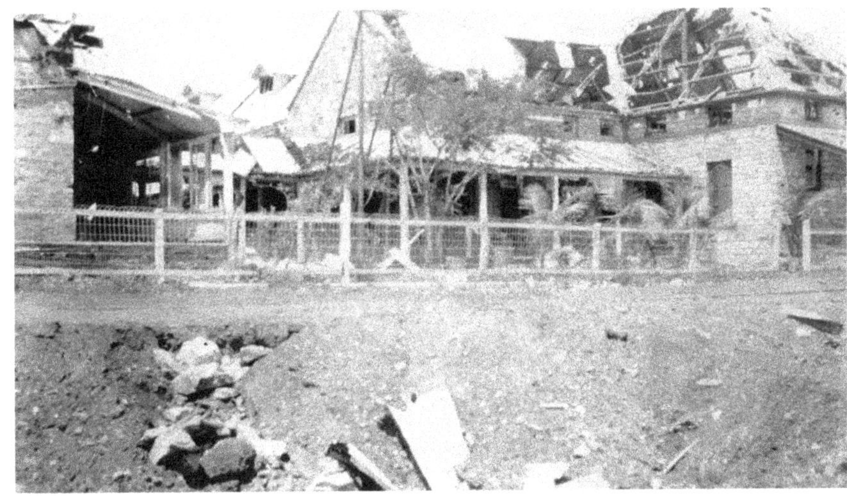

Darwin Post Office, bomb damage, 19th of February 1942. (Unknown, NTAS, GPC, NTRS 3822-P1 Folder 99.)

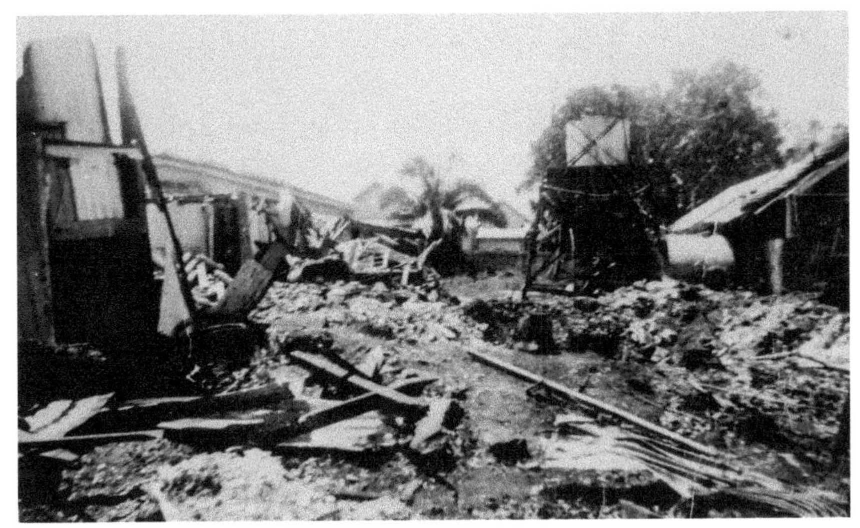

Darwin Post Office compound, bomb damage, 19th of February 1942. (Unknown, NTL, Peter Spillett Collection, PH0238/0332.)

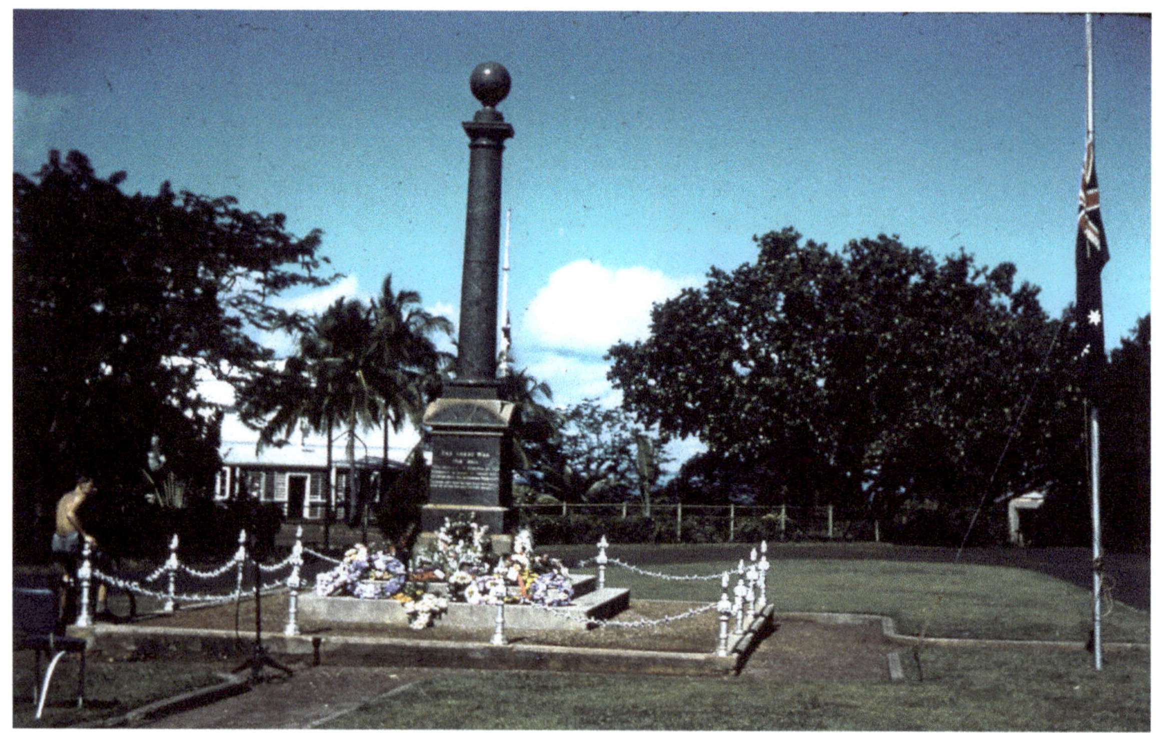

Cenotaph, Liberty Square, c1960s. (W.C. Laidlaw, NTAS, W.C. Laidlaw Collection, NTRS 317 Item 52.)

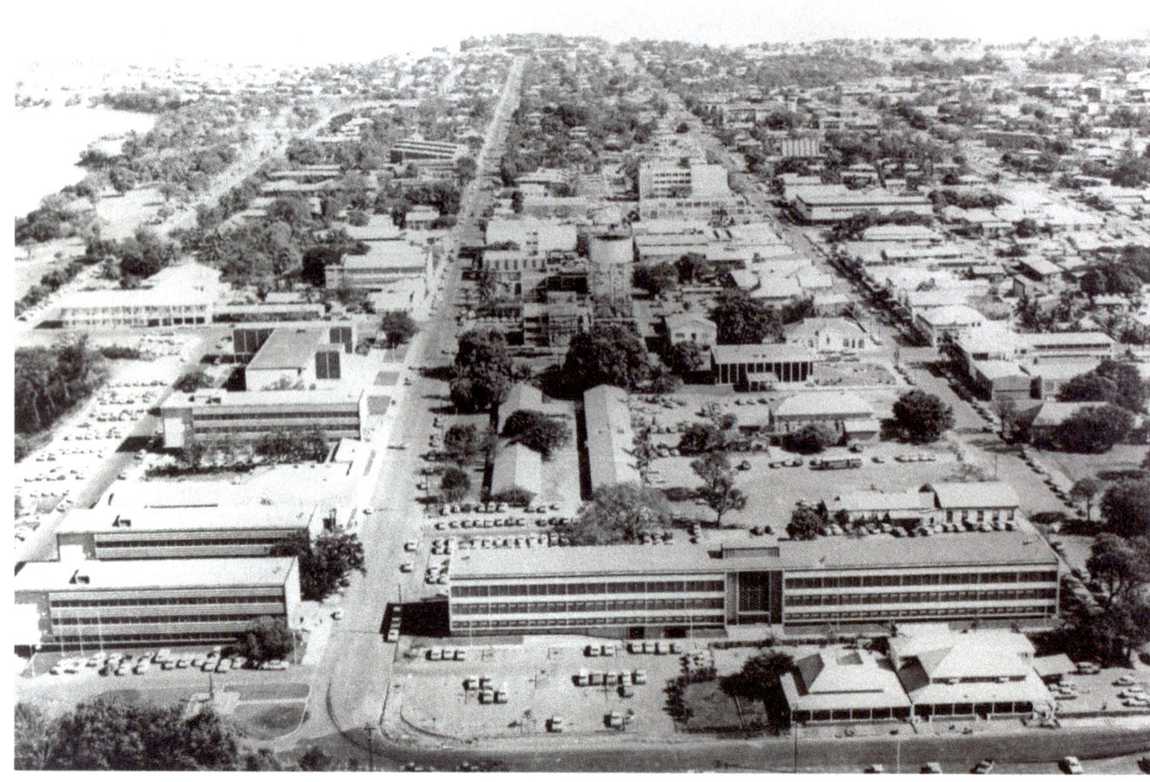

Darwin CBD with Commonwealth administration buildings in foreground, 1968. (Unknown, NTL, Peter Spillett Collection, PH0238/1582.)

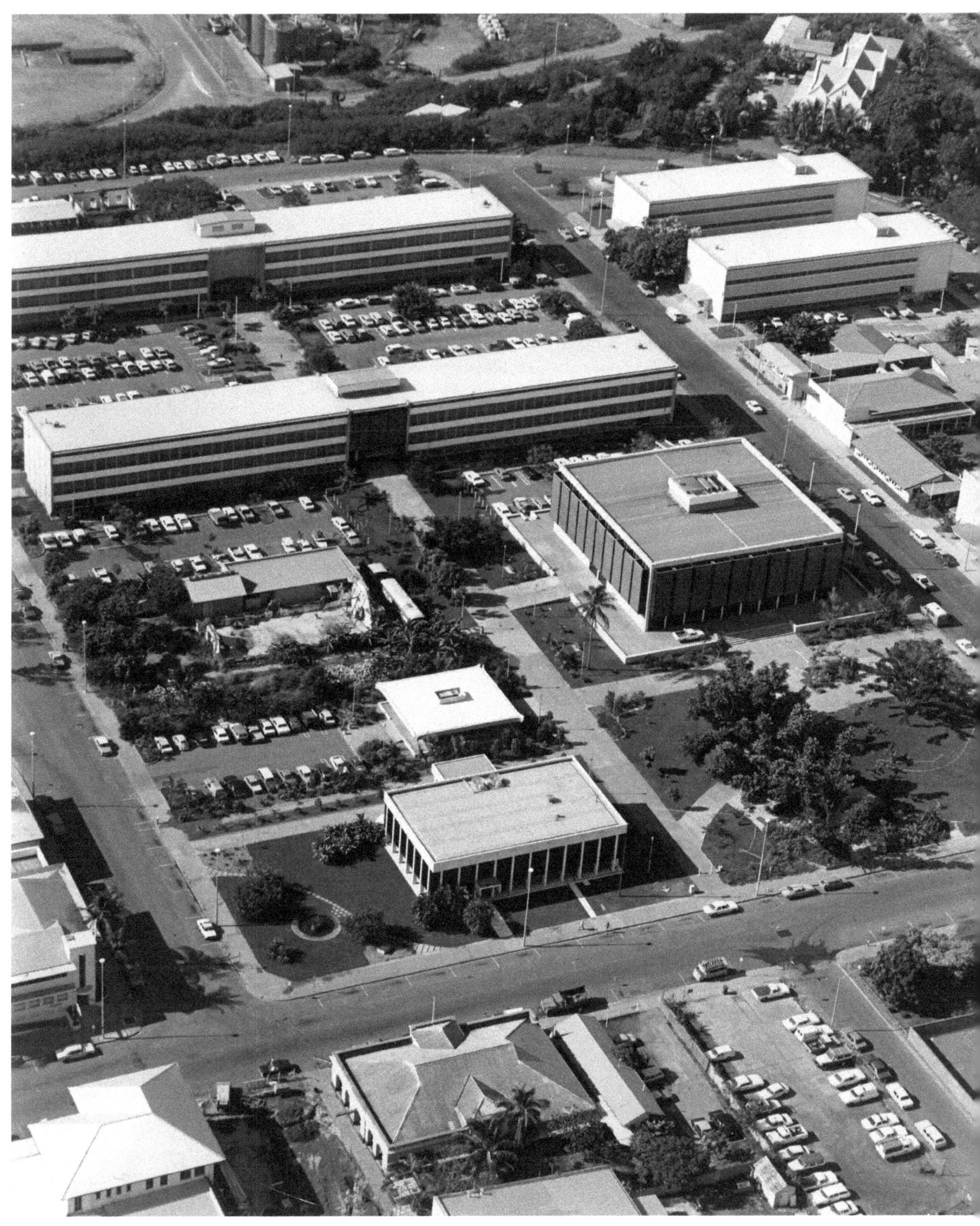

Commonwealth administration buildings and Administrator's Residence, c1980. (Unknown, NTAS, GPC Collection, NTRS 3822-P1 Folder 90 Government administration buildings.)

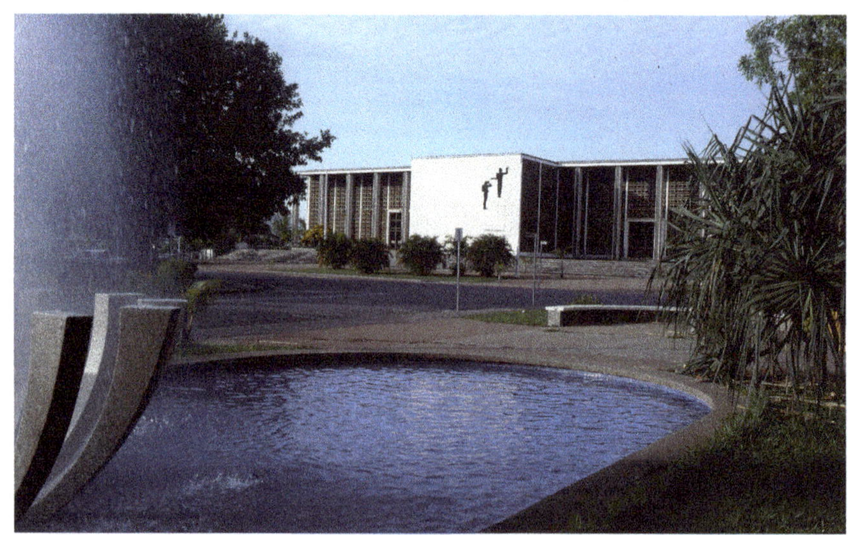

Supreme Court, Mitchell Street, 1985. (Unknown, NTAS, GPC Collection, NTRS 3822-P3 Darwin Buildings Slide LF64.)

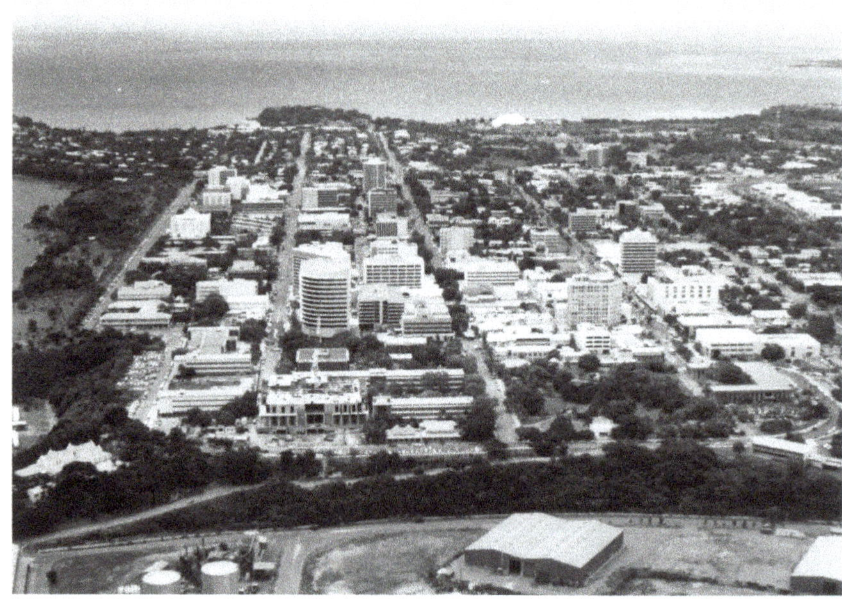

Northern Territory Supreme Court building under construction, c1990. (Unknown, NTAS, GPC Collection, NTRS 3822-P1 Folder 69 Supreme Court Building under construction.)

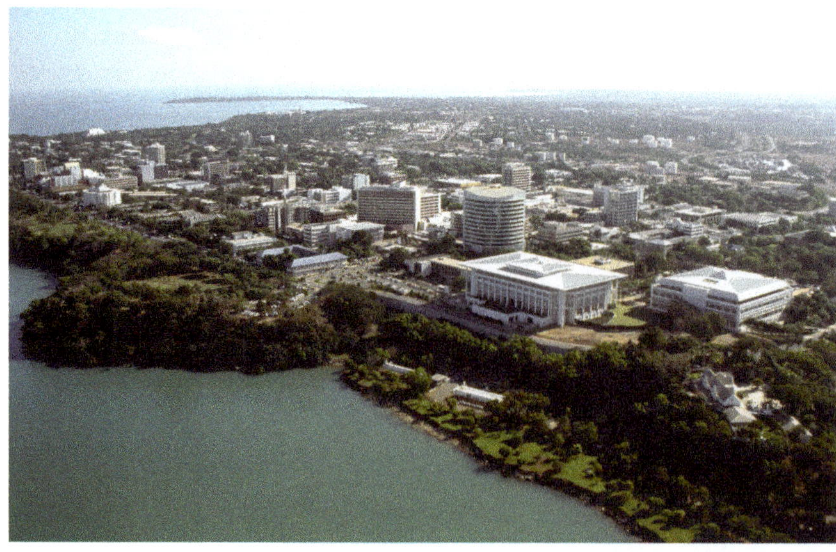

Legislative Assembly, Supreme Court and Administrator's Residence, 1995. (Unknown, NAA, Cities & Towns, Darwin from the Air, 1995, A6135, K7/8/95/346.)

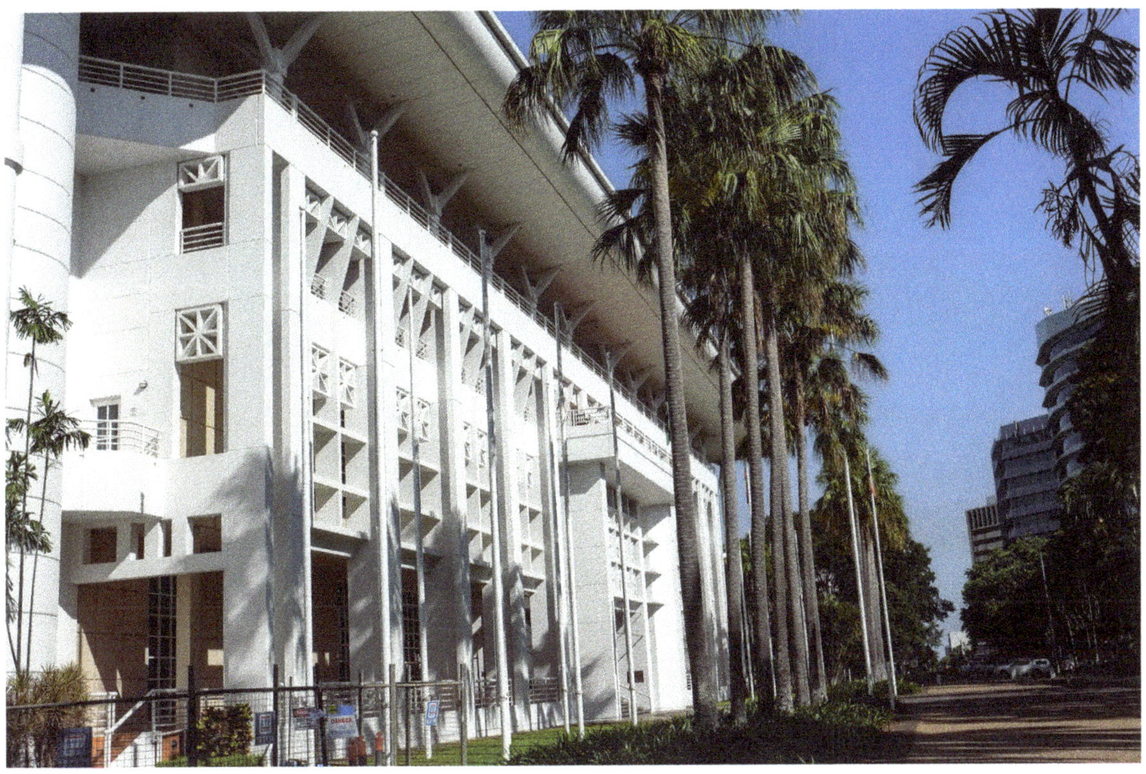

Legislative Assembly, 2017. (Martin, R., Matthew Stephen, Personal Collection, Legislative Assembly_05.)

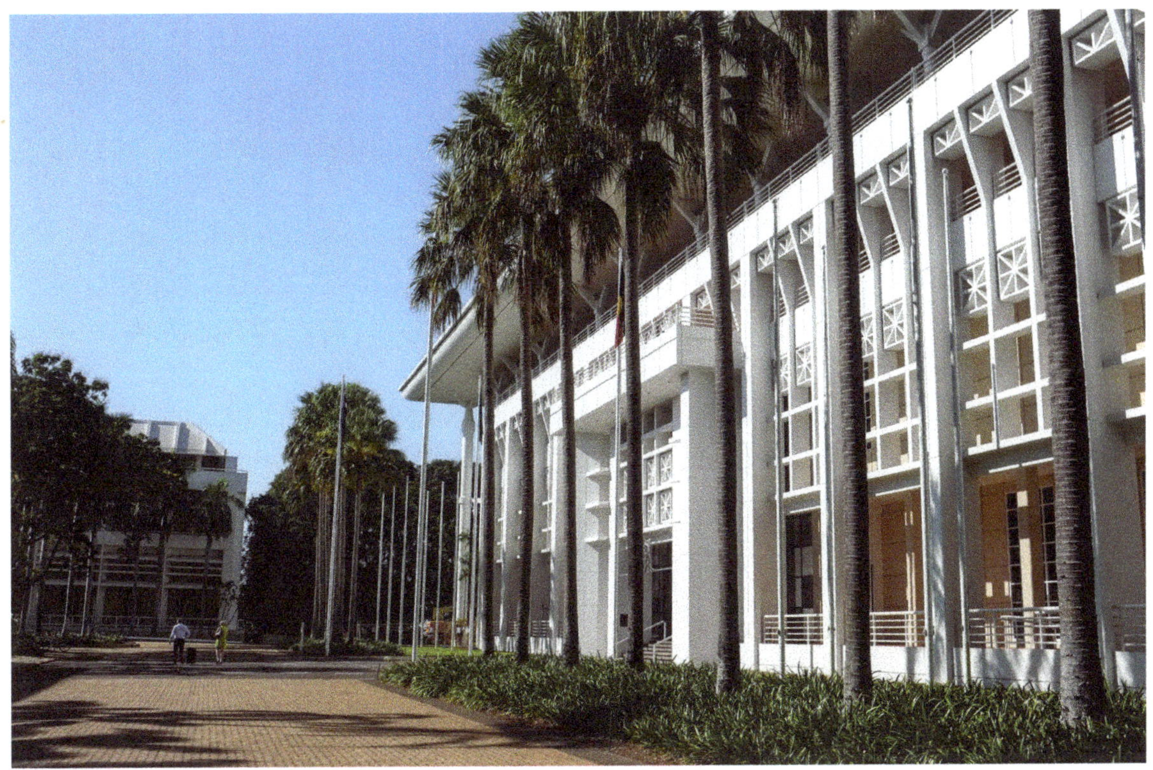

Legislative Assembly, 2017. (Martin, R., Matthew Stephen, Personal Collection, Legislative Assembly_12.)

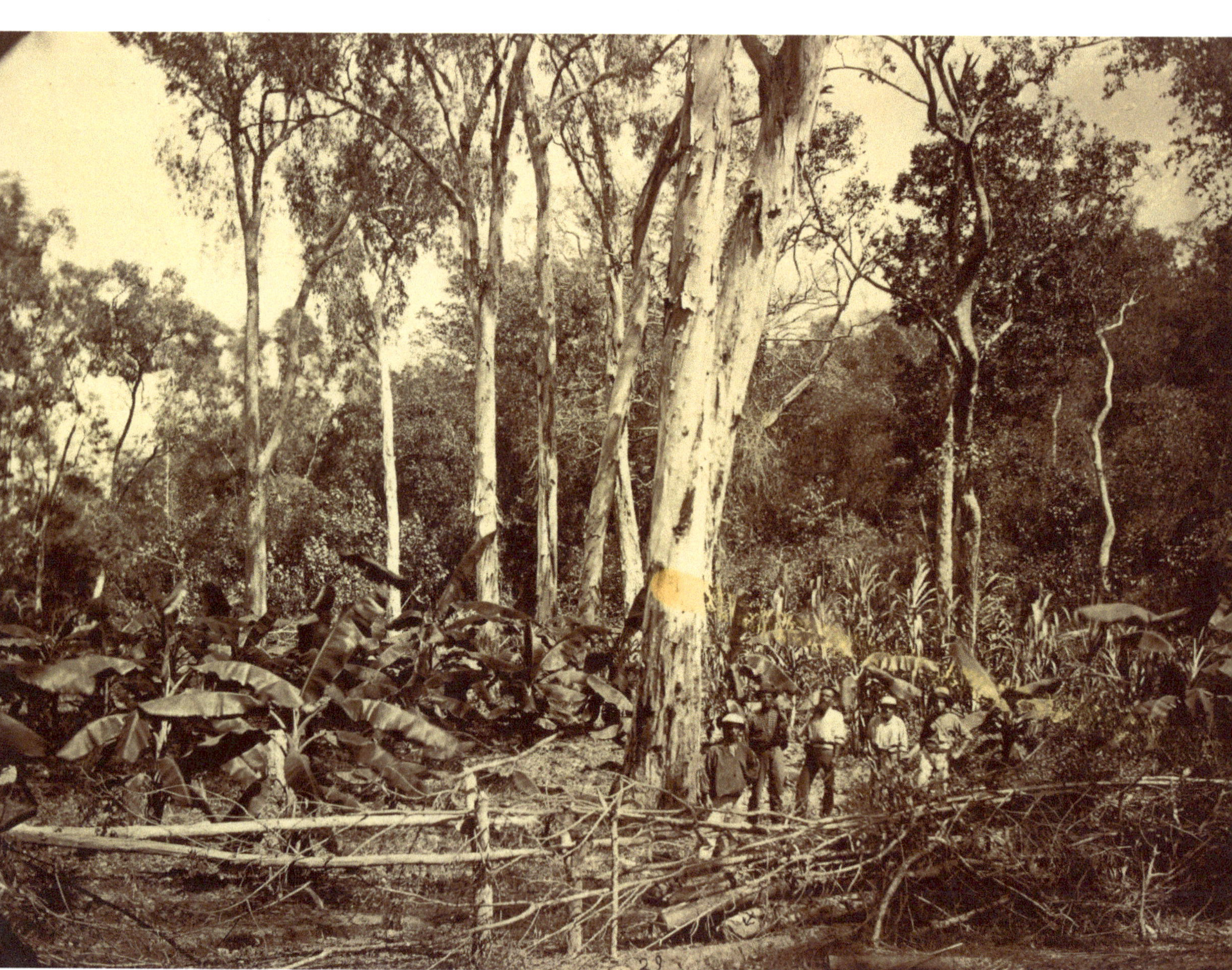

Peel's Well, c1870. (Sweet, S.W., SLV, Views of Darwin and Roper River, N.T. [picture], H141568.)

Chapter 7

The Esplanade

In the original Palmerston town survey The Esplanade facing the harbour was designated as public land. It stretched from Bennet Street to Doctors Gully and continued on to include the full southern length of Emery Point. Emery Point remained largely vacant until the 1930s when *HMAS Coonawarra* Naval Base was declared in 1932. Construction of infrastructure upon Emery Point began in 1934 and has remained under Australian Defence force control since.

Peel's Well at the north western end of The Esplanade played an important part in the early settlement of Darwin. Named after Goyder's 1869 survey party Doctor, Robert Peel, the area became known as Doctor's Gully (*Ninyji*). As a reliable well it supplied water to the early settlement, passing ships and the settlement's first food gardens. Chinese gardens were established on the gully floor in the 1870s and remained in use until World War II.[1]

A site above the western side of Doctor's Gully, was chosen for Palmerston's first hospital. Selected because it was some distance from town a wooden building housing a six bed ward and accommodation for a Matron was completed in June 1874. In 1875 a stone ward was constructed adjacent to the original building. The hospital served Darwin for 70 years until 1942 when a new hospital bounded by McKay Street and Lambell Terrace on Myilly Point was opened.

The Darwin Esplanade offered a variety of leisure options for the town's citizens. In 1873, W.H. Garson, of the Hotel Palmerston on The Esplanade, advertised 'a good pathway leading down from the hotel to a fine bathing place — a distance of about 200 yards'.[2] There was no mention of crocodiles, stingers or other marine predators!

The town oval was first established on The Esplanade in 1875.[3] It remained the epicentre of Darwin sport until the 1950s when Gardens Oval, adjacent to the Botanic Gardens, was established. The Esplanade Oval was the scene of almost all Darwin sports up until World War II and as such is the ancestral home of most Northern Territory sports. Athletics, archery, cycling, Australian rules football, hockey, rugby union, tennis, netball and baseball were all played on the ground. In 1916 the first games of Australian rules football or AFL, the Northern Territory's most popular sport, were played on The Esplanade Oval. The Esplanade Oval was one of the few convenient public meeting places so it was frequently also the site of public meetings, carnivals and the final destination of many Darwin parades. Gardens Oval became the main Darwin sports ground in 1953 and as a consequence The Esplanade Oval declined in use as a sports ground. However, the area retained its importance as public space due to its Esplanade location and beautiful outlook. In 1978 the site of the former Darwin Oval, was focal point of Northern Territory Self Government celebrations. In 1990 the Darwin

1 NT Heritage register, *Peels Well*.
2 *NTTG*, 7 November 1873.
3 *NTTG*, 29 May 1875.

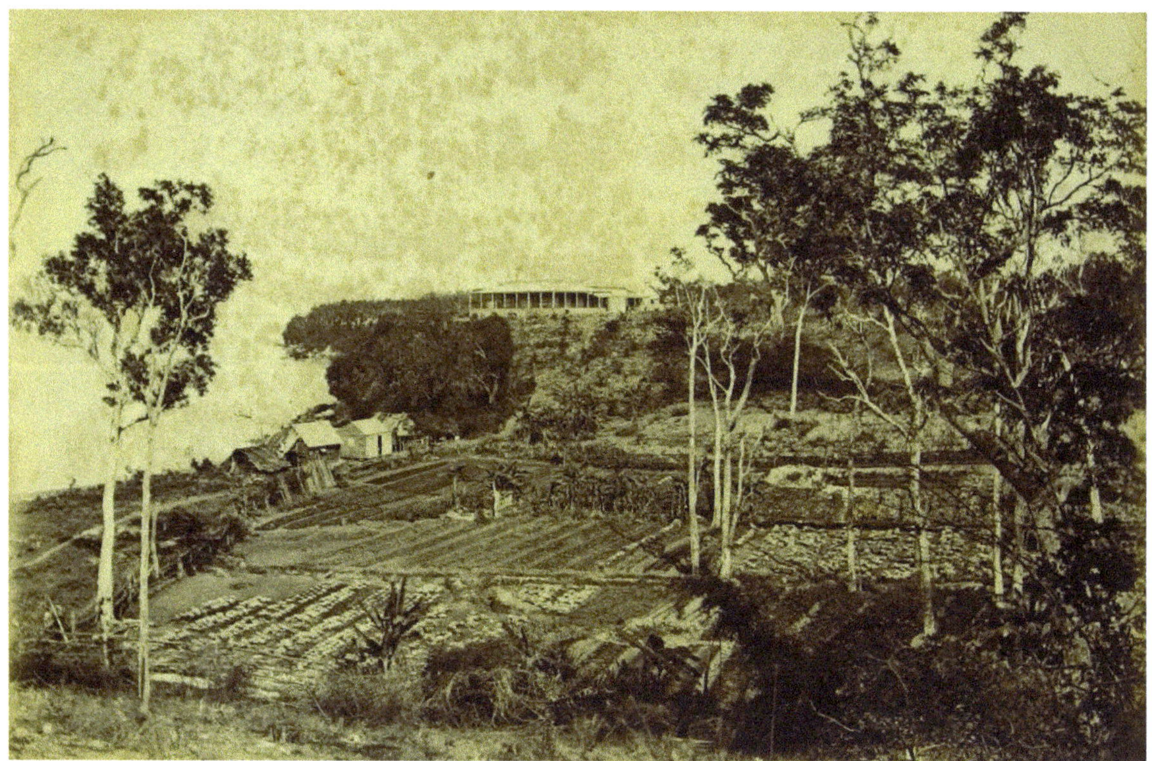

Hospital & Chinese garden, Doctors Gully, c1878. (Foelsche, P., NTAS, Foelsche Collection, NTRS 3420/P1 Item 30.)

Cenotaph was relocated to its current site on the old Esplanade Oval. Since that time it has been the site of Darwin's ANZAC Day, Bombing of Darwin, and other Military commemorations.

Lameroo is believed to be a mispronunciation of the Larrakia name, *Damoe-Ra*, for the freshwater spring in the cliff face above what is now Lameroo beach. The site had always been occupied by the Larrakia Aboriginal people.[4] In late 1911, under the Commonwealth Government *Aboriginal Ordinance*, Aboriginals in the Darwin area, including Lameroo Beach were removed from their camps around the town and moved to the Kahlin Compound. This relocation opened to way to construct swimming baths at the beach after the Fort Hill swimming baths were destroyed in a cyclone in 1919. Lameroo baths, at Lameroo beach were opened in 1922. The site was chosen because it was closer to the town and the town oval. With a concrete foundation and a fence to keep out unwelcome crocodiles the Lameroo baths were Darwin's main swimming enclosure until World War II.

Today's Darwin Esplanade is dominated by multi story hotels, and high rise commercial and Government offices. This is a relatively recent development. The first multi storey hotel on The Esplanade was completed in the early 1970s. There are few reminders of the Esplanade from earlier eras.

One of Darwin's older buildings is 'Lyons Cottage' at 74 on The Esplanade. Constructed in 1925 for the Eastern Extension Australasian and China Telegraph Company Ltd, it is the only remaining building that has clear links with Darwin's role as an international telecommunications hub. The single storey building with its sleeping quarters either side of an open central area and separate kitchen and laundry to the rear of the building is reminiscent of British colonial constructions in South East Asia. Originally occupied by the cable company's engineer the building takes

4 Bauman. *Aboriginal Darwin*, 47.

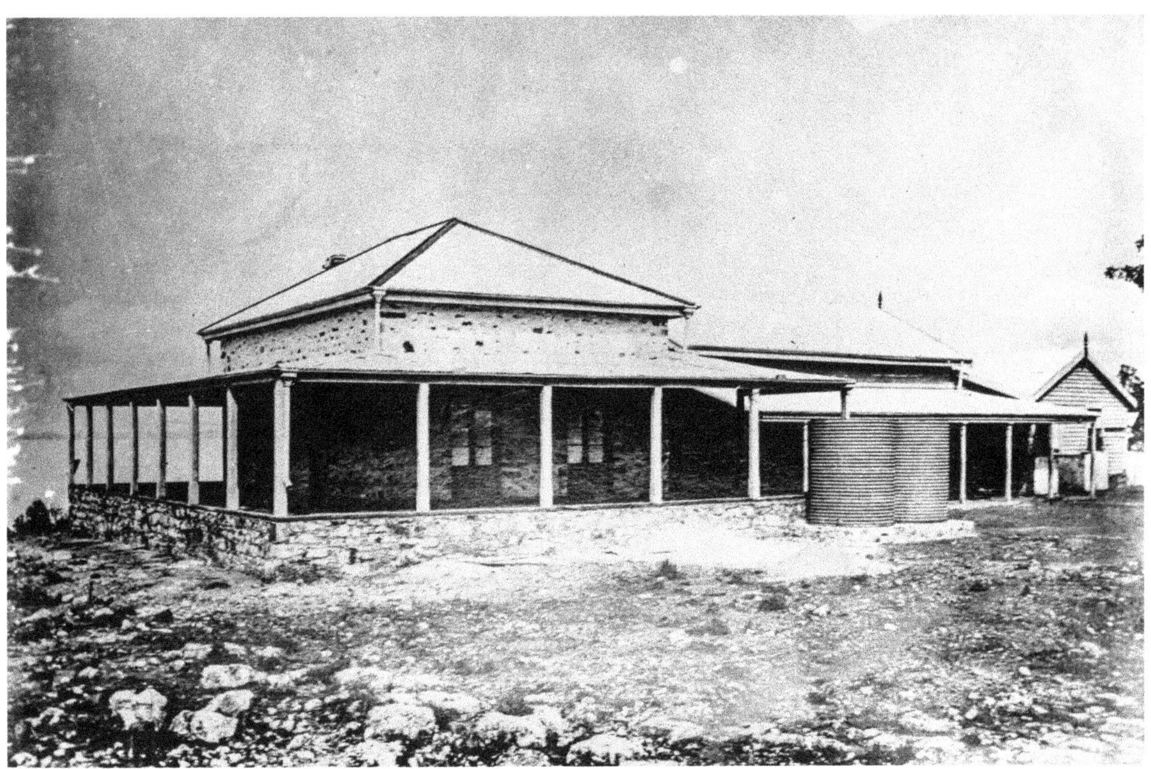

Palmerston Hospital, 1878. (Foelsche, P., NTL, Foelsche Collection, PH0111/0091.)

its name from a prominent local lawyer and politician, John 'Tiger' Lyons, who owned the property between 1948 and 1974. Lyon's was Mayor of Darwin 1958-1959 and a member of the Northern Territory Legislative Council 1963-1968.[5] During World War II the cottage was occupied by the US Army and later the Royal Australian Navy. During Cyclone Tracy the cottage lost its roof and ornate ceiling. These were repaired and in recent years the building has been used by a variety of community organisations.[6]

'Old Admiralty House' lies opposite Lyons Cottage on the corner of Knuckey Street and The Esplanade. Originally constructed in 1937 on the corner of Peel Street and The Esplanade it was the residence of the District Naval Officer. The house was moved to its current site in 1951. It is an example of a 'Type B' Commonwealth tropical design by Beni Burnett. Renovated to accommodate a modern restaurant the house provides a glimpse of 'Old Darwin' during the period just prior to World War II to the 1970s.[7]

During World War II, like so much of Darwin, large parts of The Esplanade were requisitioned for military purposes. The Esplanade Oval remained in use prior to the bombing of Darwin but had to be reduced in size to also accommodate the 14th Anti Aircraft Battery which was positioned there. Crowds were also banned from the oval and most watched football games from the front of the new Darwin Hotel. An arrangement that pleased many spectators! Doctor's Gully became a flying boat base for RAAF Marine Section and 20th, 42nd and 43rd Catalina squadrons. Workshops, a Jetty, fuel tanks and a pump house were all constructed to support the base. Three of Darwin's numerous military

5 Gibson, Lyons, John William (Tiger), *Northern Territory Dictionary of Biography*, 365-366.
6 NTG Heritage Branch, *Lyon' Cottage, Darwin, Fact Sheet*, 2011.
7 NTG Heritage Register, *Old Admiralty House*.

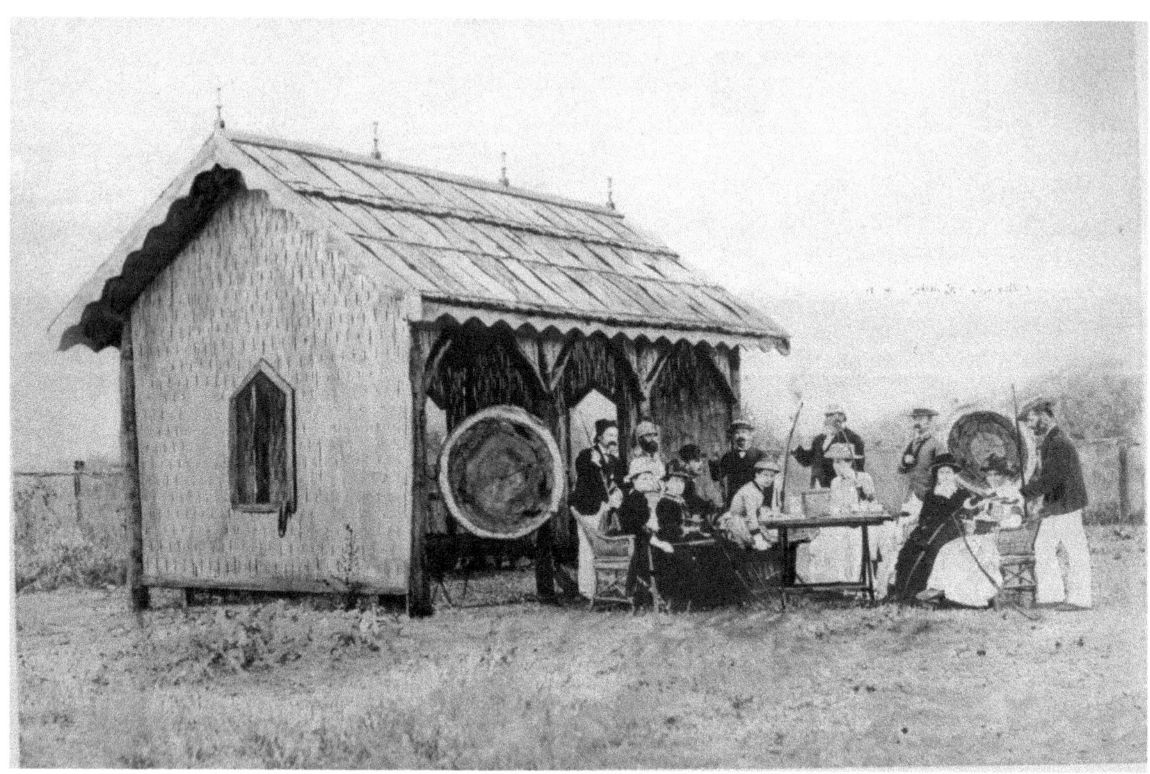

Palmerston Archery Club, The Esplanade Oval, c1886. (Foelsche, P, SLSA, Darwin Collection, B 24245.)

fuel tanks were also built in to the face of the cliffs below The Esplanade in 1944.[8]

After World War II Doctor's Gully became home to Carl Atkinson who lived there until 1979. Atkinson was a deep sea diver who ran a salvage operation from the former RAAF base. From 1946 to 1958 he salvaged the World War II wrecks in Darwin harbour. In 1959 he sold the salvage rights to the Fujita Salvage Company that removed most of the wrecks 1959 – 1960. Atkinson's lasting legacy is that he is credited with feeding the fish which is continued by Aquascene established in 1981.

At the north western end of The Esplanade, a large hostel for single women was built in 1938/39. Named Marrenah House it provided accommodation for Commonwealth unmarried female employees. After the evacuation of civilians in late 1941 the building was occupied by American Army personnel and was known as the Army Advanced Headquarters. After World War II Marrenah House returned to use as single women's accommodation. Sometimes known as the 'Virgins Retreat' in a town with a disproportionate number of men it was a well known landmark. When Marrenah House became the Northern Territory Police single men's quarters 1959-69 there were far fewer visitors! Marrenah house was demolished and replaced by the Travelodge, one of Darwin's first multi story hotels. One of the enduring images of the havoc wrought by Cyclone Tracy was the cars in the swimming pool of this newly completed Hotel on The Esplanade. In the aftermath of Cyclone Tracy The Esplanade also served as a landing ground for helicopters.

Not far from Marrenah House at the northern end of The Esplanade overlooking Doctors Gully, were the Daly Street basketball courts that were used from 1954 until 1983. Basketball was a very popular sport in Darwin, particularly in the period from 1948 to Cyclone Tracy. Games were scheduled seven

8 Pederson, *Naval Oil Tanks The Esplanade Darwin*, 6.

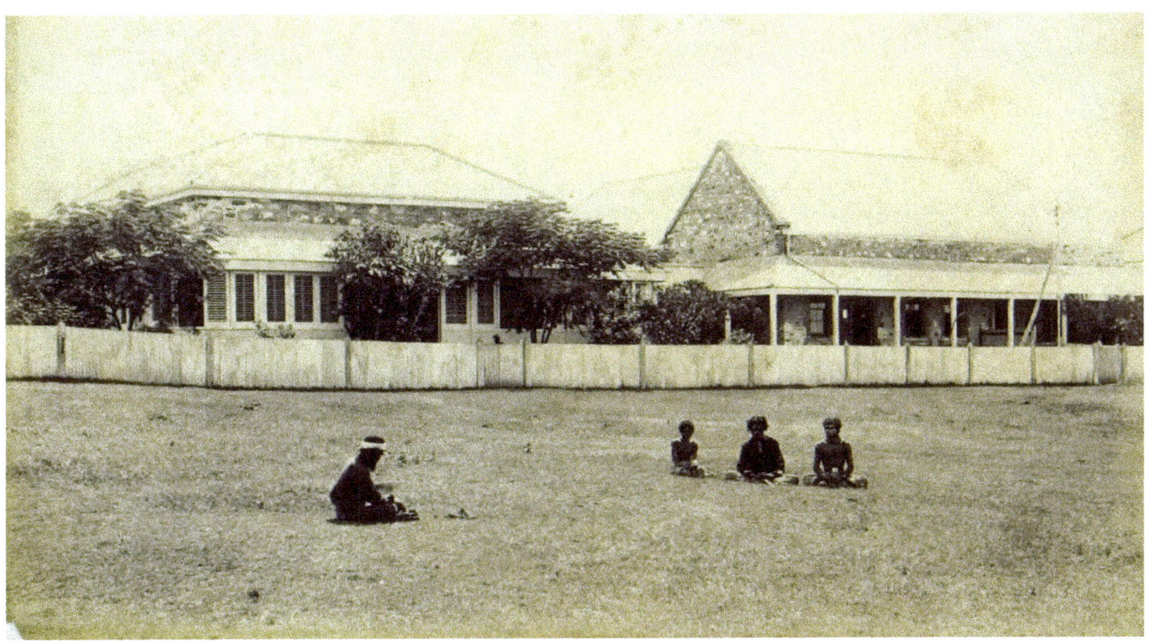

Aboriginal people sitting on The Esplanade in front of the Overland Telegraph office and Station Masters quarters, c1887. (Foelsche, P., NTAS, Foelsche Collection, NTRS 3420/P1/18.)

days a week and thousands would attend big games at the open air courts.[9]

The Darwin Hotel, 1940-1999 was a Darwin icon on The Esplanade during its lifetime. Opened in July 1940 it was heralded as 'the best tropical hotel in the Southern Hemisphere.'[10] For the next 59 years it was one of Darwin's most popular hotels. Its open ground floor entertainment area and bar, known as the Green Room in its later years, was a meeting place for locals and visitors alike. Old Darwin residents can regale you with innumerable stories of dances, music and parties at the Darwin Hotel. In 1999 the Darwin Hotel was controversially demolished in the dark of night despite the valiant efforts of many to save it.

Today The Esplanade remains Darwin's most accessible public open space. As the site of Darwin's cenotaph and many other war memorials it has an important public commemorative function. It is home to many events and festivals and continues to be the preferred end point of many city parades. With the best views of Darwin harbour and the opportunity to catch a cooling sea breeze it has always been one of Darwin's most popular destinations.

9 Austin, M., *A Brief History of Basketball In Darwin*. Also, Austin, Maisie, Personal communication, 23 September 2018.

10 *NS*, 9 July 1940.

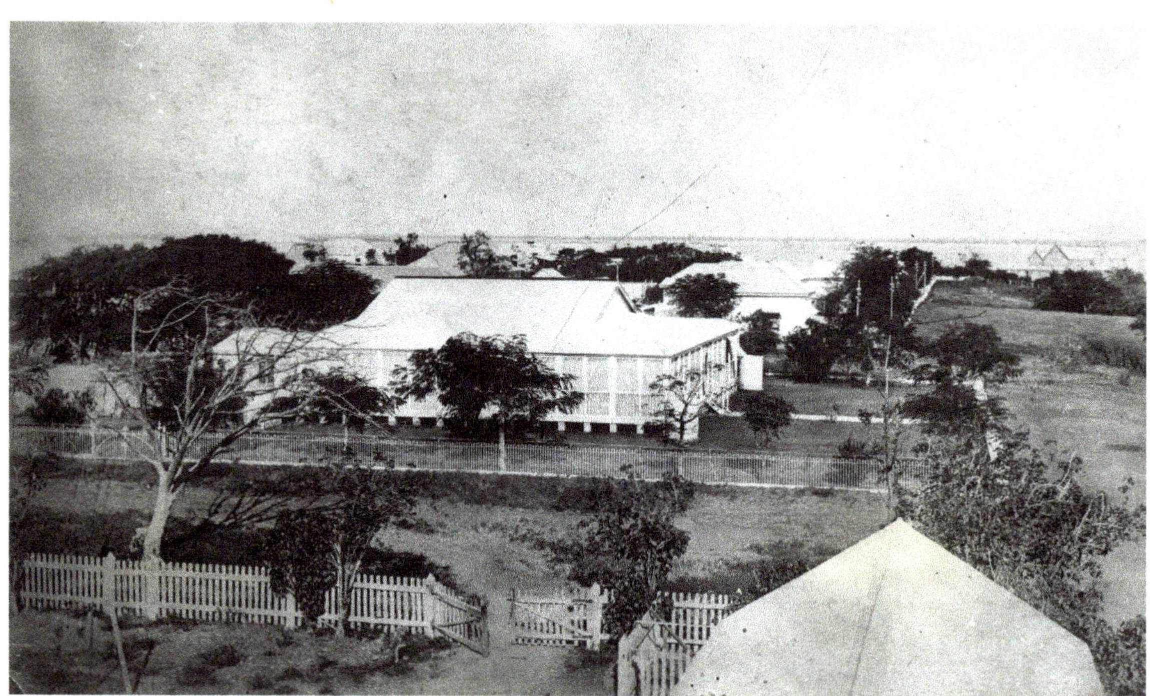

The Esplanade looking towards the Government Residence past the Cable Company Masters residence known as 'The Folly' on the corner of Knuckey St and The Esplanade, c1900. (Unknown, NTAS, GPC, NTRS 3822-P1 Folder 99 View of Esplanade.)

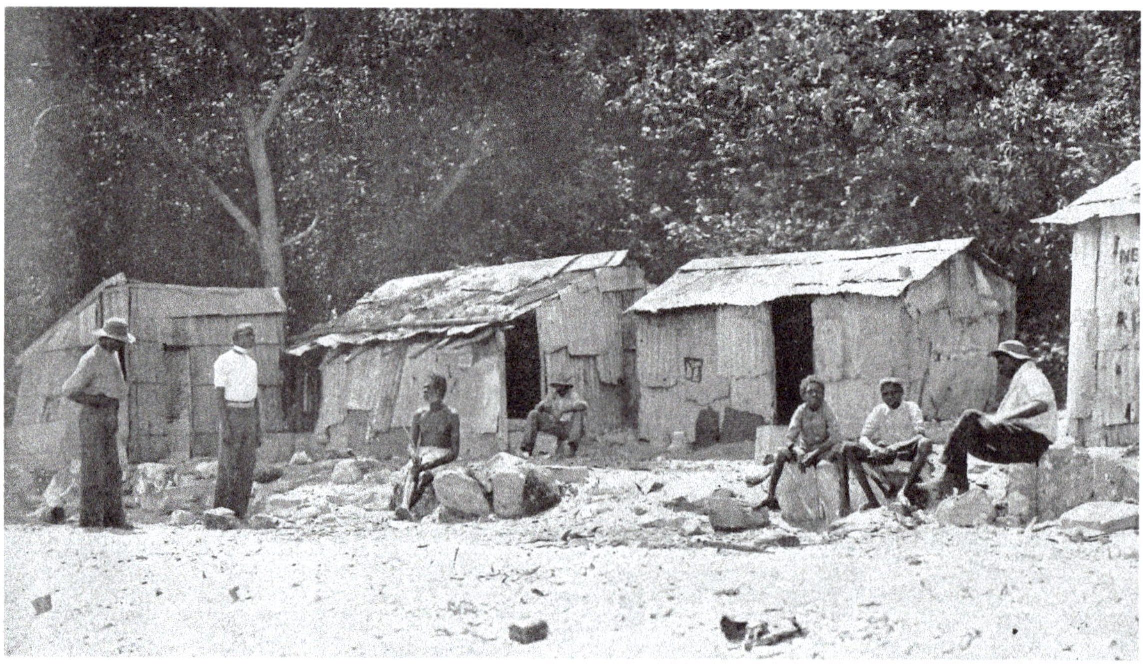

Larrakia Camp, Lameroo Beach, 1912. (Unknown, NTL, *NT Administrators Report*, 1912.)

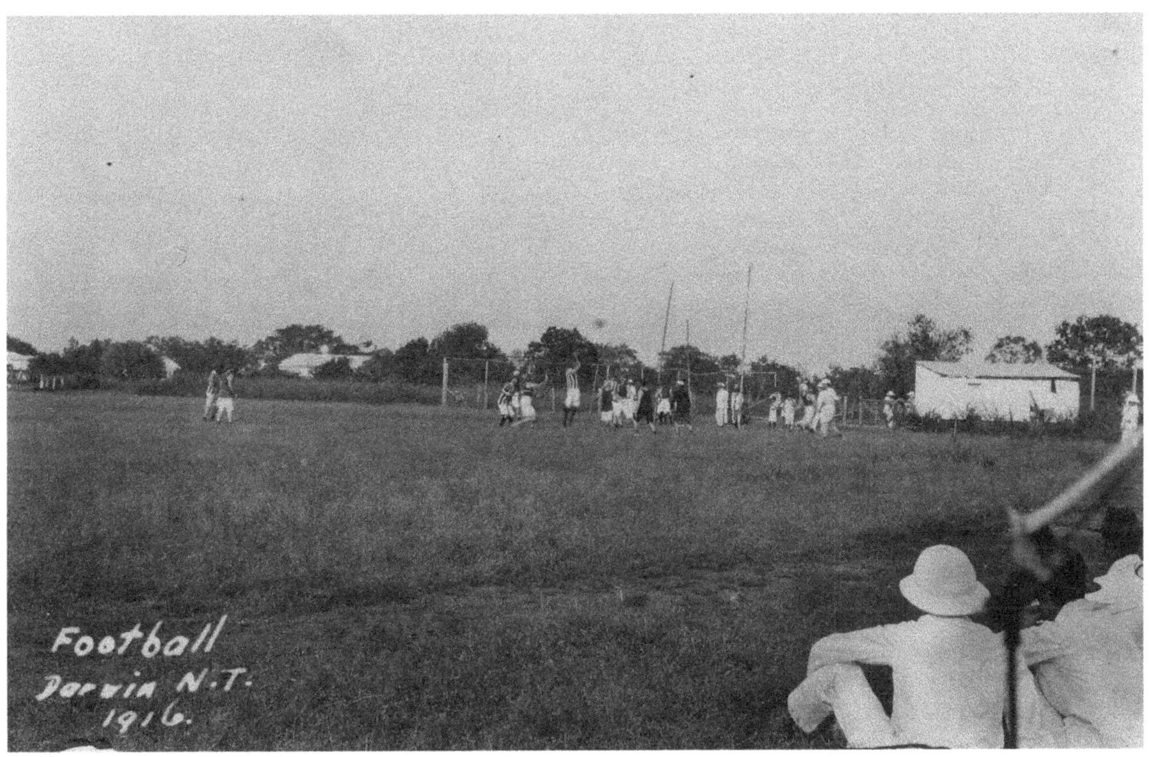

Football, The Esplanade Oval, 1916. AFL football was first played in Darwin in 1916 as a World War I fund raiser. (Unknown, SLSA, Darwin Collection, B 23025.)

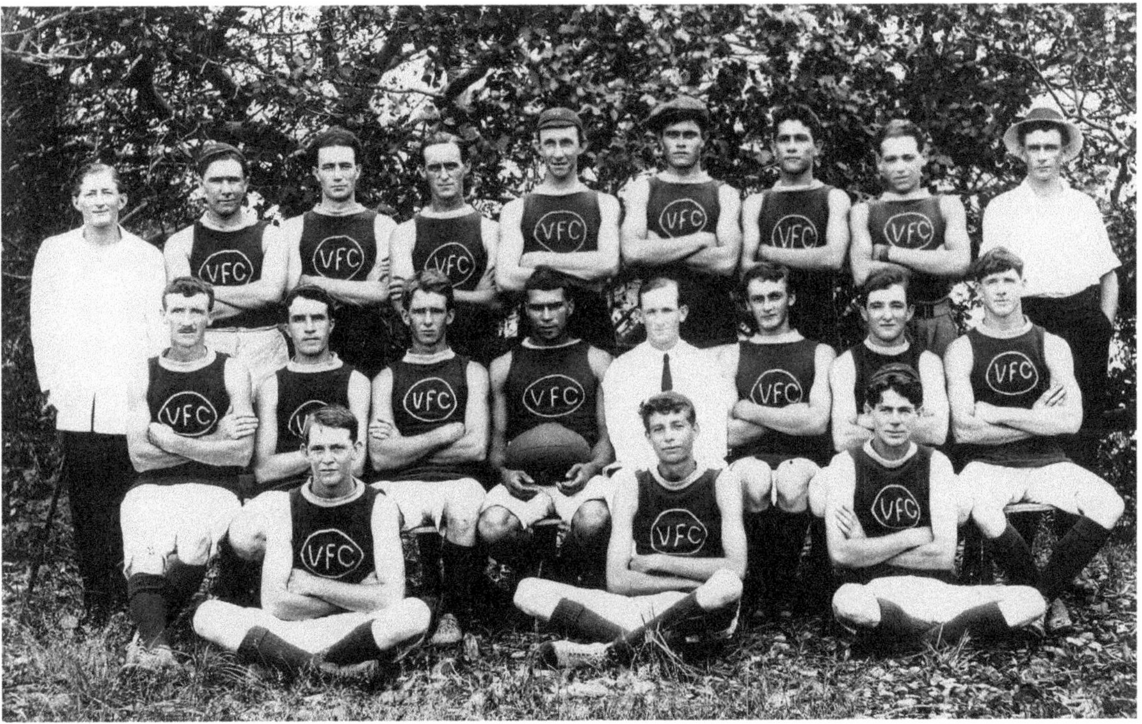

Vesteys Football Club, The Esplanade Oval, c1918. (Unknown, LNSW, E.D.W.S. Donnison Collection, MLMSS/890/3/0230.)

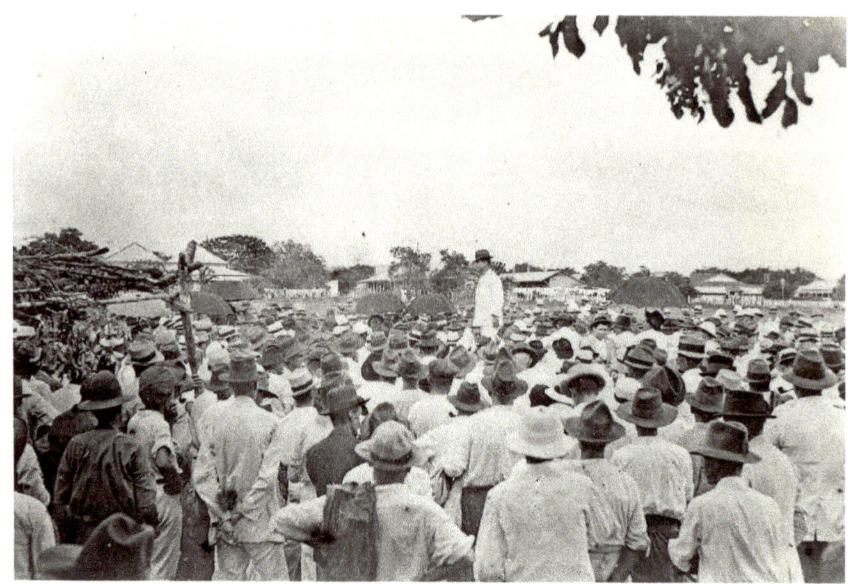

Robert Toupein, Union leader, addressing an anti-Administrator Gilruth rally on The Esplanade Oval, c1918. (Unknown, NTAS, HSNT Collection, NTRS 1854 Item 78.)

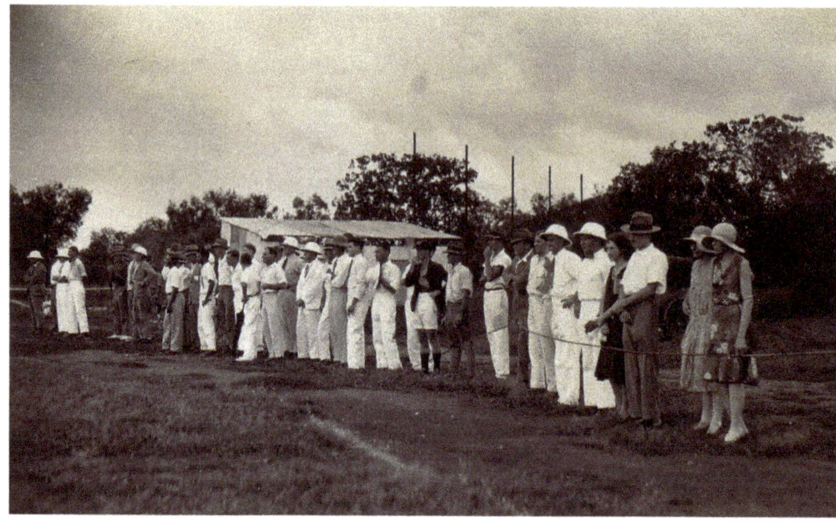

AFL football spectators at The Esplanade Oval, c1930. (Unknown, MAGNT, Gwyneth Ellenden (nee Davies) Collection, PIC520/008.)

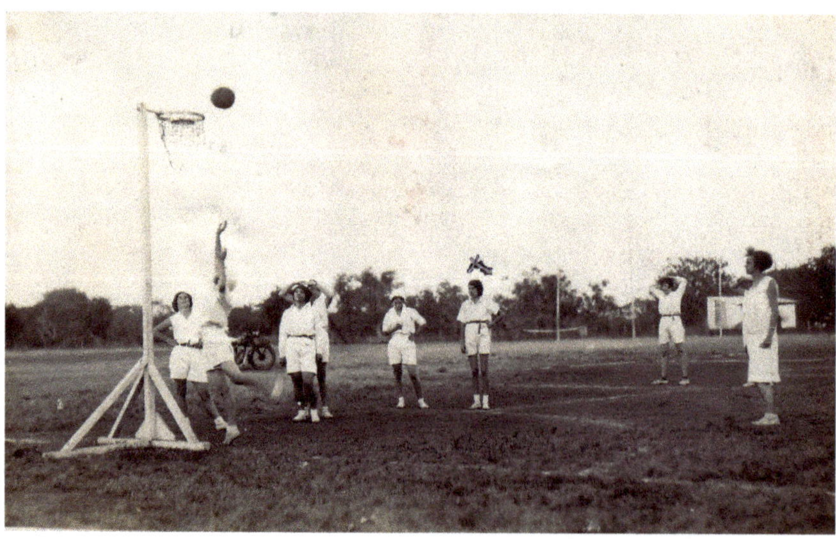

Basketball [now known as netball], The Esplanade Oval, c1928. (Unknown, MAGNT, Gwyneth Ellenden (nee Davies) Collection, PIC520/014.)

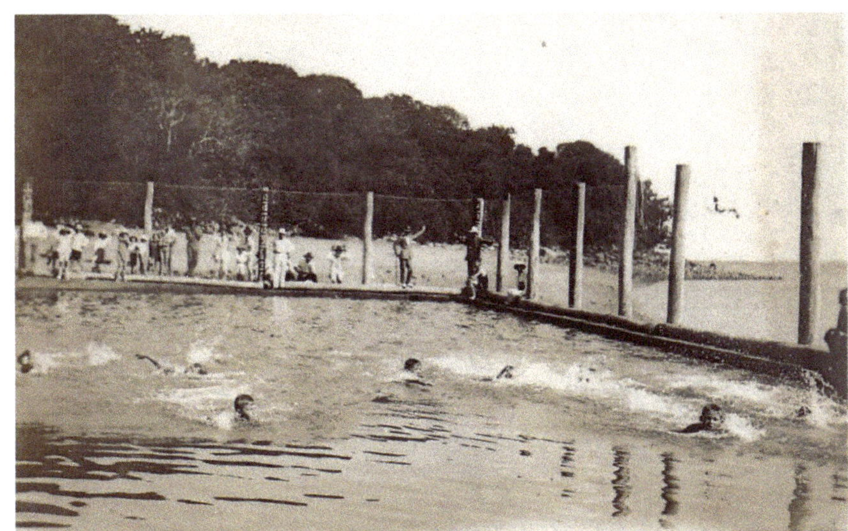

Lameroo Baths, Darwin Esplanade, c1922. (Monteith, R., MAGNT, Orr Collection, PIC521/083.)

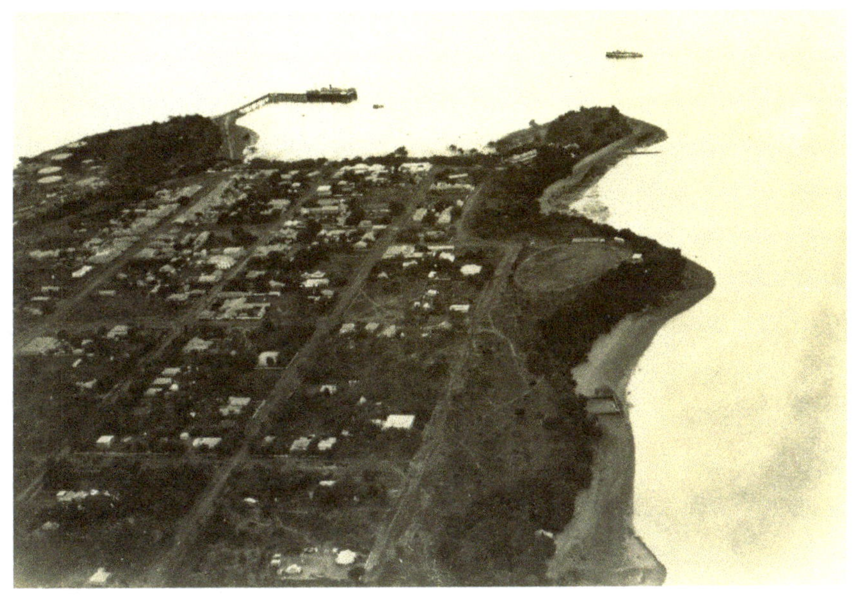

Aerial of the Darwin Esplanade showing the oval, Lameroo Beach and Baths, c1930s. (Unknown, NTAS, R.T. Cropley Collection, NTRS 2280 Item 15.)

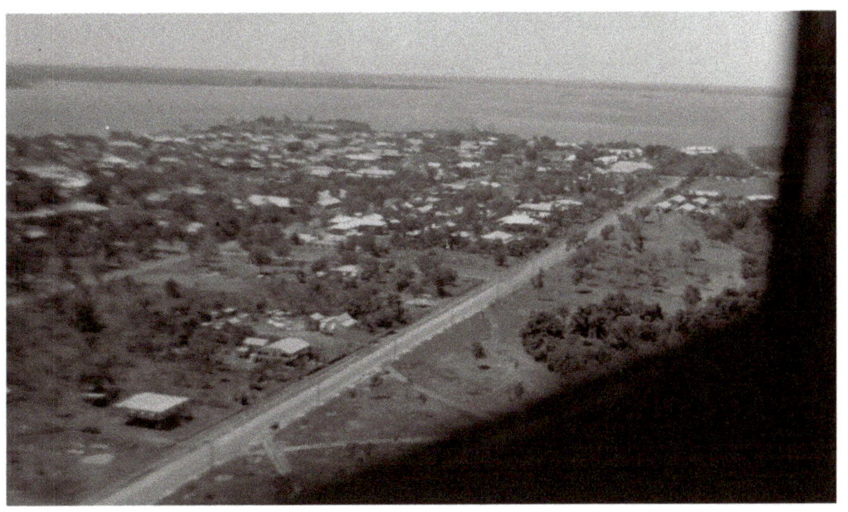

Darwin Esplanade, 1941. Note Hotel Darwin and the Army camp on The Esplanade Oval in top right corner of image. (Unknown, QANTAS, Heritage Collection.)

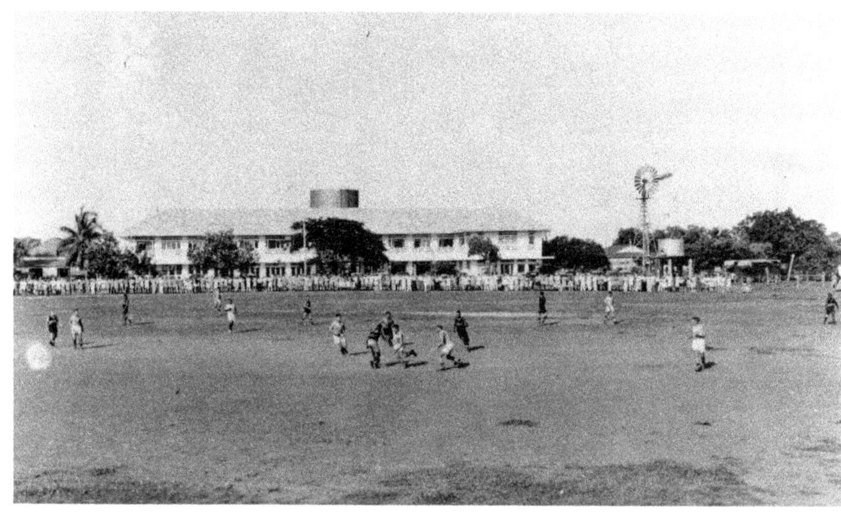

Darwin Esplanade Oval, 1941. (Unknown, NTAS, C. Knowlan Collection, NTRS 1651 Item 23.)

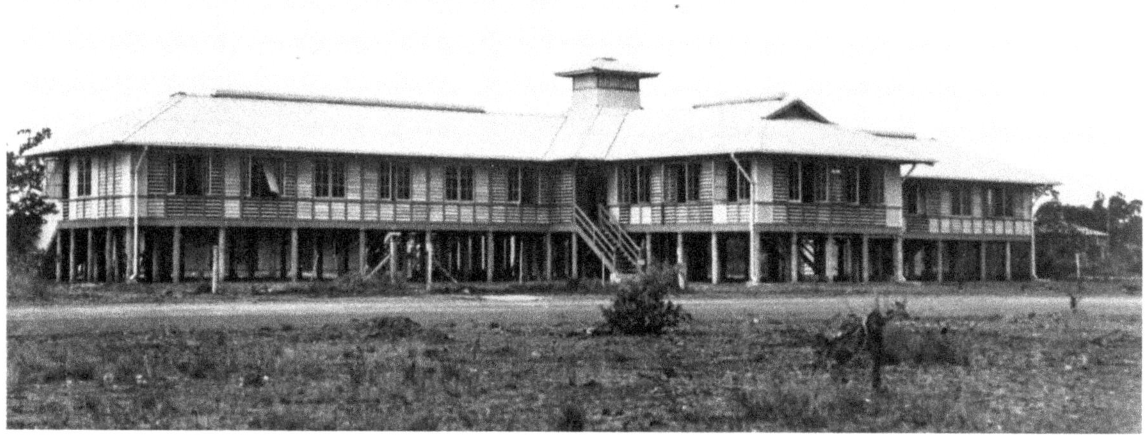

Marrenah House, single women's quarters, c late 1930s. (Copplestone, S., NTL, Hilda Copplestone Collection, PH0457/0004.)

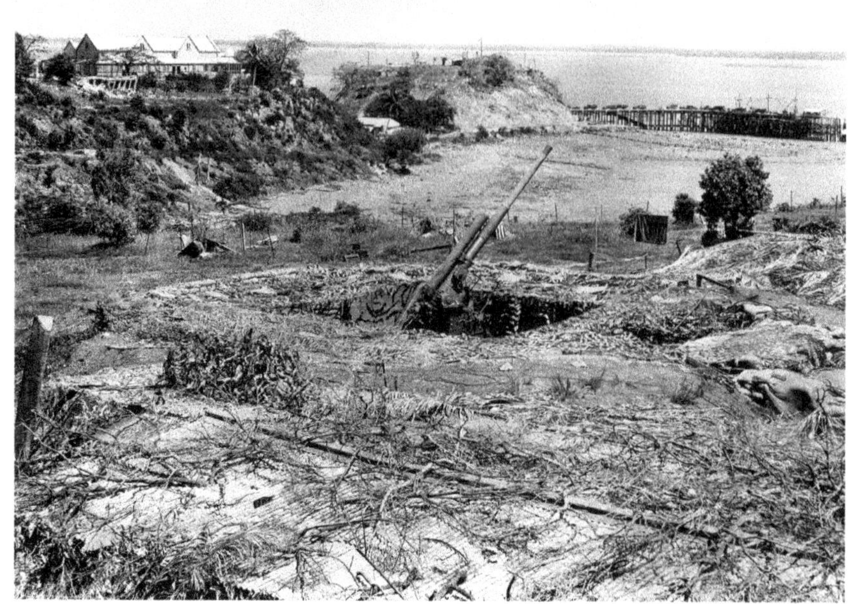

The 14th Australian Heavy Anti-Aircraft Battery position on The Esplanade near the oval, 13 November 1942. Note the Administrator's Residence on the left. To the right of that is the naval signalling station and to the right of that is the Boom Wharf. (Unknown, AWM, Photograph, 027797.)

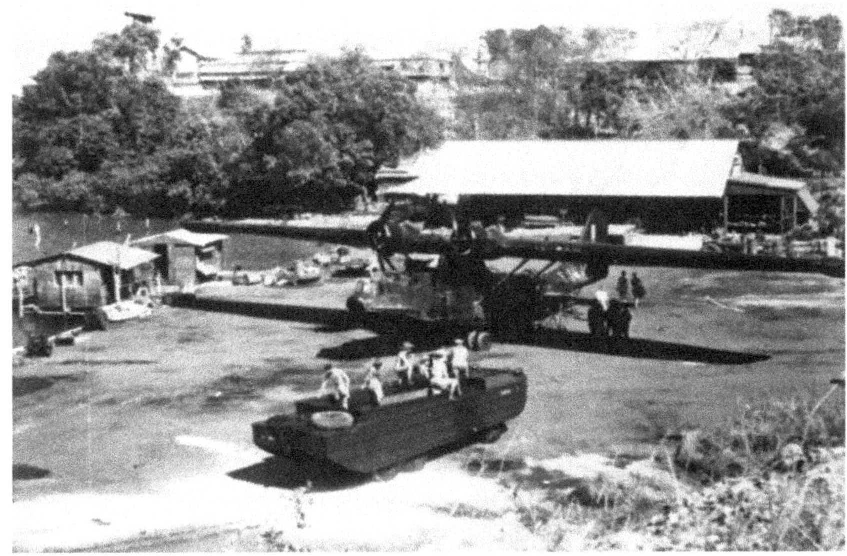

Marine Section, Doctors Gully, 1942. Note the amphibious vehicle and Catalina flying boat in foreground and the original Darwin Hospital above Doctor's Gully in the background. (Poulter, L., NTL, L. Thompson Collection, PH0022/0006.)

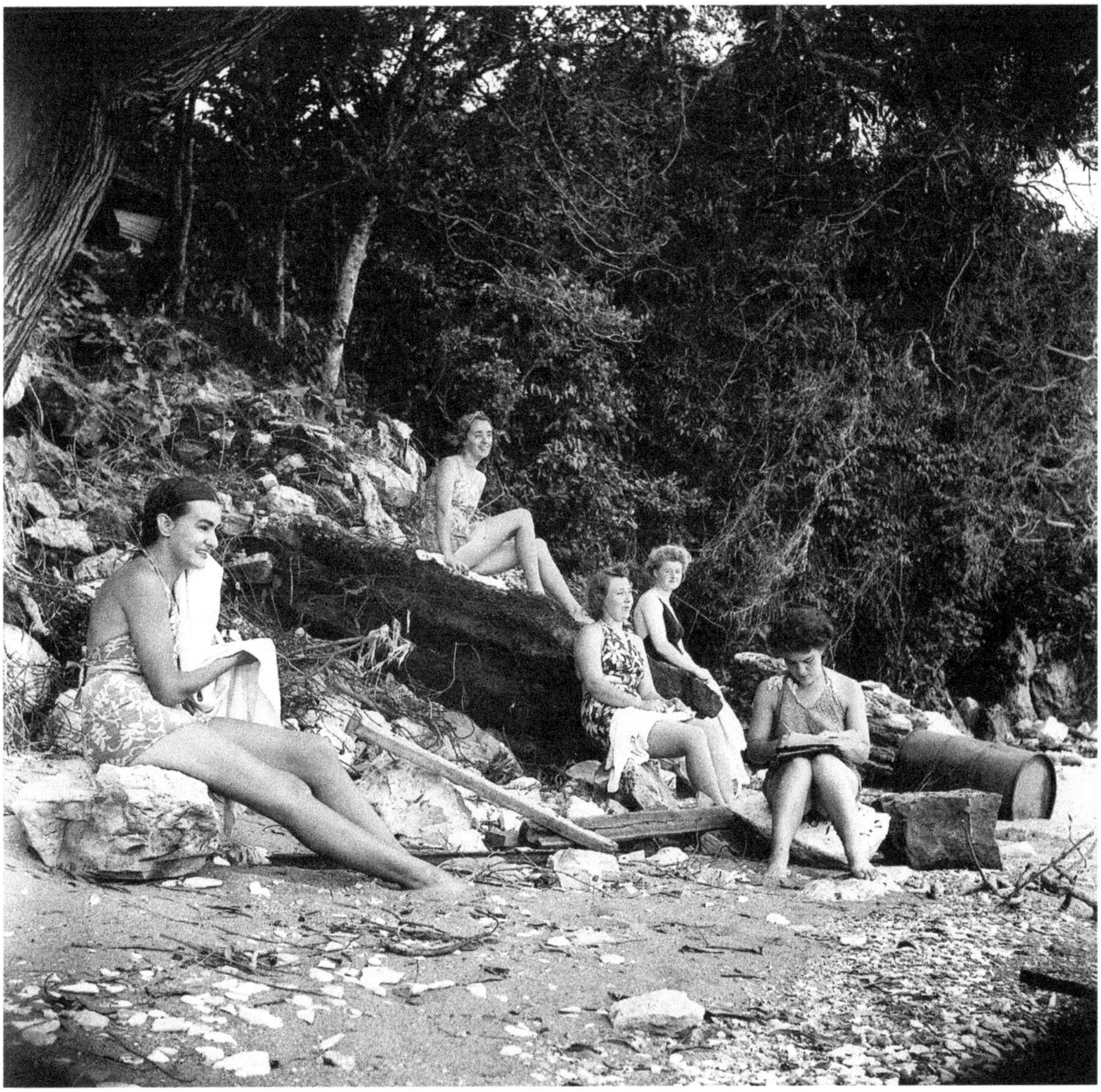

AWAS Beach, 6 May 1945. AWAS Beach was in the vicinity of Doctors Gully. AWAS is the acronym for Australian Women's Army Service. (Unknown, AWM, Photograph, 088299.)

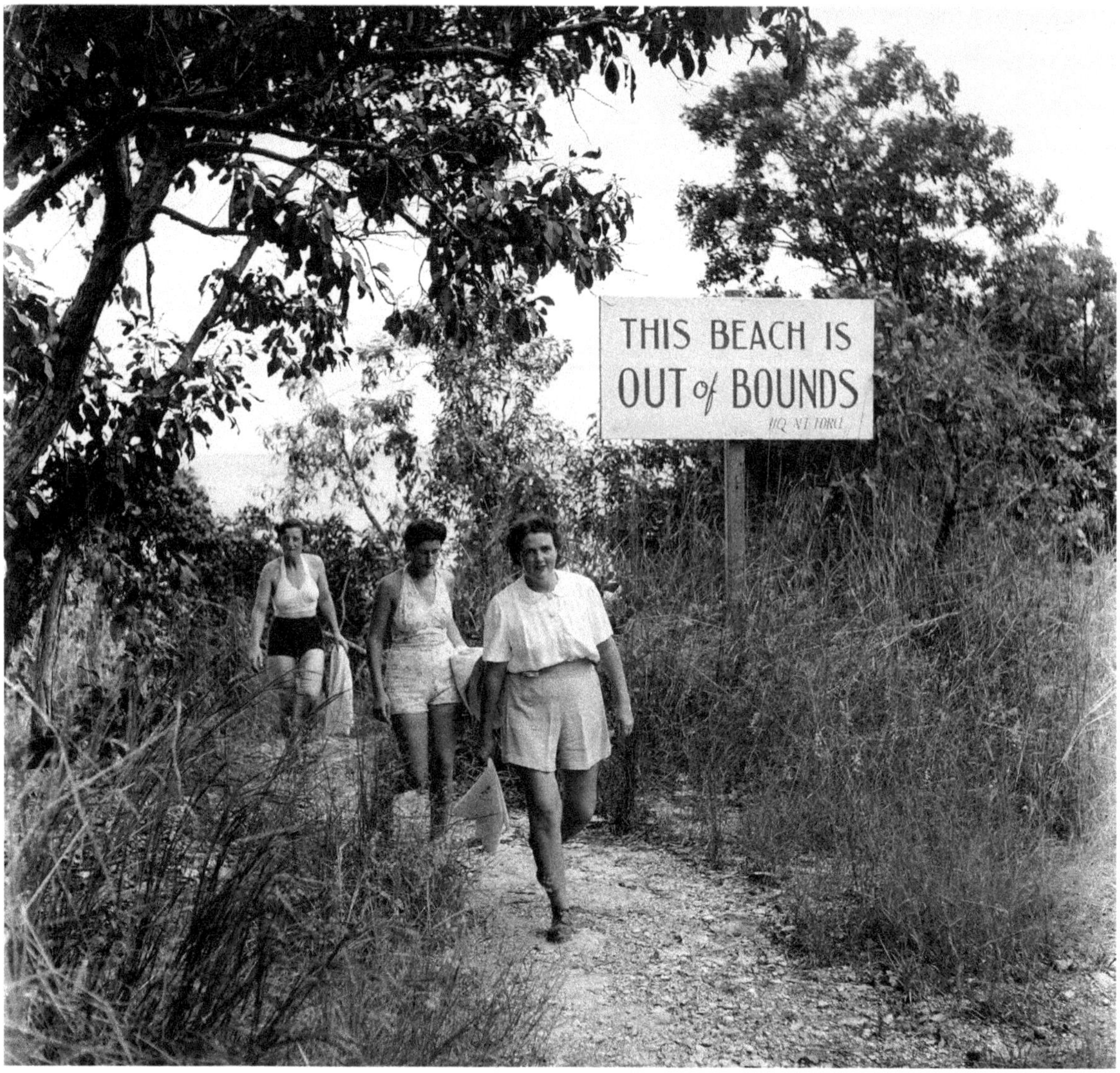

Path from AWAS Beach, 6 May 1945. Signalwoman, C. Stapleton (1) with private K. Christianson, Australian Army Medical Women's Service, Regimental Aid Post 69, AWAS Barrack (2) returning from beach. (Unknown, AWM, Photograph, 088298.)

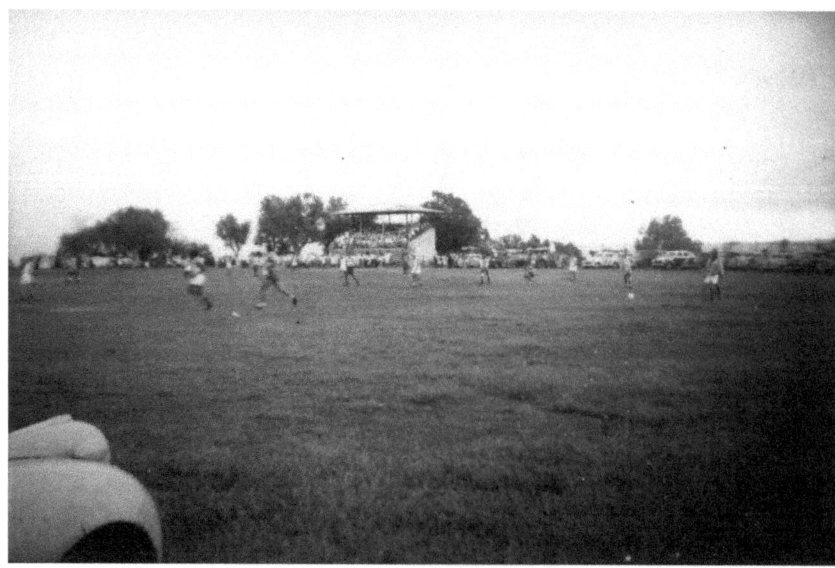

Darwin Esplanade Oval, c1950. (Harford, B.P., NTAS, B.P. Harford Collection, NTRS 1299 Item 152.)

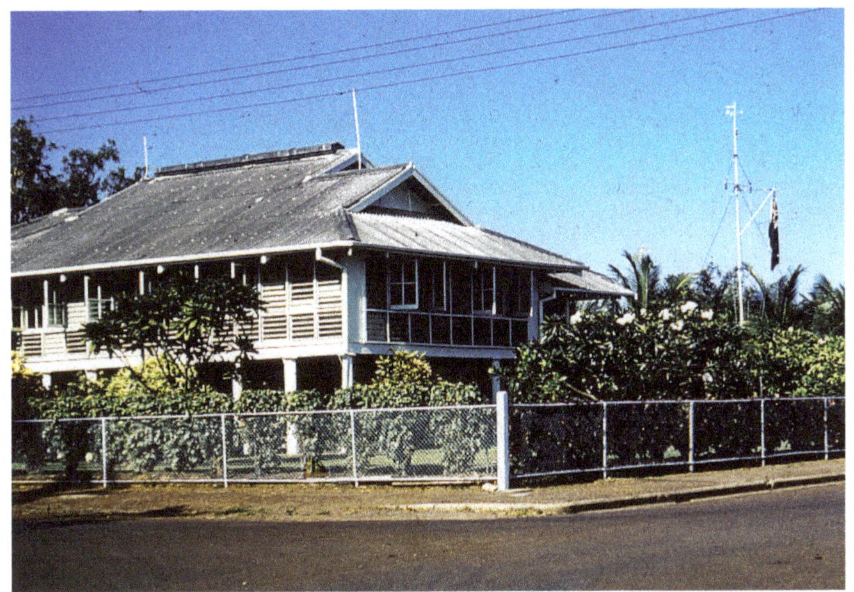

Admiralty House, Darwin Esplanade, c1960s. (Laidlaw, W.C., NTAS, W.C. Laidlaw Collection, NTRS 317 Item 36.)

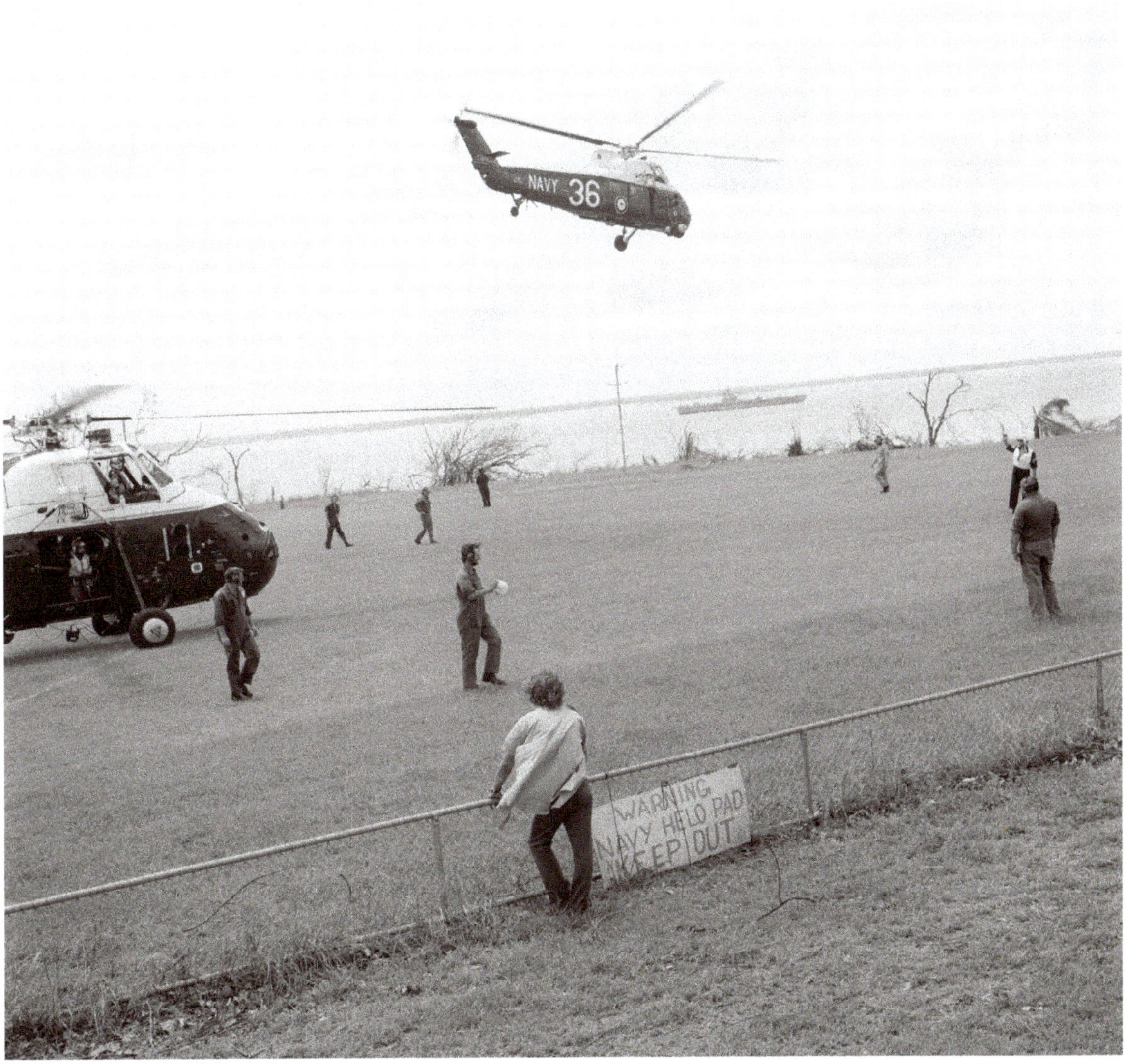

Navy helicopter pad, Esplanade, Darwin, *HMAS Melbourne* in background, following Cyclone Tracy, 1975. (Unknown, NAA, Photograph, A6180:30/1/75/30.)

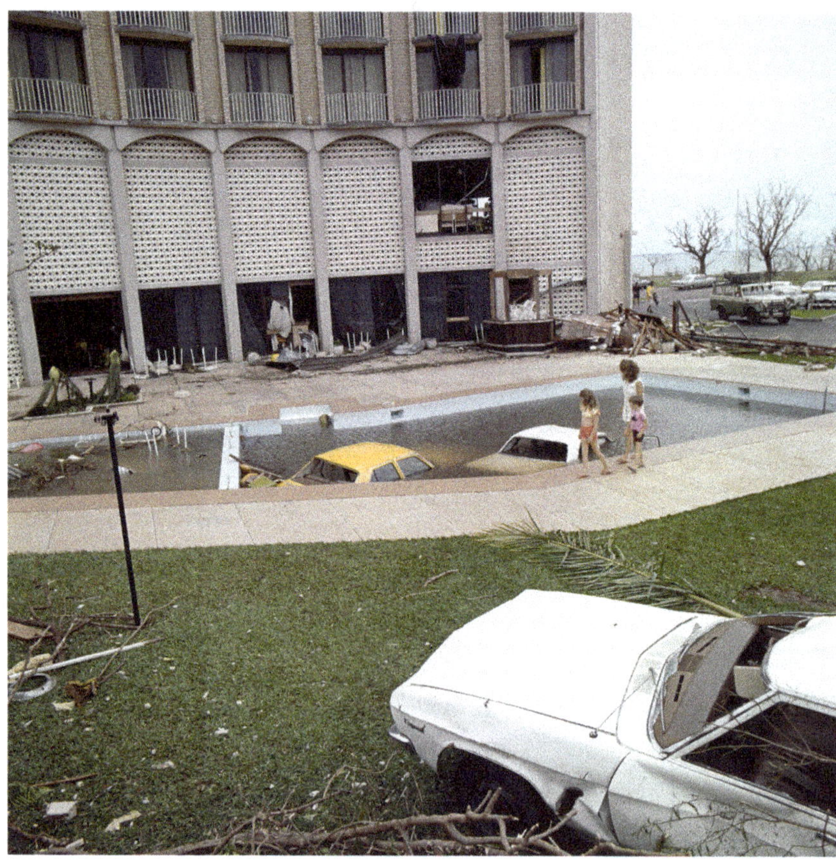

Darwin Esplanade, Travelodge pool, Boxing Day, Darwin, 1974. (Le Lievre, B., NAA, Photograph, A6135:K30/1/75/15.)

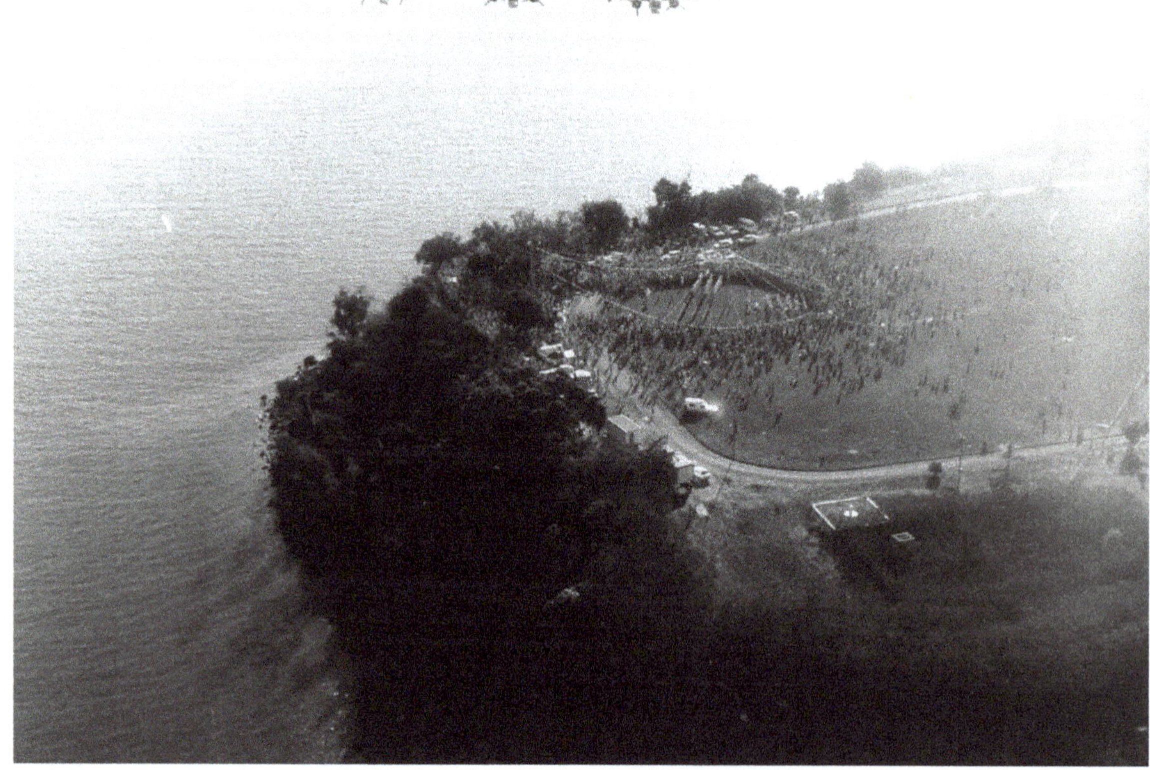

Darwin Esplanade, Self Government celebrations, 1 July 1978. (Unknown, NTAS, GPC, NTRS 3822-P1 Folder 57 Darwin Esplanade, Self-Government celebrations.)

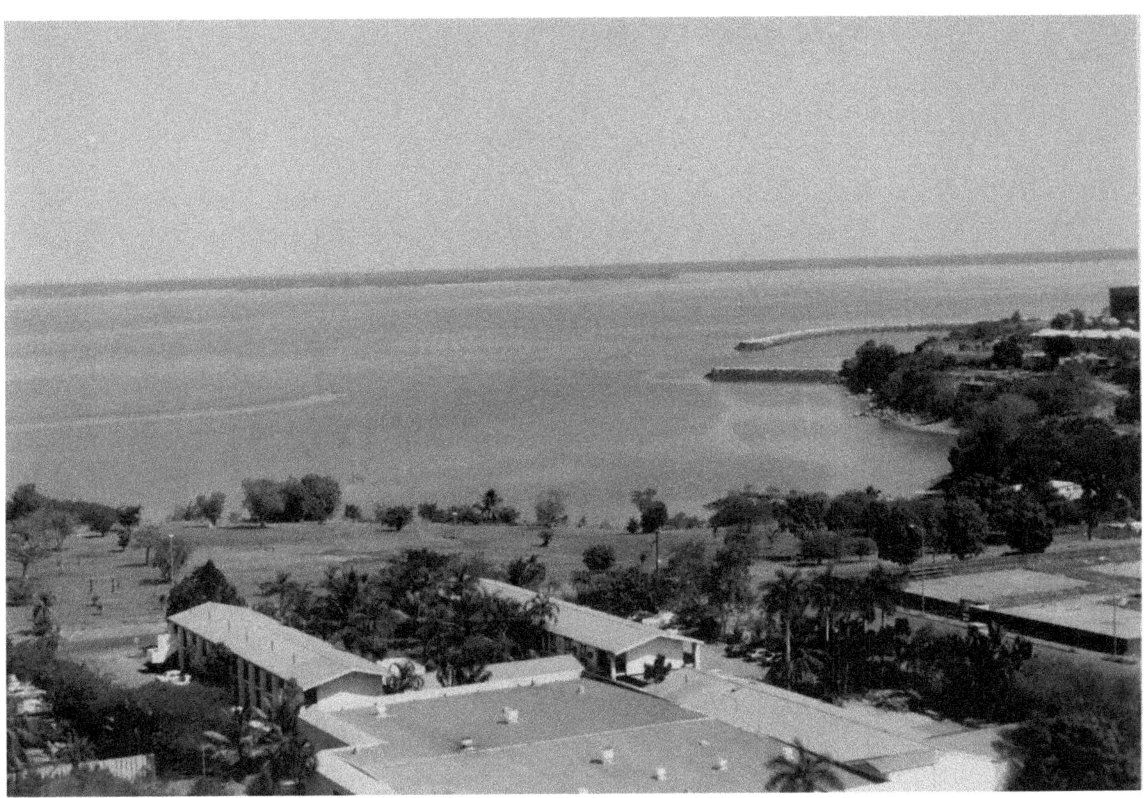

Darwin Esplanade overlooking Doctors Gully and Daly Street basketball courts, c early 1980s. (Cheater, G., NTL, Graeme Cheater Collection, PH0087/0002.)

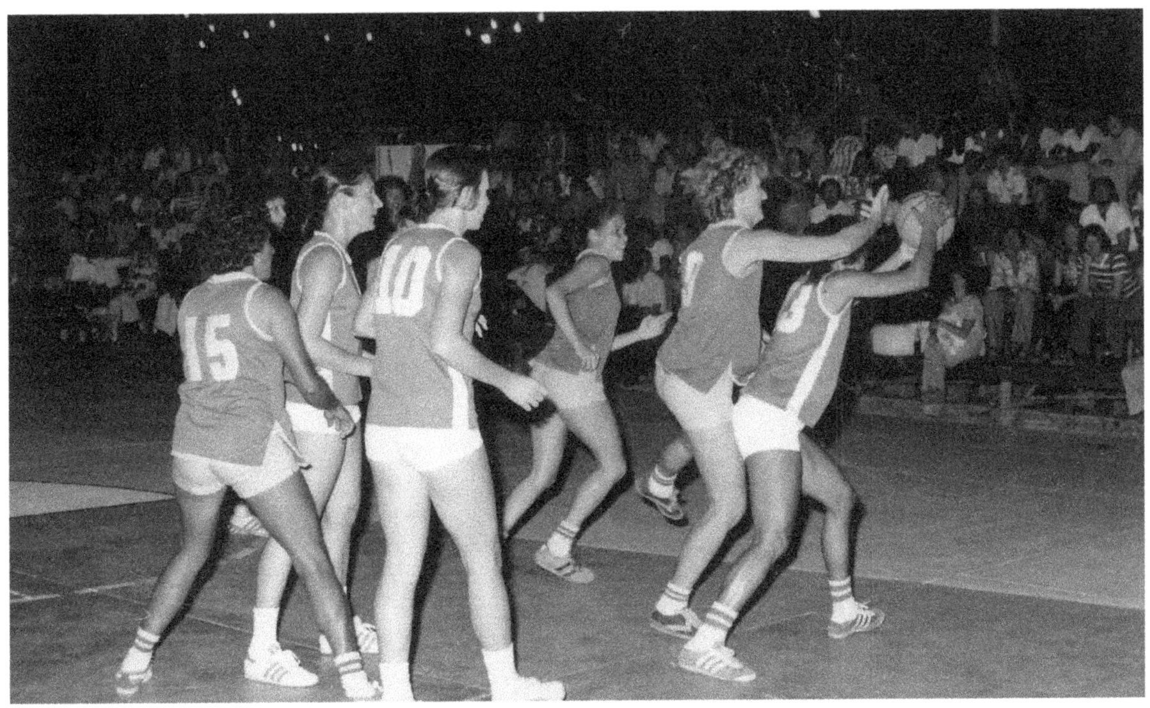

Women's basketball grand final at the Daly Street courts, c1976. (Austin, M., Maisie Austin, Personal Collection, N/A.)

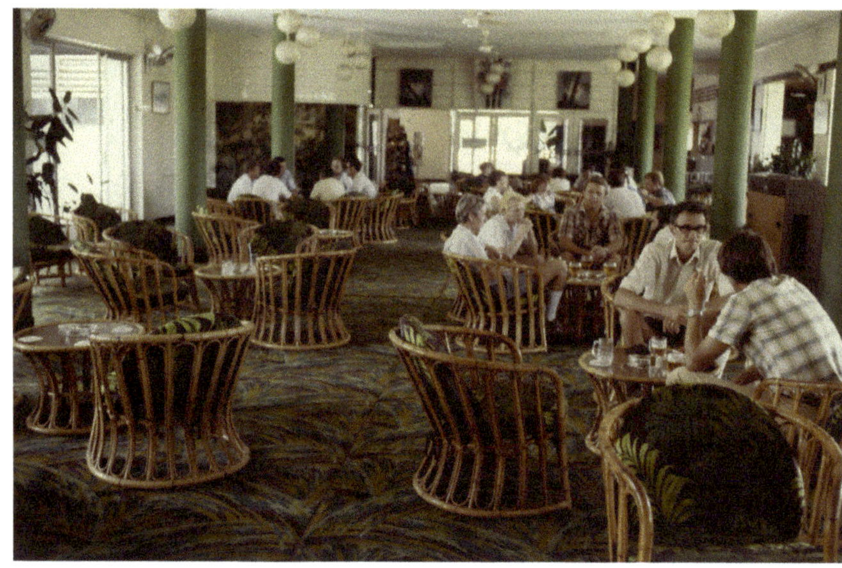

Darwin Hotel, Green Room, The Esplanade, 1982. (Wiedeman, B., NTL, Northern Territory Government Photographer Slide Collection, PH0730/1969.)

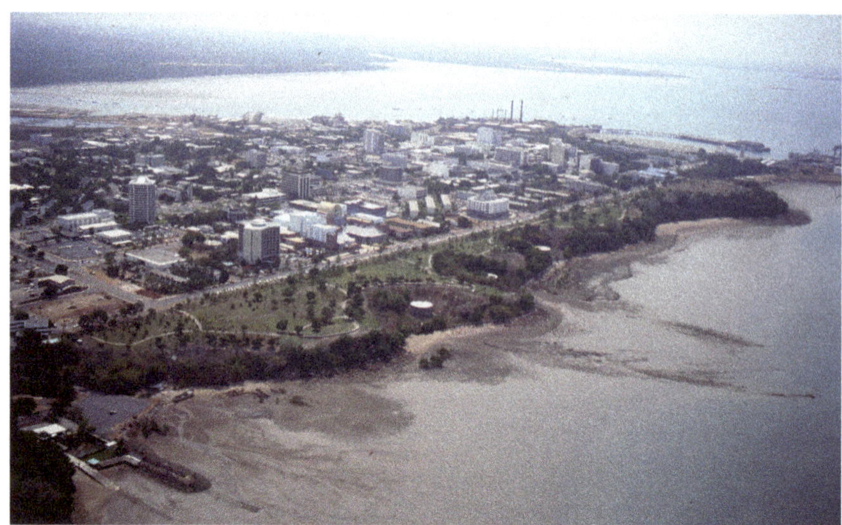

Darwin Esplanade, c1980s. (Wiedeman, B., NTL, Northern Territory Government Photographer Slide Collection, PH0730/0717.)

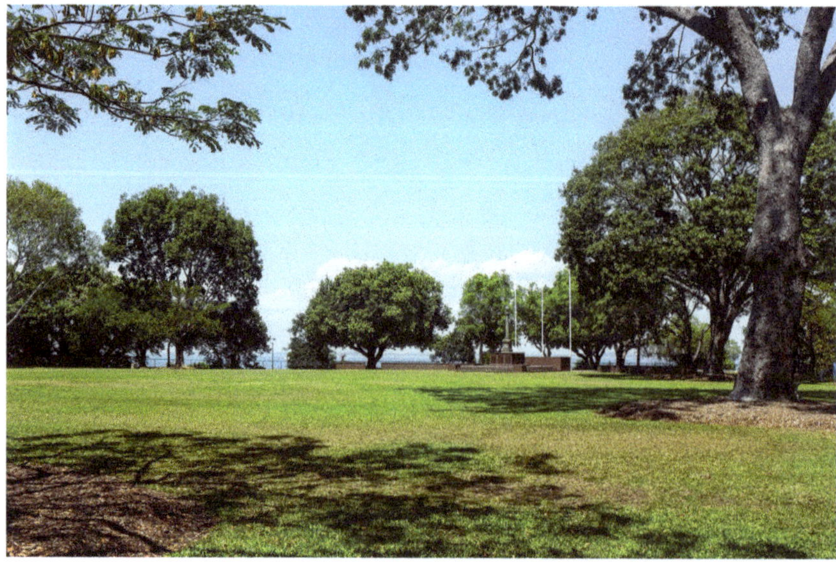

Darwin Cenotaph, Darwin Esplanade, 2017. (Martin, R., Matthew Stephen, Personal Collection, Cenotaph_11.)

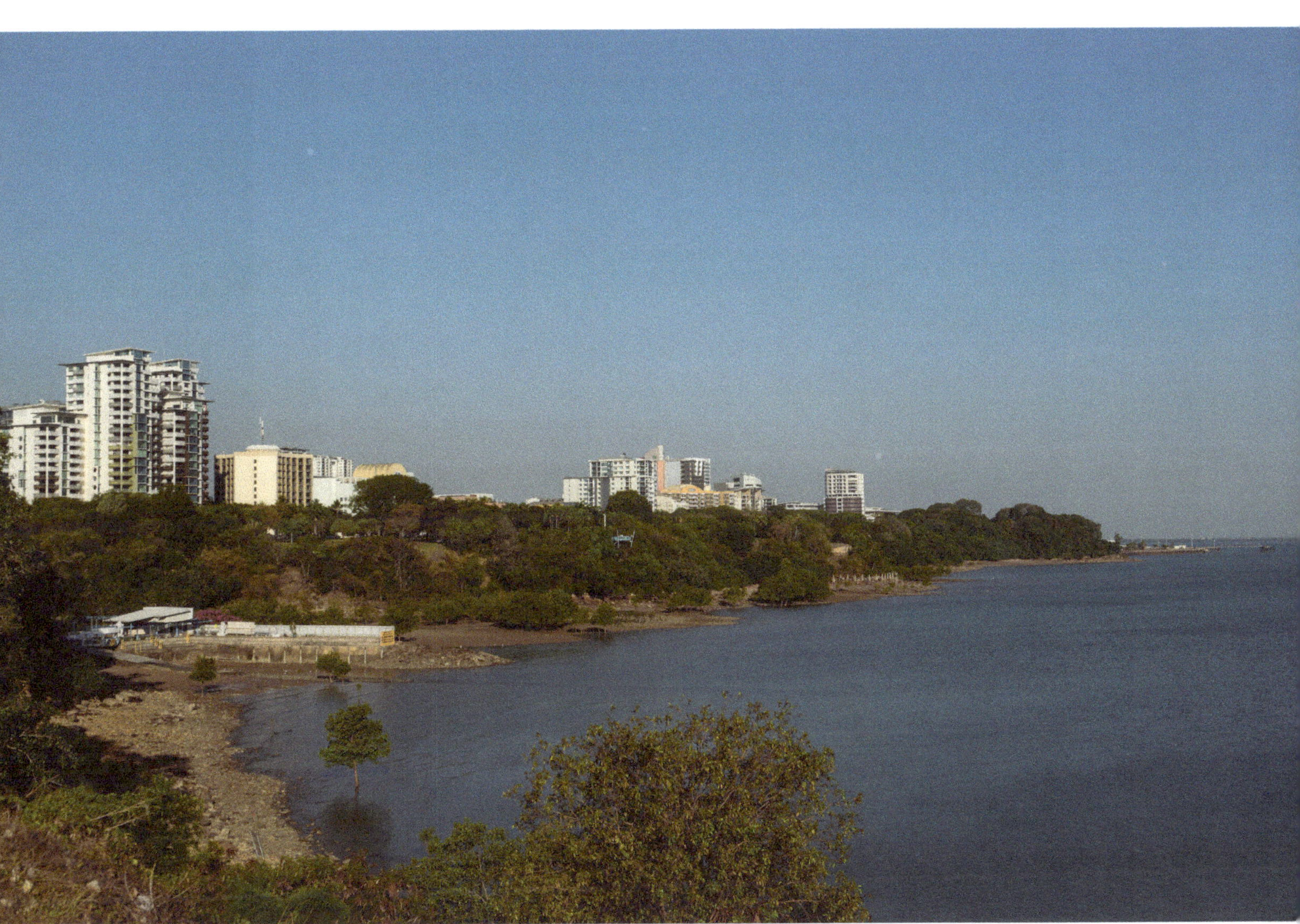

Darwin Esplanade, 2017. (Martin, R., Matthew Stephen, Personal Collection, Esplanade_07.)

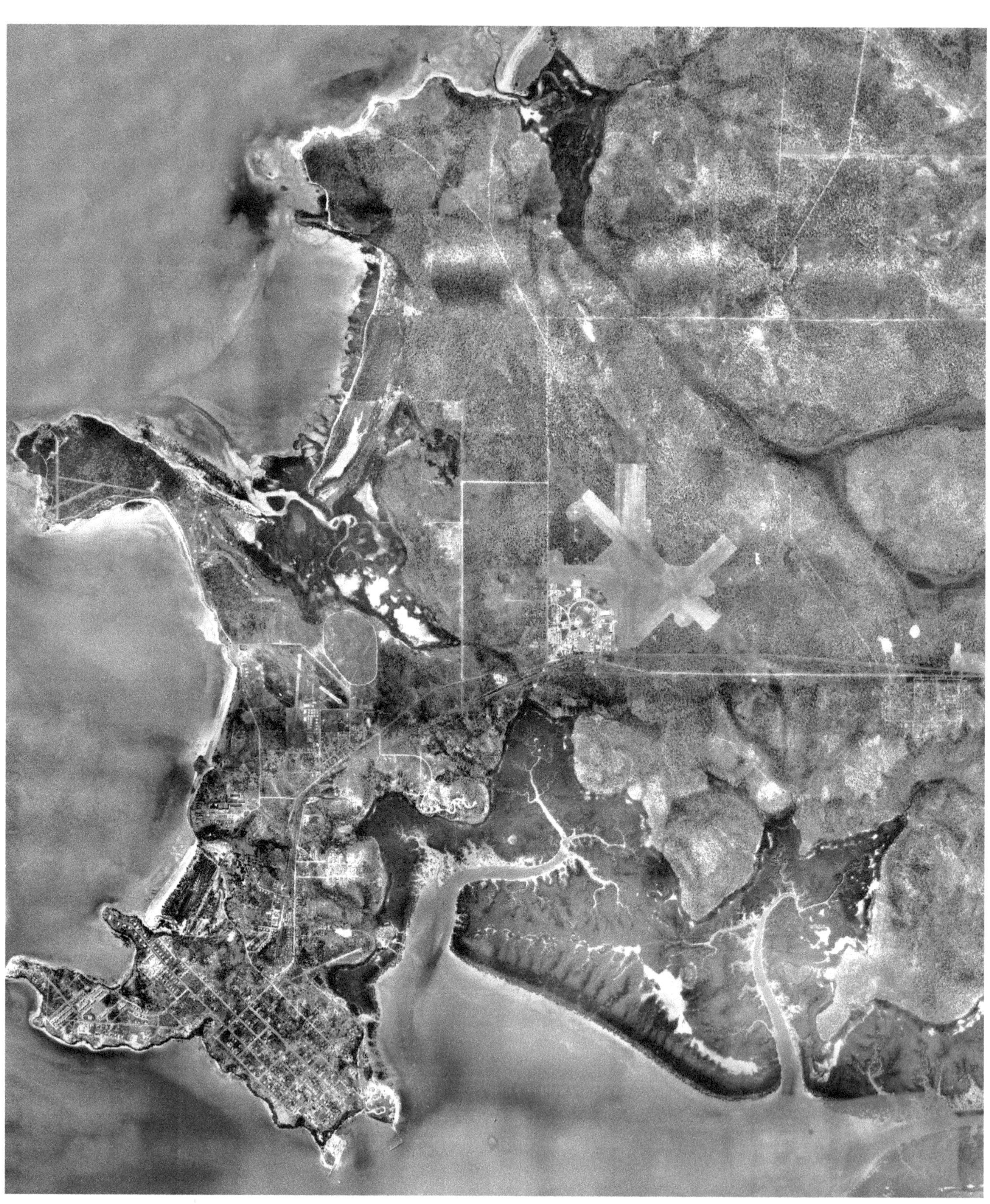

Darwin, 1941. Map courtesy NT Department of Infrastructure, Planning & Logistics, © Northern Territory of Australia. (Unknown, DIPL, Historic Images, Darwin 1941.)

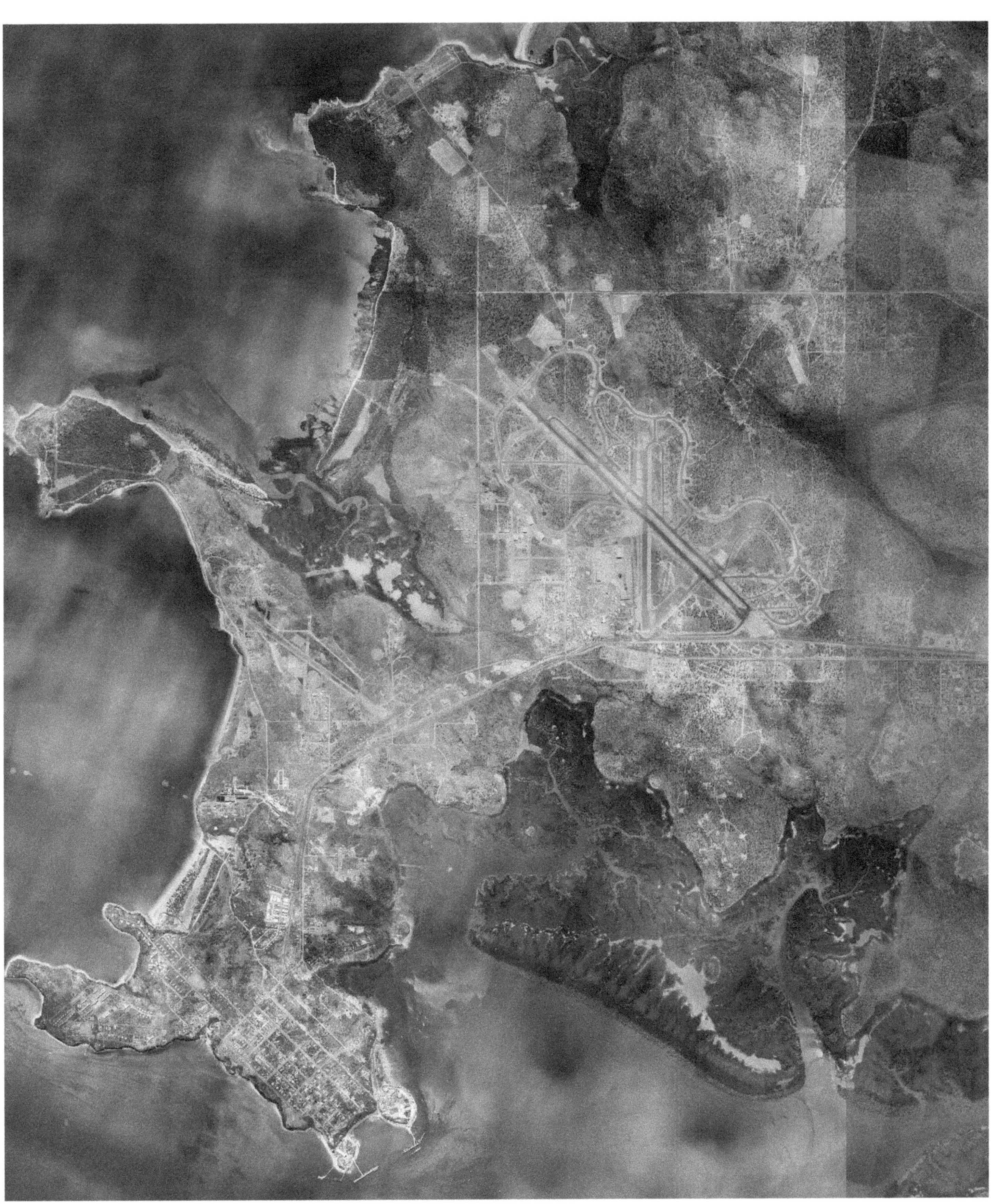

Darwin, 1945. Map courtesy NT Department of Infrastructure, Planning & Logistics, © Northern Territory of Australia. (Unknown, DIPL, Historic Darwin Images, Darwin 1945.)

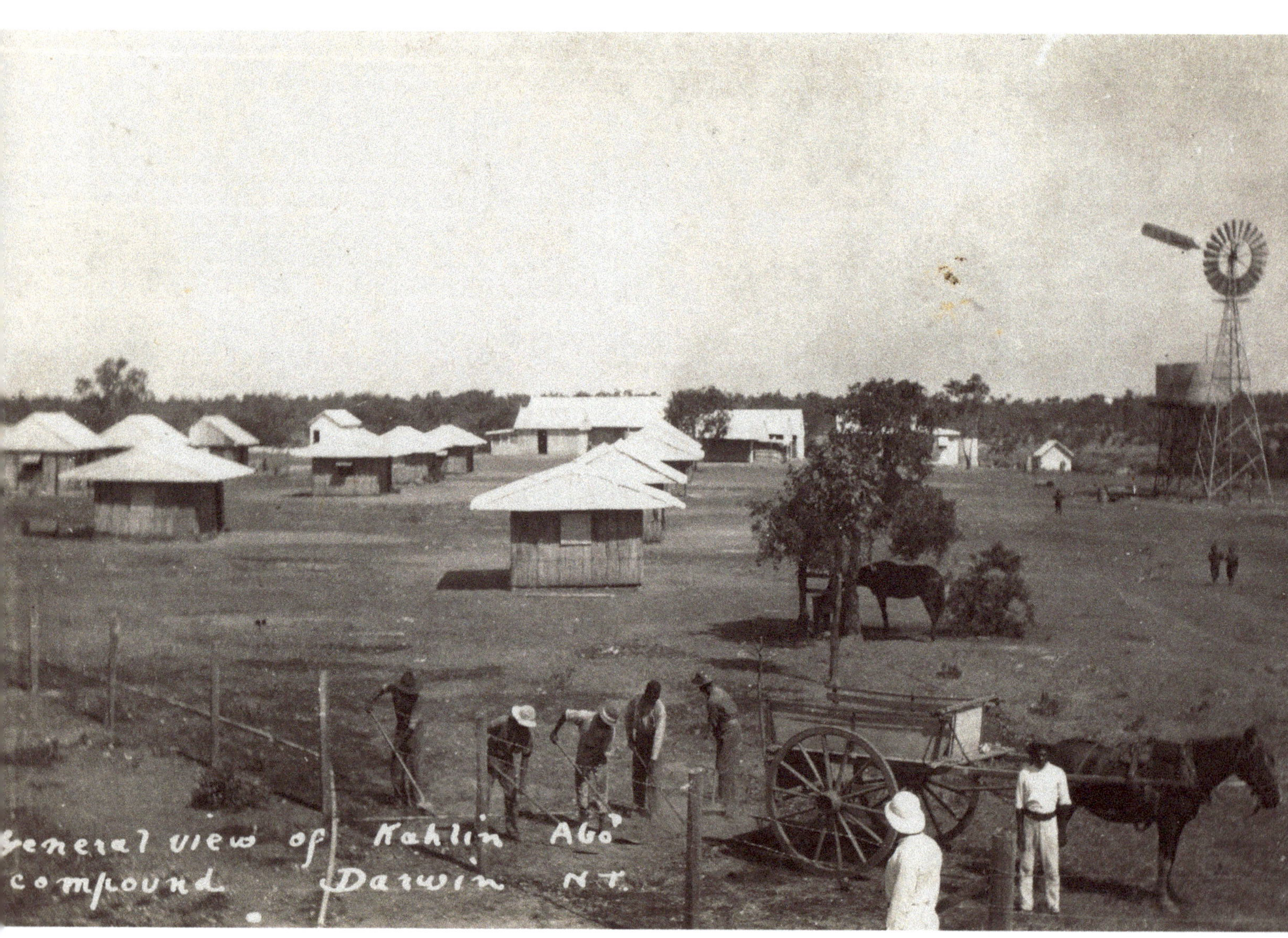

Kahlin Compound, 1915. The use of 'Abo' in the photo caption is an indication of the racism that existed in Darwin at the time. (Unknown, LNSW, E.D.W.S. Donnison Collection, MLMSS/890/3/0084.)

Chapter 8

Myilly Point ~ *Myilli*

Myilly Point is a prominent headland on Darwin Harbour yet it remained largely ignored and undeveloped until 1912. It is believed that the J.A. Gilruth, Commonwealth Administrator, named Myilly Point based on the Larrakia word for 'stones', *Myilli*.[1] Previously the point had been known locally as Dead Horse Point.[2] Development took place when the Commonwealth decided to establish an Aboriginal reserve on Kahlin beach and the adjacent plateau while also constructing housing for government officials on Myilly point.

In 1912 Kahlin Beach, the foreshore on the south-western side of Myilly Point, was selected as the site for an Aboriginal reserve under the Commonwealth *Aboriginal Ordinance, 1911*. The site which became known as Kahlin Compound extended from Kahlin Beach to the area that is now bound by Lambell Terrace and Kahlin Avenue. Under the *Aboriginal Ordinance* Professor Baldwin Spencer, Special Commissioner and Chief Protector of Aborigines used Commonwealth power to force Aborigines in the town area to relocate there.[3] In 1913 'The Compound' as it was known colloquially, was described in the Administration report.

> The Compound comprises about 13 acres ... There are now sixteen bark huts, a boys dormitory, girls dormitory, kitchen, laundry, office, storeroom, coach-house and fodder room, a fowl house, and some old dilapidated buildings in the gardens ... there were seventy six inhabitants of the compound; all these, with the exception of the Superintendent, were aboriginals or half-castes.[4]

Conditions for the Aboriginal inmates of Kahlin compound were harsh. Government policies attempted to control all aspects of their lives. Despite the hardships the survivors of Kahlin Compound are amongst Darwin's most prominent Aboriginal families who played a major role in its development.

The history of Kahlin Compound is just one example of Australia's policies towards its Indigenous people in the early 20th Century. There were many 'compounds' established throughout the Northern Territory driven by Commonwealth policy. These racially discriminatory policies were a continuation of colonial policies that set out to control the lives of Aboriginal people. One result of these policies is 'The Stolen Generation', where Aboriginal children of mixed descent were removed from their families and interred in State and Church Institutions. These policies continue to cast a shadow across Australia's record of treatment of its Indigenous people.

By 1936 Kahlin Compound was considered no longer suitable as an Aboriginal reserve 'not only because it is, being so obsolete in structure, an eyesore, but because the isolation necessary for the efficient control of inmates no longer exists'.[5] The Compound had been severely damaged in the 1937

1 NTG, Place Names Register, *Myilly Point.*
2 *NTTG*, 28 May 1914.
3 Spencer, *Report of the Administrator, 1912,* 46.
4 NTG Heritage Branch, *Kahlin Compound,* 5
5 NTG Heritage Branch, *Kahlin Compound,* 11.

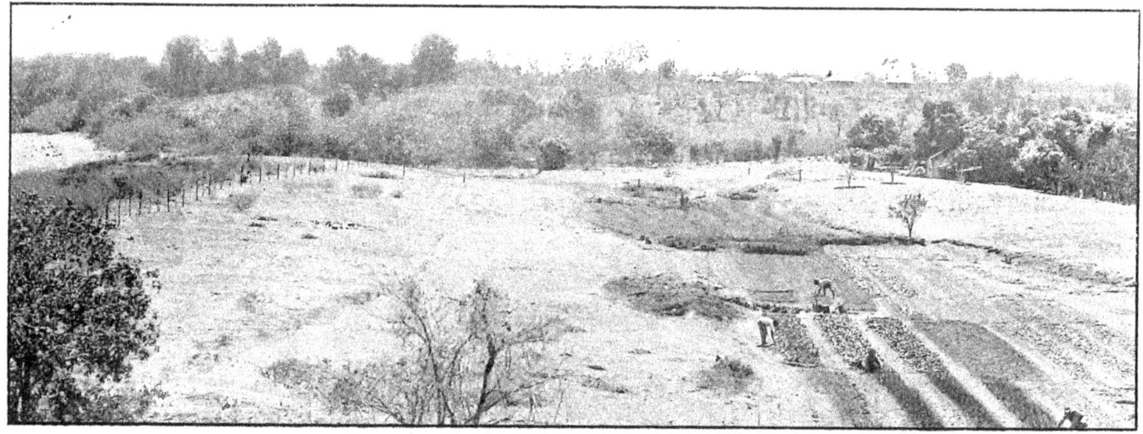

Campbell, Photo.

FIG. 16.—ABORIGINAL GARDEN AT KALIN BEACH, OUTSIDE DARWIN.

The houses in the new compound are seen in the distance on the top of the small cliff, below which the Beach can be seen on the left. The Lamaru camp is being shifted to the latter spot.

Kahlin Compound, 1912. Photo taken from what is today Kahlin Oval. (Campbell, *NT Administrators Report*, 1912.)

cyclone. An alternative site, more distant from Darwin, was selected in Ludmilla. The 360 acre property would become known as Bagot Aboriginal Reserve. By May 1938 the inmates of Kahlin were transferred to Bagot.

At the same time that Kahlin Compound was established in 1912 Commonwealth Government housing was constructed on Myilly Point despite the opposition of the Palmerston District Council. The Council believed that the land was reserved as parkland for the use of the people.[6] In 1913/14 the Commonwealth constructed five houses on an extension of Mitchell Avenue past Lambell Terrace. In 1932, Flagstaff House, known locally as the Commandant's House, because it was home to the Territory's senior army officer, was constructed on the area now known as Flagstaff Park. In the late 1960s and early 1970s the residence was home to Northern Territory Supreme Court Judge Richard Blackburn. The house, like the majority of the housing on Myilly Point was destroyed by Cyclone Tracy.

In 1938, further housing for senior Commonwealth public servants was built in the area now known as the Myilly Point Heritage Precinct. Designed by the Commonwealth's Principal Architect for Northern Australia, Beni Carr Glynn Burrnett, Audit, Burnett, Mines and Magistrate's house are fine examples of pre World War II Darwin architecture. Many of the houses on Myilly Point were damaged in Japanese Bombing raids during World War II but fortunately those in the Heritage Precinct remain to give us a glimpse of life in Darwin's pre World War II history.

In 1941 construction of a new Darwin hospital began on the former Kahlin Compound site. An 89-bed hospital bound by Lambell Terrace and McKay Street was opened on 2 February 1942 and was bombed on the 19th of February. For almost 30 years the hospital remained Darwin's main health care facility until the current Royal Darwin Hospital was completed in 1980. Between 1942 and the 1970s the hospital grew enormously and the site became intensively developed. It was also a social hub because many hospital staff were accommodated on site in housing or dormitory type accommodation. A distinctive feature of the hospital was the three story louvered nurses quarters on the corner of Lambell Terrace and Mitchell Street completed in 1952.[7] Although there has probably always been a path from the northern side of the

6 *NTTG*, 9 October 1913.

7 Carment, *Looking at Darwin's Past*, 63.

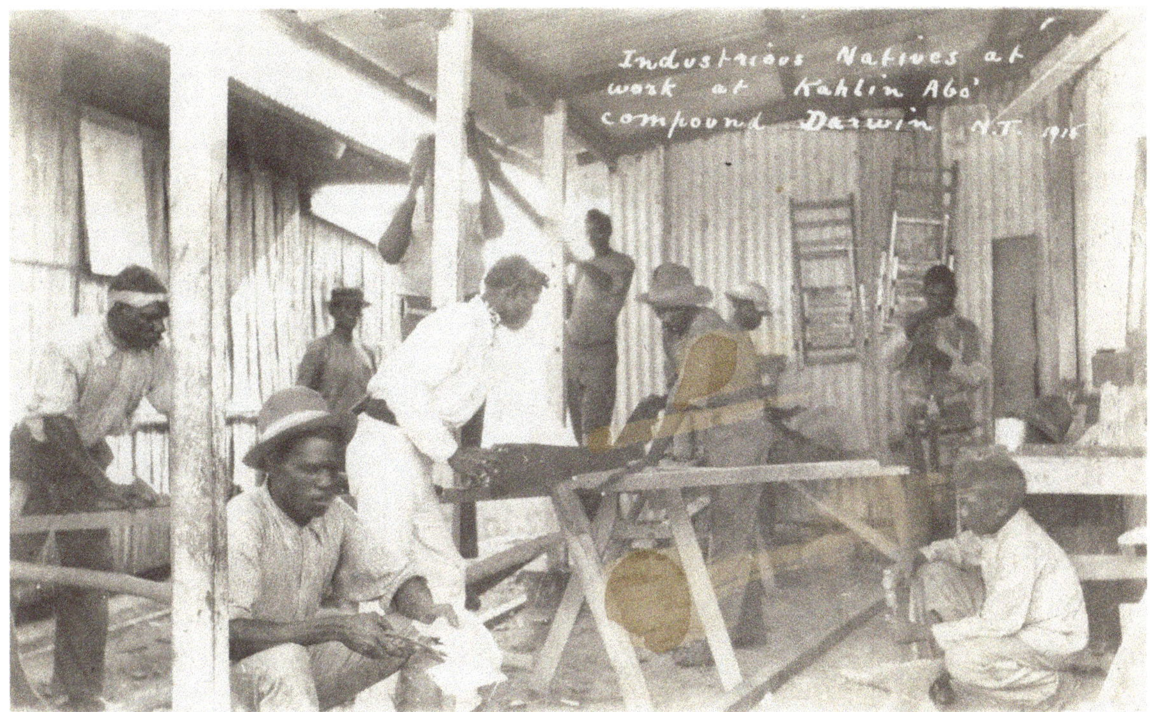

A rare photo of life inside Kahlin Compound, c1915. (Unknown, LNSW, E.D.W.S. Donnison Collection, MLMSS/890/3/0085.)

Myilly Point plateau down to Mindil beach it became known as 'Nurses Walk' during the years the hospital was in operation. Another distinctive feature of the hospital was the ground level hub and spoke design, To this day, former staff, patients and visitors alike comment that the design afforded easy access to the outdoor environment that was perfectly suited to the tropics and recovering from illness.

As Darwin's only hospital when Cyclone Tracy hit in 1974, the Lambell Terrace facilities played a critical role. Despite some damage and cuts to mains power and water the hospital was quickly back in business. The day after the cyclone its dedicated staff, all of whom had their own cyclone survival stories, treated between 500-1000 casualties and admitted 112 patients.[8]

In 1986 some years following the relocation of health services to Royal Darwin Hospital, parts of the former Lambell Terrace hospital were refurbished for the newly created University College of the Northern Territory, the predecessor of Charles Darwin University. The old nurse's quarters became student accommodation. The Myilly Point campus of the Northern Territory University closed in 1997 after new facilities were opened on the Casuarina campus used today.

Cyclone Tracy damaged all of the older housing on Myilly Point. The Paspaley House, designed by Harry Seidler, and completed in 1958, is one of the few pre-cyclone buildings that remain. The last remnants of the pre World War II era housing on Myilly Point were cleared in 1983 when Paul Everingham, the Northern Territory Chief Minister and his government, thought it would be a great location for a Casino. Public outcry thwarted the scheme but most of Myilly Point has remained vacant land since that time. The former Lambell Terrace hospital site was also cleared in the late 1990s. Although there have been numerous proposals to redevelop the Old Kahlin Compound and Darwin Hospital site none have come to fruition.

8 Carment, *Looking at Darwin's Past*, 63.

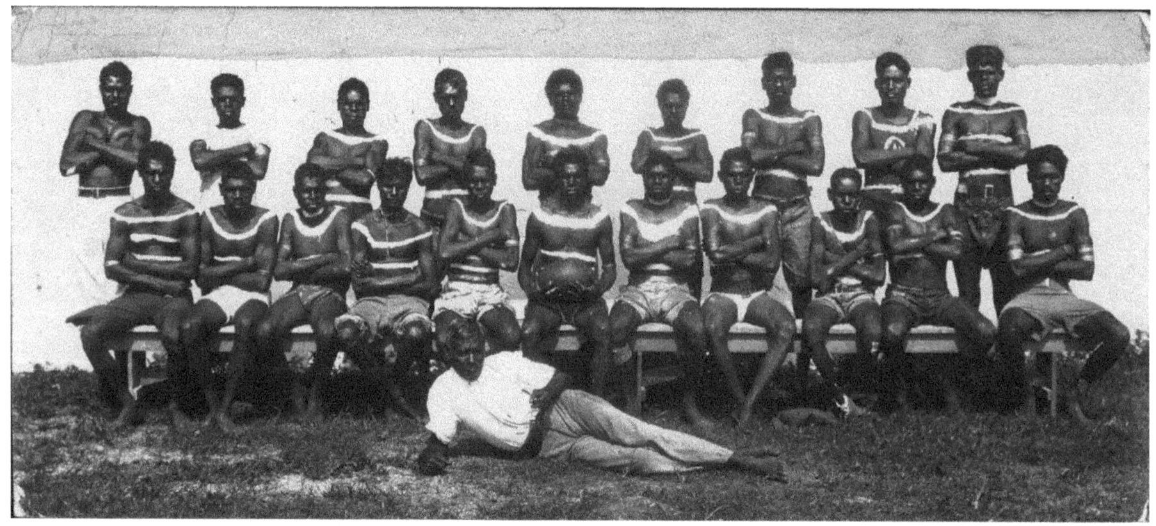

Kahlin football team, c1920s. Aboriginal people from the compound were excluded from the Northern Territory Football League until World War II. This team would have played in an exhibition game on the town oval. (Unknown, SLWA, Conigrave Collection, 2908B28.)

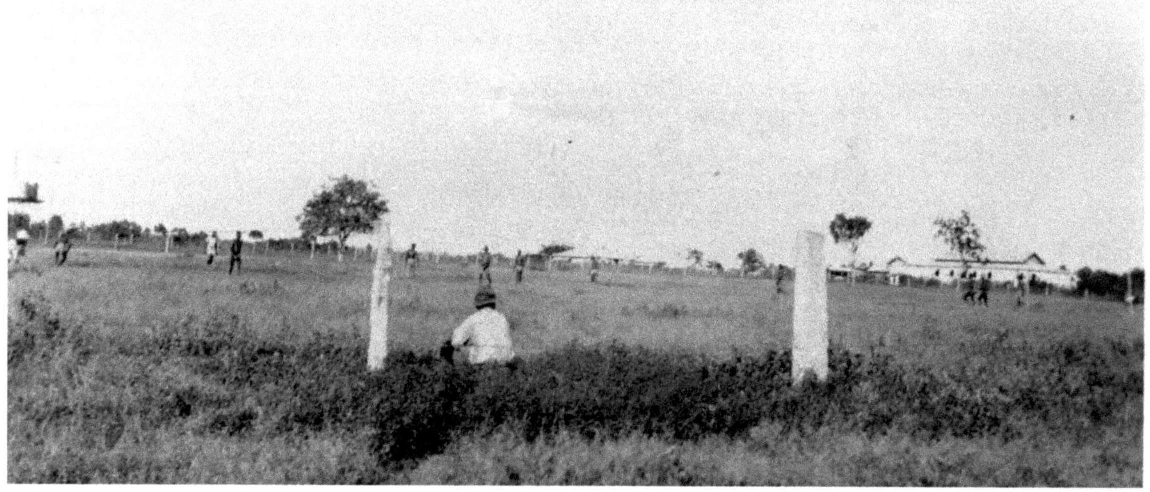

Kahlin Compound football game, c1930s. Despite being banned from the town competition there were football competitions and games at the Kahlin Compound throughout its history. (Unknown, Kendrick, D., NTL, D. Kendrick Collection, PH0518/0031.)

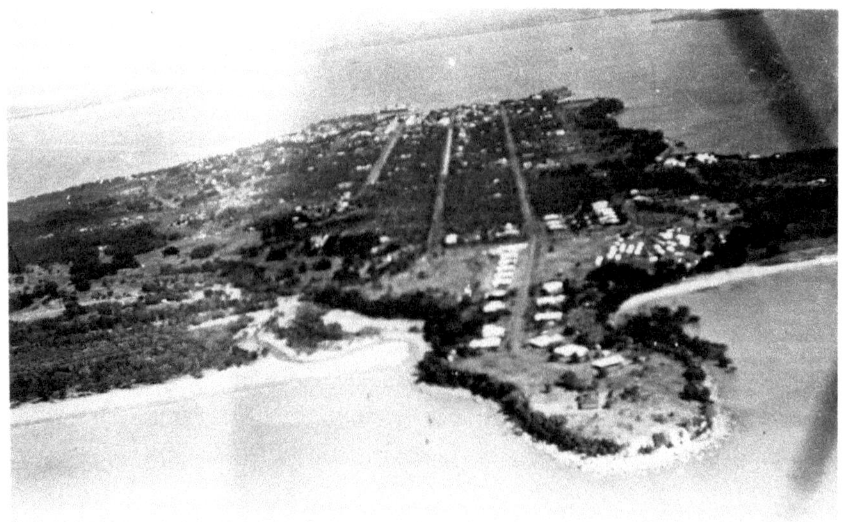

Myilly Point with Flagstaff House under construction, c1932. Kahlin Compound above Kahlin Beach. (Unknown, NTL, Murray H. Fletcher Collection, PH0251/0006.)

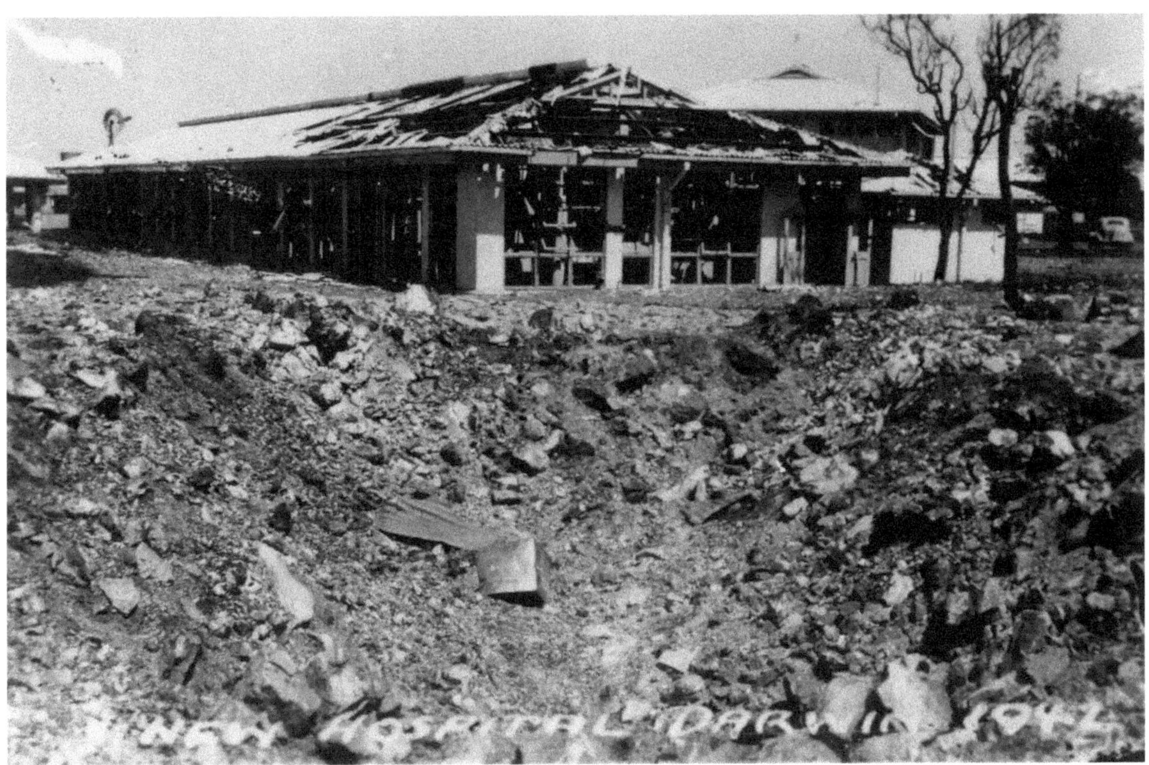

Darwin Hospital, bomb damage, Myilly Point, 19 October 1942. (Unknown, NTL, Murray and Grace Collings Collection, PH0861/0111.)

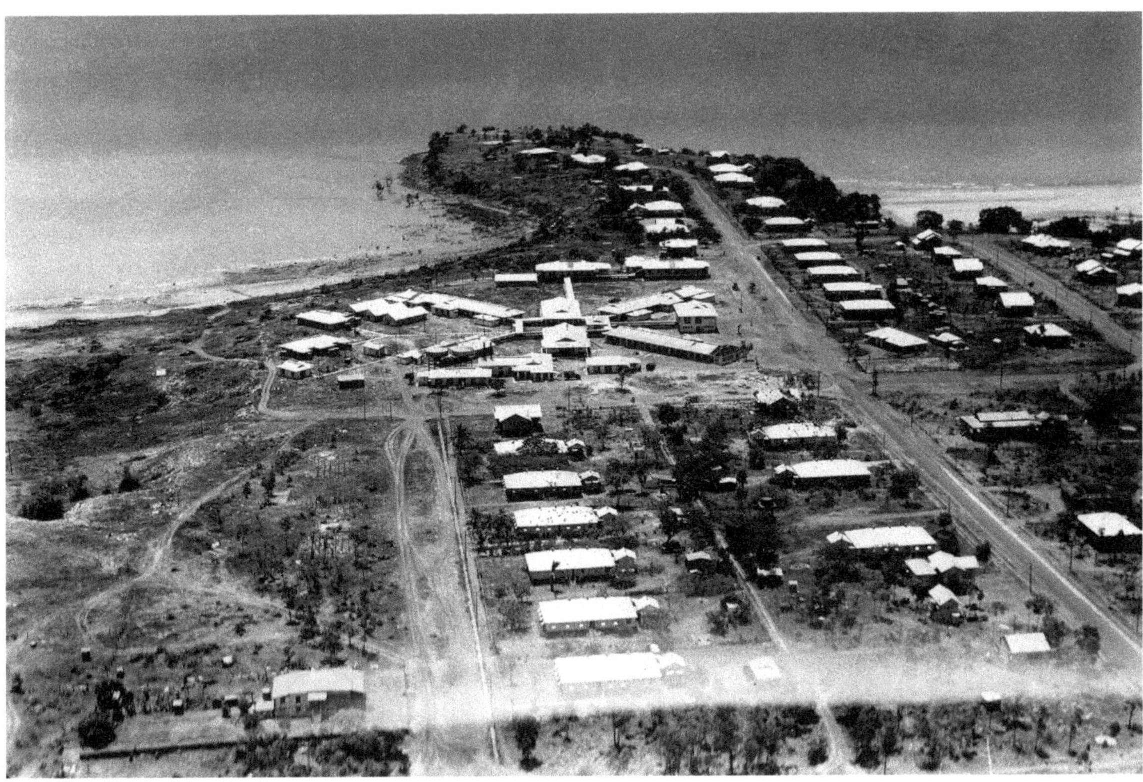

Darwin Hospital, Myilly Point, 19 October 1942. When Darwin Hospital was built the main entrance was on McKay Street, an extension of Mitchell Street. McKay Street ceased to exist in later years as the Hospital expanded. (Sanders, W.C., AWM, photograph, 027330.)

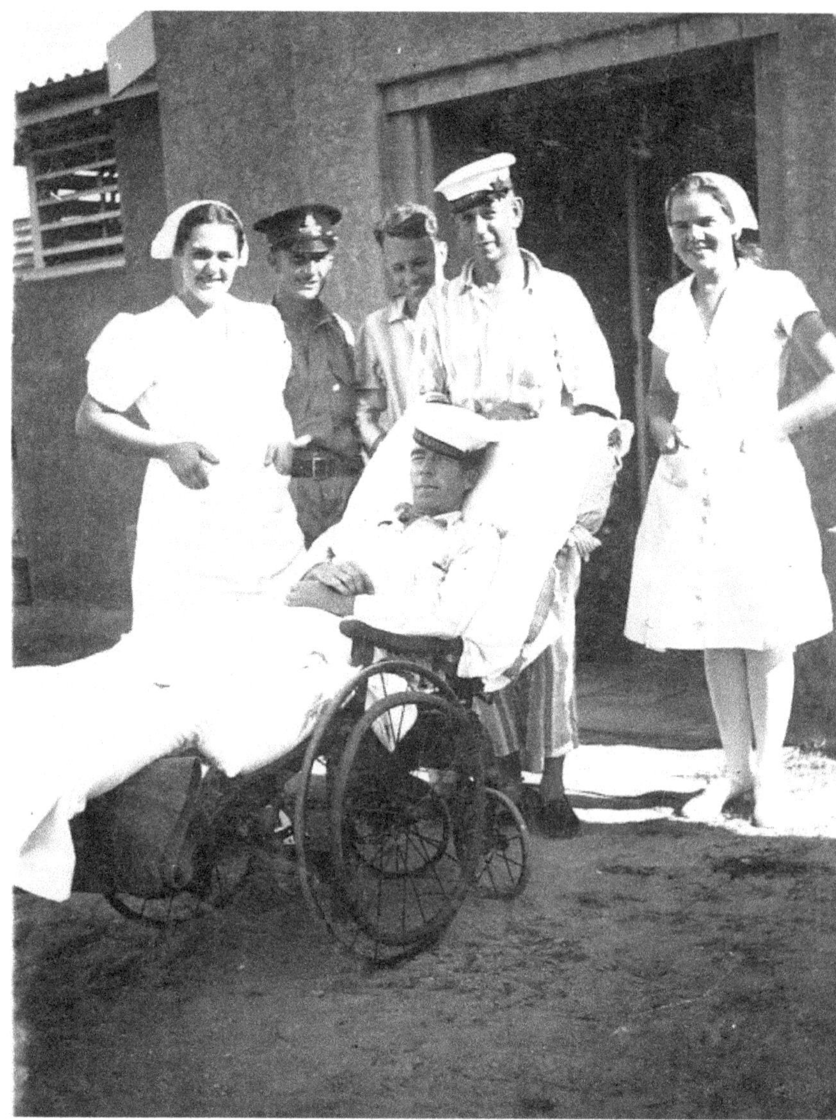

Darwin Hospital, Myilly Point, c1942. Hospital nurses and patients. (Unknown, NTAS, B. Duke Collection, NTRS 1733 Item 5.)

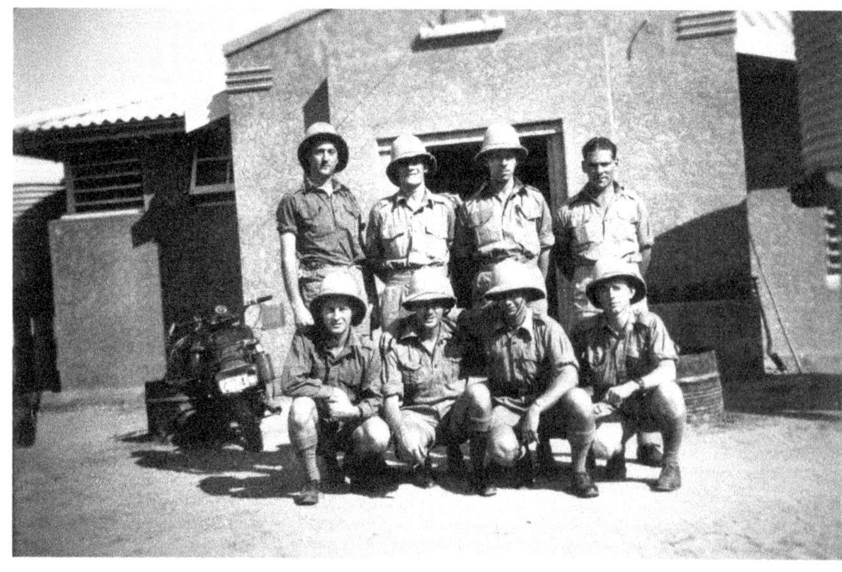

Darwin Hospital, Myilly Point, c1942. Medical orderlies at Kahlin Hospital. (Unknown, NTAS, B. Duke Collection, NTRS 1733 Item 16.)

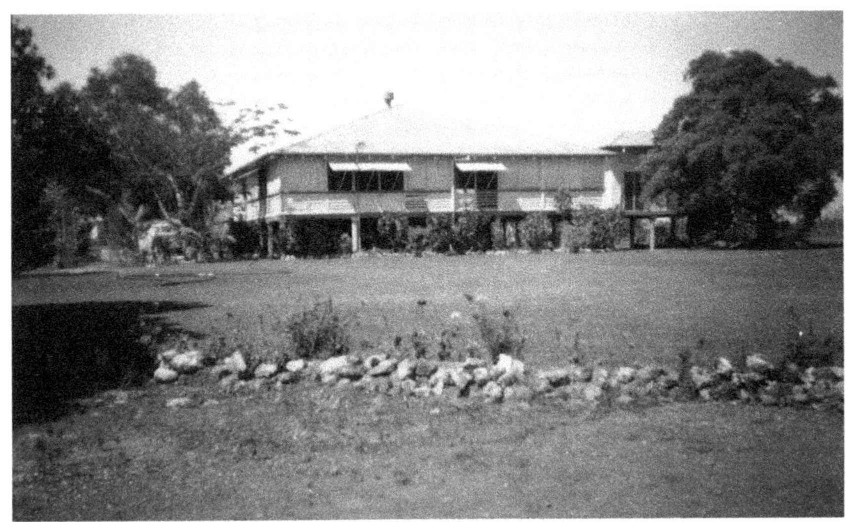

Flagstaff House, Myilly Point, 1949. (Harford, B.P., NTAS, B.P. Harford Collection, NTRS 1299 Item 94.)

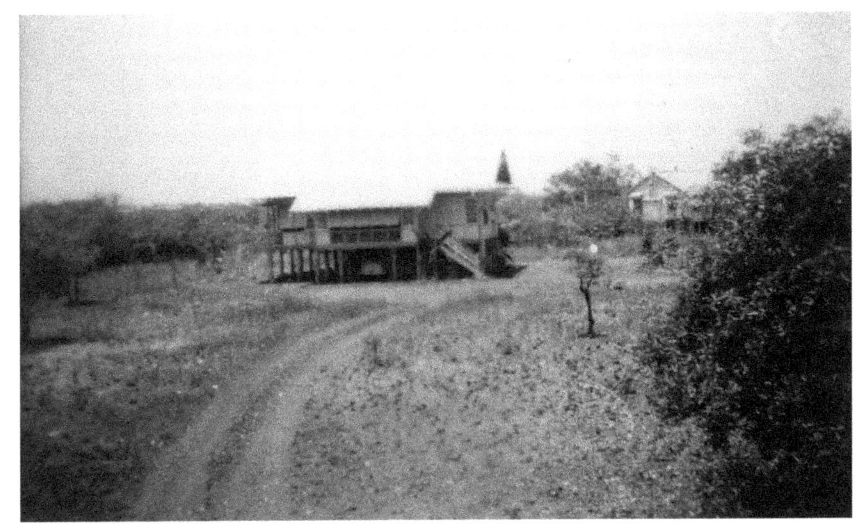

Myilly Point house, 1950. (Harford, B.P., NTAS, B.P. Harford Collection, NTRS 1299 Item 213.)

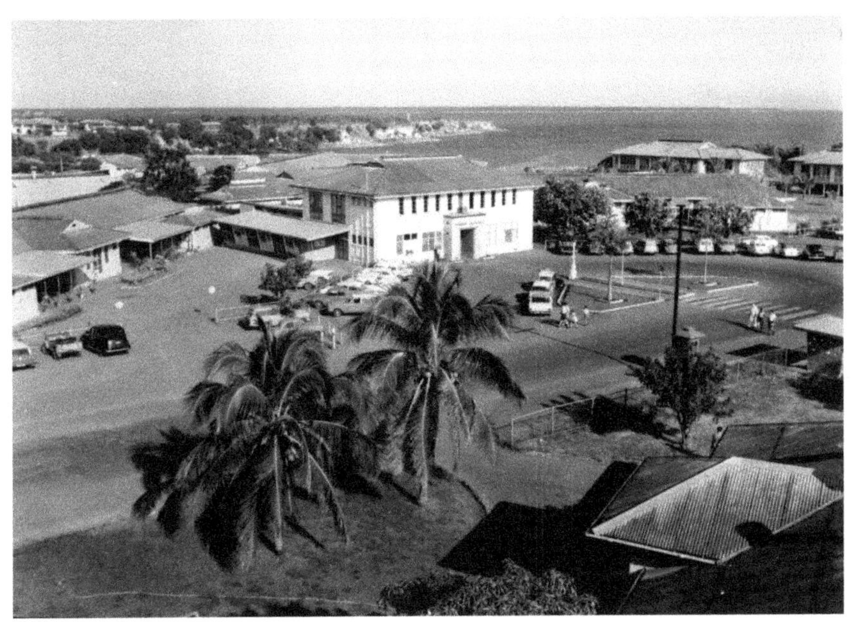

Darwin Hospital, Myilly Point, c1960s. (Unknown, NTL, Northern Territory Government Photographer Collection, PH0093/0006.)

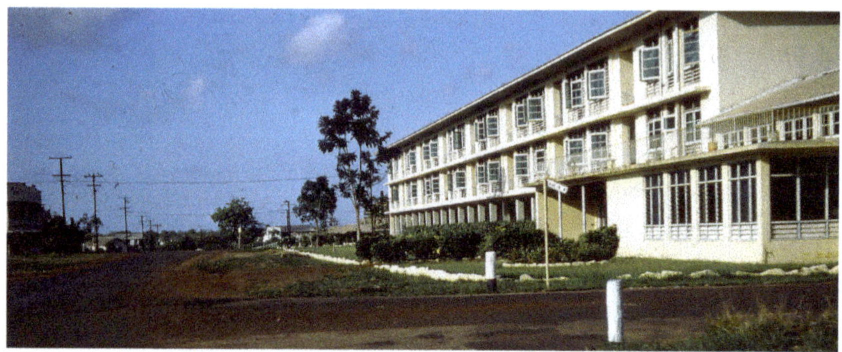

Darwin Hospital, Lambell Terrace Nurses Quarters, Myilly Point, c 1957. (Laidlaw, W.C., NTAS, W.C. Laidlaw Collection, NTRS 317 Item 30.)

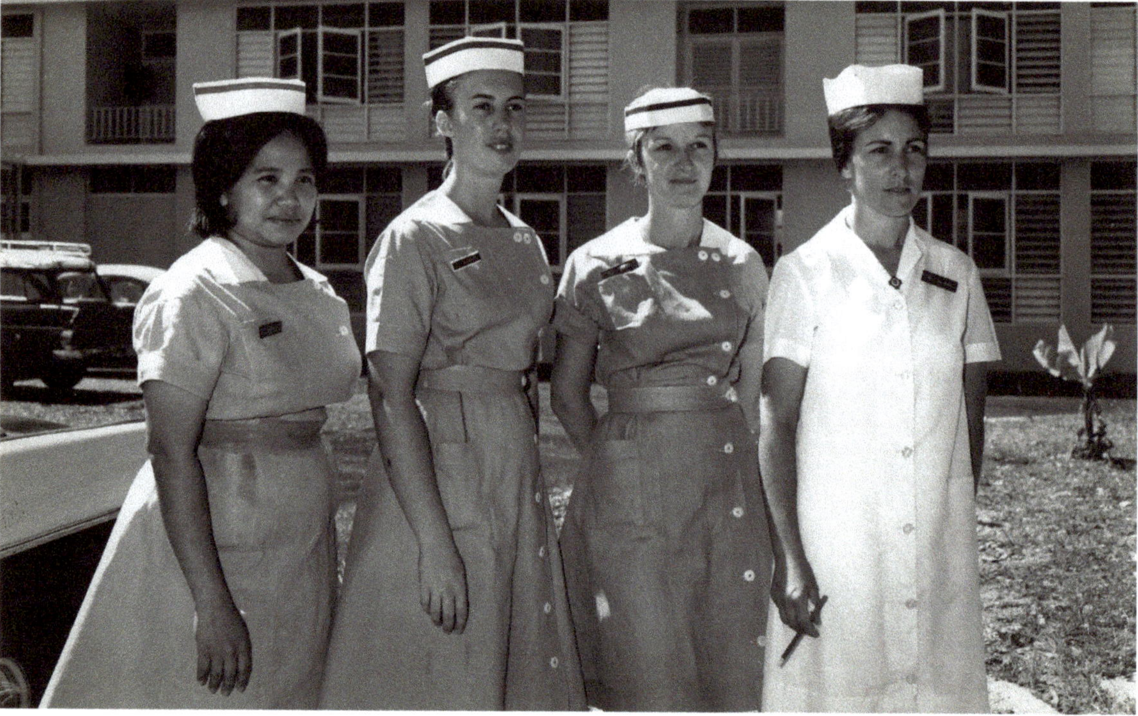

Darwin Hospital, nurses in front of Lambell Terrace Nurses Quarters, Myilly Point, c 1970s. (Unknown, NTRS 3822-P1 Folder 103.)

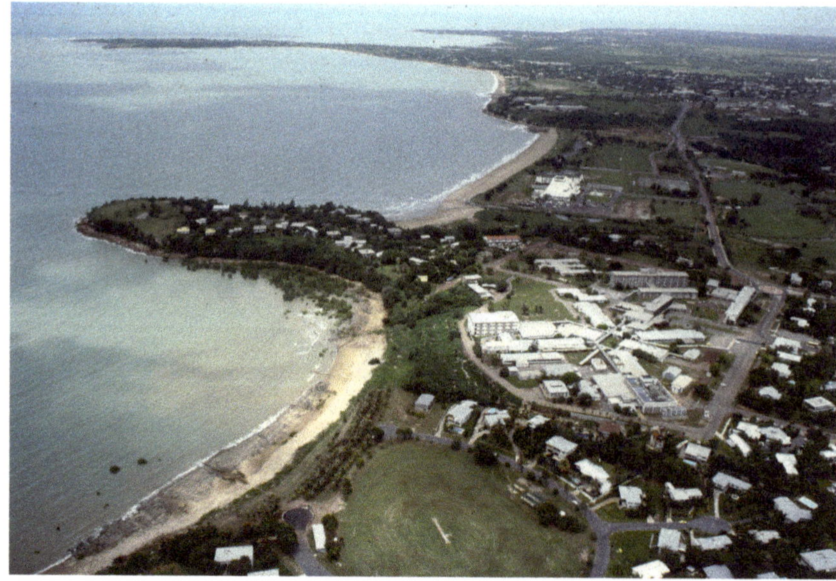

Darwin Hospital, Myilly Point, 18 December 1984. (Unknown, NTAS, GPC, NTRS 3822-P3 Darwin Aerials City Slide LF71.)

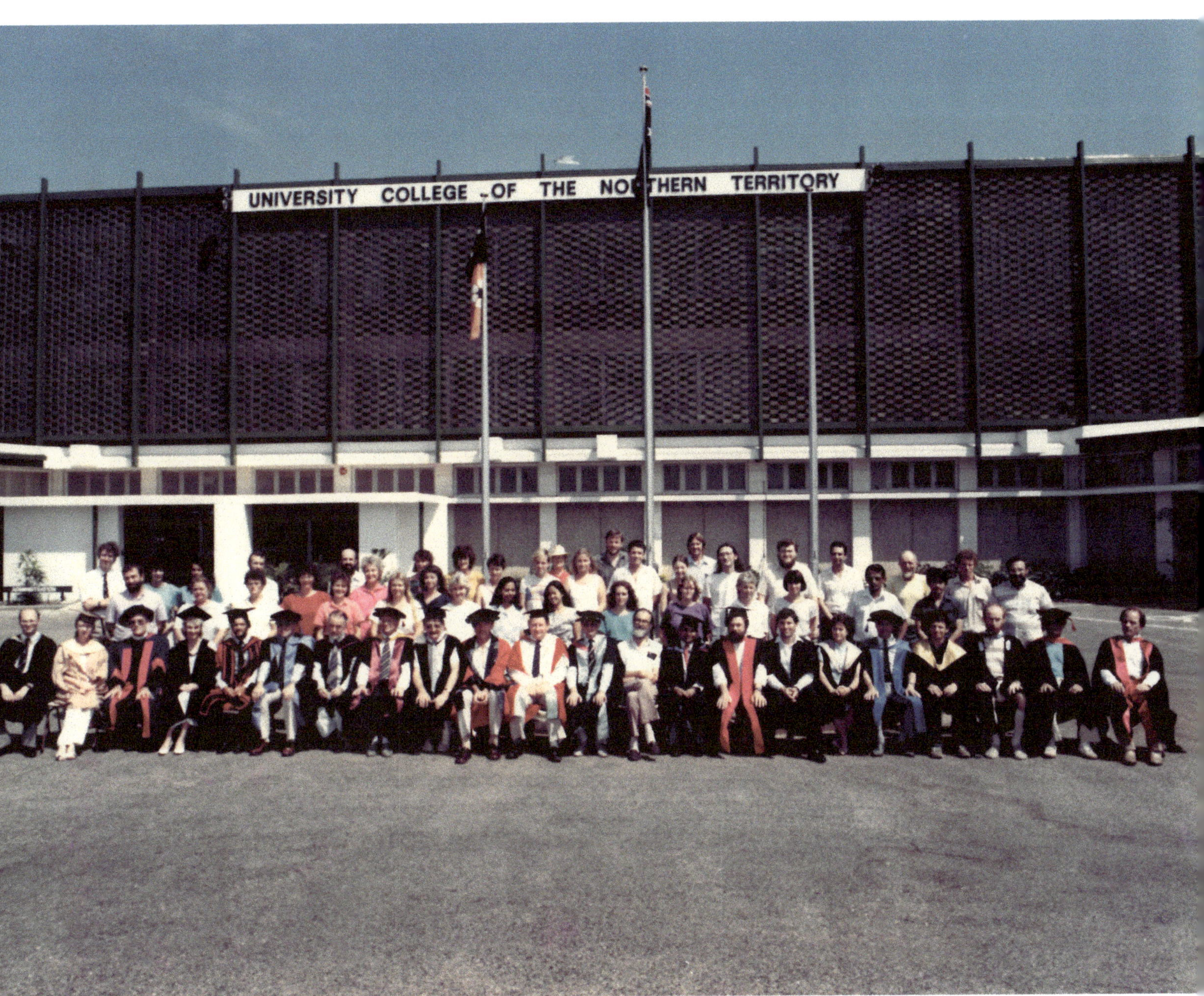

University College of the Northern Territory, inaugural staff, 1987. (Unknown, Powell, A., Personal Collection.)

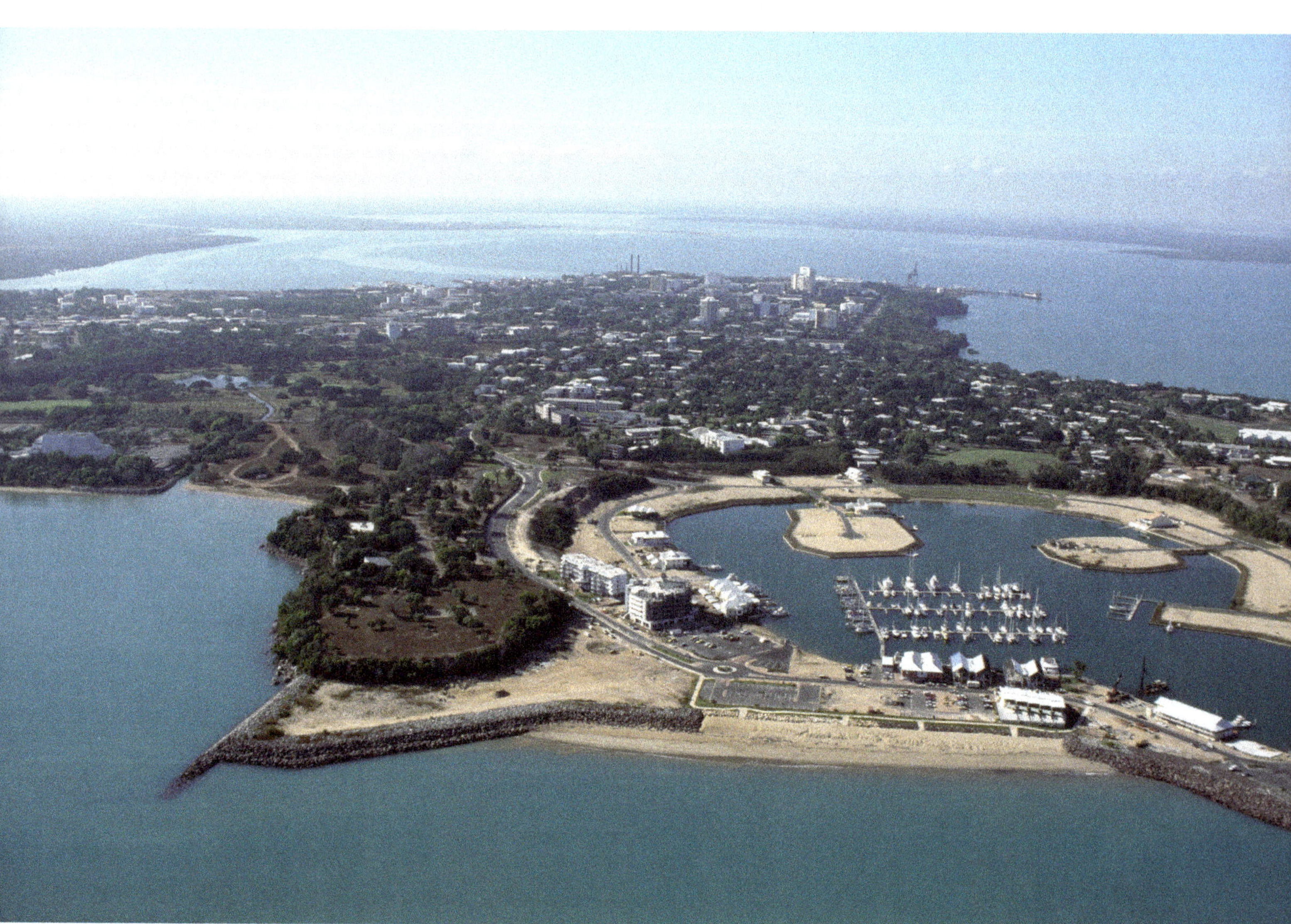

Myilly Point, construction of Cullen Bay Marina, 1995. (Unknown, NAA, Photograph, Cities & Towns from the Air, 11707446.)

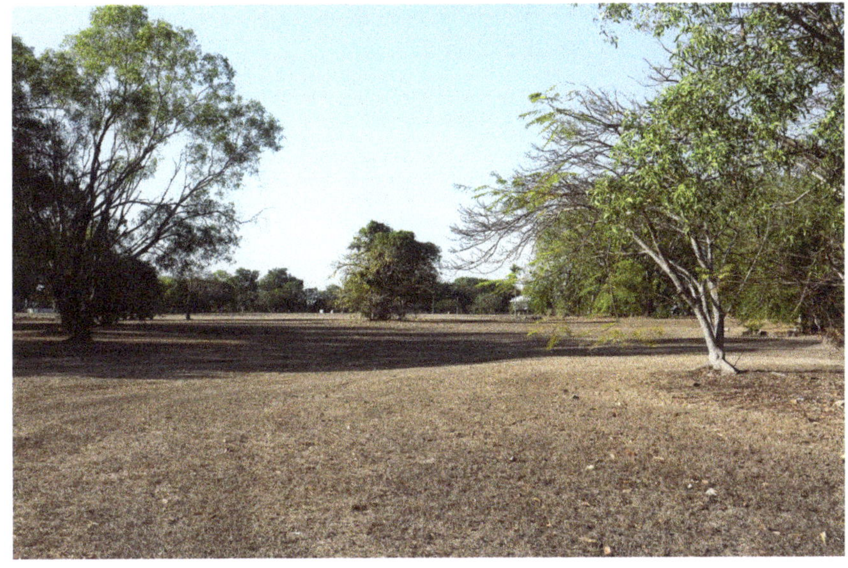

Lambell Terrace, site of the former Kahlin Compound and Darwin Hospital, Myilly Point, 2017. (Martin, R., Matthew Stephen, Personal Collection, Lambell Terrace_02.)

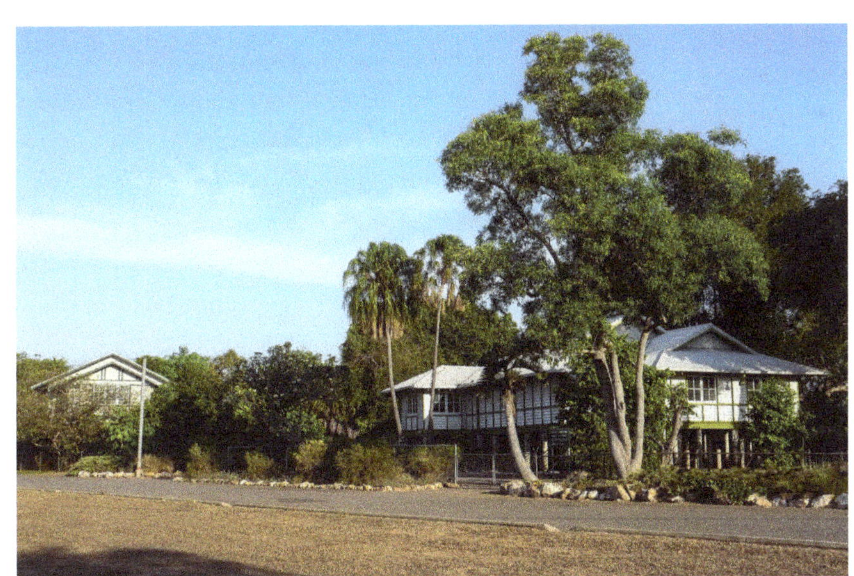

National Trust, historic precinct, Myilly Point, 2017. (Martin, R., Matthew Stephen,
Personal Collection,
Myilly Point _02.)

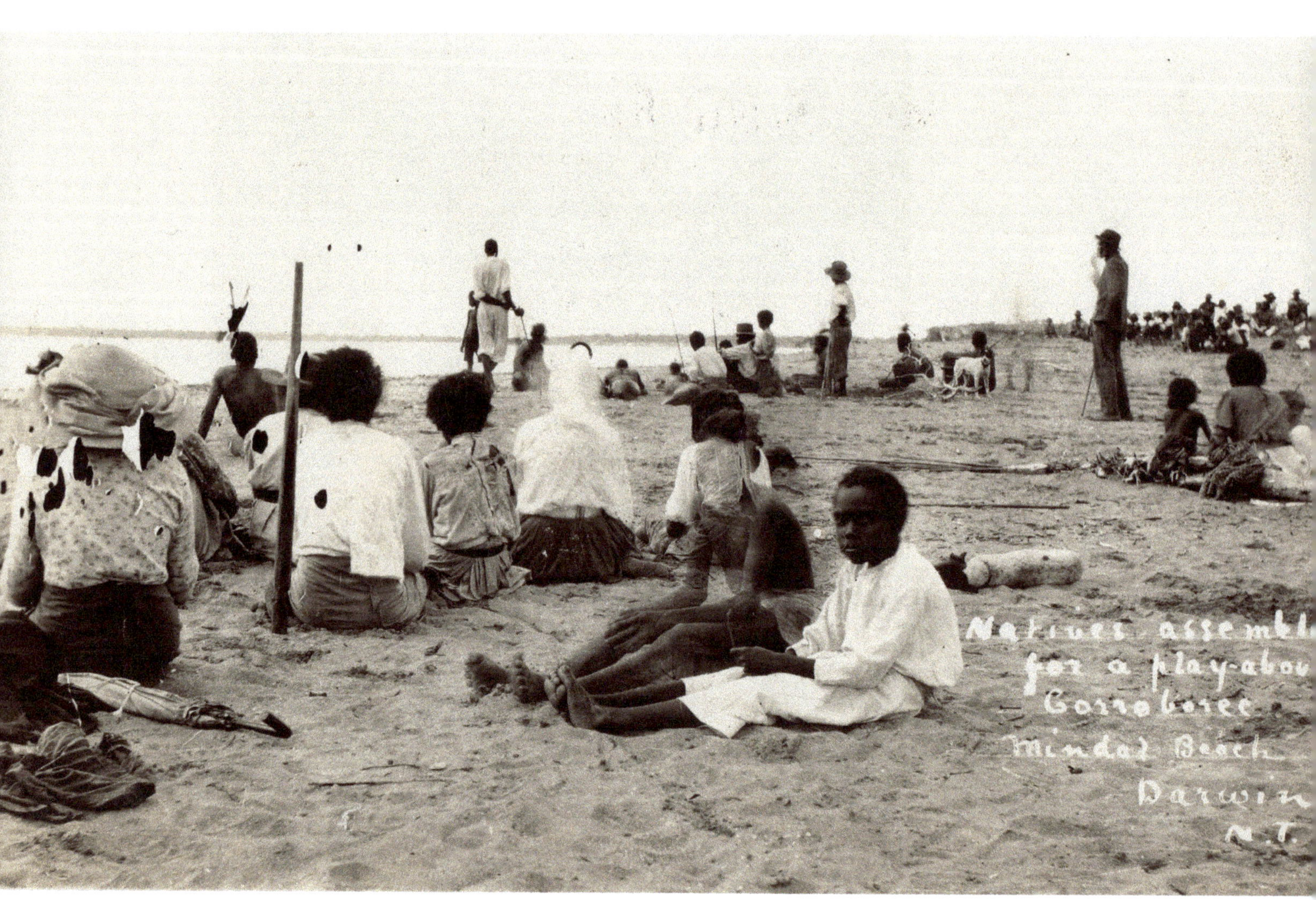

Gathering of Aboriginal people, Mindil Beach, c1915. (Unknown, LNSW, E.D.W.S. Donnison Collection, MLMSS/890/3/0053.)

Chapter 9

Mindil Beach ~ *Mindil-Ang-Gwa*

Traditionally Mindil beach was an important meeting ground for ritualised fights between Tiwi Islanders and the Larrakia. It was also an important burial site for Aboriginal people.[1] The name 'Mindil' appears on an 1871 Darwin survey map in reference to 'Mindil Swamp' in the area that is now Kahlin oval. The name was later applied to today's Mindil Beach that lies between Myilly and Bullocky Points. Mindil is believed to be derived from the Larrakia word *Min-deel* meaning sweet nut grass.[2]

Mindil Beach's clear waters, clean sands and shady foreshore have always made it popular destination for campers and day trippers. In the early days of European settlement it was soon seen as great location for swimming, sports and picnics and after 1886 Darwin residents taking a buggy trip to the beach could go via the Botanic Gardens.

Mindil Beach would be very different today had some of the alternative uses suggested been adopted. In 1872 Mindil Beach was initially selected as the site to bring ashore the overseas cable and construct the Telegraph Station because the vicinity of Fort Hill was seen to have too many obstacles to overcome.[3] In 1887 exploratory tin mining operations were commenced upon a reef just above the Mindil Beach high water mark, known to the Larrakia as *Tappilanda*.[4] Fortunately the tin mining boom predicted never materialised.

By the early twentieth century, Mindil Beach was flanked to the south by Kahlin Compound and government housing on Myilly Point and Vestey's meatworks to the north east. With Kahlin Compound and the development of housing on Myilly Point a path, now known as Nurses Walk, led down to Mindil Beach from the plateau above. The advent of the Compound was accompanied by further Commonwealth restrictions on the movement of Aboriginal people by excluding them from the beach by declaring it a 'prohibited area.'[5] This proclamation was observed more often in the breach than its adherence. Aboriginal people continued to practice their traditional rites on the beach. Up until World War II there were many reports of Aboriginal Corroborees on the beach while burial rites occurred at least up to the 1930s.[6]

In 1926 Mindil Beach became part of Darwin's aviation history in what was to be the first return flight from England to Australia. On 5 August 1926, Alan Cobham and R.W. Ward landed their De Havillard D.H. 50J-EBFO seaplane at Mindil Beach. While in Darwin the seaplane's floats were replaced by wheels to traverse Australia's interior on its flight to Melbourne. On Cobham's return journey to England he again stopped in Darwin to refit the plane's floats. He successfully completed

1 Bauman, *Aboriginal Darwin*, 83.
2 NTG, Place Names Register, *Mindil Beach*, www.
3 *SAR*, 17 February 1872.
4 *NTTG*, 19 March 1887.
5 *NTTG*, 21 October 1915.
6 Tumarkin, *Overland*, 23.

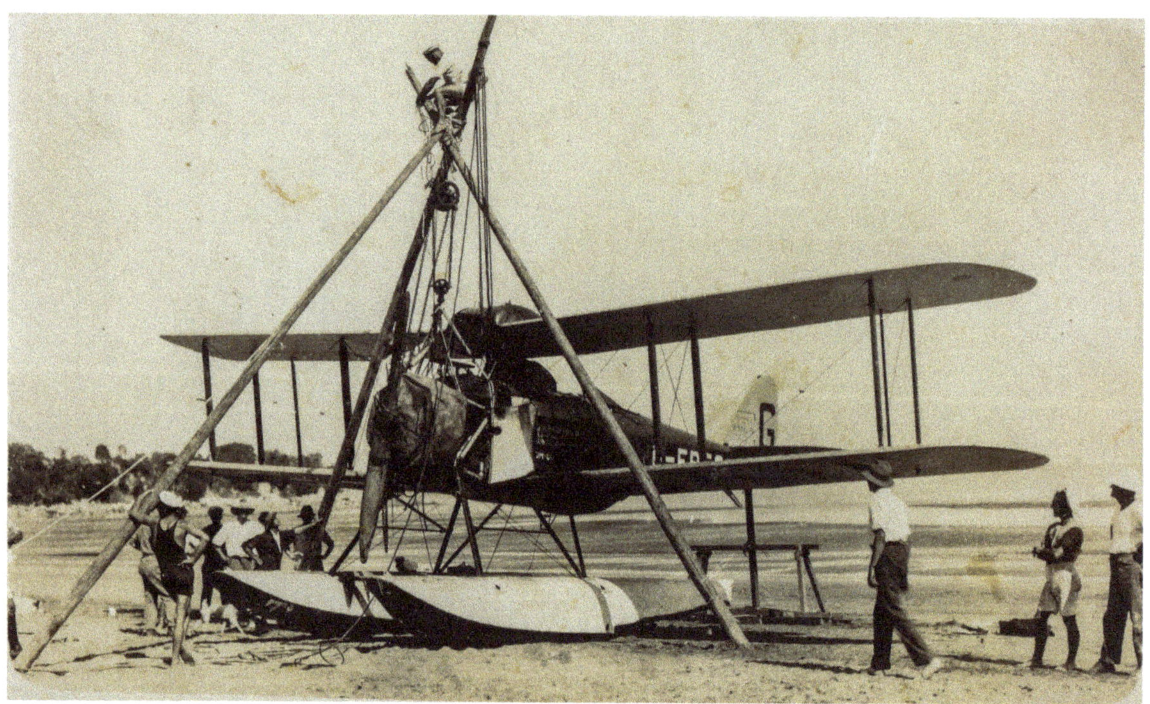

Alan Cobham and R.W. Ward, De Havilland DH50J G-EBFO, Mindil Beach, 1926. (Unknown, NTL, Robert Webb Collection, PH0782/0005.)

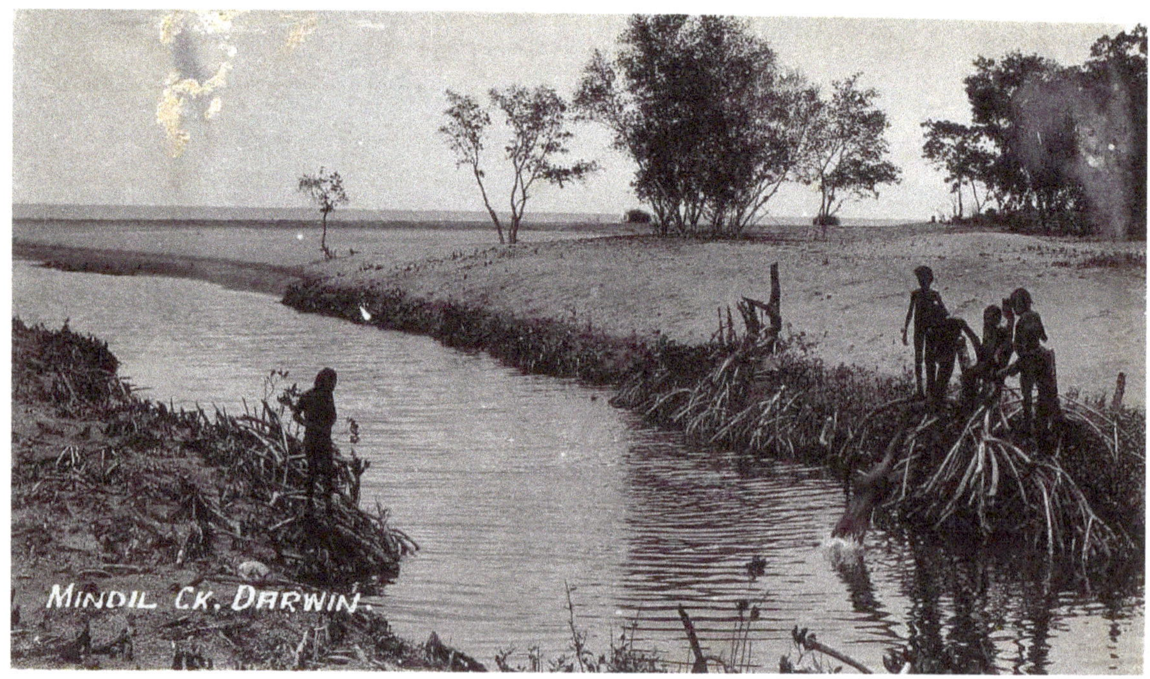

Mindil Creek, Mindil Beach, c1930s. (Unknown, MAGNT, E.M. Weir Collection, Pic001-085.)

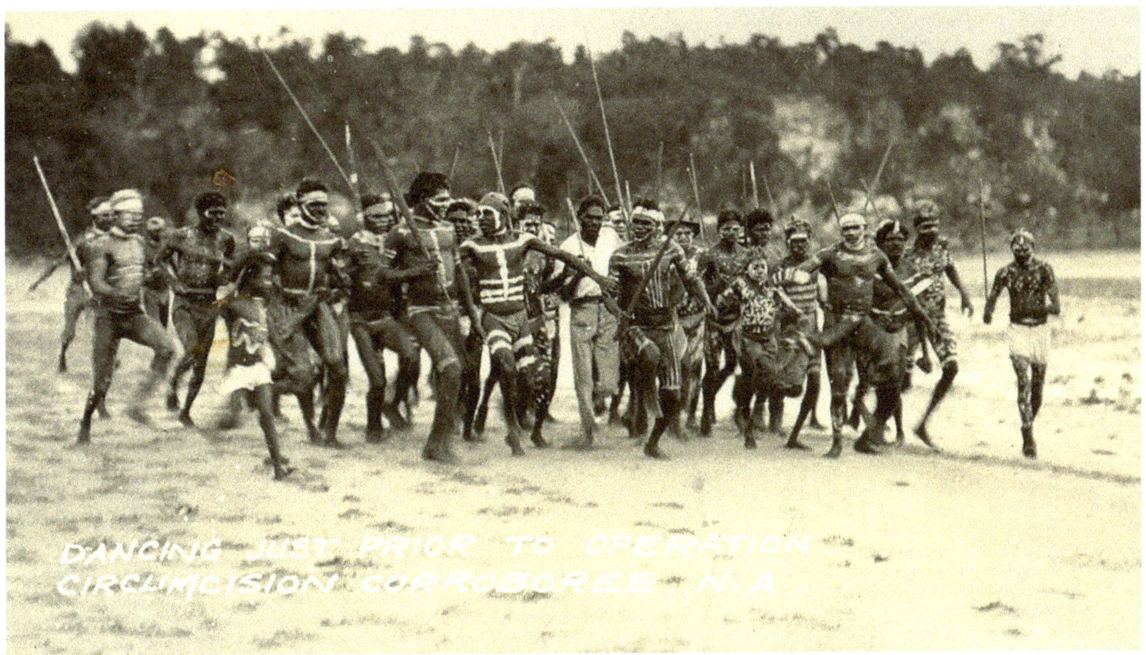

Aboriginal ceremony, Mindil Beach, c1930s. (Unknown, NTAS, Charles Wilson Collection, NTRS 3335 Item 252.)

his return journey to England on 1 October and was soon after Knighted for the achievement.[7]

Like all of Darwin Mindil Beach was affected by the Bombing of Darwin on the 19th of February 1942. Many bodies from the sunken ships in the harbour washed ashore on the beach. Soldiers were assigned to bury them on the beach as soon as possible. The bodies were recovered after the war and interred at the Adelaide River War Cemetery.[8] Despite this dark episode Mindil Beach was popular with the troops throughout the war. Many picnics and swimming excursions were held on the beach. A mobile Army canteen was often situated at the beach and in June 1945 a rotunda was erected for performances of the NT Force Band.[9] In a poignant reminder of the ravages of the war Mindil Beach hosted a picnic in September 1945 for returning Australian prisoners of war who had survived Japanese prisons in South East Asia. The prisoners of war, many of whom were bed ridden, were greeted by the NT Force Band and the Darwin soldiers were encouraged to give them a 'rousing welcome they so richly deserve [and] let them know you are proud of them'.[10] It was thought that many of the prisoners of war would like a day at the beach, something that they could only have dreamed of during their terrible time in prison.

With the return of the civilian population to Darwin after 1946 the town's reconstruction and rapid rise in population resulted in an extreme accommodation crisis. Many new arrivals initially camped on Mindil Beach. The beach was also the location for many public events such as ANZAC Day sports, learn to swim, concerts and even a Grand Gala Carnival with food stalls that was a predecessor to Mindil's now famous markets.[11] In the 1950s Mindil Beach continued to be a popular camping spot that was formalised in 1966 by the development of a Darwin City Council caravan park.[12] After Cyclone Tracy Mindil Beach again became home to some displaced and homeless people who camped

7 The Civil Aviation Historical Society & Airways Museum, www.
8 Dewar, Mickey. *A Market for Memories*.
9 *AR*, 13 June 1945.
10 *AR*, 21 September 1945.
11 *NS*, 23 May 1947.
12 Howison, Personal communicaiton, 9 May 2018.

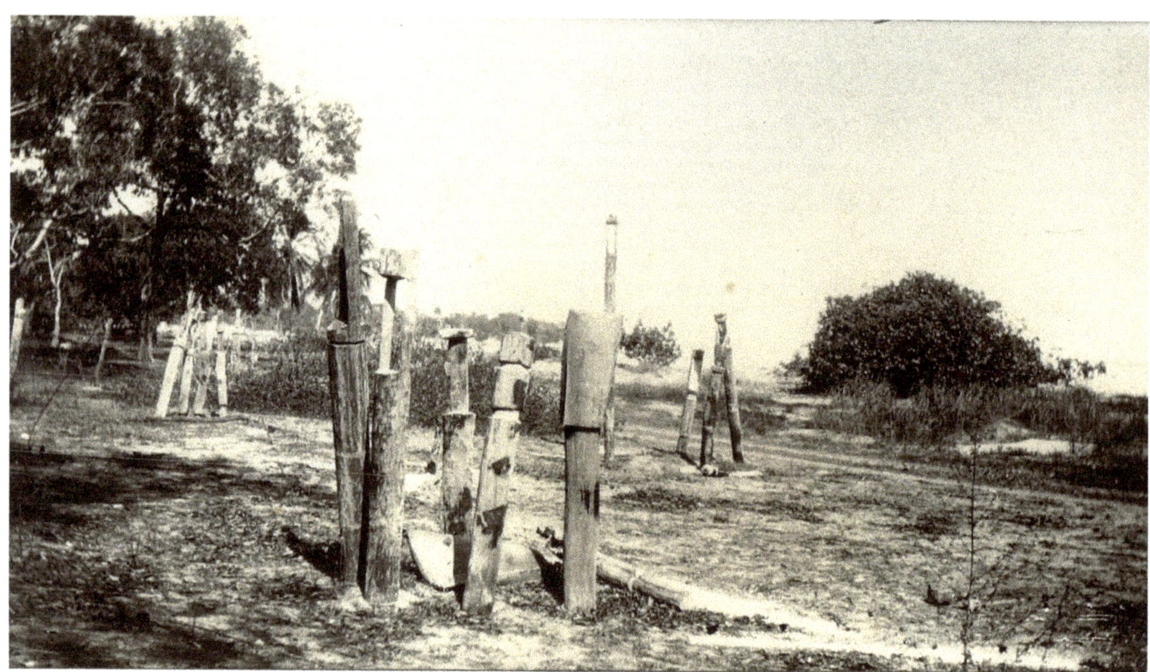

Pukamani Poles, Mindil Beach, c1930s. (Unknown, NTAS, Charles Wilson Collection, NTRS 3335 Item 263.)

there when accommodation was again very scarce. The caravan park closed when it was selected as the site of Mindil Beach Casino.

In 1974 Mindil Beach was the site chosen for the first Beer Can Regatta. Part of the Darwin Aquatic Festival, the first regatta drew a crowd of 22,000 people, about half of Darwin's population at the time, and was a great success. Perhaps more remarkably the regatta was held again in 1975, just months after Cyclone Tracy. It has since become an integral part of Darwin's events calendar.

In 1978, soon after Northern Territory Self Government, new laws were passed permitting casinos in the Territory. The first was the Don Casino, an 'interim' venue in Cavenagh Street, opened 21 September 1979, but the 'new' casino was constructed at Mindil Beach. During the construction of the casino, reminders of Mindil's past were uncovered. Human remains were found during preparatory work on the casino site.[13] A Coroner's enquiry confirmed that the human remains found were of Aboriginal people. The findings resulted in a negotiated settlement to reinter the remains on a '*memorial* island' in Mindil Creek on the casino site.[14] In May 1992 more Aboriginal graves were disturbed during excavation works for improving the Mindil Beach market area. A memorial of 'blank' Pukamani Poles was constructed at the northern end of Mindil Beach to acknowledge the presence of graves in the area. The Pukamani Poles are deliberately left 'blank' because neither the age of the burials or the origins of the remains are known.[15]

The Mindil Beach Casino opened in 1983 and has been a popular entertainment and hospitality attraction since. Mindil Beach was reinforced as one of Darwin's premier attractions by the establishment of its sunset markets in 1986. The 'Dry' season markets attract over half a million visitors each year to sample the multicultural food, view the huge variety of stalls and admire the beautiful sunsets. The markets were accorded national icon status by the Australian National Trust in 2000. The Casino and markets dominate Mindil Beach today but it should be remembered that the beach also has a long and significant continuing cultural history.

13 *CT*, 27 July 1982.
14 *CT*, 9 November 1982.
15 Darwin City Council interpretive information, Mindil Beach, 2018.

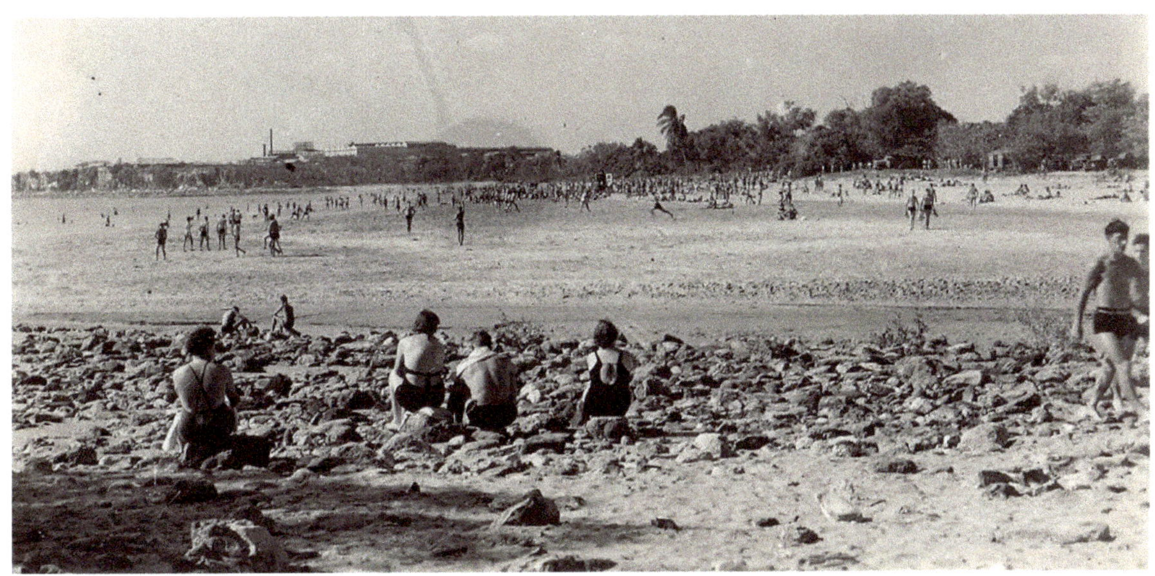

Mindil Beach, 1945. (Unknown, NTAS, J.L. Mitchell Collection, NTRS 866 Item 21.)

Mindil Beach, 21 September 1945. Picnic for former prisoners of war from Singapore who arrived in Darwin on the hospital ship *Oranje*. Private R.G. Hamson, an ex farmer from New South Wales, running soil through his hands. (Unknown, AWM, Photograph, 116630.)

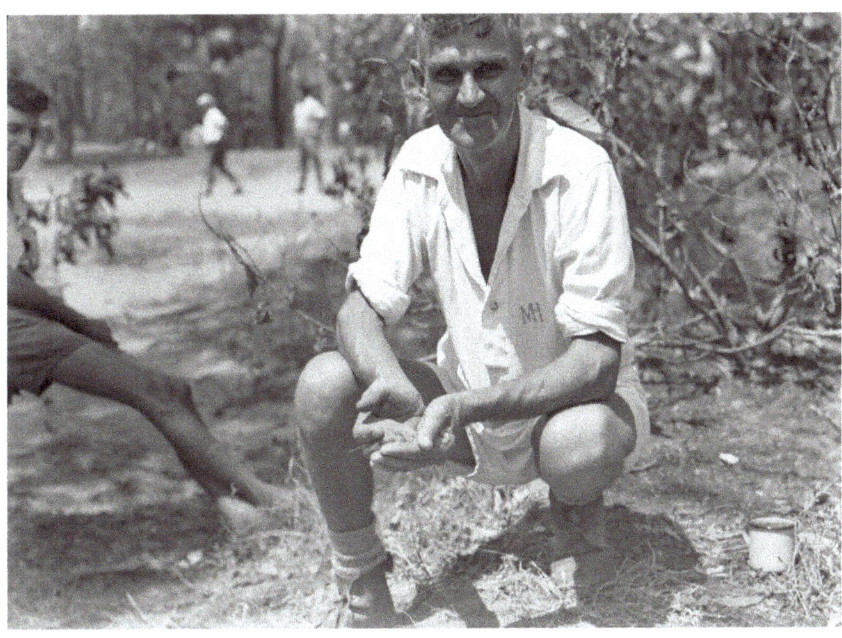

Mindil Beach rotunda, 1945. (Burns, N., NTL, Norma Burns Collection, PH0832/0024.)

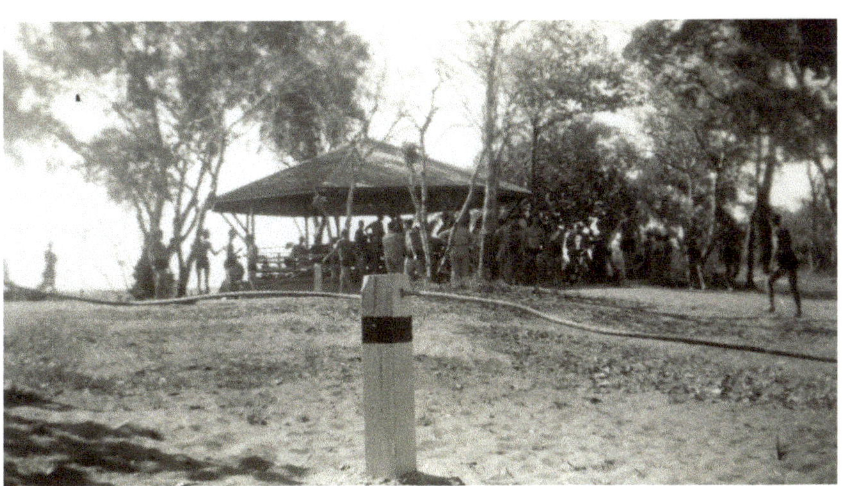

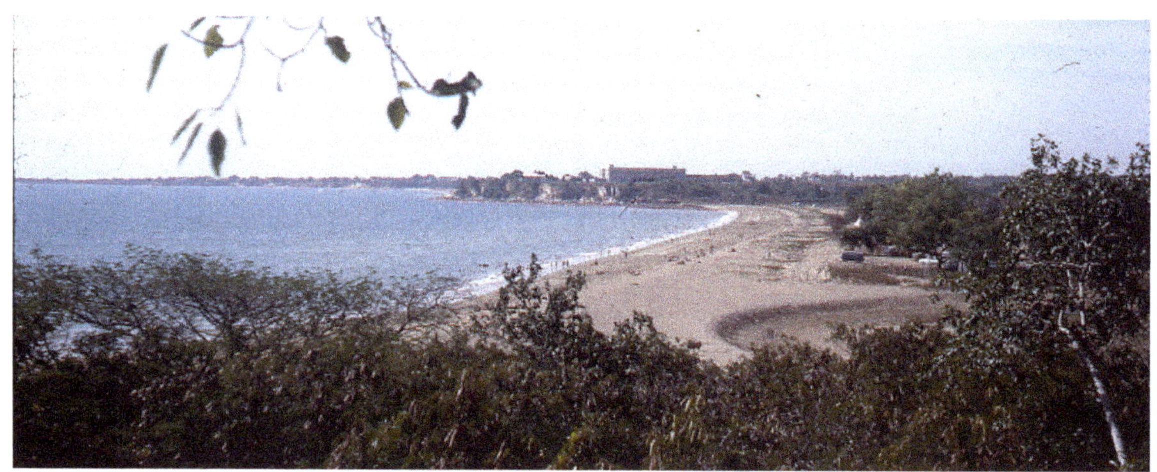

Mindil Beach, from Myilly Point, July 1964. (Graham, H., NTAS, H. Graham Collection, NTRS 3406/P1 Item 60.)

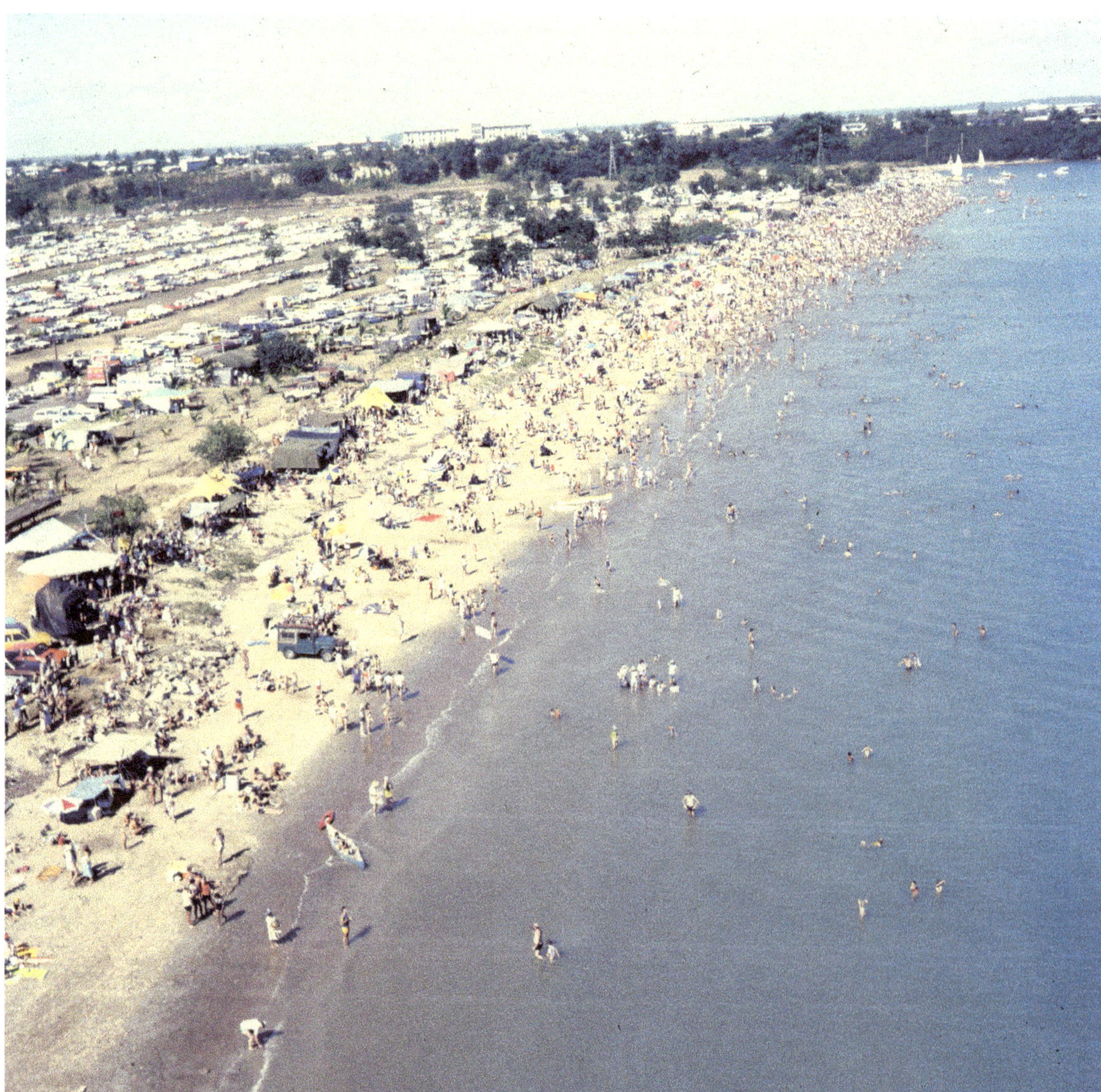

Mindil Beach, Back to Darwin Festival, Beer Can Regatta, 27 May 1978. (Wiedeman, A., NTAS, GPC, NTRS 3822-P3 Beer Can Regatta 1978 Slide 43.)

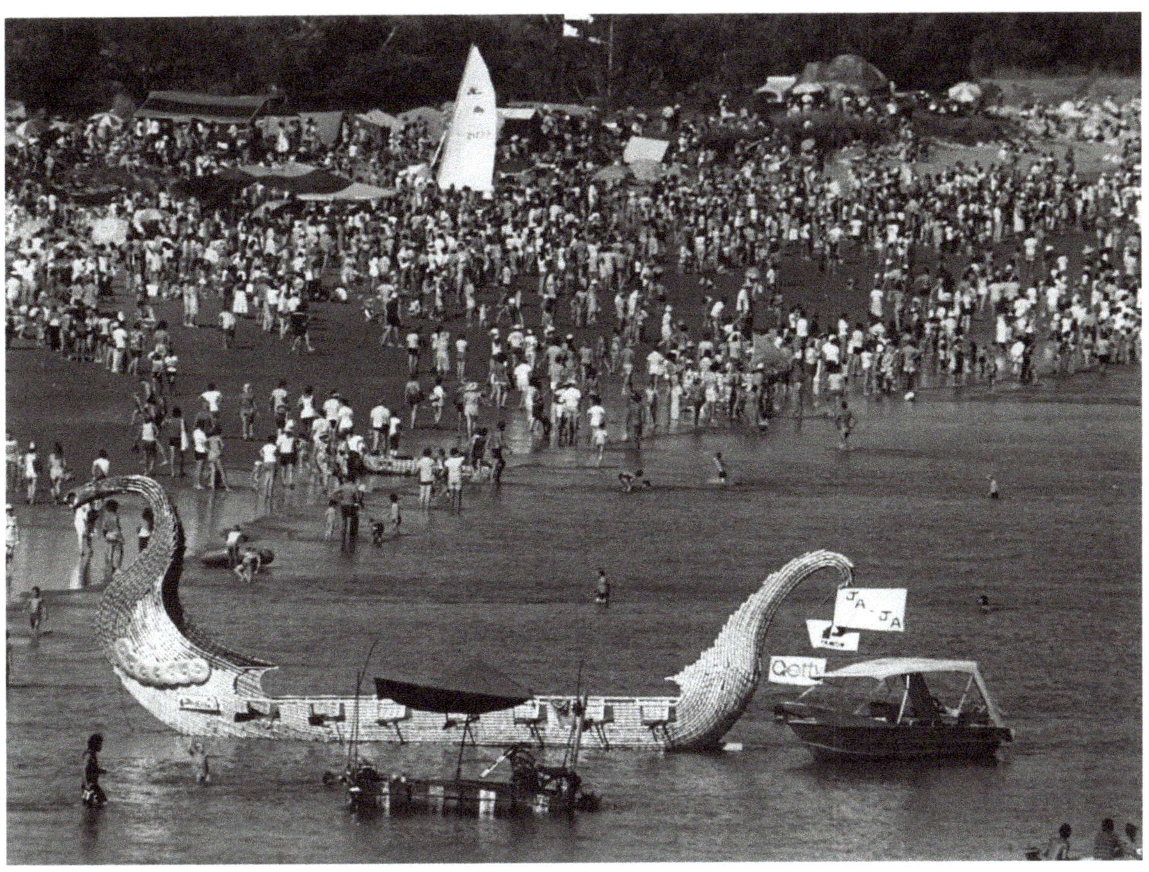

Mindil Beach, Back to Darwin Festival, Beer Can Regatta, 27 May 1978. (Unknown, NTAS, GPC, NTRS 3822-P1 Folder 23 Beer Can Regatta 1978.)

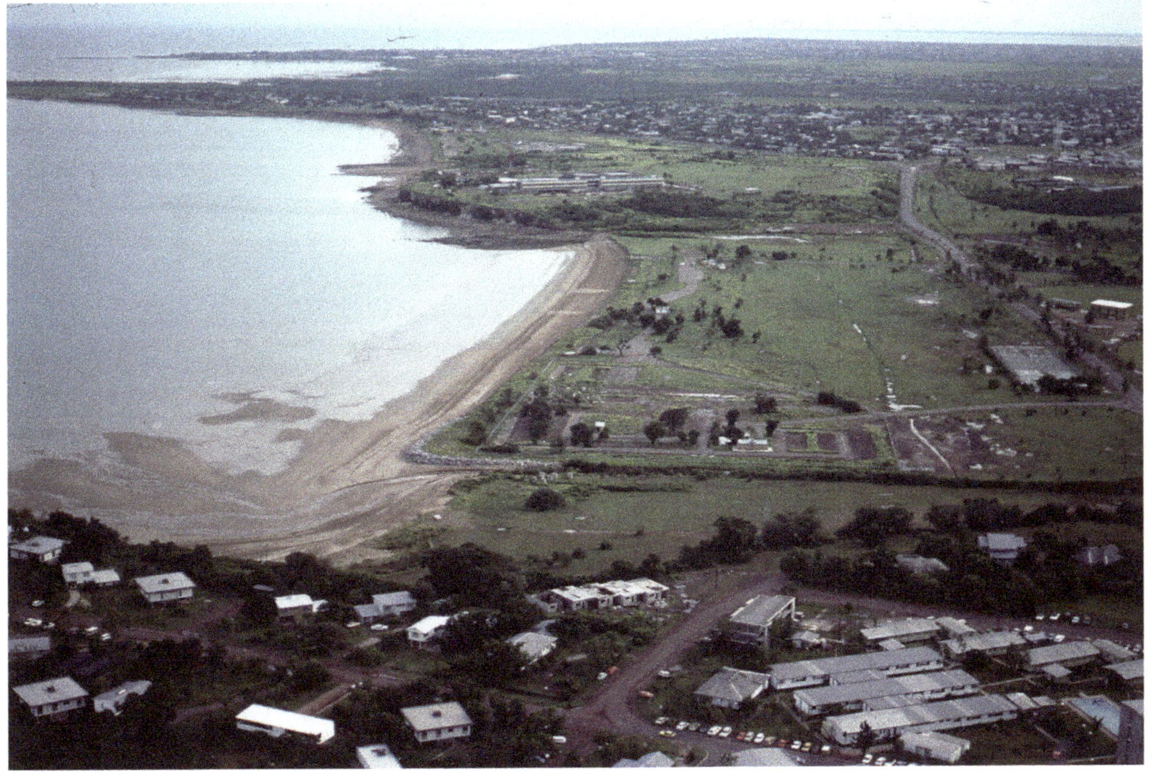

Mindil Beach, c1980. (Wiedemann, A., NTAS, GPC, NTRS 3822-P3 Darwin Aerials Suburbs Slide 116.)

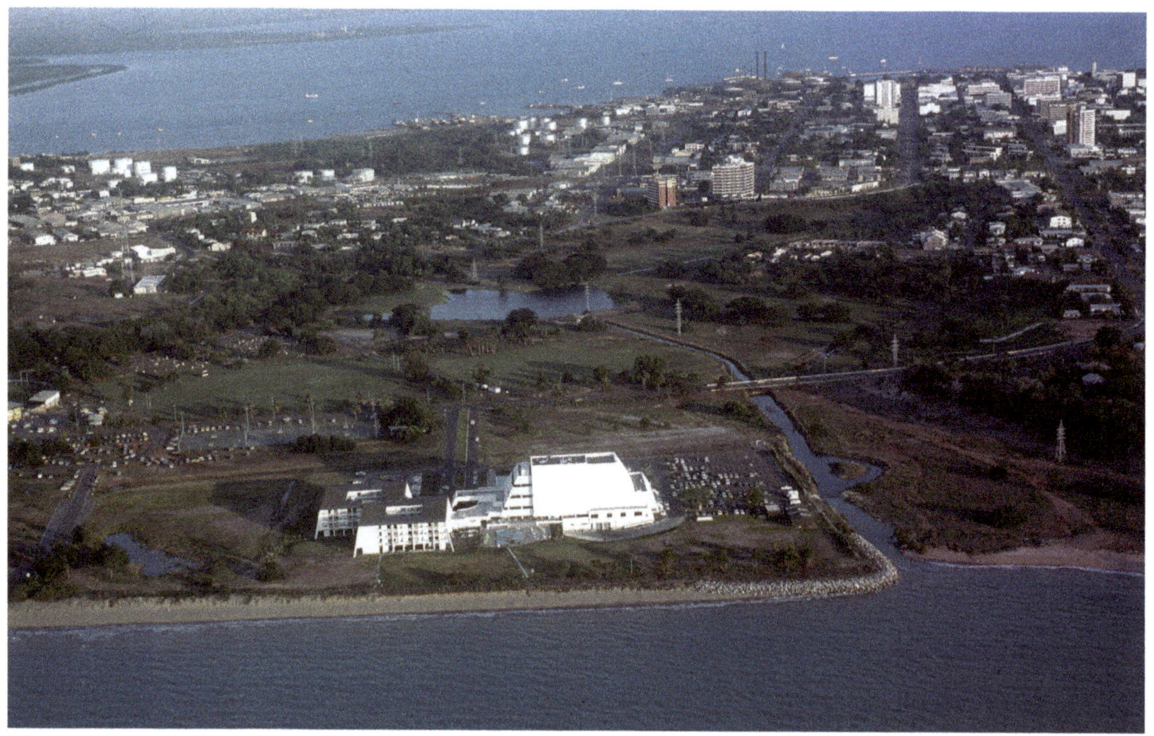

Mindil Beach, c1980. (Wiedemann, A., NTAS, GPC, NTRS 3822-P3 Darwin Aerials Suburbs Slide 116.)

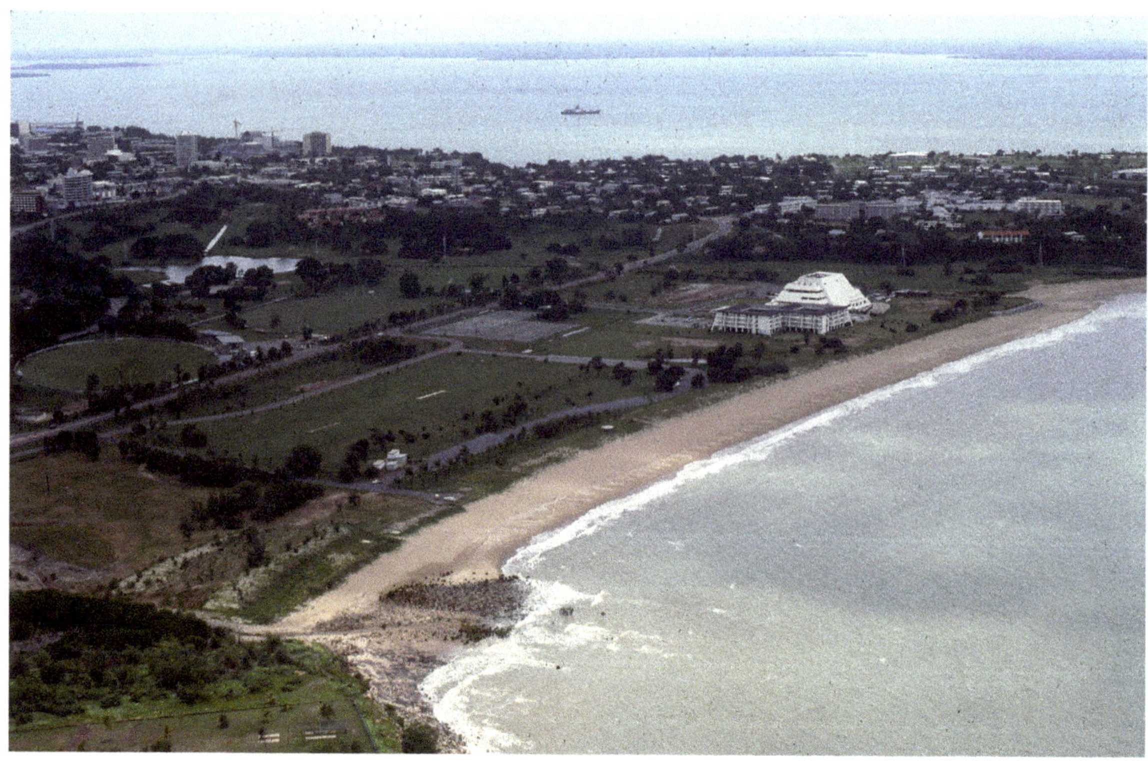

Mindil Beach, 1984. (Unknown, NTAS, GPC, NTRS 3822-P3 Beaches & Coastlines Slide LF9.)

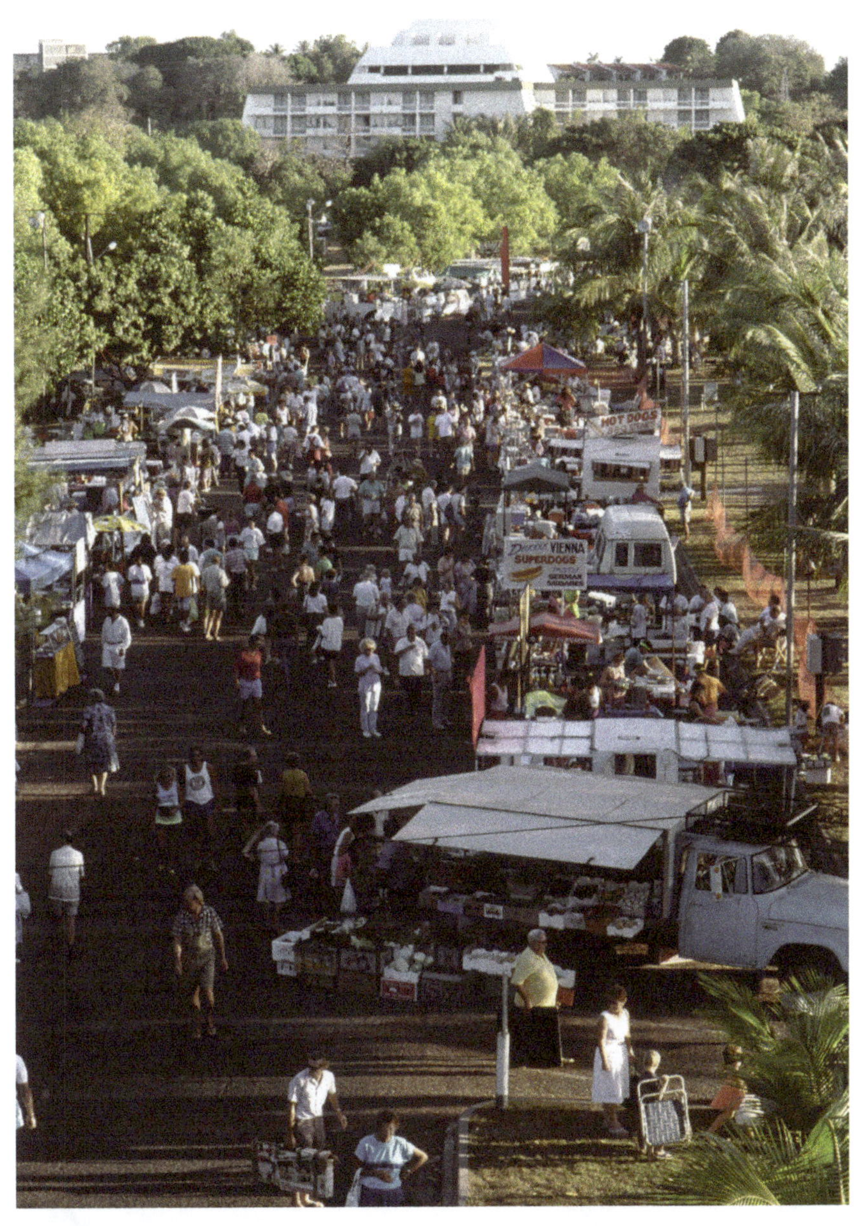

Mindil Beach Markets, 1991. (Unknown, NAA, Photograph, A6135, K29/7/91/111.)

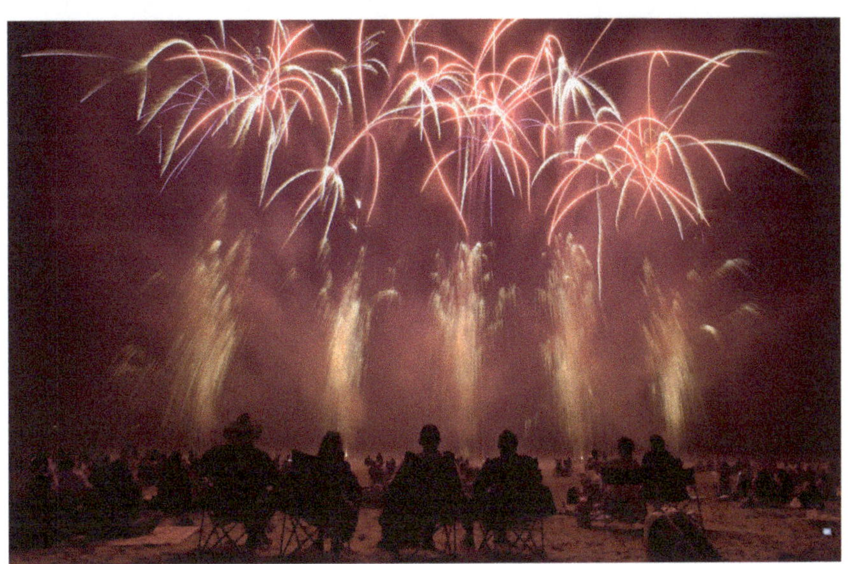

Mindil Beach, Territory Day, c1 July 2016. (Eve, P., Tourism NT, Tourism NT Collection, 100435-3.)

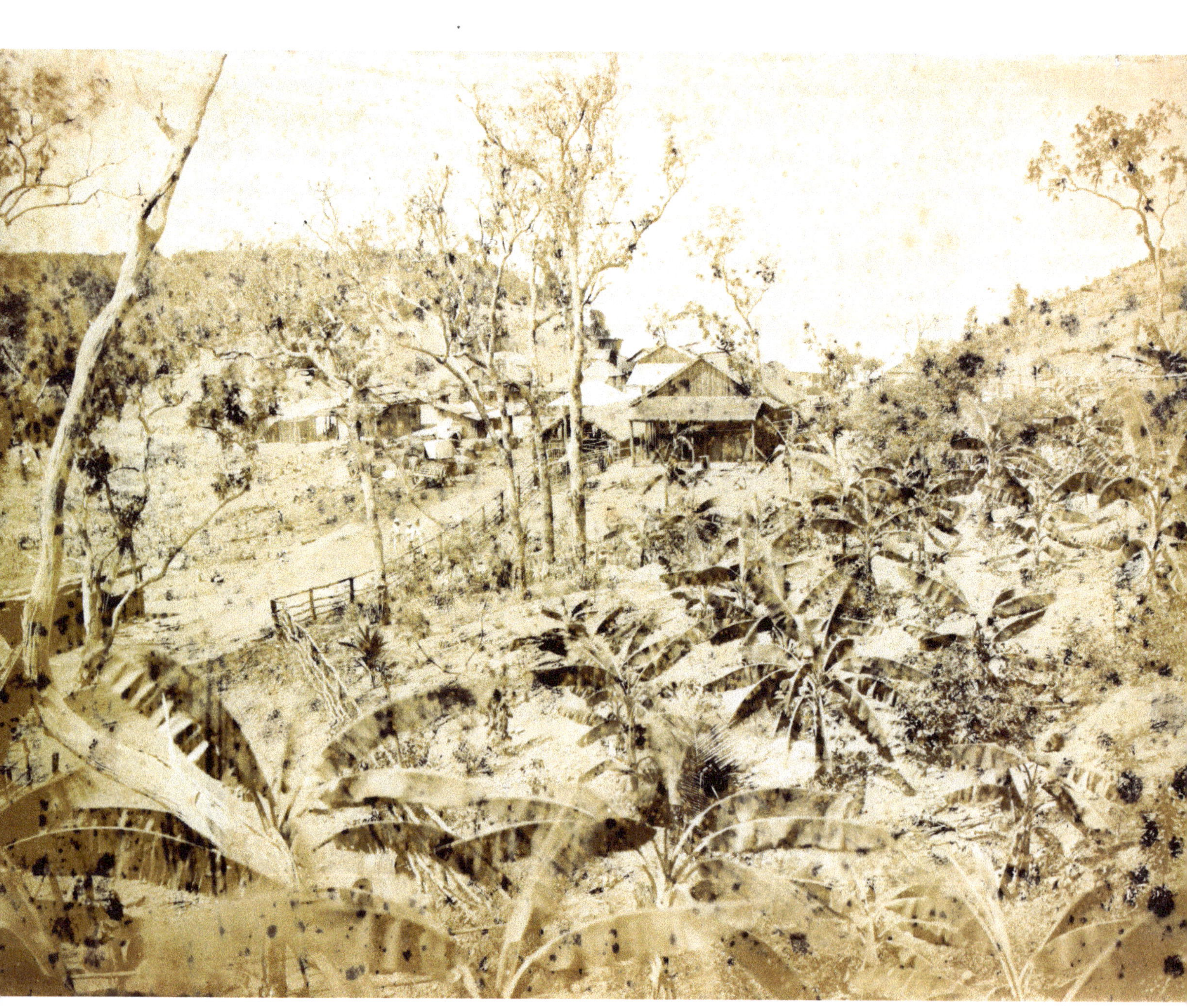

Government Garden, Francis Bay, overlooking the Surveyors Camp at Fort Hill, c 1870. (Sweet, S.W., SLV, Views of Darwin and Roper River, N.T. [picture], H10704.)

Chapter 10

The Botanic Gardens & Gardens Oval

The area stretching inland from Mindil Beach to the Gardens Golf Course and the George Brown Botanic Gardens is one of Darwin's major parklands and recreation areas. In the early years of European settlement up to World War II much of the area was mangrove swamp and tidal back waters. In the early 20th Century some of the swamp became a sanitary reserve for the town's sewage. In the post World War II period, as Darwin developed, the area was reclaimed and developed into the parklands of today.

The George Brown Botanic Gardens have not always been on their current site. The first Government Garden was established at Doctor's Gully soon after the South Australian survey party arrived in 1869. Due to a fire through the area the Government Garden moved to a site near the Surveyors Camp on the foreshore of Frances Bay near Fort Hill. The garden at Doctor's Gully was replanted in 1870 and another garden was also established in 1871 at the corner of Greene Terrace and Daly Street on the main road to Fred's Pass, now the Stuart Highway.[1]

In 1878 Maurice Holtze, was appointed Acting Government Gardener in charge of the Botanical Gardens.[2] The Holtze family would be connected to the Botanic Gardens until 1913. In 1879 the Government Garden moved to a larger location at Fannie Bay near the Fannie Bay Gaol. The site was not well chosen due to poor soil and water supply so in the early 1880s the Government moved the gardens again. Maurice Holtze selected a site near Mindil Beach mid way between Palmerston and Fannie Bay. By 1886 Holtze had relocated many of the plants from the Fannie Bay Garden. The new gardens like those before were not initially designed as a recreational area but as 'experimental gardens' to demonstrate the agricultural potential of the Northern Territory. Many experimental tropical crops such as sugar cane, coffee, rice and cotton were grown successfully in the gardens under the supervision of Holtze. However, his results could not be reproduced on a commercial scale anywhere in the Territory. Maurice Holtze was curator of the Botanic Gardens until 1891 when he was appointed Director of the Botanic Gardens in Adelaide. He was succeeded by his son Nicholas who served in the role until his premature death in 1913.

Since the Botanical Gardens were moved to their current location on Garden's Road, they were a cool lush haven for Darwin residents. Due to a lack of water and poor stony soils in the town area private gardens were very difficult to grow and were not a feature of the town until reticulated water was available after World War II. All manner of social events from picnics to soap box derbies, sports and Aboriginal Corroborees were held at the gardens over the years.

A major addition to the Botanic Gardens was the construction of a sound shell which was completed in 1965. The Amphitheatre, as it is known today, was a popular venue and the only one in Darwin for many years that could cater for large crowds. In 2000 the former Weslyan Methodist Church, originally

1 Bisa. *Remember Me Kindly*, p.29-35.
2 *NTTG*, 20 July 1878.

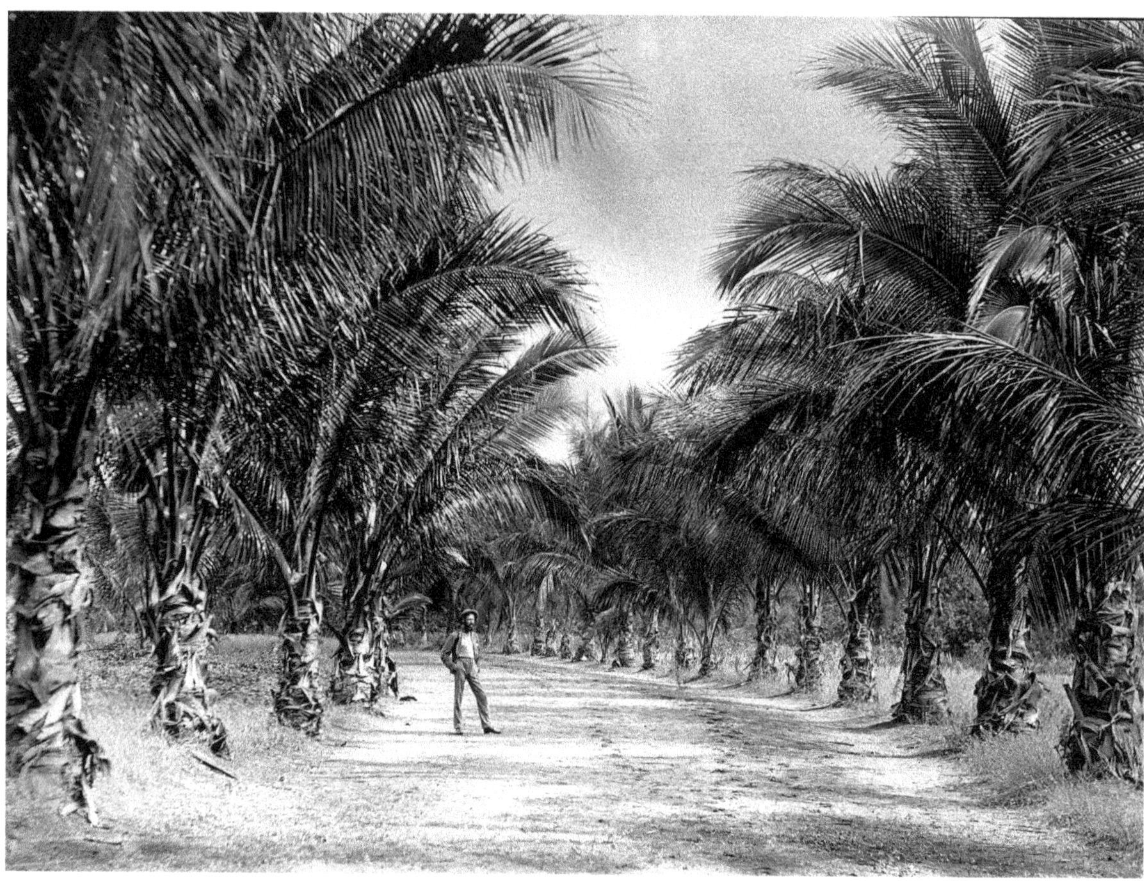

Botanic Gardens, c1900. (Bleeser, F., NLA, Florenz Bleeser Collection, PIC/9981/138.)

constructed in Knuckey Street, Darwin, in 1897 was moved to the Botanic Gardens and is now a cafe. Prefabricated in Adelaide, South Australia, and transported to Darwin it is one of the few remaining examples of colonial era architecture in Darwin.

The Botanic Gardens are named in honour of George Brown who cared for the Gardens from 1970 to 1990. Brown's tenure included the restoration of the Gardens following Cyclone Tracy when 78 percent of the trees and shrubs were lost along with the nursery, fern house and original curator's cottage. Brown was also credited with playing a key role in the post Cyclone Tracy greening of Darwin.[3] After his career at the Botanic Gardens he served as Darwin's Lord Mayor 1992-2002.

The Botanic Gardens were the main development in the area, but not the only one. In 1913 the Darwin Maritime Coastal Station (VID) was constructed on what is now the Golf Course on Gardens Road near the intersection of Hood Terrace and McMinn Street. The Darwin station was part of a national network of 19 coastal radio stations designed in response to the sinking of the *RMS Titanic*. Some categories of ships were required to maintain continuous radio watch monitored by shore stations. The radio station or Wireless Station as it was known locally, was also recognition of Darwin's strategic location. It was taken over by the Australian Navy during World War I and again in 1942 when it transmitted messages to the Darwin naval base, *HMAS Coonawarra*. The Wireless Station ceased operations in June 1950.[4]

A 'wireless' station of another kind was established on Gardens Hill adjacent to the Botanic Gardens when the Australian

3 NTG, Heritage Branch, *George Brown Botanic Garden's Fact Sheet*.
4 Boland, *Know Where You Stand, 1*.

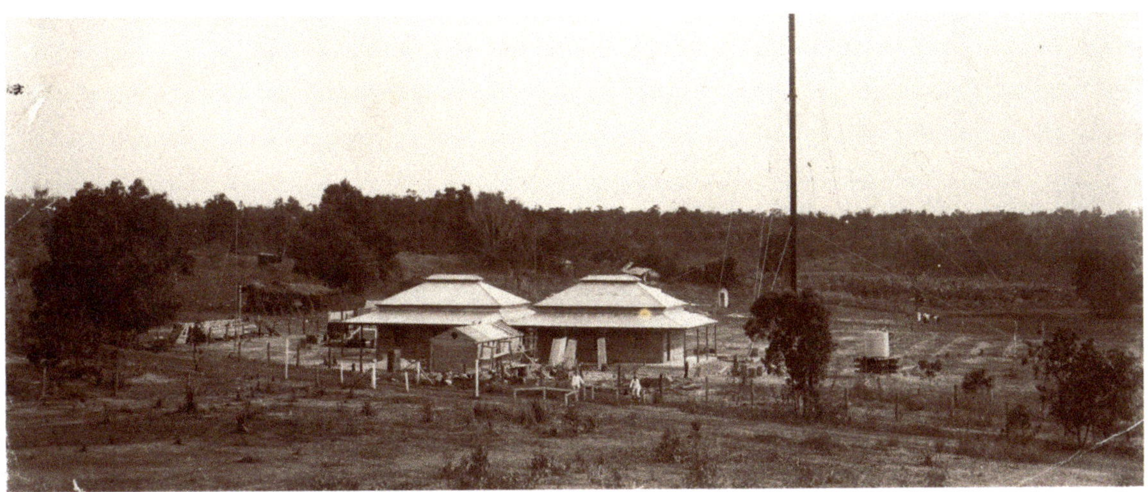

Darwin Coastal Radio Service under construction, 1913. (Unknown, MAGNT, Waldron Collection, PIC058.)

Broadcast Corporation station 5DR commenced transmissions in March 1947. The site was later known as Blake Street. 5DR was originally an Australian Army Amenities Service, created in 1943, to broadcast to armed services to maintain morale. During wartime it was located at Lee Point on Darwin's northern beaches. ABC 5DR and later 8DR transmitted from Blake Street site until 1967 when it transferred to its current location in Nichols place (Cavenagh Street).[5]

In 1919, 23 acres of land between the Botanic Gardens and the Myilly Point escarpment were set aside as a sanitation reserve for the towns sewage. 'Night-soil' collected from Darwin's outside toilets was collected and dumped in the reserve and covered with sand from Mindil Beach. During this era many Darwin residents were reliant on 'Flaming Furies'; outdoor toilets which required the pit to be dowsed in kerosene and set alight from time to time. It was not until the 1950s and the development of a modern sewage system that this service was no longer required.

Gardens Road Cemetery was also opened in 1919 after the closure of the Palmerston Cemetery on Goyder Road. It remained in use until 1970. A visit to the cemetery provides a glimpse into the town's history during this period. The diversity of cultures interred at the cemetery tells you just how multicultural Darwin has been throughout its history.[6]

The shift of sporting activities from the Esplanade Oval to The Gardens Oval in 1953 was an indicator of the growth and development of Darwin in the post war period. The Esplanade Oval had been the main football ground since 1916 but it was unpopular with players because it was more gravel than grass resulting in players enduring painful cuts and grazes every game.[7] The first game played on Gardens Oval was 20th October 1953. There were some teething problems with Gardens Oval. The first Northern Territory Football League grand final played there in 1953-54 between Waratahs and Buffaloes was almost cancelled because the ground was a quagmire.[8] Such were the drainage problems that bait fish were sighted around the ground on a monsoonal high tide![9] Fortunately the ground was constantly improved over the years to become the scene of many football triumphs. Despite the

5 *5DR (8DR) Darwin at Blake Street, 1946-1965*, See also Woodrow, *The Broadcaster*, 18. Parker, Phillip, Personal communication, 18 May 2018.

6 NTG, Heritage Register, *Gardens Road Cemetery*.

7 Felsenthal, Ian. Personal communication, November 2015. Ian was Works and Housing Football Club captain coach in 1952-53.

8 *NTN*, 9 March 1954.

9 Bob Elix, Personal communication, 12 January 2016.

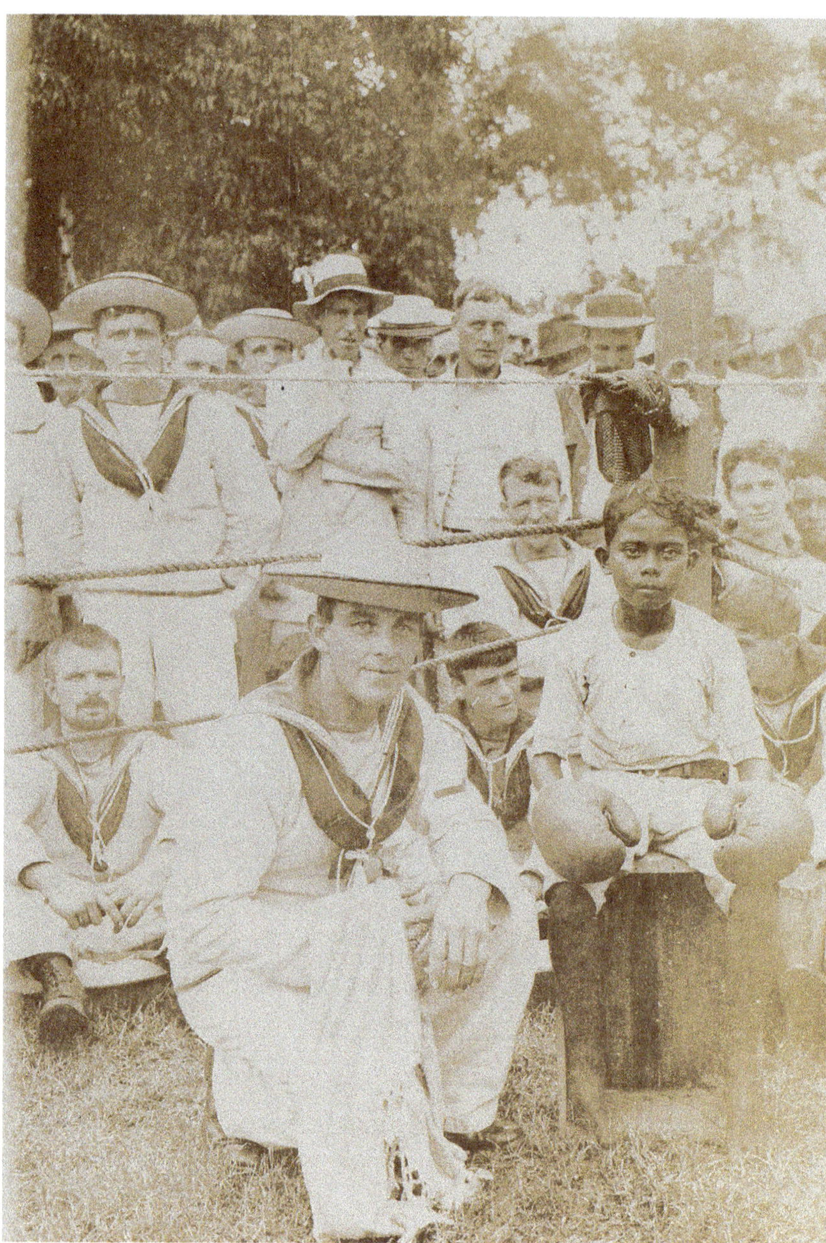

Botanic Gardens, boxing match between Ponto Cubillo and 'Young Nelson' during visit of *H.M.S Cornwall*, February 1916. (Unknown, E.D.W.S Donnison Collection, LNSW, ML MSS 890/3/02224.)

construction of a modern football stadium in Darwin's northern suburbs at Marrara in 1990 many Darwin locals still love watching sport at the Garden's Oval, which must be one of the most picturesque in Australia.

The extensive parkland visible today combines the Botanic Gardens, Garden's Oval and the Gardens Park Golf Course. The golf course, which opened in 1970, was not always the green belt it is today. The area included a garbage dump which was closed in 1963 when Darwin City council drained and levelled the area. The site was named 'Palmerston Park' in 1966 when discussions also began to establish a municipal golf course.[10]

The Botanic Gardens and Gardens Park are a verdant haven in the centre of the city. They provide an important recreation area and green space for locals and visitors alike. Like all of Darwin its history may not be immediately obvious but closer inspection reveals a rich social and cultural legacy.

10 Howison, Personal communication, 10 May 2018.

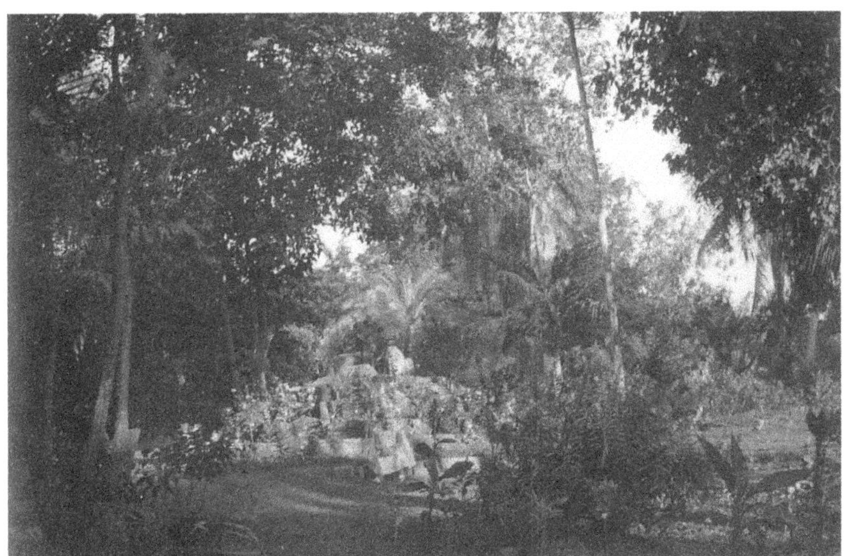

Botanic Gardens, c1939. (Garrard, NTAS, Major & Mrs Garrard Collection, NTRS 1204 Item 21.)

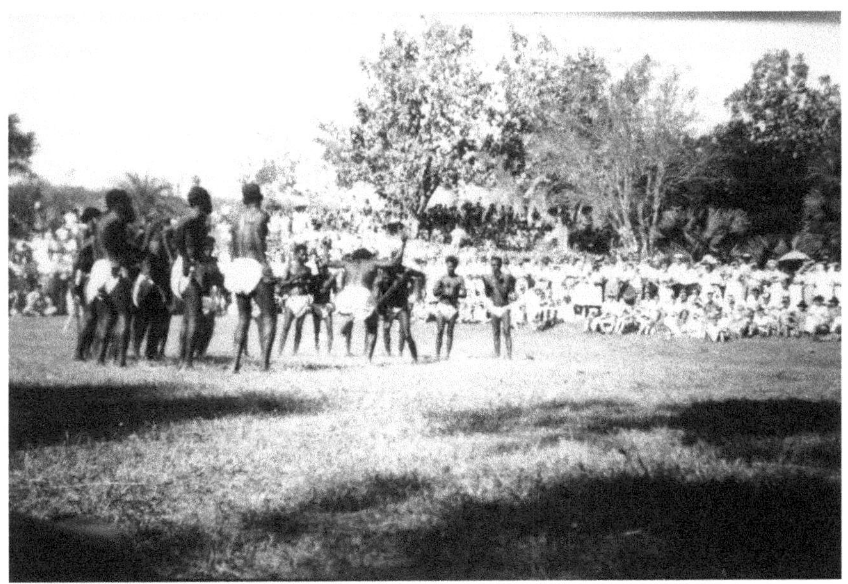

Botanic Gardens, Aboriginal Corroboree, 1949. (Harford, B.P., NTAS, B.P. Harford Collection, NTRS 1299 Item 100.)

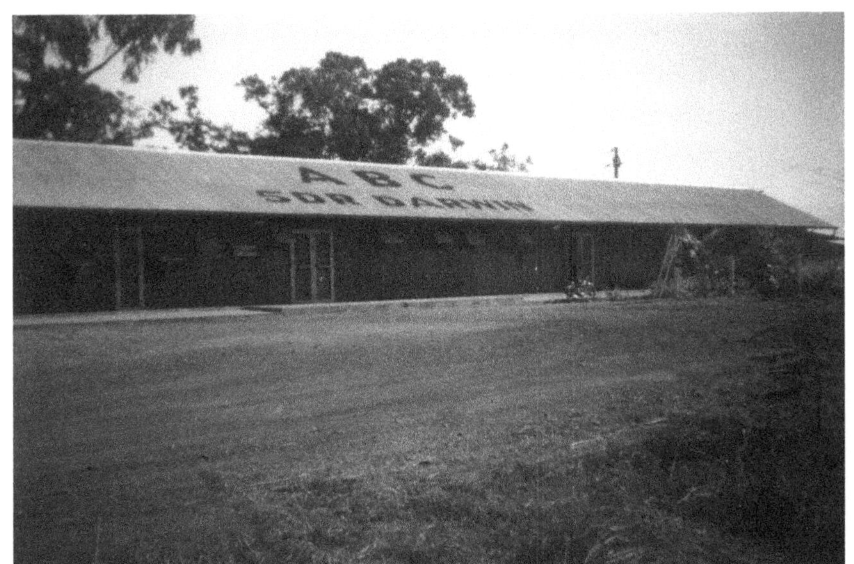

ABC radio studios, Blake Street, 1949. (Harford, B.P., NTAS, B. Harford Collection, NTRS 1299 Item 62.)

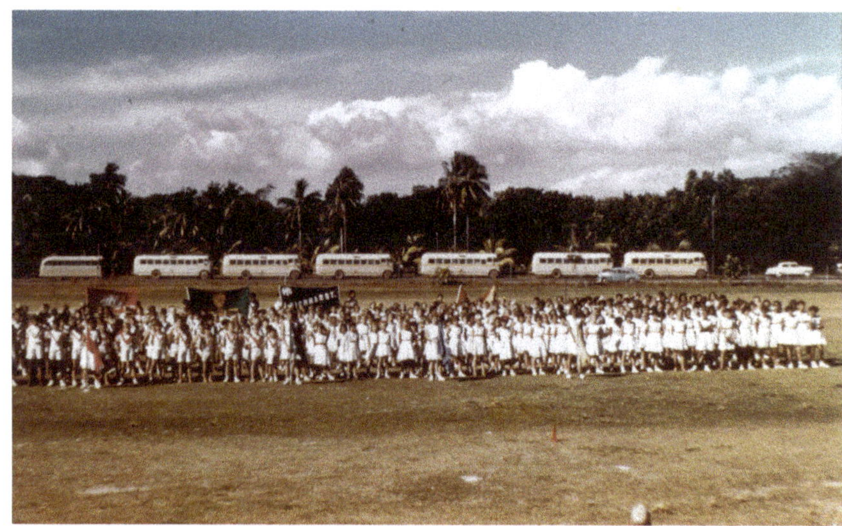

Gardens Oval, Darwin High School sports day, 1957. (Peck, D., NTL, N.C. Pearce Collection, PH0088/0137.)

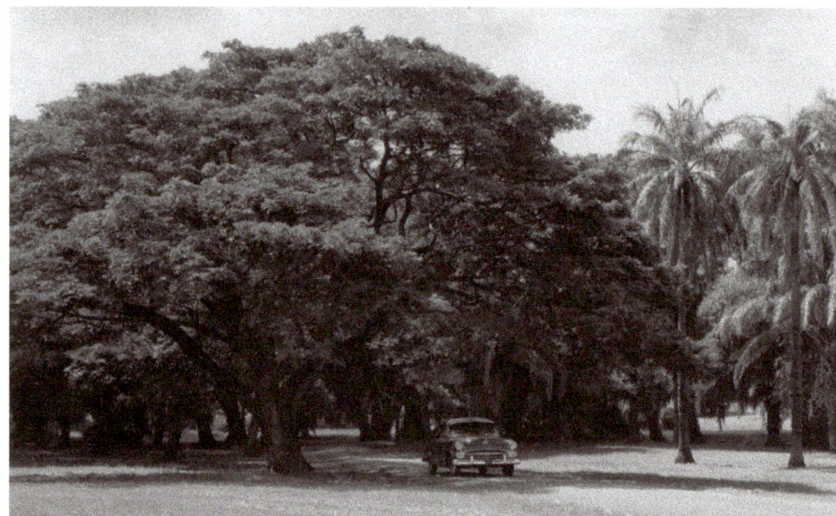

Darwin Botanic Gardens, 1957. (Unknown, QANTAS, Heritage Collection, N/A.)

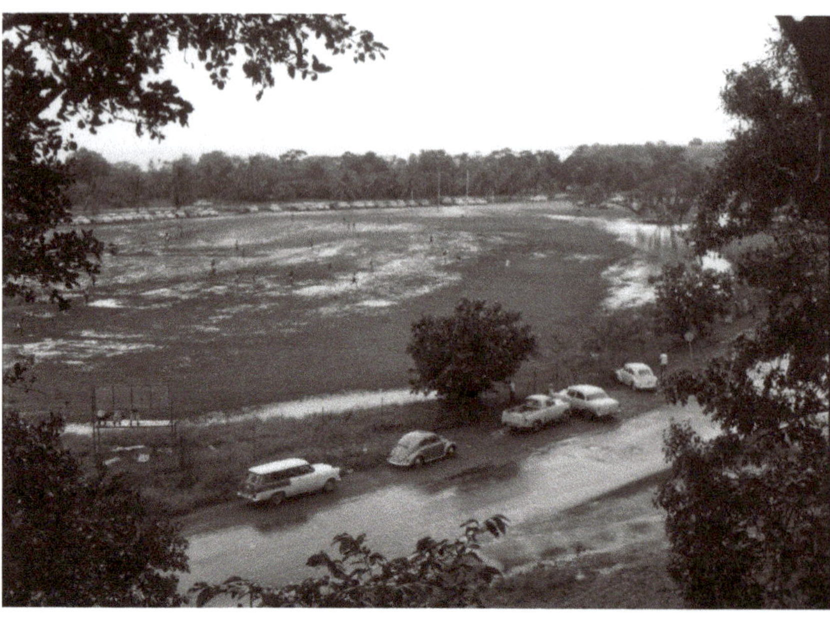

Gardens Oval, c1960s. (Unknown, NTL, NT Government Photographers Collection, PH0093/0036.)

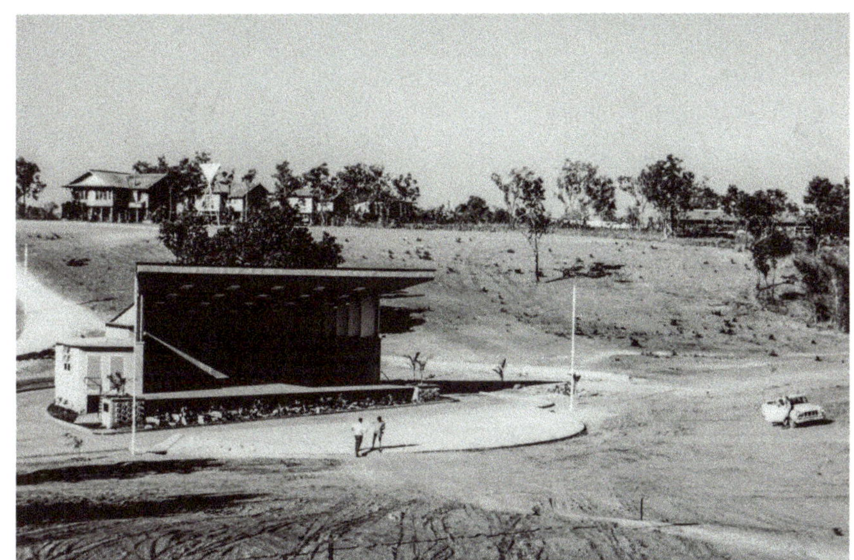

Botanic Gardens, Amphitheatre, 1965. (Unknown, NTL, David Veal Collection, PH0258/0033.)

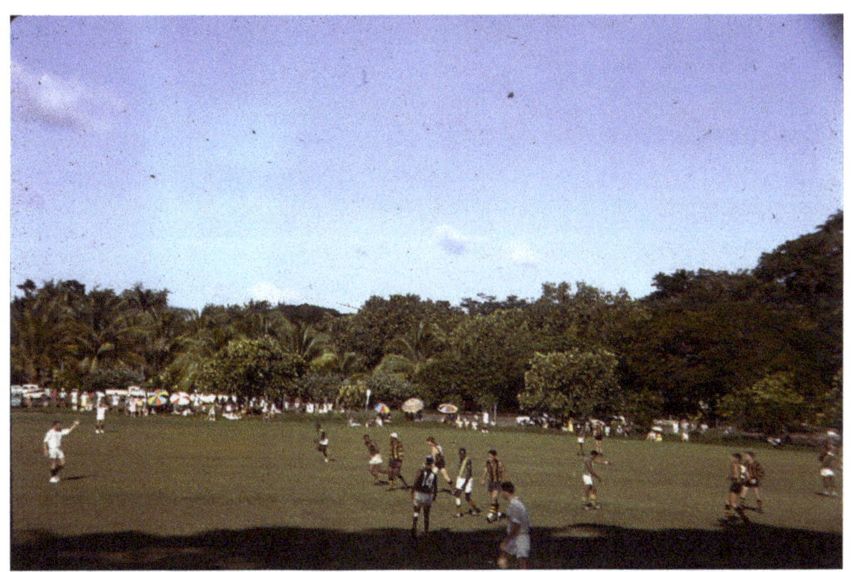

Football match, Gardens Oval, c1966. (Unknown, NTAS, H, Graham Collection, NTRS 3406/P1 Item 47.)

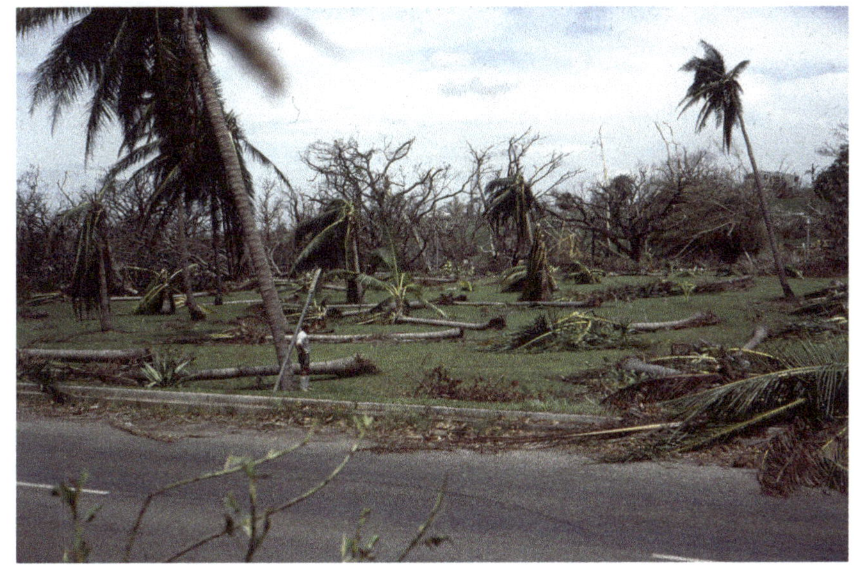

Botanic Gardens, post Cyclone Tracy, 1974. (Adams, L., NTAS, Leo Adams Collection, NTRS 3128/P1 Item 23.)

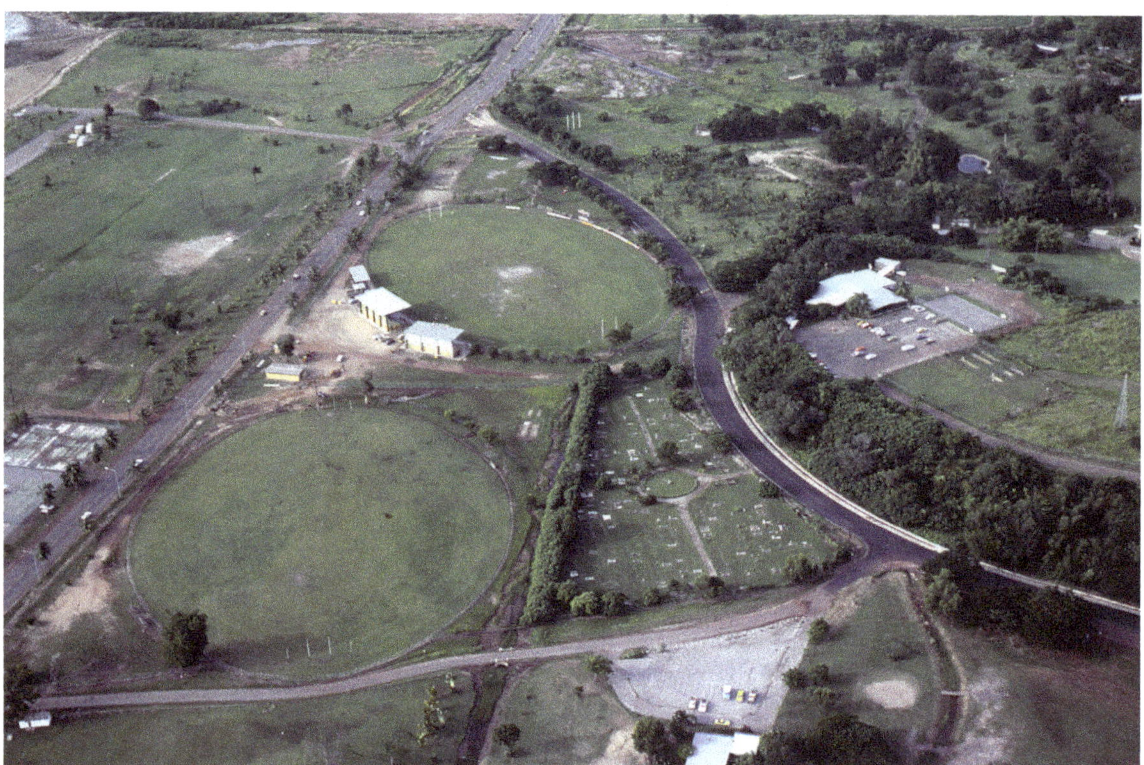

Gardens Oval, Cemetery and Botanic Gardens, 1980. (Unknown, NTAS, GPC, NTRS 3822-P3 Darwin Aerials Suburbs Slide 89.)

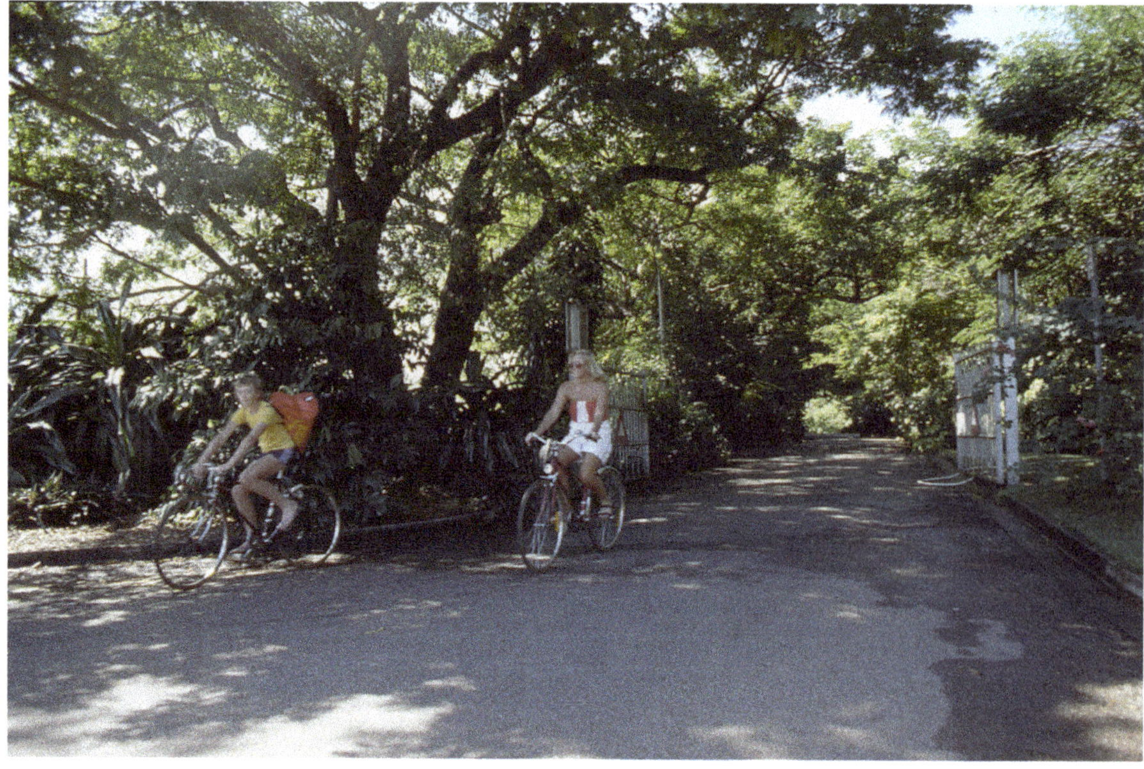

Botanic Gardens, 1981. (Unknown, NTAS, GPC, NTRS 3822-P3 Botanic Gardens Slide 6.)

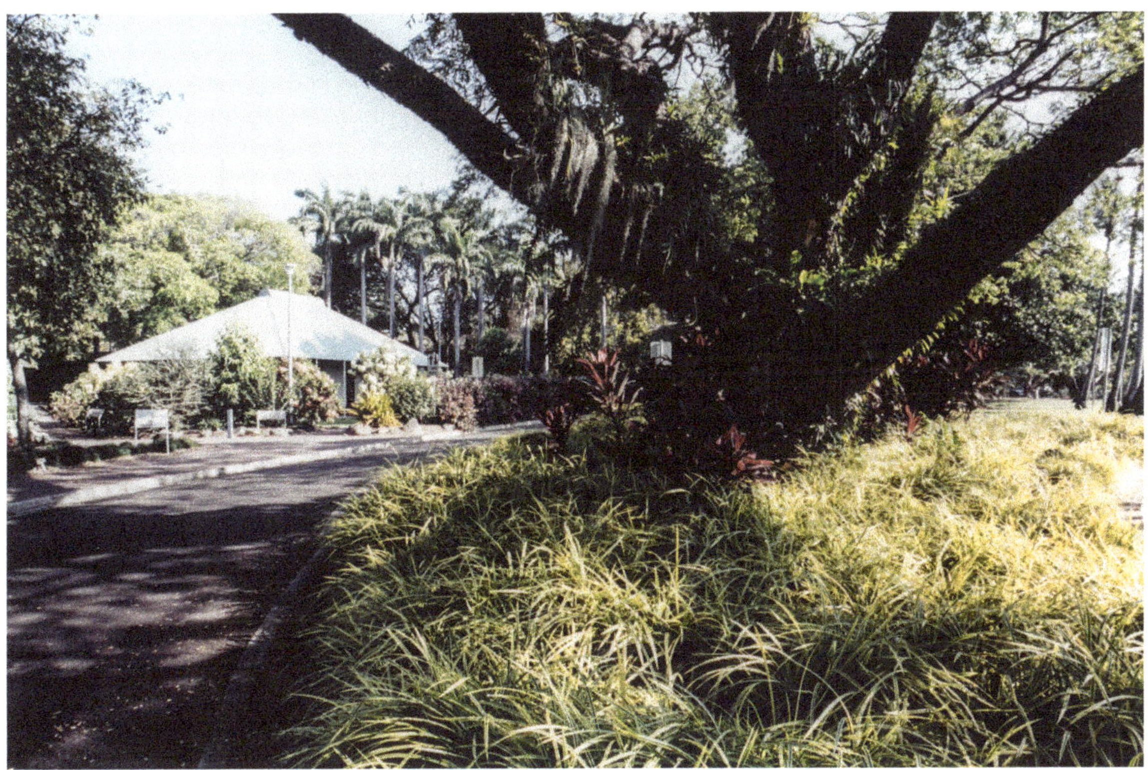

George Brown, Botanic Gardens, 2002. The former Weslyan Methodist Church, now a cafe, is in the background. (Carrington, S., NTL, Darwin 2002 Collection, PH0757/0227.)

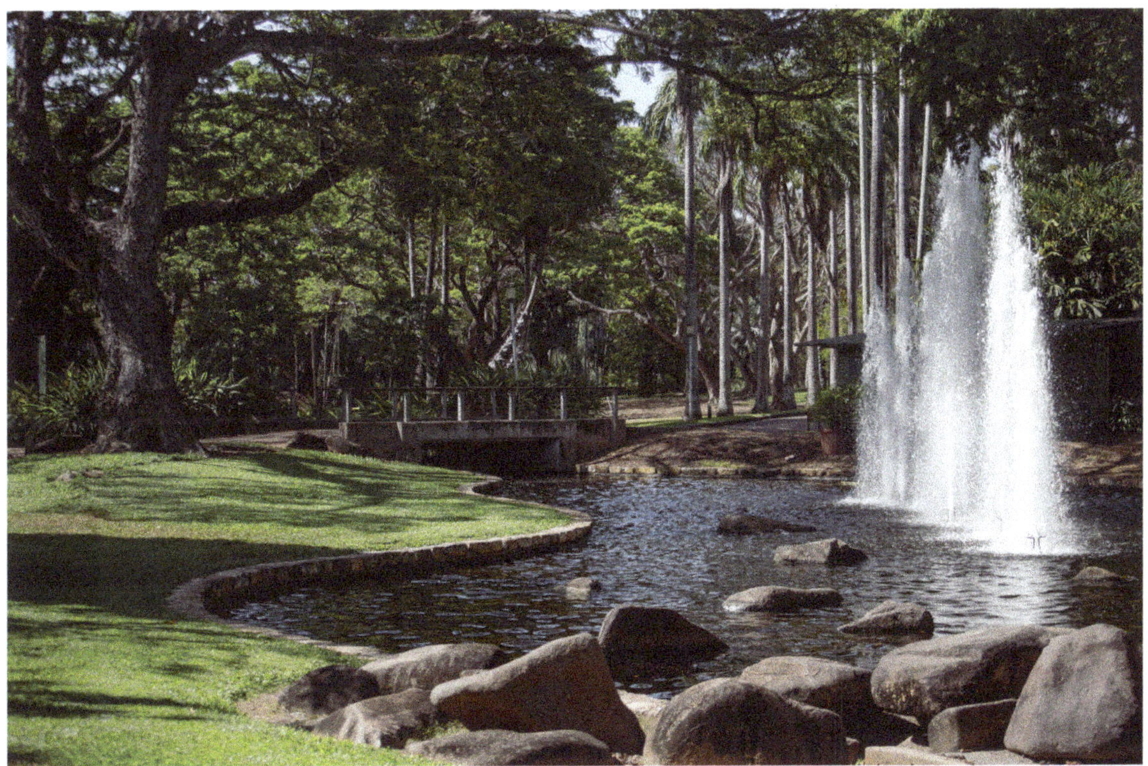

George Brown, Botanic Gardens, c2015. (McNaught, S., Tourism NT, Tourism NT Collection, 121228-2.)

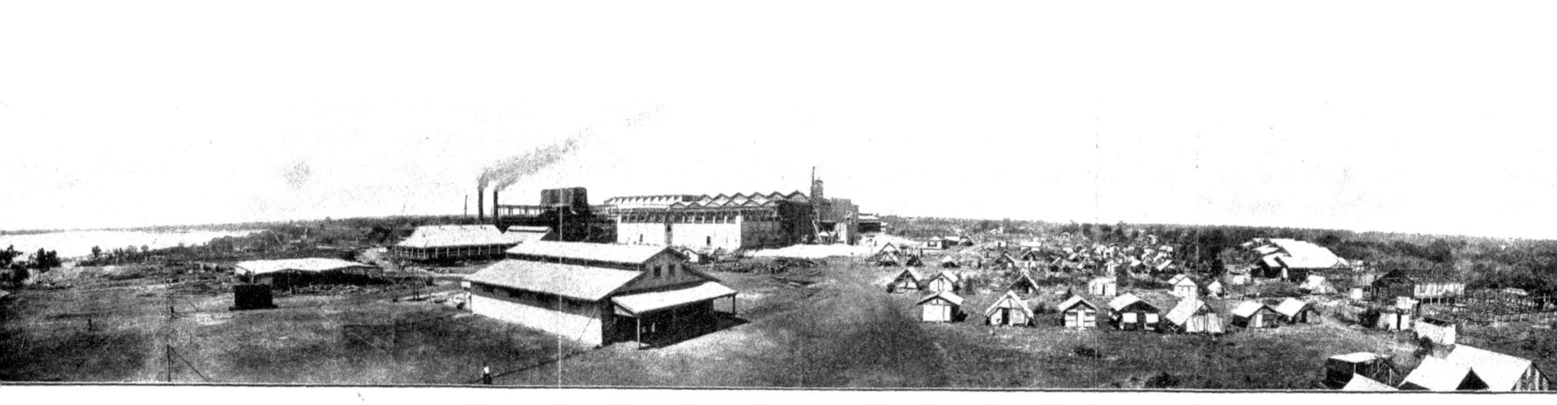

Panoramic View of Freezing Works at Paraparap, with Retail Grocery Store in Foreground.

Vesteys Meatworks, Bullocky Point, 1915. (*NT Administrators Report*, 1915.)

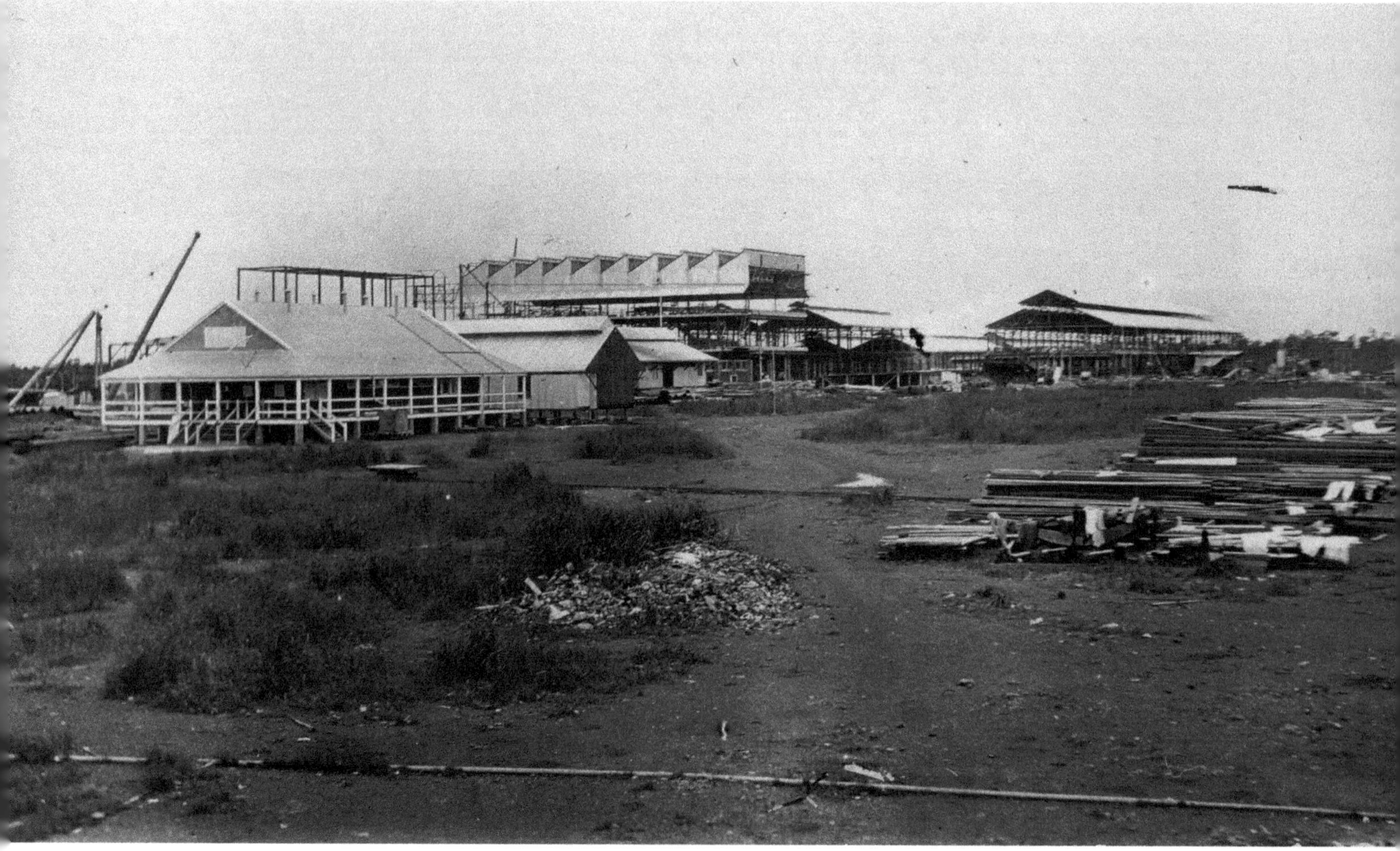

Vesteys Meatworks under construction, Bullocky Point, c1915. (Unknown, LNSW, E.D.W.S Donnison Collection, ML MSS 890/3/0191.)

Chapter 11

Bullocky Point

Although Bullocky Point is believed to have been named during the period when Vesteys Meatworks dominated the site during World War I the name appears on plans from the 1880's.[1] Up until 1914 the site remained undeveloped being relatively distant from the road linking the town to Fannie Bay Gaol. Although there were some market gardens in the vicinity of Bullocky Point and what is now Vesteys beach, the area was rarely mentioned.[2] This all changed dramatically in 1914.

In April 1914, Vestey Brothers (known as Vesteys), a British multinational meat conglomerate, agreed to establish a meat-processing and freezing works in Darwin. Negotiations to establish the meatworks began in 1912. It was hoped that the massive project would provide some much needed stimulus to the Northern Territory economy that had been stagnant since the turn of the century.[3] The agreement to develop the meatworks included the passing of the *Pine Creek to Katherine River Railway Act 1913*, which further boosted the economy. The construction and operation of Vesteys meatworks, from 1914 to 1919, transformed the social, political and economic landscape of Darwin. In a sense it was the Northern Territory's Industrial Revolution. The industrialisation of the Darwin workforce resulted in a trebling of the White population (concentrated in Darwin) from 1173 in 1911 to 3767 in 1918.[4]

Establishing Vesteys Meatworks resulted in an economic boom. The cost of construction was almost one million pounds. The plant covered ten acres of floor space, a four storey accommodation block for 300 single men, two hundred huts for married couples and massive water tanks that remain today as a high school gymnasium. The refrigeration section capacity was nearly a million cubic feet.[5] A railway spur was built to the plant. Vesteys opened in April 1917. In its first season of fourteen weeks 19,000 cattle were slaughtered. However, the life of Vestey's Meatworks was short. It closed its operations in 1920 plunging Darwin into economic depression. Although it opened again briefly in 1925 the site remained derelict until 1932 when the single men's accommodation was used for temporary accommodation by the newly created military unit, The Darwin Detachment.

In the 1930s Bullocky point played a brief role in a 'Golden Age' of Australian Aviation history. From the early 1930s to 1940 the QANTAS rest house on Bullocky Point provided accommodation to its passengers and crew while in Darwin. Situated at the tip of Bullocky Point with some of the finest views of Darwin Harbour, the two renovated elevated houses were originally built in 1914 to accommodate Vesteys Executive Manager and General Manager. The rest house was in use by 1935-36 to service passengers

1 NTG, Place Names Register, *Bullocky Point.*
2 Mitchell. *Bullocky Point*, 27.
3 Alcorta. *Darwin Rebellion 1911–1919*, 19.
4 Northern Territory, *Report of the Administrator, 1918*, 15.
5 Gibson, Eve. *Beyond the Boundary*, 23.

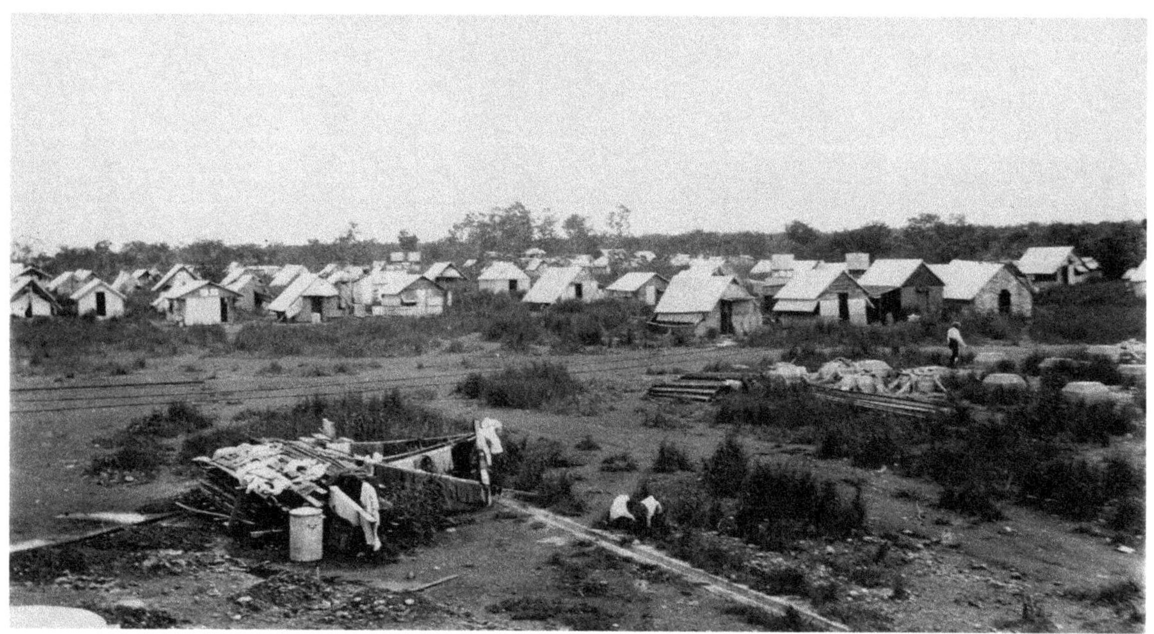

Vesteys Meatworks, workers camp, Bullocky Point, c1915. (Unknown, LNSW, E.D.W.S Donnison Collection, ML MSS 890/3/0190.)

and crew on the De Havilland 86 passenger service between Brisbane and Singapore. In 1938 the De Havillands were replaced by Short Empire C Class flying boats. The QANTAS Empire flying boats were a first class only service which had lounge chair style seating, a promenade cabin, a gallery cabin to take in the views and a wine cellar. Passengers were served by uniformed stewards in the fashion of luxury ocean liners. The service did not travel at night and so required overnight accommodation.[6] Upon arrival in Darwin Harbour the flying boats would anchor near Stokes Hill Wharf where passengers would disembark into tenders which conveyed them to shore. Passengers would then travel by vehicle to Bullocky Point. The QANTAS rest house on Bullocky Point was superseded as flight staff and passenger accommodation by the Hotel Darwin when it opened in 1940. International passenger services from Darwin ceased in February 1942.[7]

In the build up to World War II Vesteys Meatworks site became accommodation for many military servicemen despite its dilapidated and primitive conditions. In 1939 the newly formed Darwin Mobile Force set up a base there, as did RAAF personnel. Commandeered by armed service personnel they not only used existing buildings and accommodation they also constructed their own camps on the Vesteys site.[8] Such was the development that by the war's end the site contained over three hundred and fifty dwellings in the form of cottages and dormitories.[9] Vesteys was not only an accommodation area but served a number of purposes during the war including a supply and transport depot,[10] field bakery, field butchery,[11] and a reconnaissance and survey photographic darkroom laboratory.[12]

In the post World War II period the Vestey's site became home for many returning civilians and was used by the Northern Territory public

6 Sydney Museums, *Flying Boats: Sydney's Golden Age of Aviation*. www.
7 Crotty, David, Personal communication, 31 July.
8 Gibson, Eve. *Beyond the Boundary*, 39.
9 Mitchell. *Bullocky Point*, 30.
10 Caudle, Rex, Oral History Interview, NTAS, 2.
11 Greentree, Geoffery, Oral History Interview, NTAS, 9.
12 Tilson, Clyde, Oral History Interview, NTAS, 3.

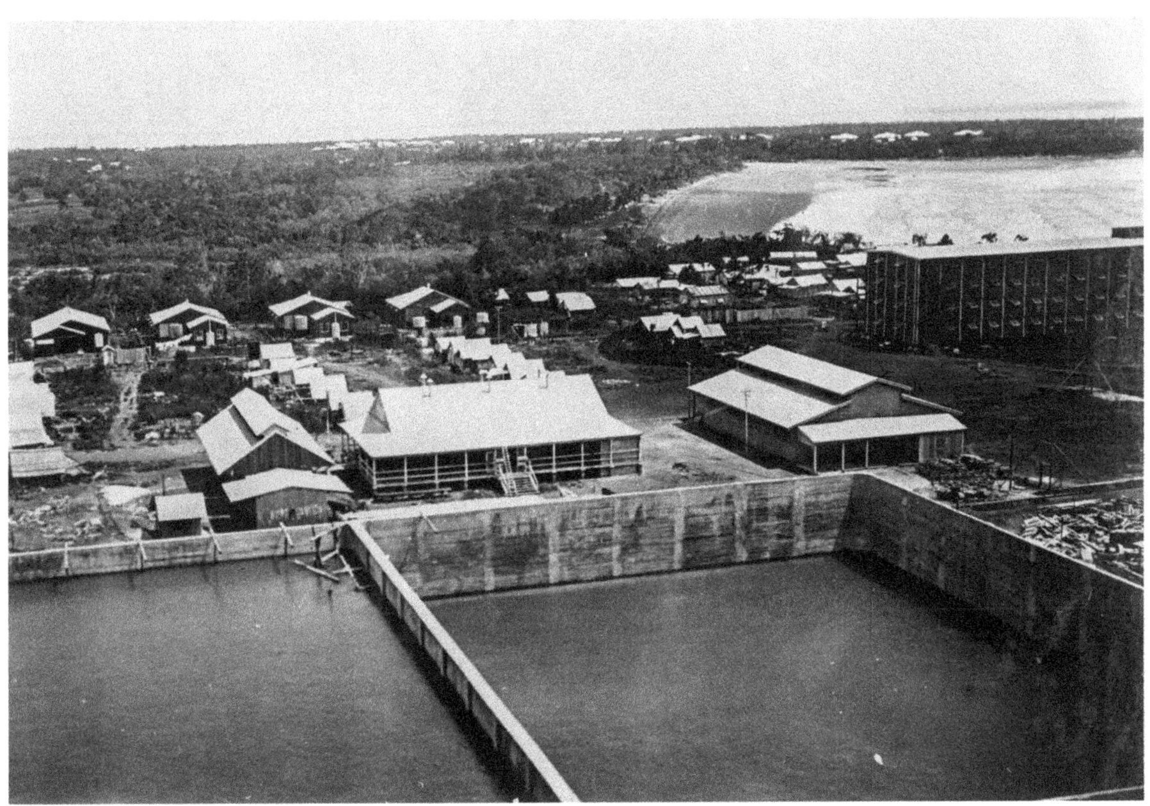

Vesteys accommodation looking towards Mindil Beach, c1920s. Note the water tanks in the foreground and single men's quarters to the right. (Unknown, NTL, Roy Edwards Collection, PH0274/0663.)

service.[13] These arrangements were temporary because the site was the subject of legal dispute between the Vestey Company and the Commonwealth.[14] Nevertheless, Vesteys became a small community in its own right with both residential and small businesses on the site. One very well known business was the DX Bakery, named after three former NT soldiers. DX was the army designation for soldiers enlisted in the Northern Territory. They took over the army bakery located at Vesteys during the war and operated on the site until 1956.[15]

By the 1950s Darwin's post war reconstruction was well underway and the population was growing rapidly. Between 1947 and 1957 Darwin's population had doubled from 5208 to 10807.[16] As the town grew so did the demand for recreational activities. In 1952 the Arafura Power Boat Association was the first civilian aquatic club established for water sports on Fannie Bay. In the 1950s and 1960s water skiing was a popular activity on Fannie Bay. The Darwin Water Ski Club has been located at Bullocky Point since the early 1960s. One of a number of clubs on Fannie Bay it is a great location to watch Darwin Harbour and take in the sunset. The Darwin Bowls and Social Club was established in 1959 on its current site.[17] One of the Northern Territory's first bowls club it was further indication of Darwin's growing and rapidly diversifying sporting community.

The old Vesteys Meatworks buildings were extensively damaged by fire in 1956. This prompted the demolition and clearance of the site in 1959 with the exception of the 'Tank' which was retained as an emergency water supply. Although initially considered

13 Mitchell, *Bullocky Point*, 33
14 Gibson, *Beyond the Boundary*, 57.
15 Richards, Joe. Oral History Interview, NTAS, 6-7.
16 Gibson. *Beyond the Boundary*, 73.
17 Darwin Bowls & Social Club, www.

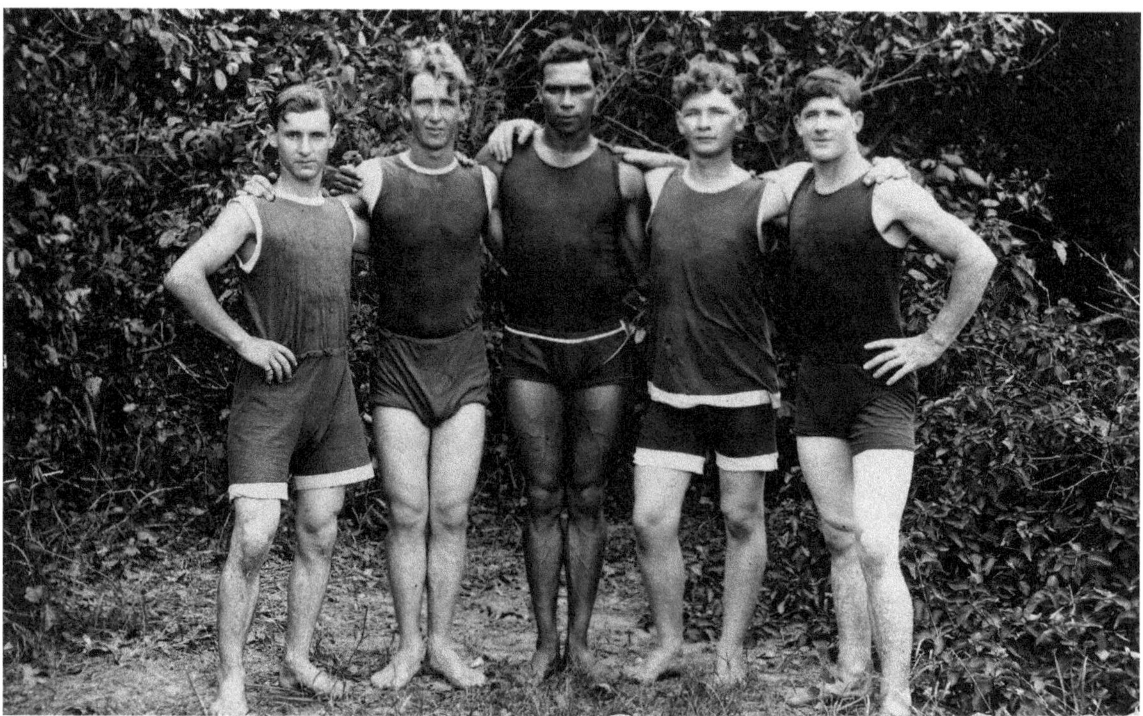

Northern Territory Swimming Championship competitors, Parap, 1919. The swimming events were held in a 'reservoir' at Vesteys Meatworks. The man in the centre of the photograph is Rueben Cooper who won the Northern Territory Swimming Championship. Cooper is an inductee of the Australian Aboriginal and Islander Sports Hall of Fame. (Unknown, E.D.W.S Donnison Collection, LNSW, ML MSS 890/3/0214.)

a beautiful location for residential use it was chosen as the site for Darwin High School.[18] Darwin Higher Primary School was established in 1948 as part of the Darwin Primary School on Cavenagh Street. In 1956 the High School was relocated into temporary accommodation adjacent to the primary school. In 1959 Bullocky Point was home to approximately 200 people who were not keen to move because alternative accommodation was expensive and difficult to obtain. Many refused to move and had to be evicted. The last residents remained until their power and water was cut off while others remained until their rooves were being demolished. Construction of the High School began in 1961 and the first students moved into the new premises in September 1963.[19] Darwin High School was officially opened in 1966.[20] The Vestey's Tank, the last vestige of Bullocky Point's tumultuous history as a meatworks, was integrated into the school in 1987 when it was converted into a gymnasium.

The Museum and Art Gallery of the Northern Territory (MAGNT) was created by the Legislative Council of the Northern Territory in 1966. It was initially housed in the old Darwin Town Hall on Smith Street but this was destroyed by Cyclone Tracy in 1974. After Cyclone Tracy the museums activities continued in temporary premises. When the Northern Territory gained self government in 1978 the Commonwealth had already committed to a museum and art gallery on Bullocky Point. Opened in 1981 the MAGNT at Bullocky Point is Darwin's premier museum and art gallery. However, the Museum and Art Gallery of the Northern Territory also includes the Fannie Bay Gaol, Defence of Darwin Experience, Museum of Central Australia and Lyon's Cottage. The MAGNT at Bullocky Point

---

18 *TCA*, 9 December 1959. See also, NTG, Heritage Brach *Vestey's Tank: Background Historical Information*, ,April 2010, 15 & Mitchell, *Bullocky Point*, 34.

19 Boland, *Bullocky Point History*, 134.

20 Gibson, *Beyond the Boundary*, 79.

has extensive collections of traditional and contemporary Indigenous art, Australian and Northern Territory art and South East Asian art. There are also important natural history, maritime history and Northern Territory history collections. The permanent Cyclone Tracy exhibition gives visitors a glimpse of the Cyclone and how it has shaped Darwin's history. The Indigenous art gallery and changing exhibitions showcase the art of extraordinary traditional and contemporary Indigenous artist, many of whom call the Northern Territory home. The galleries changing exhibitions also show a wide variety of Northern Territory, Australian and international art.

It is appropriate that Bullocky Point is home to MAGNT. Vesteys meatworks changed the face of Darwin forever. The events that transpired during the meatworks short lifetime shaped the character and identity of the Northern Territory for much of the twentieth century. Today's MAGNT exhibitions give a glimpse of Darwin and the Northern Territory's evolving role and character as the fulcrum of North Australia's development.

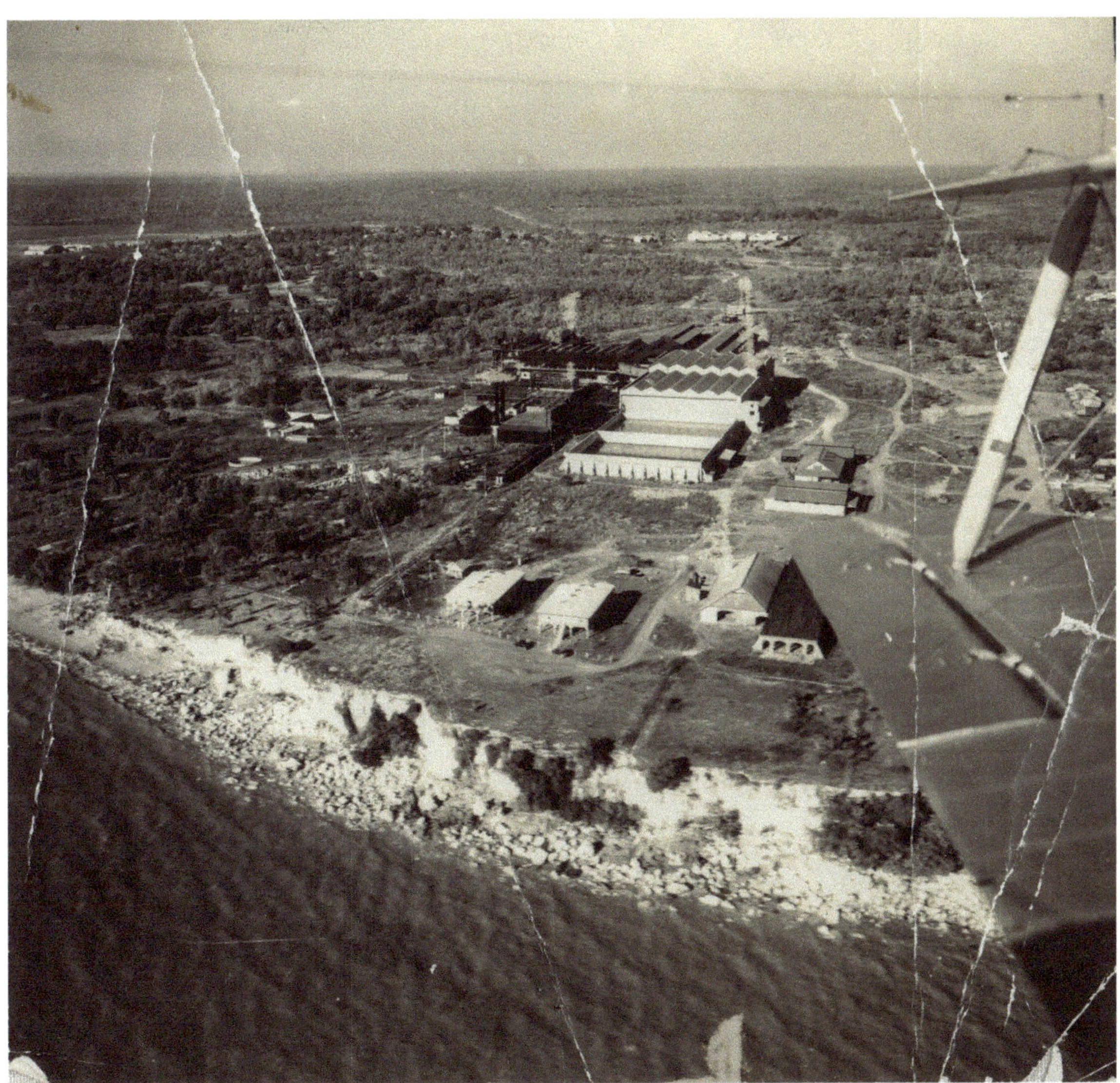

Vesteys Meatworks, c1930s. Parap Loco Depot and Major Repairs Workshop in background. (Unknown, NTL, Charles Micet Collection, PH0708/0006.)

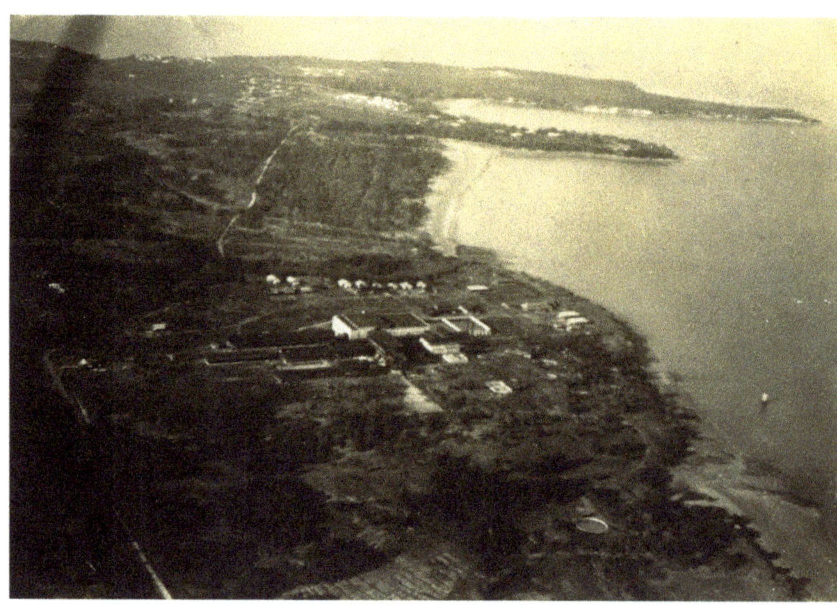

Vesteys Meatworks, c1933-35. (Unknown, NTAS, R.T. Cropley Collection, NTRS 2280 Item 3.)

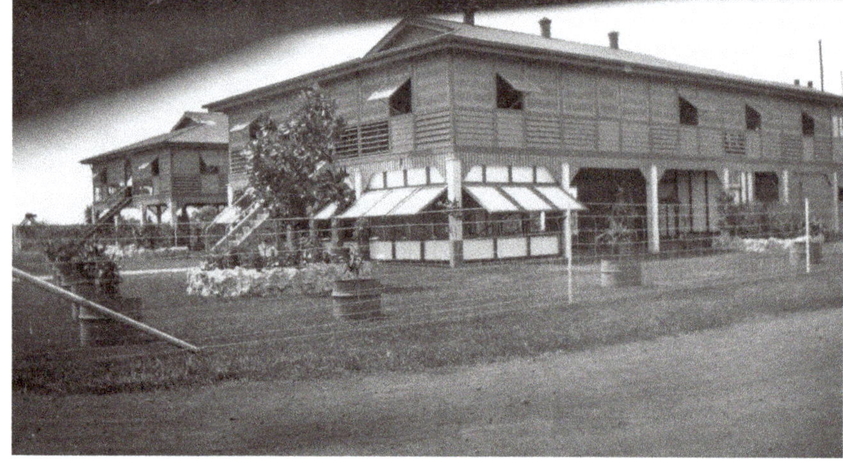

QANTAS, Darwin Rest House, Bullocky Point, c1938. Note the two buildings at the tip of Bullocky Point in the previous images. These became the QANTAS, Darwin Rest House. (Unknown, QANTAS, Heritage Collection, N/A.)

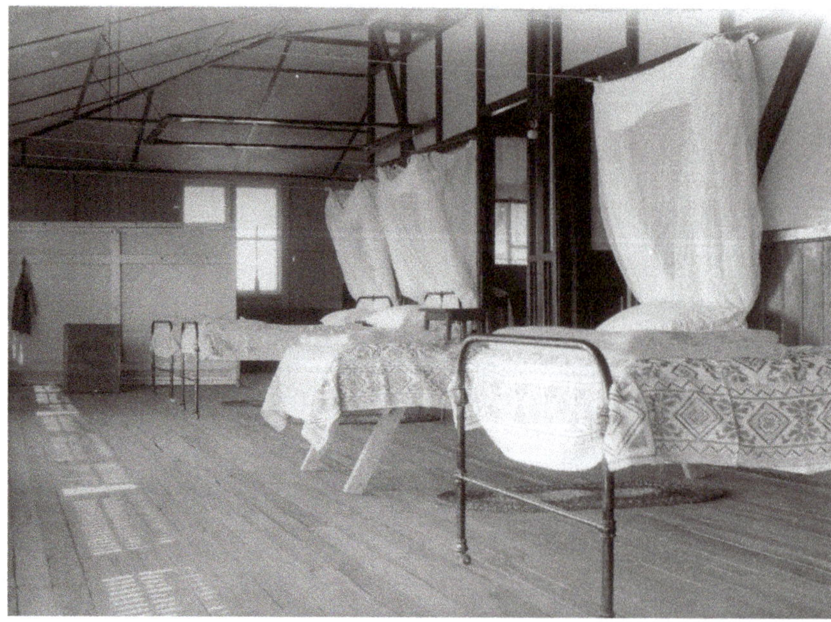

QANTAS, Darwin Rest House, interior, Bullocky Point, c1938. (Unknown, QANTAS, Heritage Collection, N/A.)

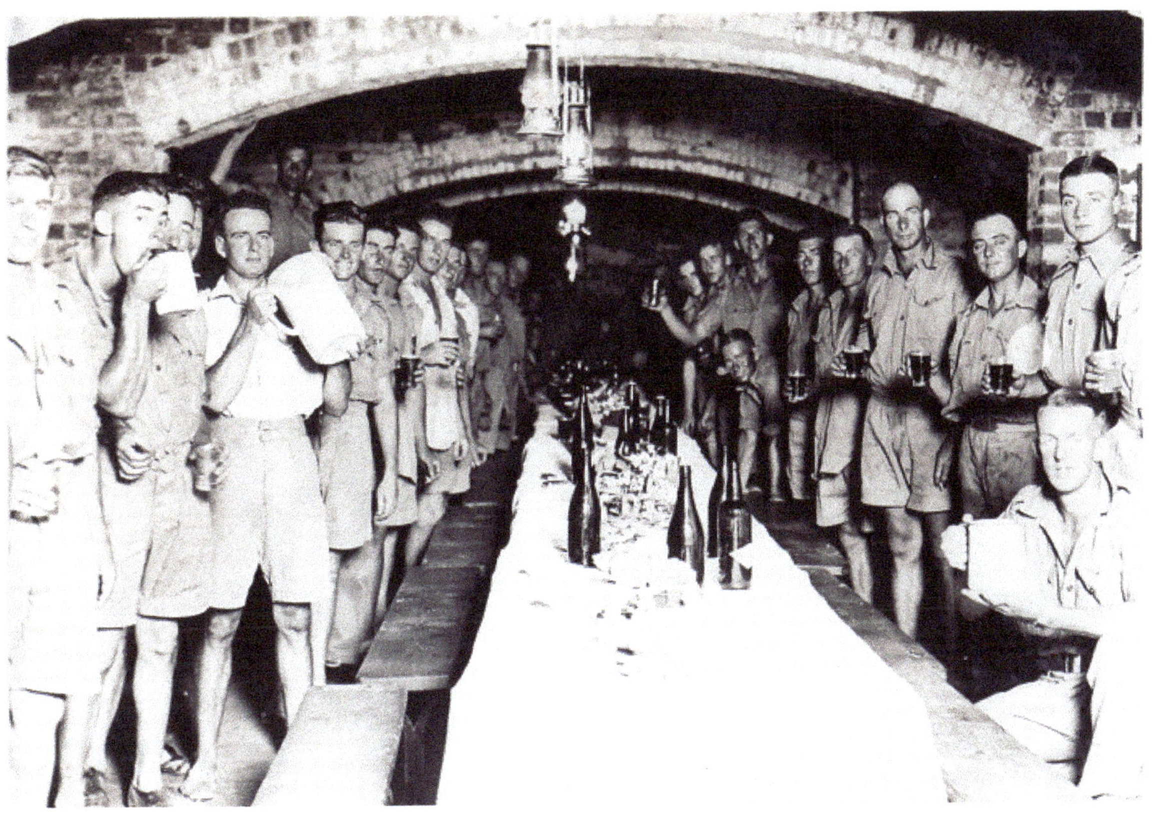

Darwin Mobile Force Christmas party at Vesteys, 1934. (Unknown, Angus Bird, Personal Collection, 15.)

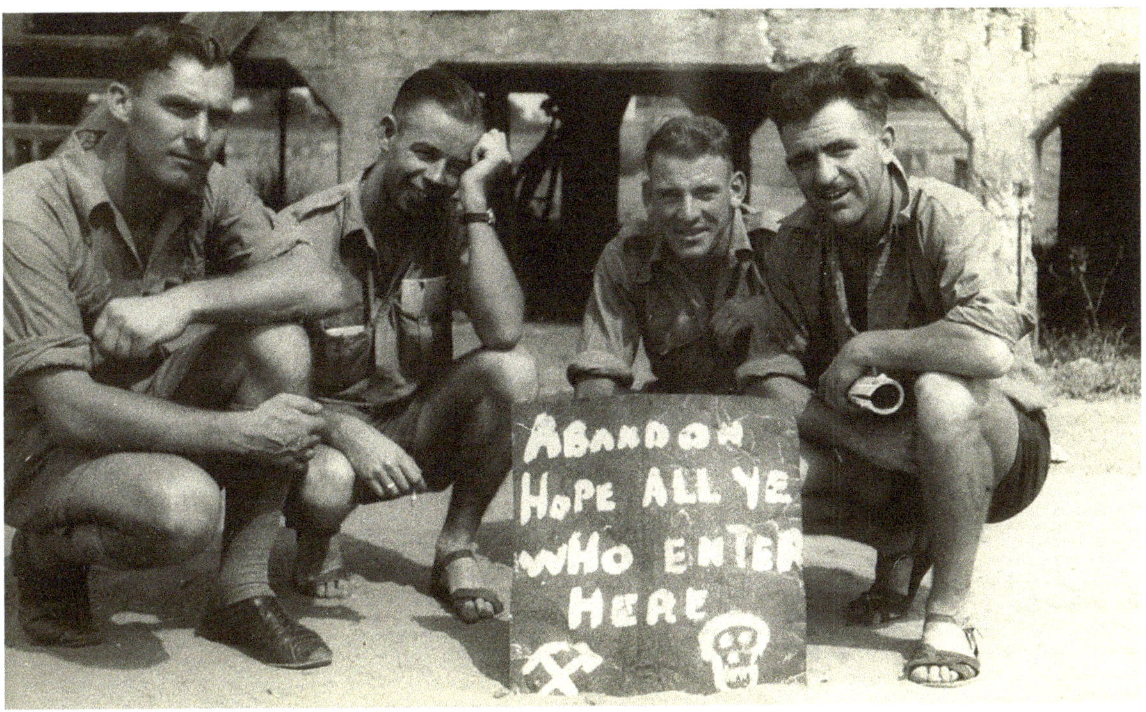

Soldiers of the Darwin Mobile Force, accommodated at the abandoned Vesteys Meatworks, Bullocky Point, 1938. (Unknown, NTAS, B. Humble Collection, NTRS 1168 Item 50.)

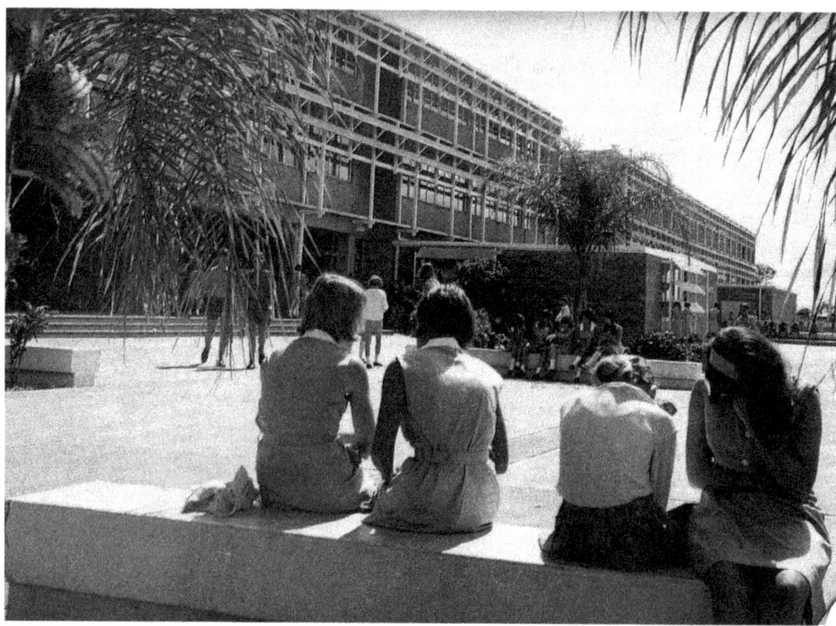

Darwin High School, c1965. (*NT Administration Report*, 1965, 71.)

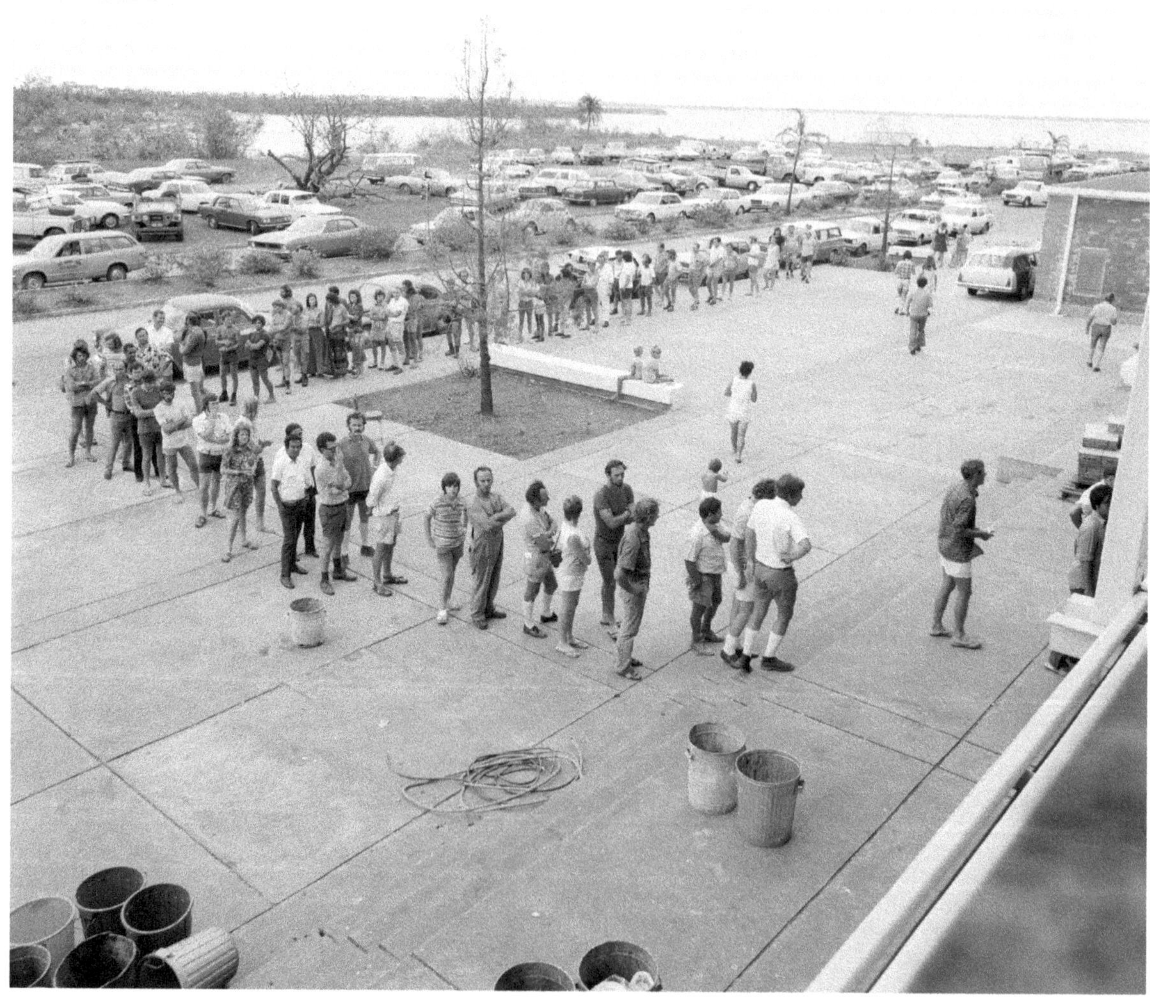

Darwin High School was one of a number of school emergency centres that provided food and services for survivors after Cyclone Tracy, 1975. (Unknown, NAA, Photograph, A6180:29/1/75/40.)

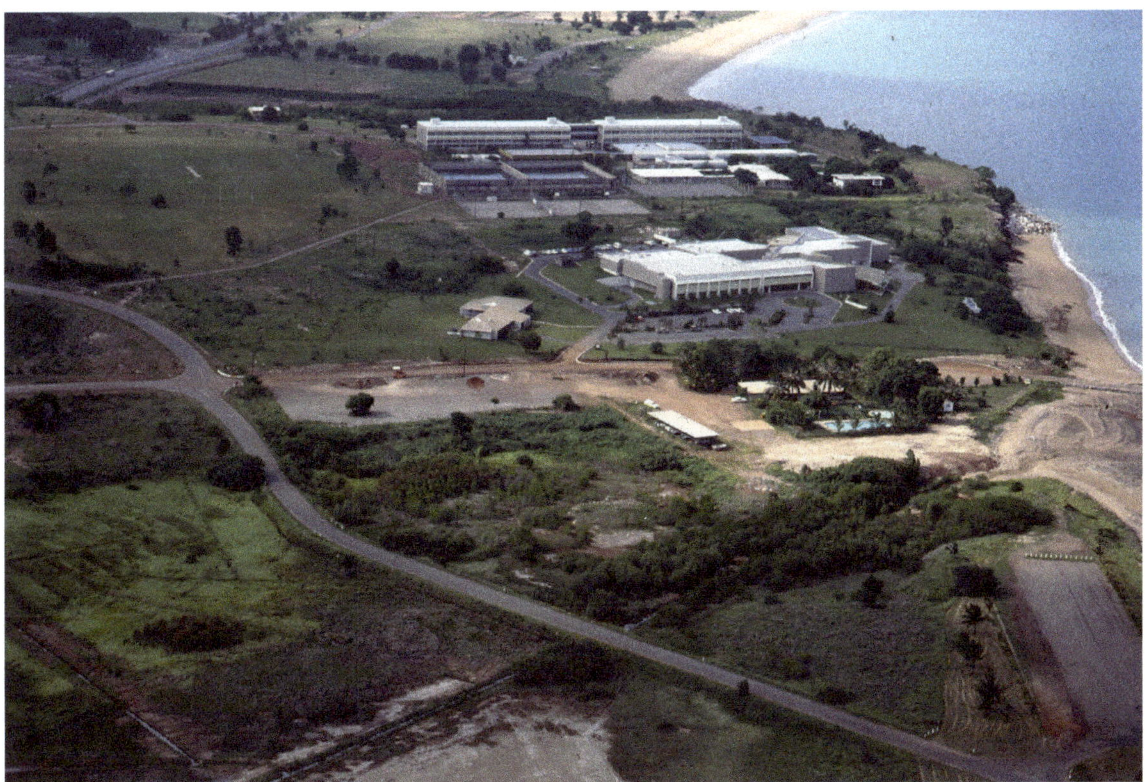

Darwin High School, Museum and Art Gallery of the NT and Darwin Water Ski Club, Bullocky Point, 1982. (Unknown, NTAS, NTRS 3822-P3 Darwin Aerials Suburbs Slide LF53.)

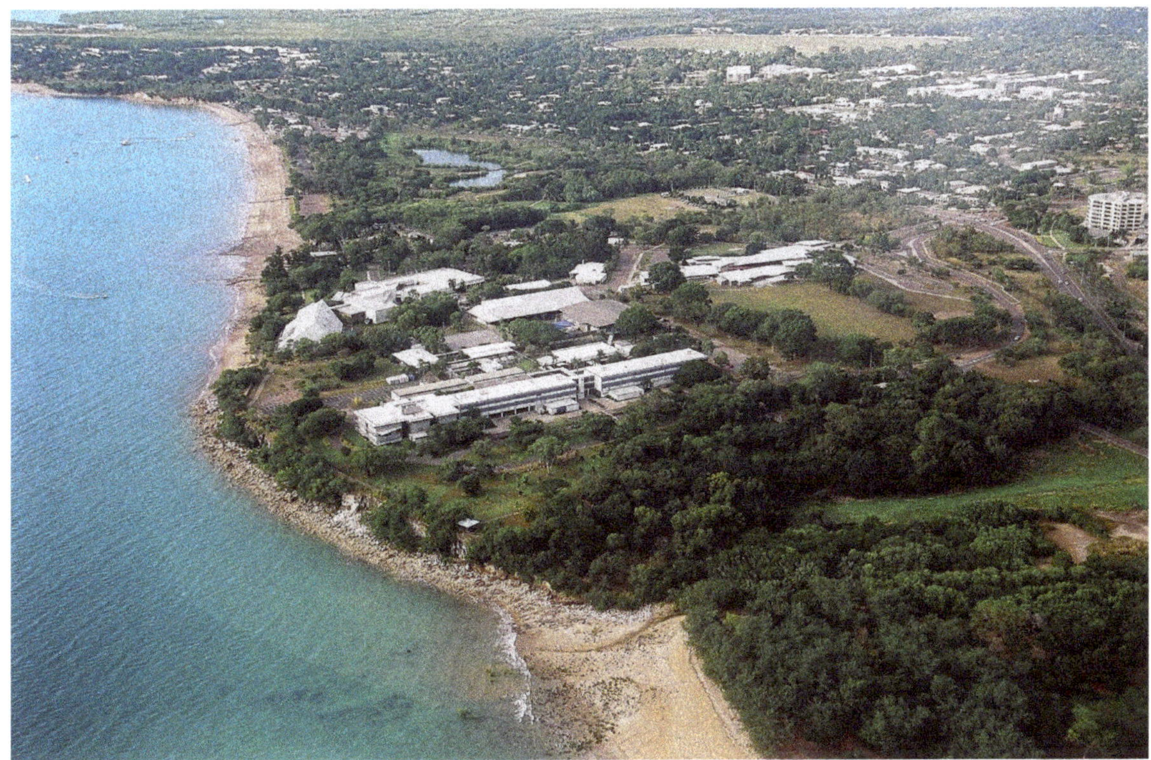

Darwin High School, c2016. (Boland, J., Boland, J., Personal Collection, aero_2.)

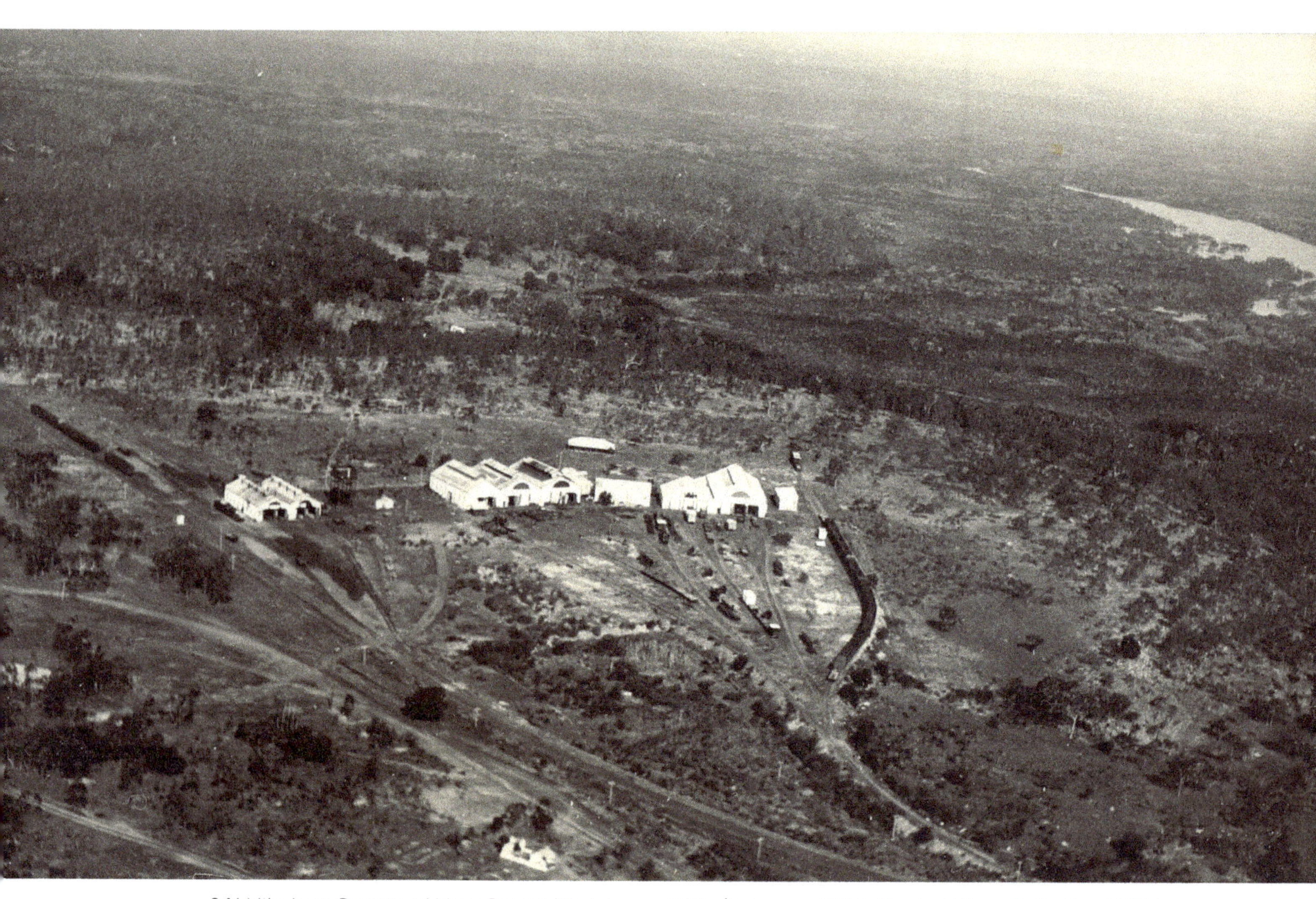

2 ½ Mile, Loco Depot and Major Repairs Workshops, c1930s. (Unknown, NTAS, Charles Wilson Collection, NTRS 3335 Item 290.)

Chapter 12

Darwin's First Suburbs: Parap & Fannie Bay

Fannie Bay is believed to be named after Fanny Carandini, a popular opera singer in Australia during the 1860s and 1870s. It seems that a number of Goyder's survey party had attended a concert of the well known Carandini's sing group who had performed in Adelaide in 1868.[1] Perhaps one or some of the surveyors were quite taken with Fanny, or Fannie as she was often known, and felt compelled to name one of Darwin harbour's most scenic bays after her.

Parap was initially named Paraparap in 1912 by Administrator Gilruth after the Victorian Parish of Murroon but after 1919 it was shortened to Parap.[2] Prior to this time the area now known as Parap was known locally as the Two and a Half Mile, after the Loco Depot and Major Repairs Workshops established there in 1887.

In the early days of European settlement Fannie Bay was considered quite distant from the town but was a popular destination for excursions and picnics. Harriet Douglas Daly, daughter of the Government Resident, Captain William Bloomfield, describes impromptu horse racing and rifle shooting contests on Fannie Bay beach in the early 1870s.[3] The first organised horse races in Darwin were also held at Fannie Bay in 1873.[4] The exact location of the first race course is not known but may have been in a location between Bullocky Point and what is now known as Vestys Beach. A second race course was located in the vicinity of today's East Point Reserve. Horse racing settled on a racecourse in the vicinity of the current Fannie Bay Racecourse since the mid 1870s and the land was formally granted to the Northern Territory Race Club in 1887.[5]

The Government Gardens, originally established in the Palmerston town centre, were moved to Fannie Bay in 1879 to approximately the area now occupied by today's Fannie Bay shopping centre.[6] The site was not well chosen because it proved to be deficient in both water and soil.[7] Mr Maurice Holtze, the curator at the time, moved the gardens to the site of the current Botanic Gardens in 1886.[8]

The Fannie Bay Gardens and Experimental Nursery were a factor in the decision to relocate the gaol to the same area. It was anticipated that prison labour could be employed in manufacturing using some of the raw material grown there.[9] The Gaol opened in January 1884 on the same site occupied by the Fannie Bay Gaol Museum today. Fannie Bay Gaol and its inmates played a significant role in the development of Darwin. Many

1 NTG, Place Names Register, *Fannie Bay*, www.
2 NTG, Place Names Register, *Parap*, www.
3 Daly, *Digging, Squatting, and Pioneering Life in the Northern Territory of South Australia*, 62.
4 *SAA*, 14 July 1873.
5 *NA*, 21 May 1887.
6 Bisa. *Remember Me Kindly*, 45.
7 NT Government Resident, *Quarterly Report*, 1884, 9.
8 NT Government Resident, *Half-Yearly, Report*, 1886, 20.
9 *NT Report of the Government Resident*, 1881, 2.

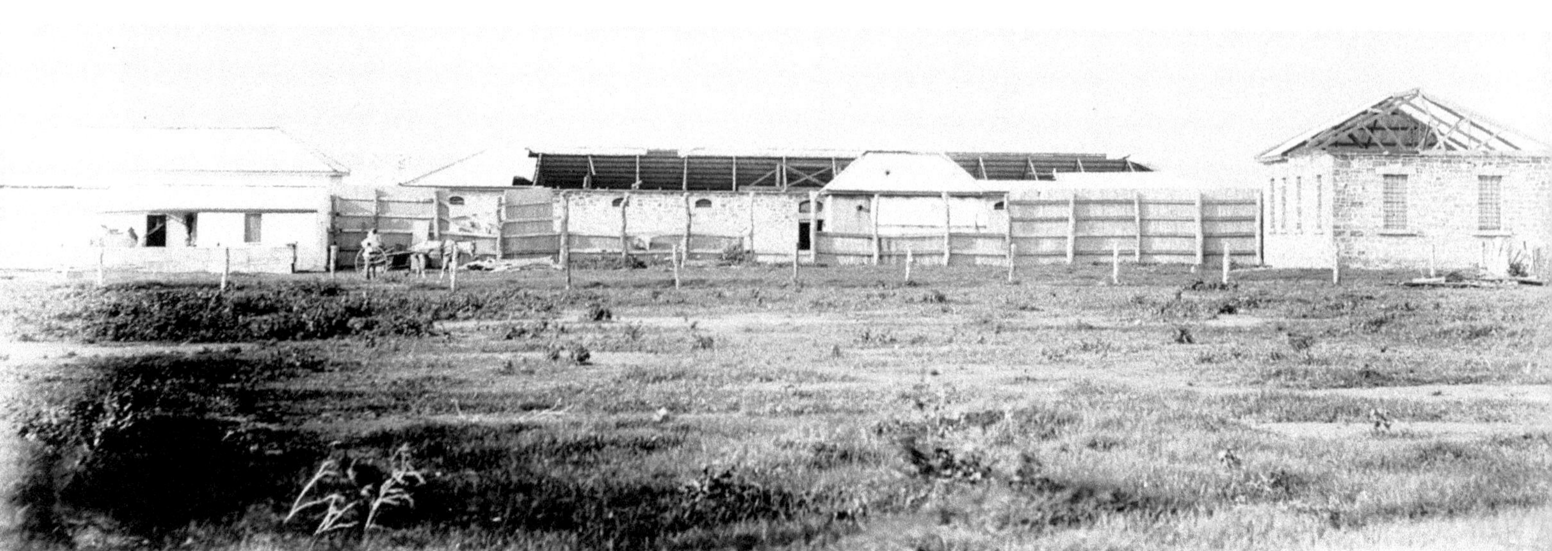

Fannie Bay Gaol, after the 1897 cyclone. (Bleeser, F., NLA, Florenz Bleeser Collection, PIC/9981/73.)

projects around the town relied on the labour of gaol inmates. Fannie Bay was also famous for its rather 'flexible' security with prisoners known to break out of and into the gaol with some regularity!

The Fannie Bay Gaol was the scene of some important events. In 1888 the art work of Aboriginal inmates was exhibited at the Melbourne Centennial International Exhibition in what is recognised as the first Aboriginal art exhibition in Australia.[10] In 1913, C.J. Kirkland, editor of the *Northern Territory Times and Gazette* was gaoled for contempt of court and fined £100 for criticising decisions by Judge Bevan. Public indignation at this attack on the press resulted in a collection to pay Kirkland's fine and upon his release he was carried back to town in a cavalcade of vehicles accompanied by 'wild cheering, the strings of fluttering bunting and continuous fireworks.'[11] In 1921 the well known Australian Workers Union organiser, Harold George Nelson and others, were gaoled for not paying their taxes in a campaign to gain Northern Territory political representation in the Commonwealth Parliament. Demonstrations outside the gaol included the singing of the Marseillaise and a Nelson led version of the 'Red Flag.'[12] Nelson and his co protestors were eventually released and their campaign rewarded. Nelson was elected as the first Northern Territory representative in the Commonwealth House of Representatives albeit with no voting rights. Northern Territory members of the Commonwealth House of Representatives would not receive full voting rights until 1968.[13]

During the bombing of Darwin on 19 February 1942 the gaol was strafed. For their own protection the inmates of Fannie Bay Gaol were released with the instructions 'every man for himself.'[14] For the remainder of the war the gaol was used by the Army and Air Force. The last hangings at the Fannie Bay Gaol in 1952 were those of Jerry Coche and John Novotney, convicted of killing a local taxi Driver. In Cyclone Tracy Fannie Bay Gaol was badly damaged but the prisoners played their part in the clean up after the cyclone. The Gaol was operational until 1979 when its functions were relocated to the Berrimah Gaol. In 1984 the Fannie Bay Gaol was restored and opened as part of the Museum and Art Gallery of the Northern Territory.

10 Boland, *Know Where You Stand*, 8.
11 *NTTG*, 1 May 1913.
12 *NS*, 7 June 1921.
13 NAA, *Electoral Franchise and Territorians*, Research Guide, www.
14 Hall, *Darwin 1942*, 129.

A north to south transcontinental railway had been the subject of public debate in Australia since the 1850s. This became reality when the South Australian Government commenced the southern section of the railway from Port Augusta to Farina in 1879. Tenders were let for the construction of the northern section from Palmerston in 1886. As part of the project the Loco Depot and Major Repairs Workshops, were constructed at the two and a half mile mark of the line. A number of houses were also built in the vicinity for railway workers. The North Australia Railway eventually reached Birdum in 1929 and operated until 1977. The Two and a Half Mile Loco Depot and Major Repairs Workshops and its workers were an integral part of Parap throughout the railway's history. When the Transcontinental Railway did finally reach Darwin in 2004 the northern terminal was at the East Arm Port.

When Paraparap was first named in 1912 development in the area had centred on the Fannie Bay Gaol and the Two and a Half Mile Railway workshops. The only other significant site in the area was the Palmerston Cemetery, now on Goyder Road, the town's main cemetery from 1870 to 1919. This all changed with the announcement of the Vesteys Meat-processing and Freezer Works on Bullocky Point. The impact of Vesteys extended much further than Bullocky Point. The dramatic increase in population associated with the Meatworks resulted in the need for a primary school in the area. Paraparap Primary School opened 3 August 1917 on the corner of Mckillop and Stokes Street catering for the children from Vesteys and Two and Half Mile communities.

In the 1930s development in the Parap area increased along Parap Road. In 1931, George and Mary Seale took over the Parap Club on Parap Road. Initially a members only club it was granted a liquor license in 1934 to become the Parap Hotel. By 1936 the population of Parap had grown to 514 when Darwin's population at the time was 1992.[15]

Development in Parap rapidly increased when construction began on a new Royal Australian Air force base on the current Darwin Airport site in 1938. The civilian airport also underwent upgrades in 1939 to cater for military use as World War II loomed. A 'Tin City' sprang up in the vicinity to house the new infrastructure and servicemen. In 1940 a new Parap Police Station was built on the corner of Parap Road and the Stuart Highway.[16]

Darwin has always been linked to Australia's aviation history. In June, 1919 William 'Billy' Hughes, Prime Minister of Australia initiated The Great Air Race, where the Commonwealth Government offered a prize of ten thousand pounds for the first aeroplane crewed by Australians to fly from Britain to Australia within thirty days before the end of 1919. On 10 December 1919 an ex Vickers Vimy heavy biplane bomber crewed by Ross and Keith Smith, Jim Bennett and Wally Sheirs won The Great Air Race when they landed on an airstrip recently developed on a paddock near the Fannie Bay Gaol. Almost the entire population of Darwin turned out to greet them.

In the years that followed many famous aviators including Bert Hinkler, first solo aviator from Britain to Australia (February, 1928), Amy Johnson, first female solo aviator from Britain to Australia (May, 1930) and Amilia Earhart (June, 1937) were all greeted at the Parap aerodrome. In 1934, Qantas Empire Airlines (QEA), a joint venture between QANTAS and the British company Imperial Airways were granted the contract for Australia's Overseas Air Service. QEA were granted a lease of land at Parap for the construction of an aircraft hangar. A Civil Aviation Administration building was constructed and a second runway cleared. Regular QEA flights began in 1935. The main runway was sealed in the same year. During this period the Civil Aviation drome became a hub of activity in the Parap / Fannie Bay suburbs that developed around it.[17]

15 *NS*, 20 October 1936.
16 *NS*, 12 March 1940.
17 Gibson, *Beyond the Boundary*, 33-37.

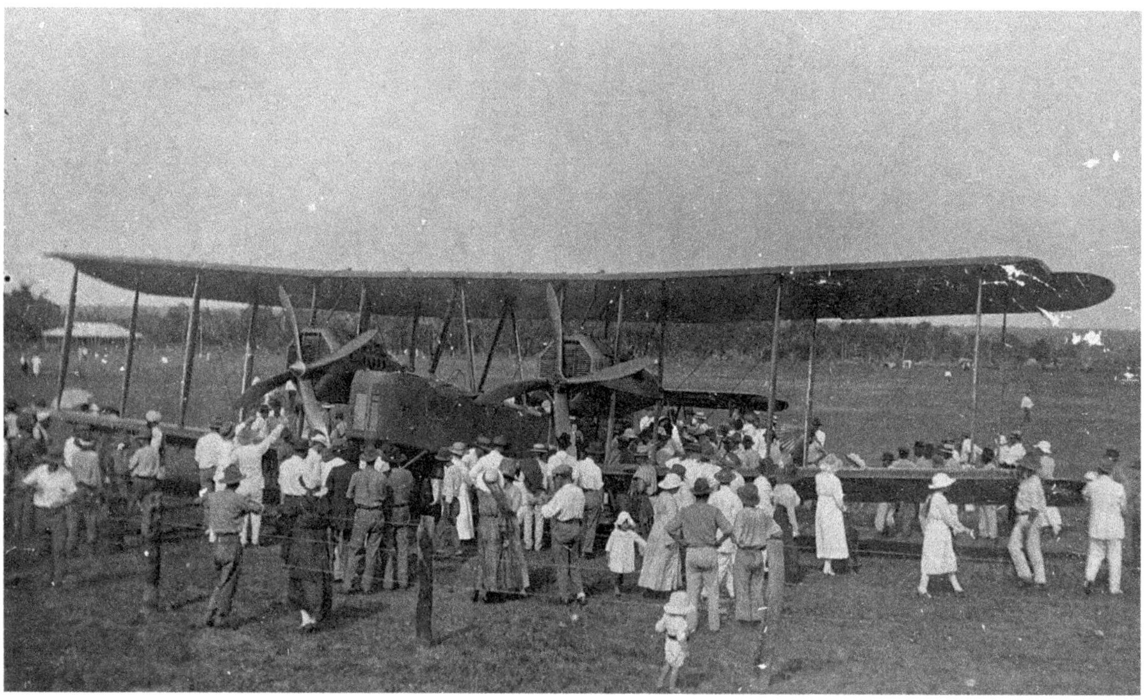

10 December 1919, Ross and Keith Smith, Jim Bennett and Wally Sheirs, land their Vickers Vimy in Darwin to win The Great Air Race. (Unknown, QHC, Darwin Collection, N/A.)

On the 19th of February 1942 the Civilian Aerodrome and RAAF base were strafed in the first bombing raid destroying or damaging the infrastructure there. The few fighter planes in Darwin were also destroyed. In the second raid 80 minutes later the RAAF base was patterned bombed adding further damage to the already crippled facilities. There were 64 Japanese air raids on Darwin between the 19th of February 1942 and November 1943. Many targeted Darwin's RAAF base but it remained in service throughout the war. During this time Allied forces gradually wrestled back control of Australia's Northern skies.

Planning for the Parap Fannie Bay area post war began during the war. It was recognised that the Civil Aviation Aerodrome, Vesteys Meatworks and the Fannie Bay Gaol were all impediments to the development of the area for residential purposes. Redevelopment was made easier by the *Commonwealth Darwin Lands Acquisition Bill* in August 1945 that resulted in the compulsory acquisition of Darwin freehold land giving planners a free rein. By 1946 the Department of Aviation had closed the Civil Aviation Aerodrome at Parap and transferred the civilian operations to the military airfield in Winnellie. The 1934 QANTAS Hangar at Parap is the last remnant of the Civilian Aviation Aerodrome.

Civilians began to return to Darwin from mid 1946. Families returning to Darwin after their evacuation in late 1941 and early 1942 found that their former homes were destroyed, severely damaged or occupied by military or Commonwealth authorities. Accommodation was in such short supply that most had to find housing in the numerous military camps that now laid deserted around Darwin. The largest, Camp 118, also known as Parap Camp, was situated in what is now Stuart Park. Another camp in the Fannie Bay racecourse area became known as Paradise Flat.[18] Housing was usually in the form of Sydney Williams huts, a type of pre fabricated hut used extensively by the military throughout Darwin. The huts were constructed in six metre sections upon a steel frame and clad with corrugated iron, an A frame roof and iron doors at each end. There were push out shutters set alternatively high

18 Austin, *Quality of Life*, 7.

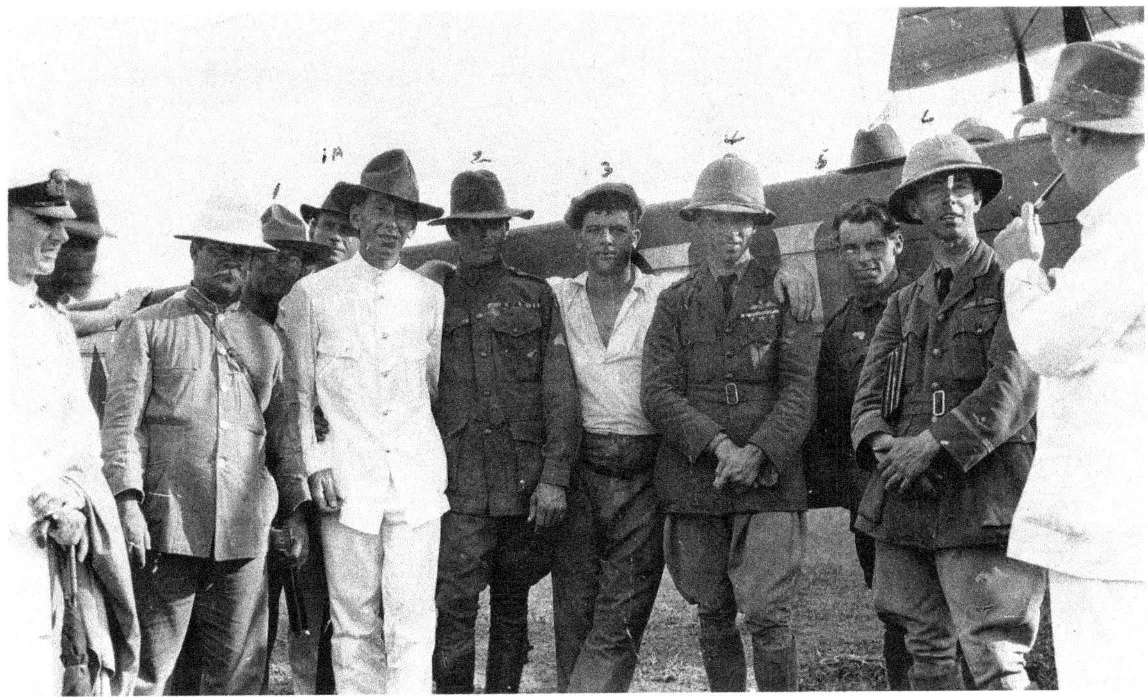

Larry Donnison was part of the crowd to greet the winners of The Great Air Race at the Parap airfield. He identified himself and his friends with the crew [On reverse of the postcard).
1. L. Donnison 1A Tapper, 2. Bennett, 3. Houstan, 4. Ross Smith, 5. Wallie Shiers, 6. Keith Smith
(Unknown, E.D.W.S Donnison Collection, LNSW, ML MSS 890/3/0205.)

and low for ventilation. The sections could be joined to form larger units up to almost twenty five meters. Depending on the size of the huts in Darwin's camps they could be partitioned in two for a family in each half. Darwin's growing population made do in such conditions until new housing could be built or found. Despite the difficult conditions those who lived in the camps developed a strong sense of community that remains until this day.

A sign that race relations were changing after World War II was the activities of the Australian Half-caste Progressive Association reformed in 1951.[19] Many of those involved lived in Darwin's camps. In 1952 the Half-Caste Progress Association was not just a political organisation it had a social brief as well. The parish hall at the Parap Camp became known as the Sunshine Club which became the scene of innumerable weddings, social functions and regular dances where the diverse crowds danced the night away to the sounds of the local 'string bands' largely made up of musicians drawn from the Aboriginal, Filipino and Torres Strait communities.

After years of residential housing shortage in Darwin the Commonwealth established the Northern Territory Housing Commission in May 1959.[20] New housing became available in Darwin's growing suburbs in the early 1960s resulting in the various World War II era camps being phased out and replaced by new development.

The late 1950s and 1960s was a period of rapid growth and development for Darwin and the suburbs of Parap and Fannie Bay in particular. The Commonwealth embarked on a significant housing construction scheme in the late 1950s to house its employees that resulted in 500 houses being built in

19 Stanton, *The Australian Half-Caste Progressive Association,* 43. The Northern Territory Half-Caste Association was formed in 1936 but its activities largely ceased during World War II. The Association was reformed in approximately 1951. See *CA*, 13 April 1951.

20 NAA, Northern Territory Housing, Research Guide, www.

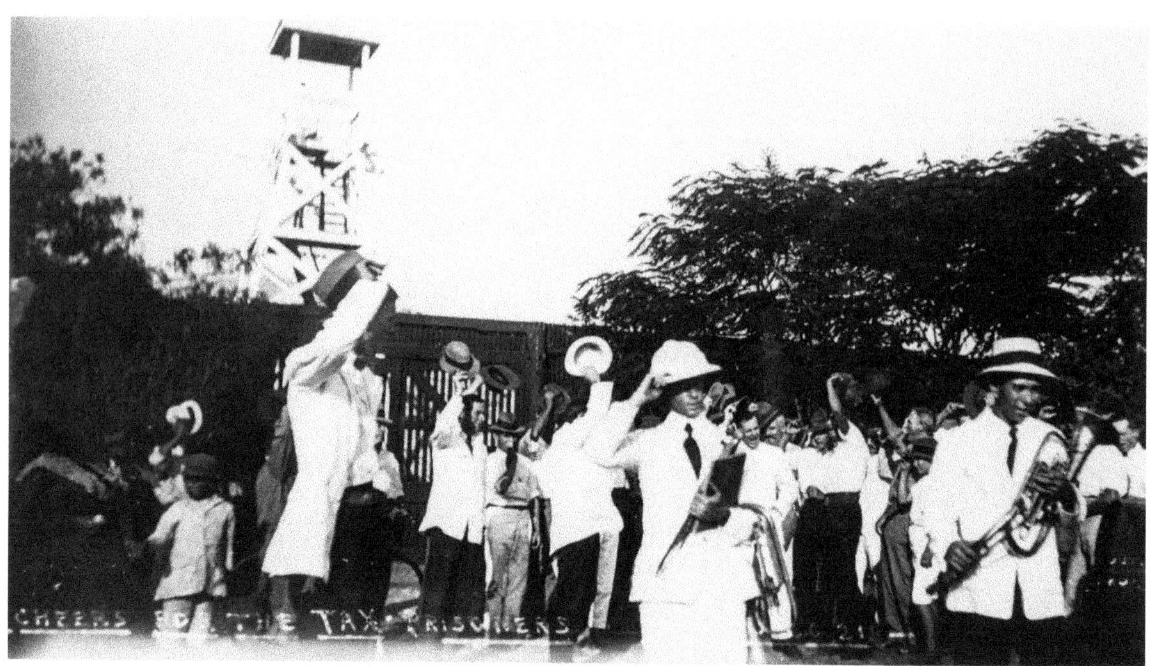

'3 Cheers for the Tax Prisoners'. Brass band and group gather outside the Fannie Bay Gaol. Protesters gathered outside the gaol to encourage those imprisoned during the 'no tax with no representation' campaign for a House of Representatives seat in the Federal Parliament, 1921. (Buscall, J.C., NTL, Buscall Collection, PH0170/0075.)

Parap and Fannie Bay. Many of the homes built were elevated louvered homes known as 'Government Greys' due to the use of unpainted asbestos fibro panels. After 1959 the Northern Territory Housing Commission was established to focus on public housing. This included both residential family homes and numerous blocks of flats which had not been common in Darwin until this time.

The development in Parap and Fannie Bay was not restricted to residential housing. In 1957, the NT Wholesale Drug Company, purchased two blocks where the Parap Shopping Village now stands. The shopping precinct of today began with the construction of five shops, including Barden's Chemist.[21] The 'new' Parap Primary School on Parap Road was opened in 1958.[22] The Darwin Olympic Swimming Pool, on Ross Smith Avenue, Parap was opened 14 May 1960. Darwin's first public in ground swimming pool opened with a 'spectacular' aquatic display that included diving and a water ballet.[23] The Parap shopping centre was enhanced by the Parap open air picture theatre in April 1961.[24] It was the first time since the late 1920s that Darwin could offer two picture theatres. The Parap shopping centre became the home of the Parap Markets in 1982.[25] The markets are a Saturday morning Darwin institution that showcases international cuisine and locally grown produce.

Compared to other suburbs of Darwin the Parap / Fannie Bay area was not as badly affected by Cyclone Tracy. Most of the relatively new Commonwealth housing stood up well to the devastating winds with only about a third damaged beyond repair, whereas the rate of damage in Darwin's northern suburbs was almost 100%.[26] Nevertheless Cyclone Tracy did leave its mark on Fannie

21 Parap Village, www.
22 Boland, *Know Where You Stand,* 16.
23 *NTN*, 17 May 1960.
24 Gibson, *Beyond the Boundary,* 78.
25 Parap Village, www.
26 Gibson, *Beyond the Boundary,* 85.

Bay and Parap. The Fannie Bay Hotel was extensively damaged and did not reopen after Cyclone Tracy. Proposed post-cyclone planning changes in the area, particularly a highway to link Fannie Bay to Casuarina via Nightcliff through established residential areas were strongly opposed by local residents.[27] People power prevailed and the new road as proposed did not eventuate.

Today the suburbs of Parap and Fannie Bay enjoy the reputation of being amongst Darwin's oldest and most established suburbs. Although some government and private businesses have chosen to move out of the city centre into Parap and Fannie Bay they remain largely residential suburbs. The proximity to the city and Fannie Bay means the residents are close to most of Darwin's amenities and attractions. Even closer, scattered through the streets are constant reminders of Darwin's extraordinary history.

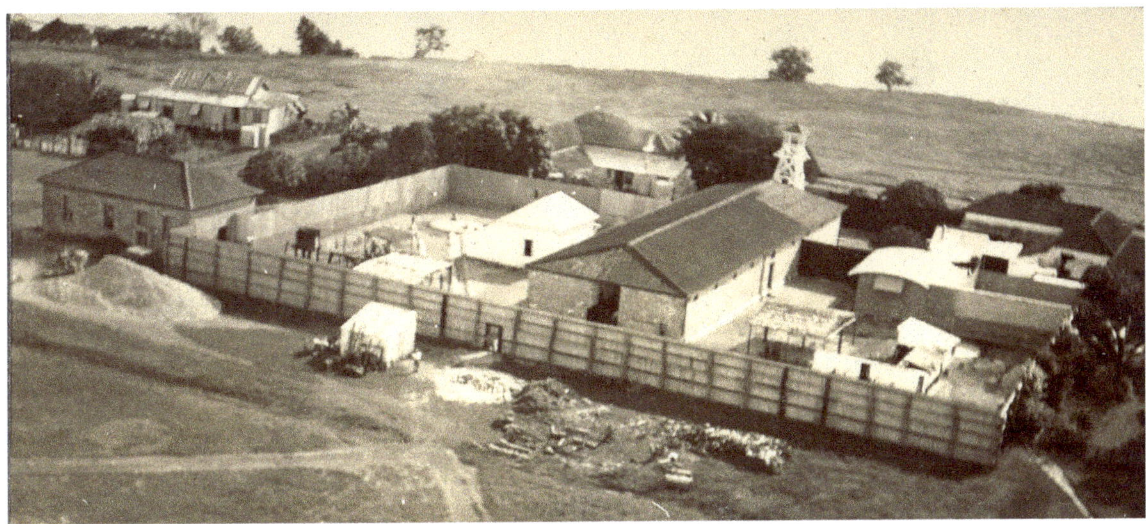

Fannie Bay Gaol, c1930s. (Unknown, NTAS, Charles Wilson Collection, NTRS 3335 Item 288.)

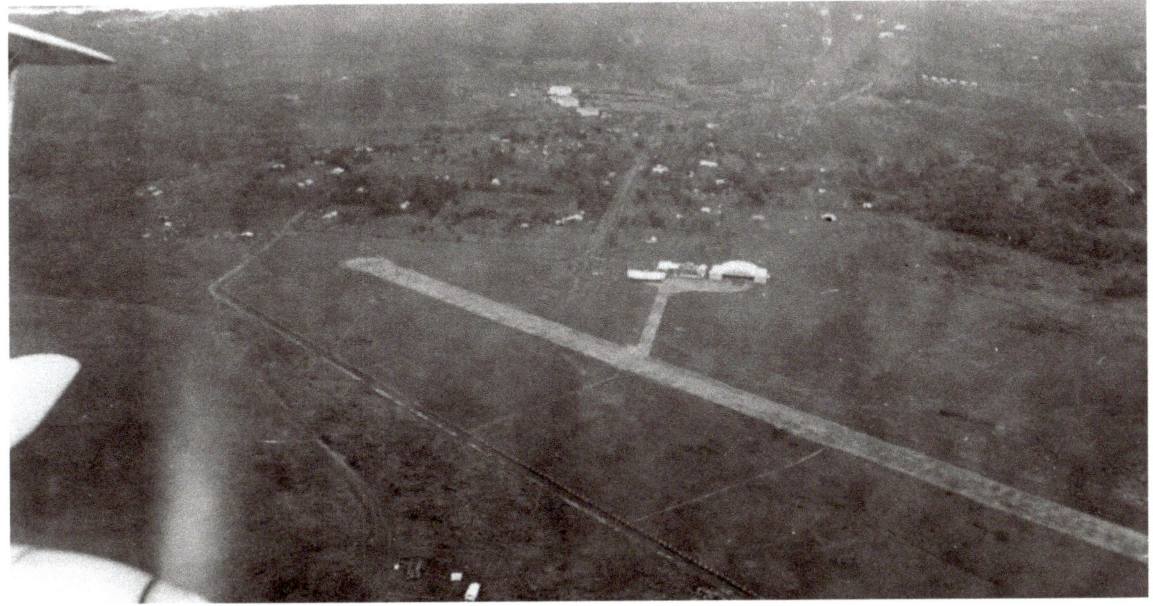

Civil Aviation Authority Aerodrome and Parap, c1930s. (Unknown, QHC, Darwin Collection, N/A)

27 Smith & Nicholls, *Darwin Golf Club*, 51. A highway linking Fannie Bay and Casuarina via an East Point University was first proposed in 1963.

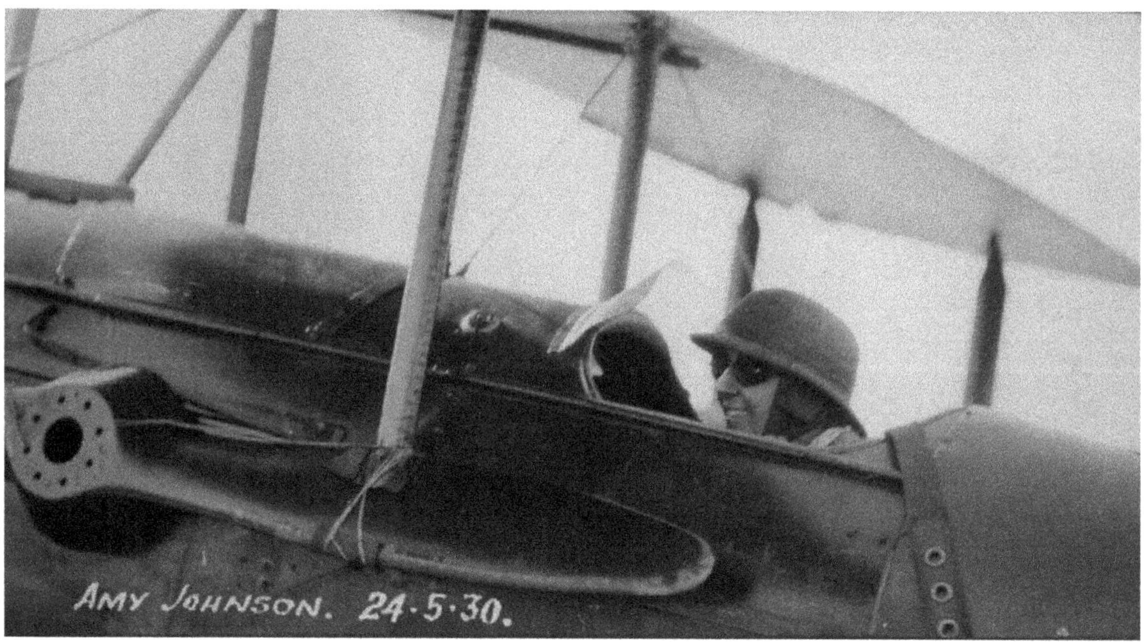

Amy Johnson, first female solo aviator from Britain to Australia, May, 1930. (Unknown, NTAS, Charles Wilson Collection, NTRS 3335 Item 32.)

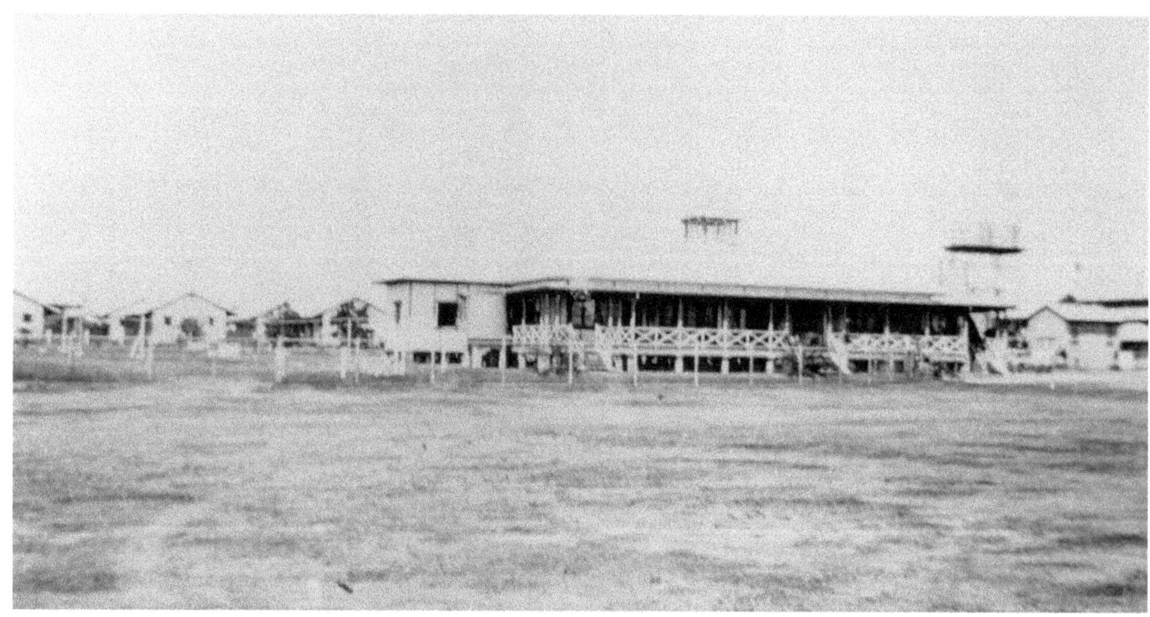

Darwin Civil Aviation Aerodrome, Control building, Parap, 1940. (Unknown, QANTAS, Heritage Collection, N/A)

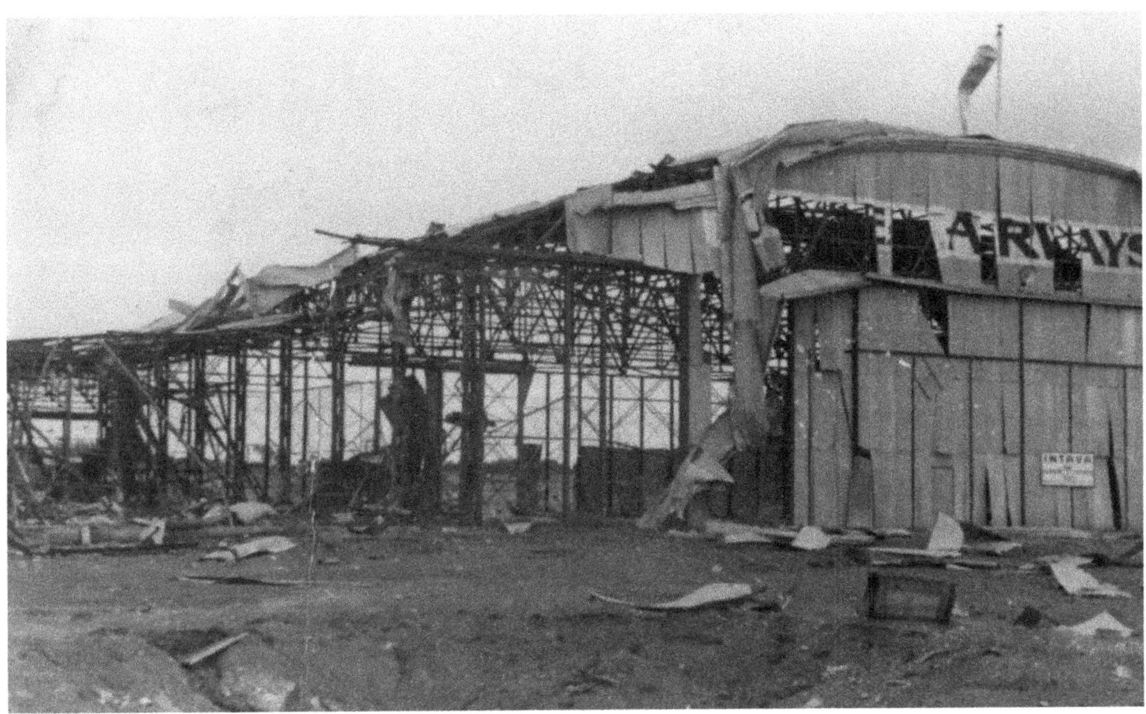

QANTAS Hangar, Darwin Civil Aviation Aerodrome, bomb damage, 19 February, 1942. (Unknown, QANTAS, Heritage Collection, N/A.)

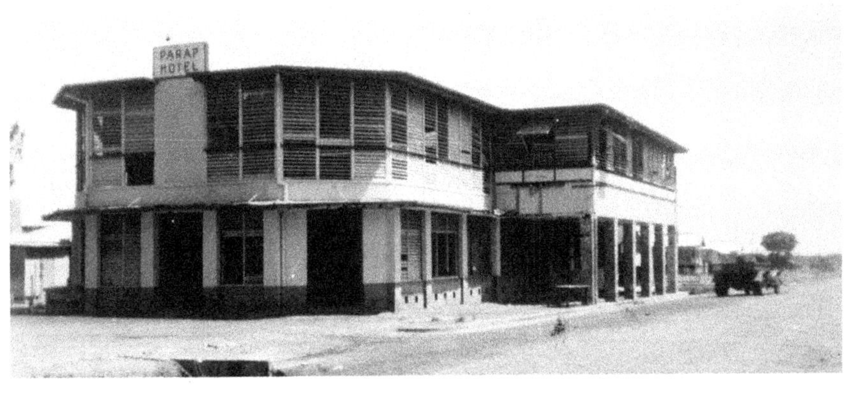

Parap Hotel, c1940s. (Unknown, NTL, Lyndon Thomas Collection, PH0696-0051.)

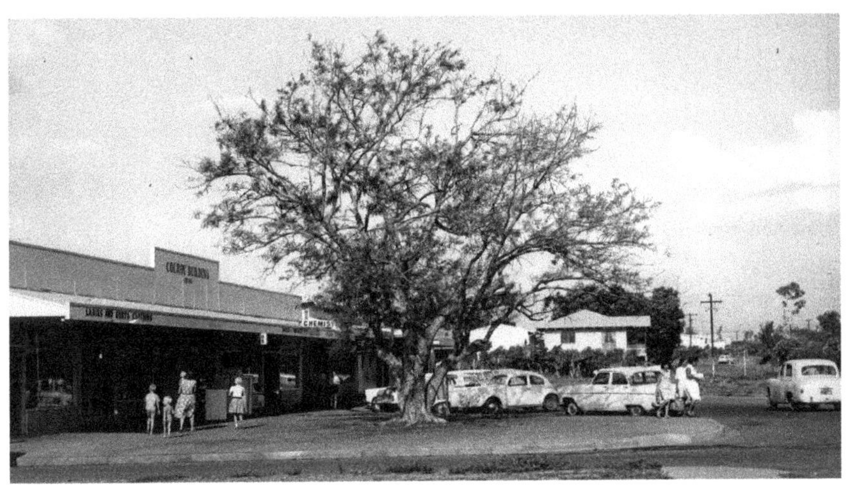

Parap Shopping Centre, c1960s. (Unknown, NTAS, GPC, NTRS 3822-P1 Folder 73.)

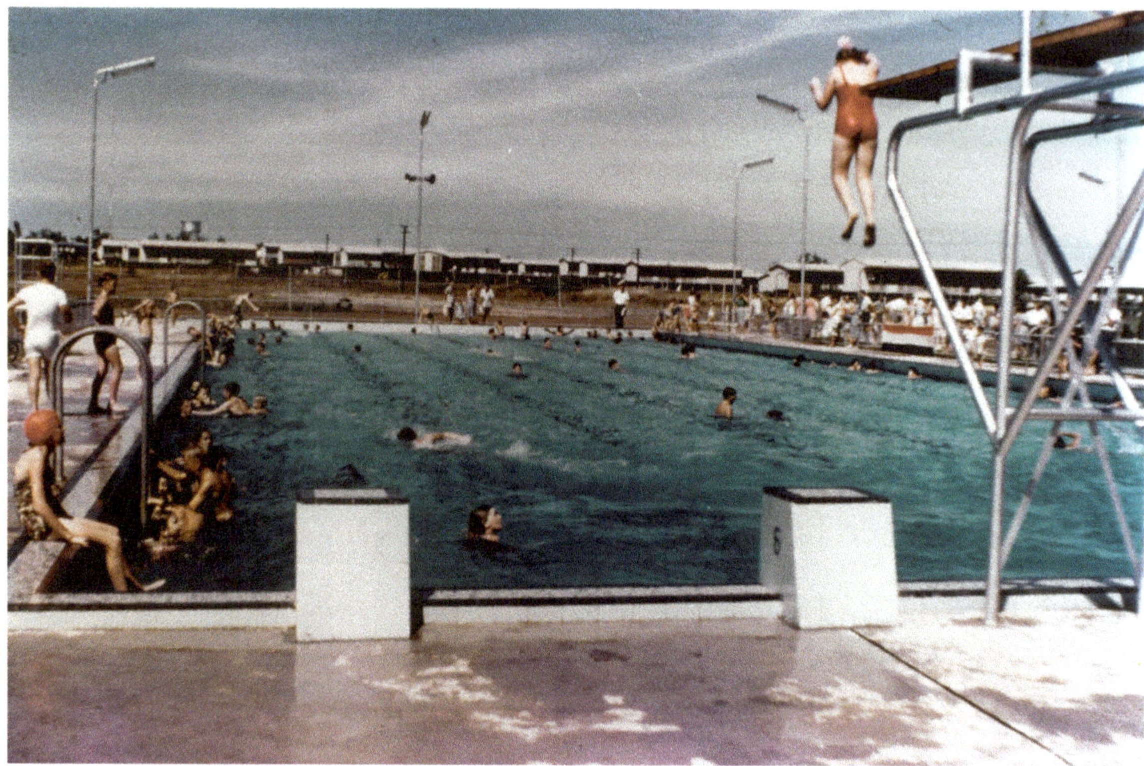

Parap Pool, opening day, 1961. (Helyar G. & F., NTL, Lois & Geoff Helyar Collection, PH0092/0276.)

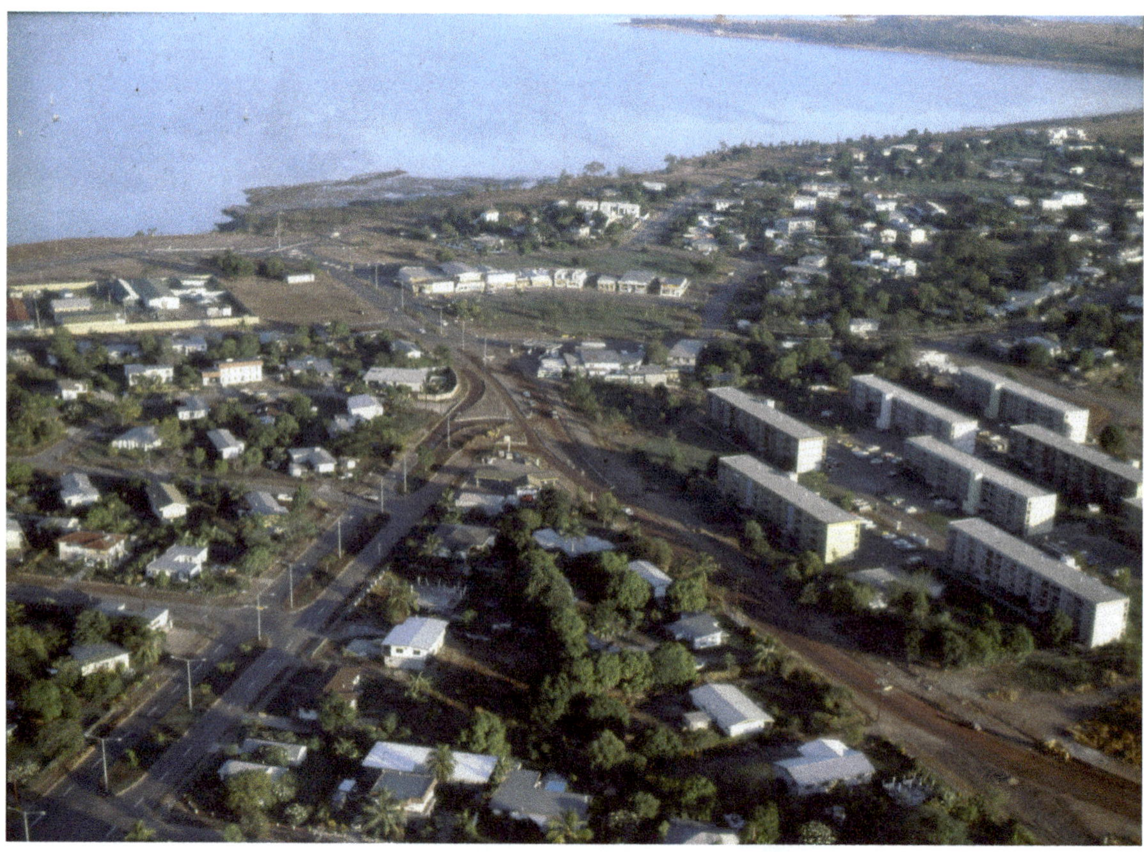

Fannie Bay Gaol, Shops and Kurringal Flats, c1980. (Wiedemann, A., NTAS, GPC, NTRS 3822-P3 Darwin Aerials Suburbs Slide 41.)

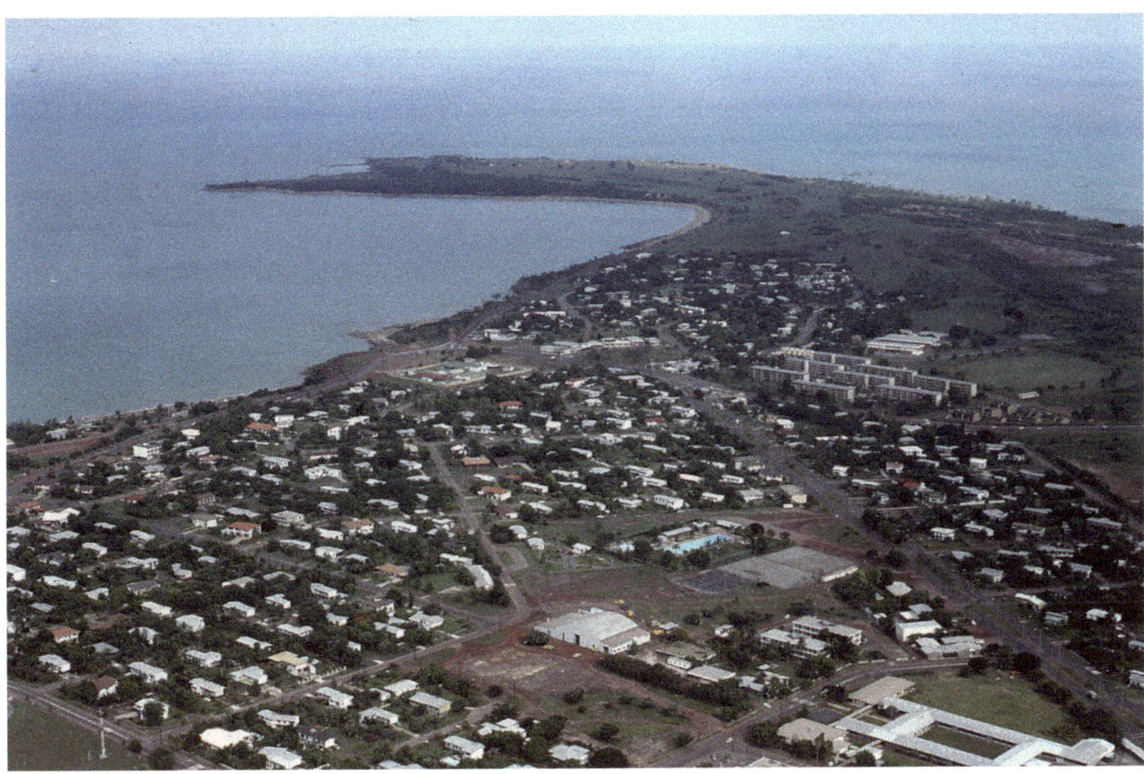

Parap, Fannie Bay & East Point, 1982. (Unknown, NTAS, GPC, 014_NTRS 3822-P3 Darwin Aerials Suburbs Slide 311.)

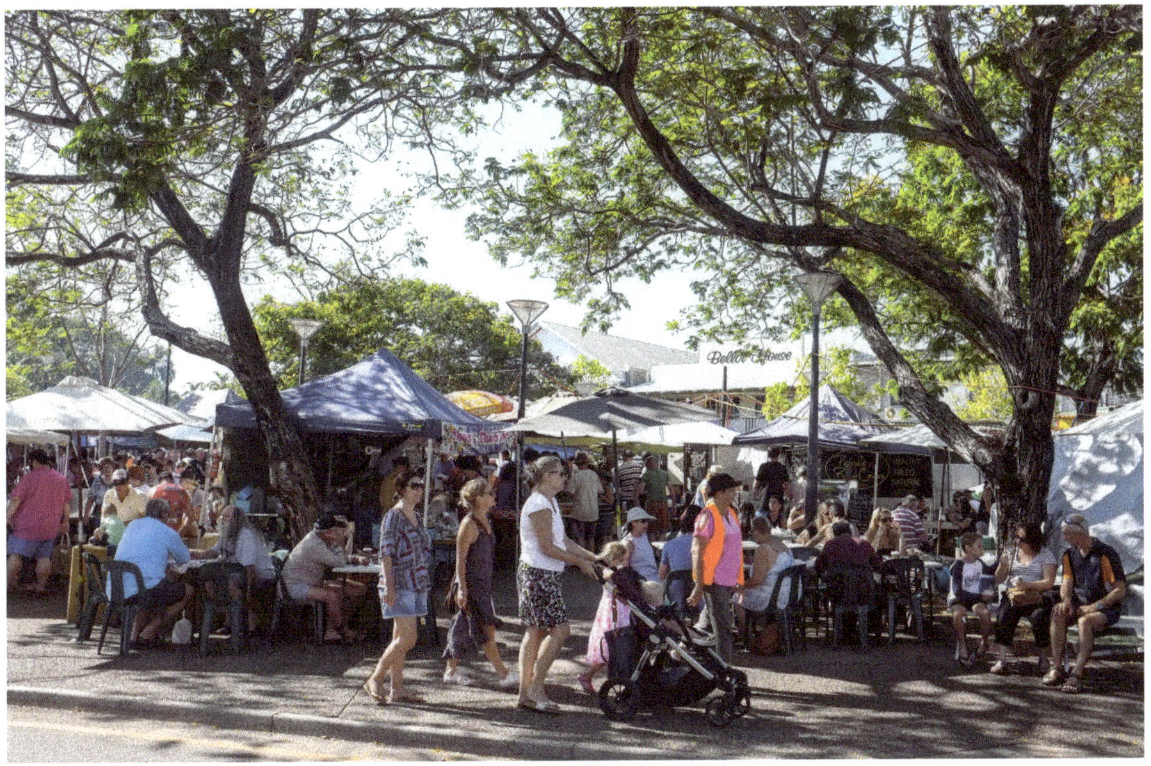

Parap Markets, 2017. (Martin, R., Matthew Stephen, Personal Collection, ParapMarket_20)

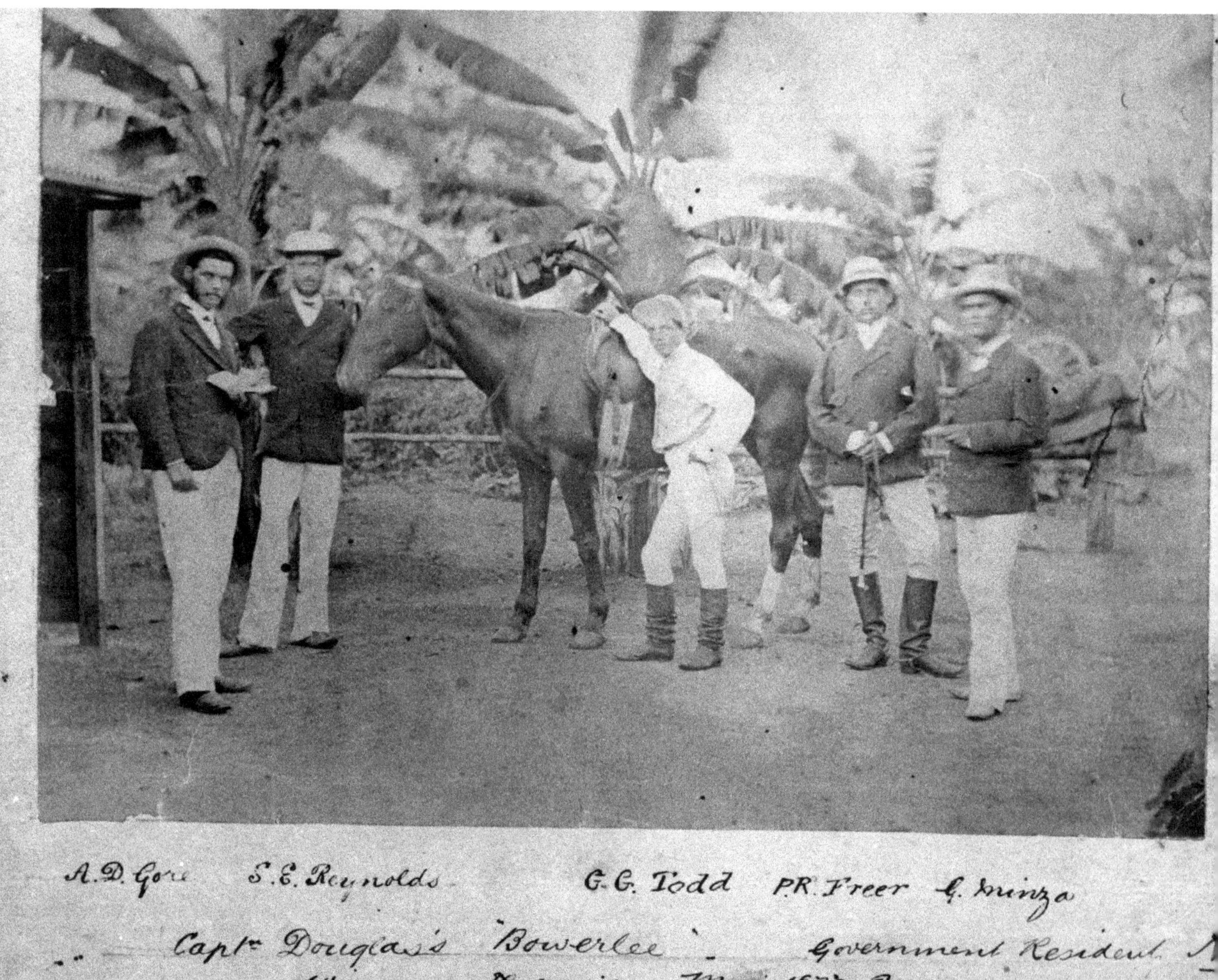

Griffith George Todd, dressed as a jockey, L-R A.D. Gore, S.E. Reynolds, Todd, P.R. Freer, G. Minza: Capt. Douglas's "Bowerlee" winner of the Maidens, May 1873. (Unknown, SLSA, Darwin Collection, B11947.)

Chapter 13

The Fannie Bay Coast & East Point ~ *Meyirrang*

During the colonial period East Point was considered distant from the town of Palmerston and was used mainly as a recreational area for picnics and outings. The first horses races held in Palmerston were on Fannie Bay beach.[1] A colonial era institution, the Annual Palmerston Church Picnic, was often held at Fannie Bay from the 1870s to the turn of the 20th century.

In 1917, Eustratos Haritos established the Darwin Salt Works on salt pans on East Point to supply the Vesteys Meatworks.[2] The natural salt pan was fed by the tidal movements of Ludmilla Creek. The basin would flood with salt water, the water eventually evaporating leaving the remaining salt to be harvested. The edges of the salt pan were built up to deepen and contain the flooding. A pump was installed to increase the water volume and sluice gates controlled the flow of water between sections of the salt pan. A hand pushed cart on rails across the salt pan was used to haul the salt to a shed for bagging. [3] The salt works remained in business until World War II when civilians were evacuated from Darwin.

In 1932 East Point became the focal point of a defence infrastructure construction program that transformed Darwin both socially and economically. The first phase of construction of the coastal defences, or Fortress Darwin as it became known, were built in 1932-34 to protect the naval oil tanks at Stokes Hill and The Esplanade. This work was carried out by the Darwin Detachment made up of members of the Royal Australian Artillery (RAA) and the Royal Australian Engineers (RAE). The military installations at East Point included the construction of a road to the site, wells to supply water, six inch gun emplacements, command post, searchlights, magazines, engine rooms to drive the searchlights and guns, observation and gunfire control towers and accommodation for the garrison.[4] The construction works were the largest undertaken in Darwin since Vesteys Meatworks and civilian and Aboriginal prison labour were employed to assist the military personal. In 1933 the Darwin Detachment was relieved by the Darwin Garrison (RAA & RAE) and the work continued unabated. The six inch guns at East Point were test fired in May 1934.[5]

Amidst the military build up the new Darwin Golf Club links at East Point were opened in 1935.[6] The club's first course, constructed on the Civil Aviation Aerodrome in 1930, had to relocate when QANTAS announced the commencement of a regular England to Australia air service in 1934.[7] The Golf Club

---

1 Catchlove, *Diaries*, 11.
2 Boland. *Know Where You Stand*, 7.
3 NTG, Heritage Register, *Ludmilla Salt Pans.*
4 Raynor, *Darwin Detachment*, 27.
5 Cramp, *The Silence of the Guns*, 16.
6 *NS*, 9 July 1935.
7 Smith & Nicholls, *Darwin Golf Club*,15.

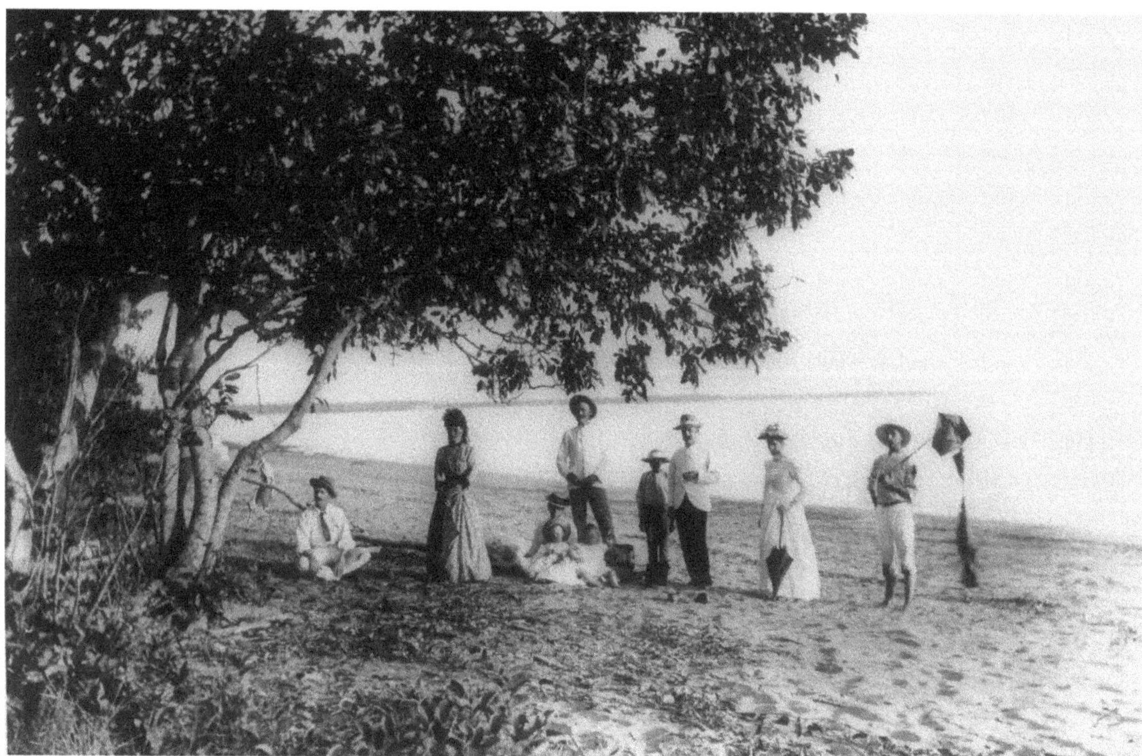

Fannie Bay Beach picnic, c1890s. (Foelsche, P., SLSA, Northern Territory Collection, B 46851.)

was granted 35 acres of land, which includes the area now covered by Lake Alexander. Golf was played at East Point up until November 1941 when the civilian evacuation of the town began.[8]

The development of the military infrastructure at East Point gained pace in the late 1930s as a response to the growing Japanese threat. The Port War Signal Station, which greatly enhanced communications with ships at sea, was operational in late 1939. The construction of an anti submarine boom net across the entrance of Darwin Harbour, with the eastern anchor point at East Point, began in 1937 but was not completed until late 1942.[9] In late 1941 two additional 6-inch guns with protecting machine gun pits were installed and test fired in August. Also in 1941 defence plans called for the installation of two 9.2 guns at East Point. Work was well under way by January 1942.

The coastal defences of Fortress Darwin at East Point were designed to repulse a naval attack. When the Japanese attacked Darwin on the 19th of February 1942, the East Point coastal defence complex was strafed by one Zero fighter with no casualties reported.[10] Work at East Point ceased for approximately the next four months while military priorities shifted elsewhere. Fortress Darwin had been rendered obsolete by air attack and was not subject to targeted bombing raids for the remainder of the war, although it was occasionally strafed by Japanese air crew.[11] Although some work at East Point recommenced the construction of the 9.2 gun emplacements and their installation did not resume until March 1943. The massive guns were finally tested in April 1944 but, soon after, the order was given to cease manning both the 9.2 and 6-inch guns. Later in 1944 all anti-aircraft guns were withdrawn from Darwin and coastal artillery reduced to one 6-inch and one 6-pounder

8 *AN*, 23 November 1941.
9 Forster, *Fixed Naval Defenses of Darwin Harbour 1939-1945*.
10 Cramp, *The Silence of the Guns*, 42.
11 Cramp, Personal communication, 1 August 2018.

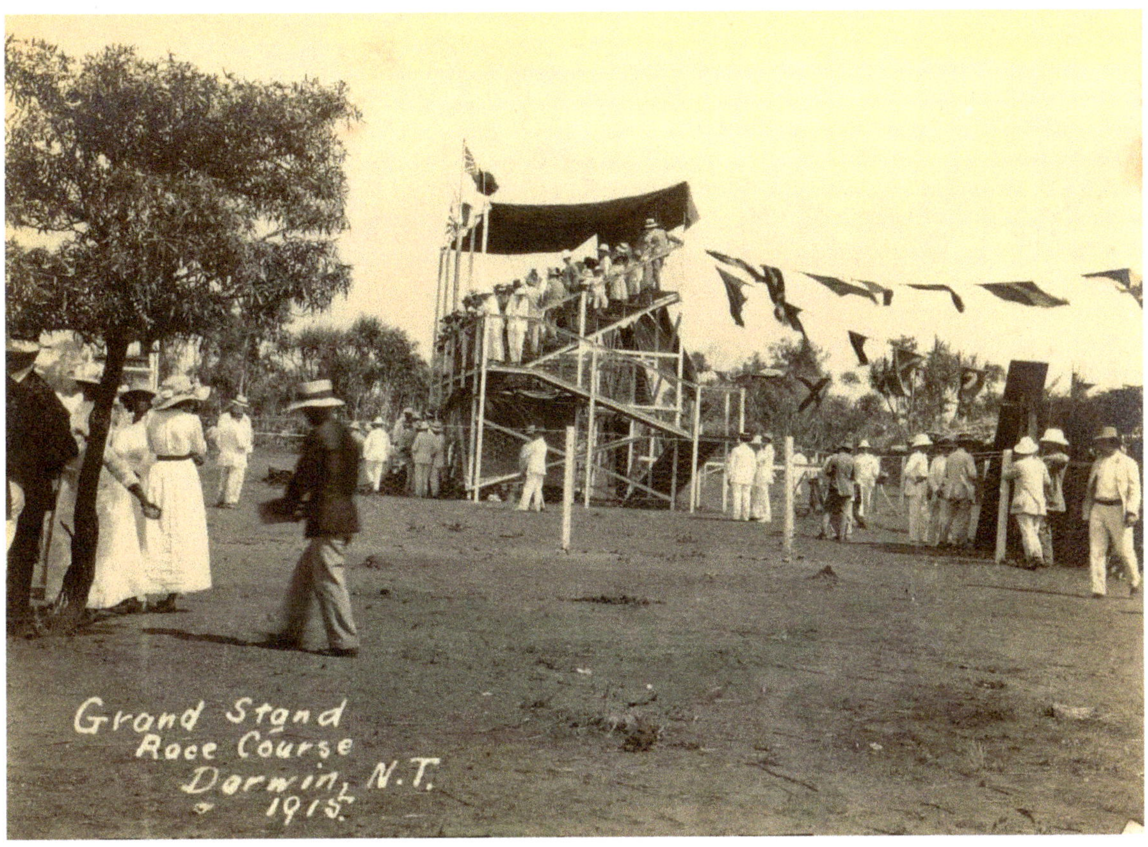

Fannie Bay Race Course, grandstand, 1915. (Unknown, NTAS, Roden Collection, NTRS 1744 Item 339.)

gun. Consequently, defence personnel levels were also reduced as troops were deployed elsewhere. [12]

As a British port aquatic sports have been a feature of Darwin since European settlement. The earliest sailing regattas featuring rowing and sailing races were held in Francis Bay from the 1870s until World War I. Many of the regattas in the late 19th Century included 'Lugger' races between pearling luggers and Chinese 'Sampan' races. Sailing disappeared from the sporting calendar between the World Wars but re-emerged at the end of World War II. As the war became more distant from Darwin and defence force levels decreased the East Point / Fannie Bay area resorted to its earlier role as a recreation area. Defence force units were involved in many sports including the East Point Bowls Club, which hosted a number of events in 1944,[13] as did the Fanny Bay Sailing Club in 1945.[14] Few records of the clubs remain but in the closing period of World War II armed forces personnel must have had time to have some fun in their spare time. When World War II came to an end on 2 September 1945 activity at East Point and the shores of Fannie Bay, military and social, almost ceased.

It was not until the late 1950s that there were new developments on the shores of Fannie Bay. The Arafura Power Boat Club established in 1952 and the Darwin Water Ski Club were mentioned in relation to Bullocky Point. The Darwin Trailer Boat Club was formed in 1958.[15] Soon after, in 1959 The Fannie Bay Hotel was opened. The Darwin Sailing Club

12 Cramp, *The Silence of the Guns*, 43-50.
13 *AN*, 23 October 1944 to 14 November 1944.
14 *AN*, 1 July 1945 to 11September 1945.
15 Darwin Trailer Boat Club, www.

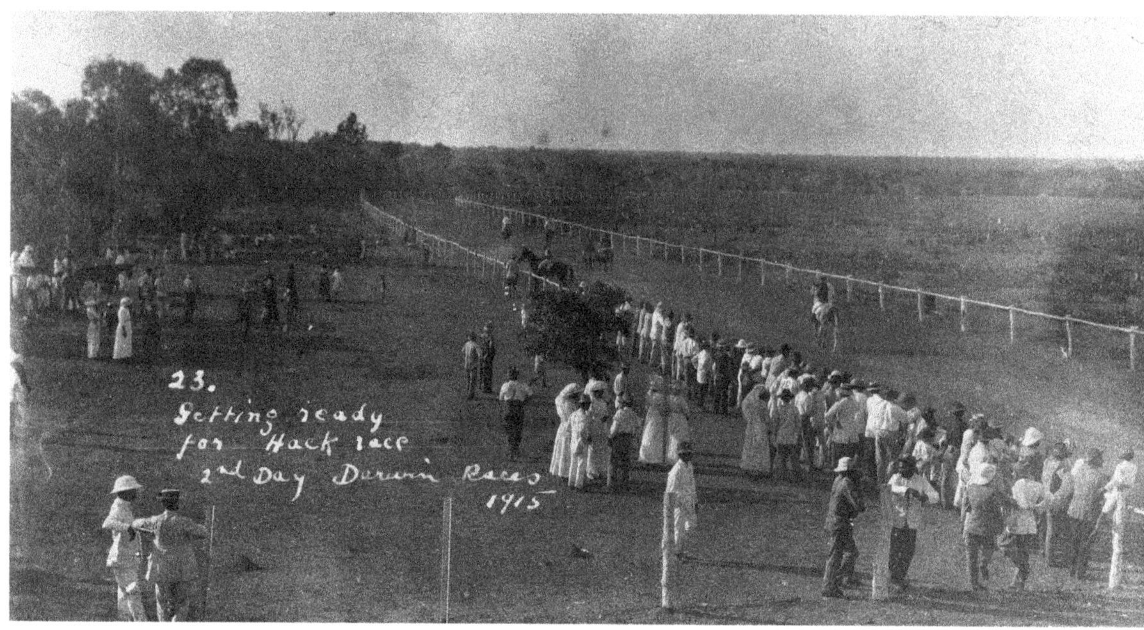

Fannie Bay races, 1915. (Unknown, LNSW, E.D.W.S Donnison Collection, ML MSS 890/3/0202.)

was formed in 1963 and built its first club house on its current site in 1966.[16] Common to all these locations is a fantastic outlook on to Fannie Bay and Darwin's beautiful sunsets. Although the Fannie Bay Hotel has gone the sailing and motor boat clubs remain to give everyone the opportunity to take in a sunset with a drink and meal.

Immediately after World War II East Point remained an Army reserve.[17] However, due to the severe housing shortage throughout the Darwin area civilians soon began to squat in the abandoned military facilities where many remained until the 1950s.[18] The Darwin Golf Club also resumed its activities at East Point in 1947. In the early 1960s government plans for a University at East Point and the construction of a highway linking East Point and Casuarina via Nightcliff prompted the Club to consider other locations.[19] It vacated the Fannie Bay course in April 1974 for its current location at Marrara in Darwin's northern suburbs.

By the early 1960s the East Point area, under the management of a board of trustees, was largely unkempt and unloved. Many of the military buildings had fallen into disrepair and considered dangerous. Seeing this Lt Colonel Haydon, who had served in Darwin during World War II, began a tireless campaign to preserve the military history of East Point. By 1967 he had enlisted the support of others and the Royal Australian Artillery Association (NT) was established. The RAAA-NT continued with the vision of an East Point military precinct by continually restoring and maintaining as many military sites as they could through the hard work of members while also lobbying the board of trustees and the government for support. In April 1968 the RAAA-NT had determined that the best way forward was to establish a military museum at East Point and by December the board of trustees had agreed to the RAAA-NT's submission for land covering East Point's military history. The East Point Military Museum was opened on 16 August 1969 and continues on the site to this day.[20] In 2012 the Defence of Darwin Experience, was added to the precinct to use technology to showcase the military history of Darwin.

16 Darwin Sailing Club, www.
17 *NS*, 9 August 1946.
18 Cramp, *The Silence of the Guns*, 52-56.
19 Smith & Nicholls, *Darwin Golf Club*, 51.
20 Cramp, *The Silence of the Guns*, 61-69.

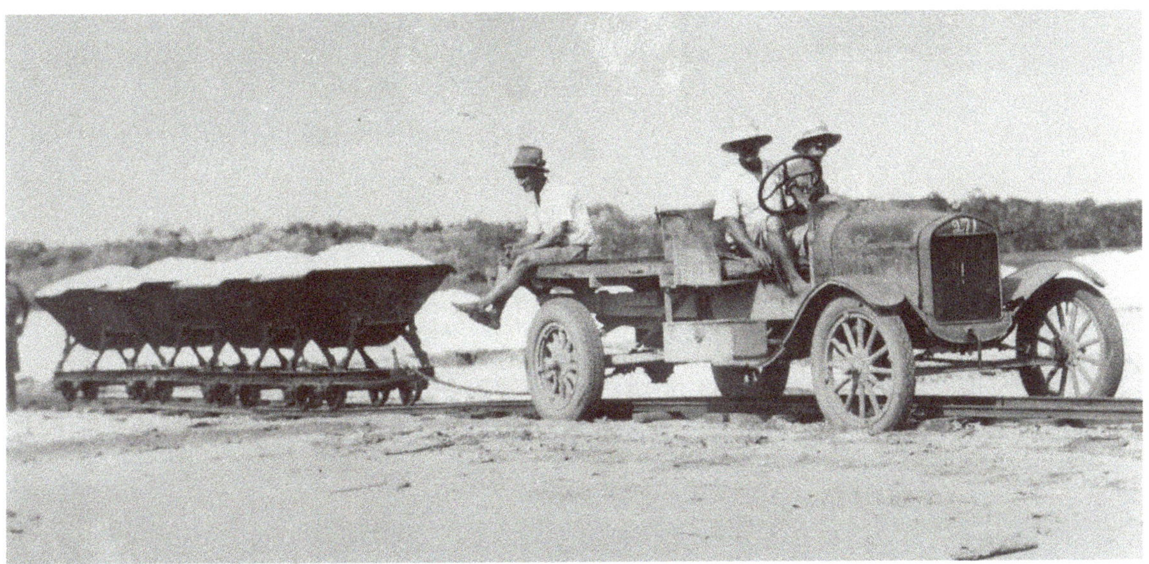

East Point salt pans, c1930s. (Unknown, NTAS, P. Murphy Collection, NTRS 1685/49.)

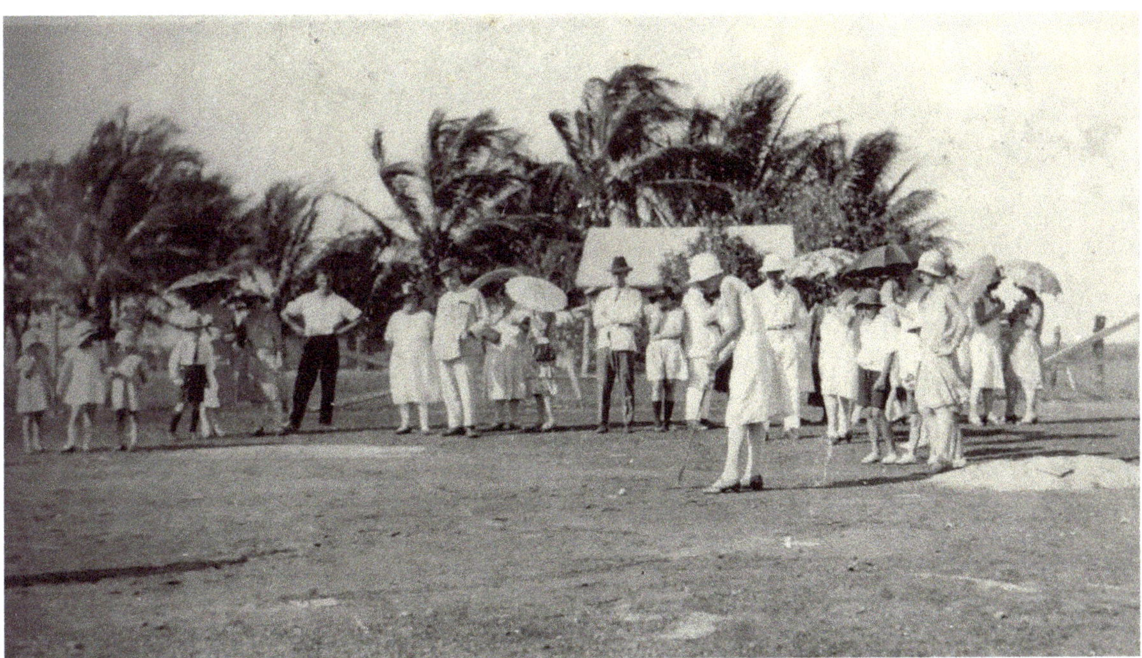

Fannie Bay Golf Course opening day, East Point, 1935., (Unknown, NTAS, HSNT Collection, NTRS 1854 Item 846.)

Lake Alexander, named in honour of Alec Fong Lim, Lord Mayor of Darwin from 1984 to 1990, was opened in July 1991. The manmade 3.5 hectare lake created from a coastal marsh transformed the East Point landscape. It now provides swimming and recreational waters to the public that are safe from the crocodiles, stingers and sharks that inhabit all of Darwin city's surrounding seas and rivers. Lake Alexander is just one of reasons that East Point is one of Darwin's most popular recreation areas. It is rare that there is not a cool breeze, and there are many great locations for a picnic. The coastal path and bikeway gives some of the best views of Darwin across Fannie Bay. Interpretive information along the way also provides a fascinating glimpse into the lives of those stationed at Fortress Darwin during World War II.

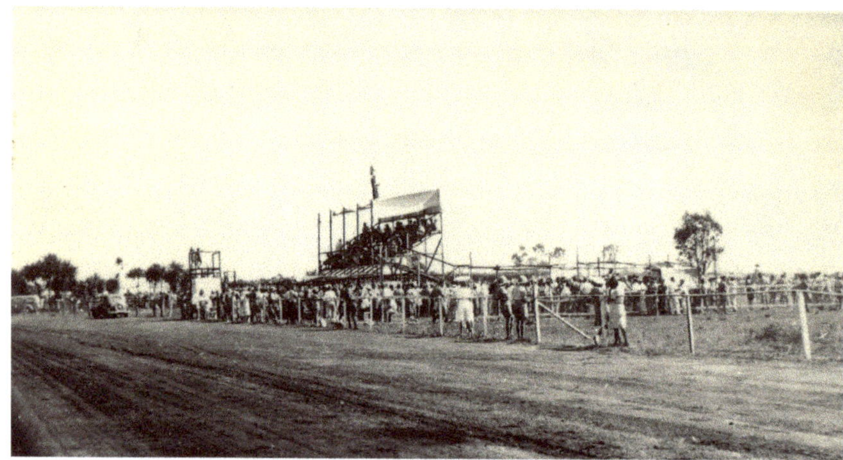

Fannie Bay Race Course, Grandstand, c1930s. (Unknown, NTAS, HSNT Collection, NTRS 1854 Item 660.)

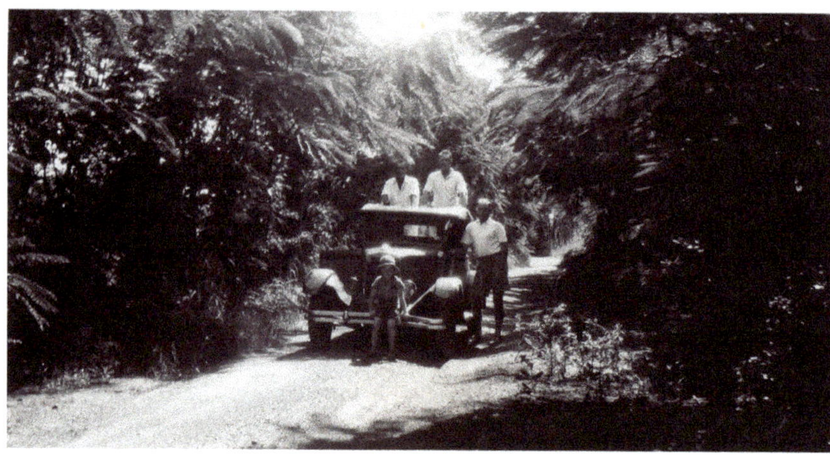

Sergeant Kelly's car, East Point Road, 1935. (Unknown, Angus-Bird, Personal Collection, 19.)

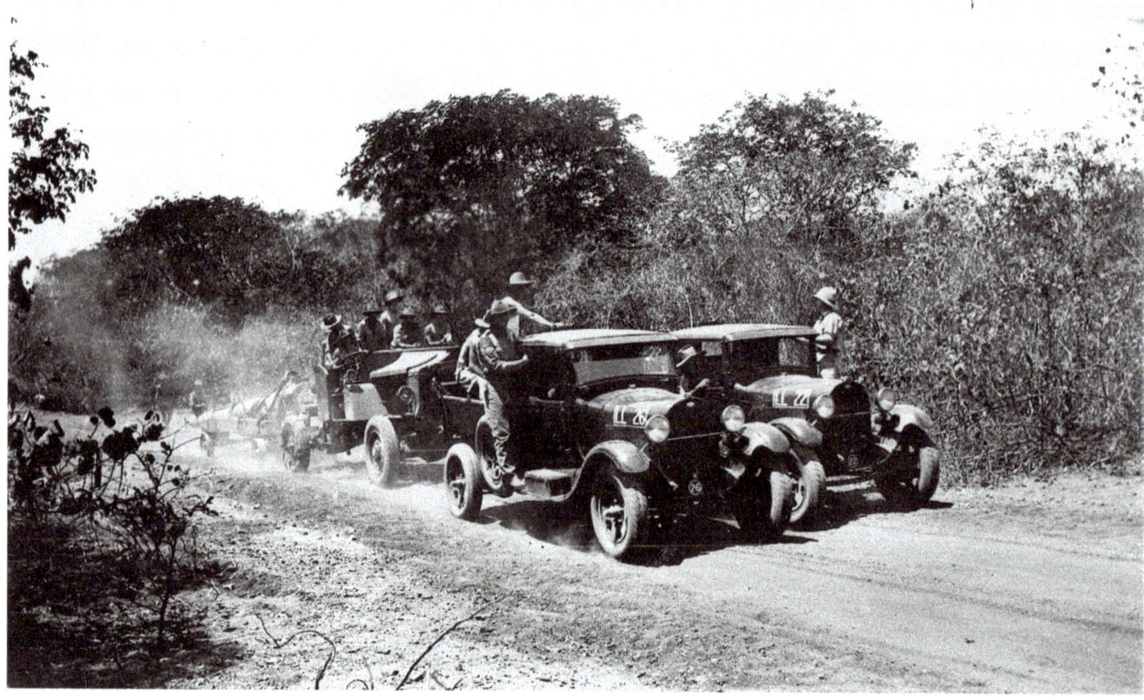

East Point Road, building coastal defences, 15 December 1934. Two 30cwt Ford trucks are hitched side by side in front of a Thorneycroft Hathi tractor towing a low wheeled trolley carrying a 6 inch gun. (Unknown, AWM, Photograph, PO2024.31.)

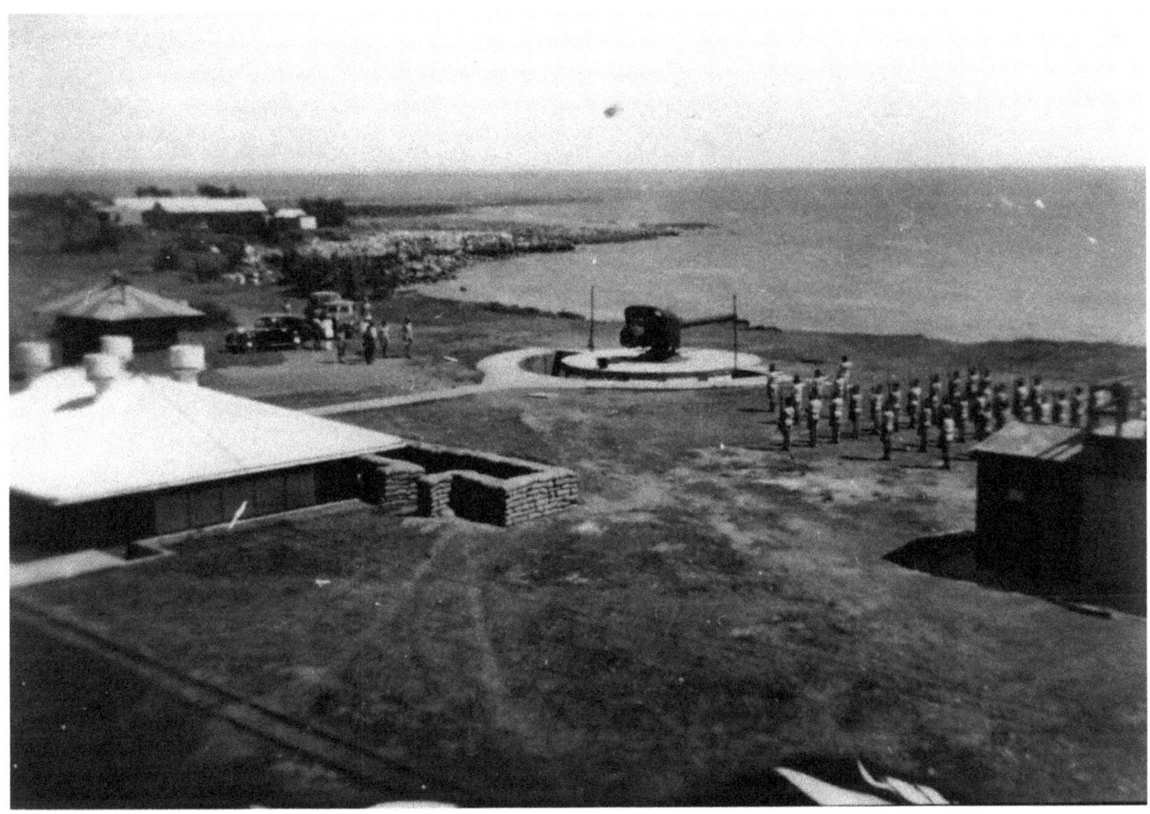

East Point, defences, 1940. (Unknown, NTL, L. M. Berry Collection, PH0277/0019.)

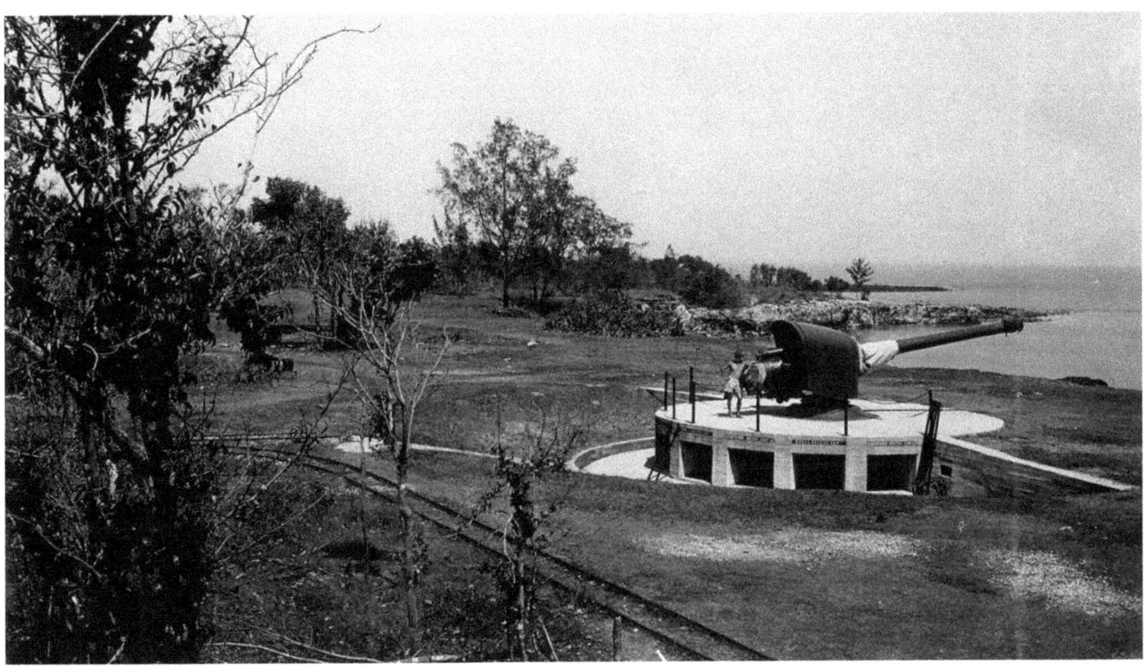

No.2 6 inch gun at East Point, c1936. (Unknown, Angus-Bird, Personal Collection, 9.)

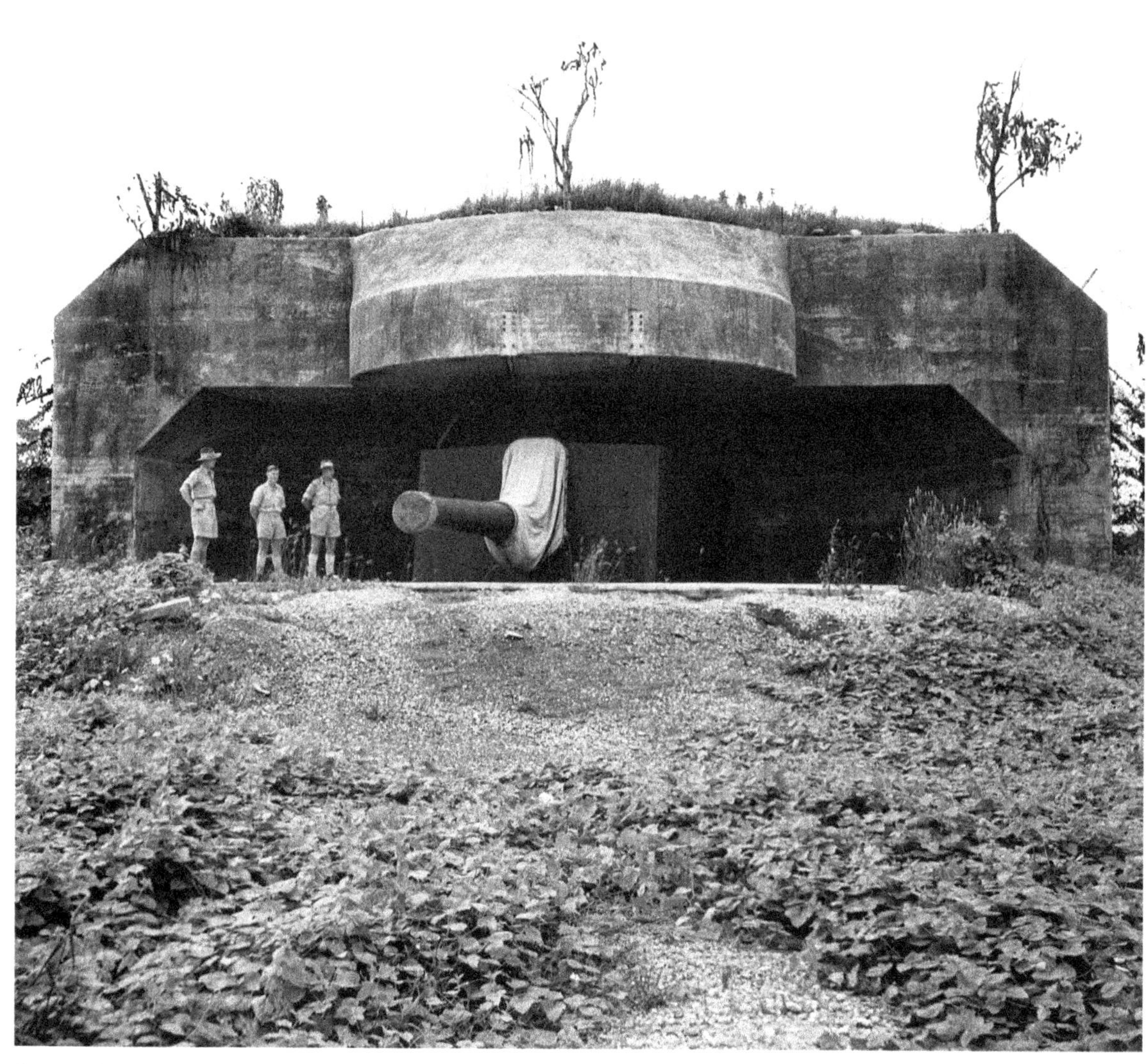

Darwin Fixed Defences, 5 March 1946. 9.2 inch guns & turret, East Point. (Unknown, AWM, Photograph, 126155.)

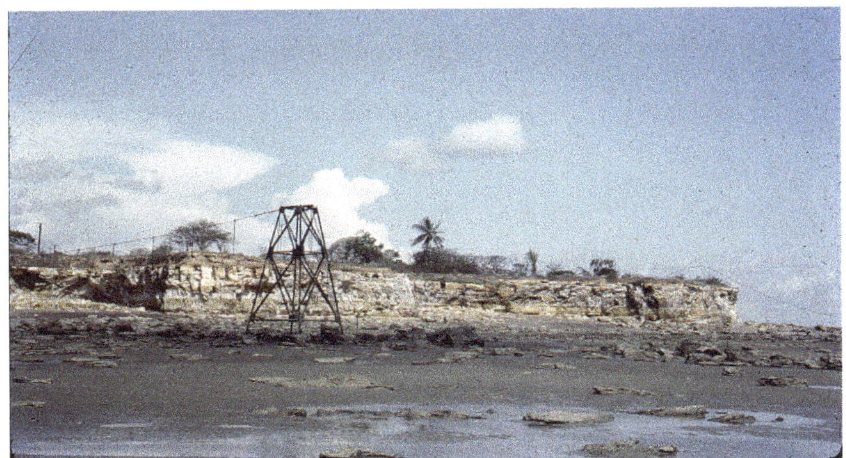

East Point, remains of the Submarine Boom, 1950s. (Graham, H., NTAS, H. Graham Collection, NTRS 3406/P1 Item 65.)

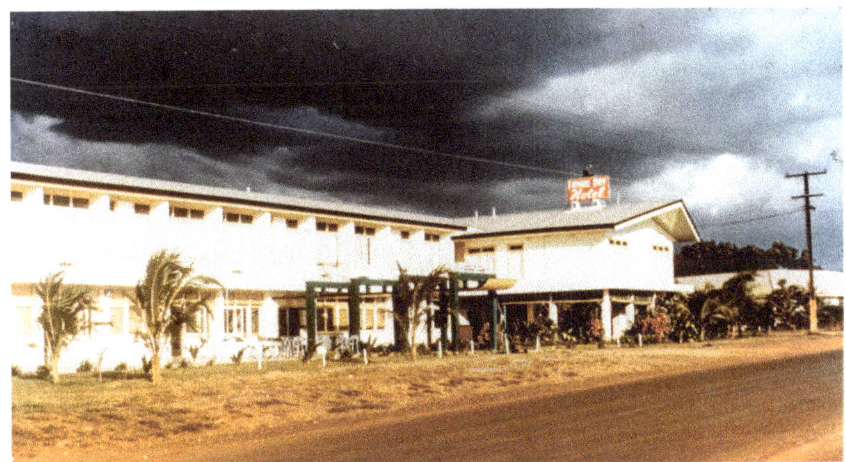

Fannie Bay Hotel, 1959. (Helyar, G. & F., NTL, Lois & Geoff Helyar Collection, PH0092-0196.)

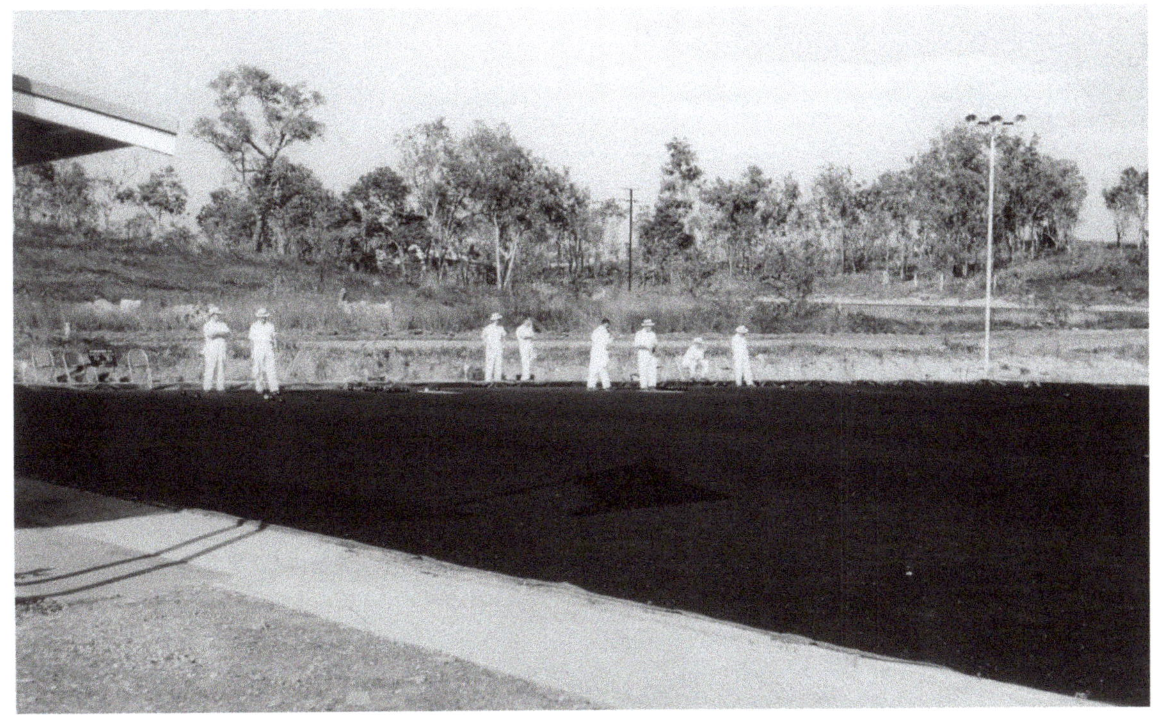

Darwin Bowls Club, 1961. (Unknown, NTL, David Veal Collection, PH0258-0007.)

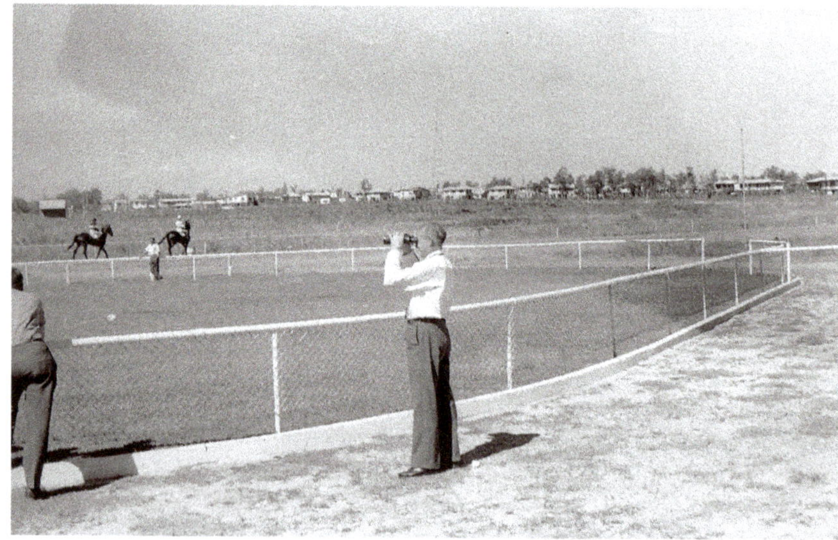

Eric Izod on duty as a judge at the Darwin Turf Club, Fannie Bay, c1961. (Unknown, NTL, Izod Collection, PH0748/0029.)

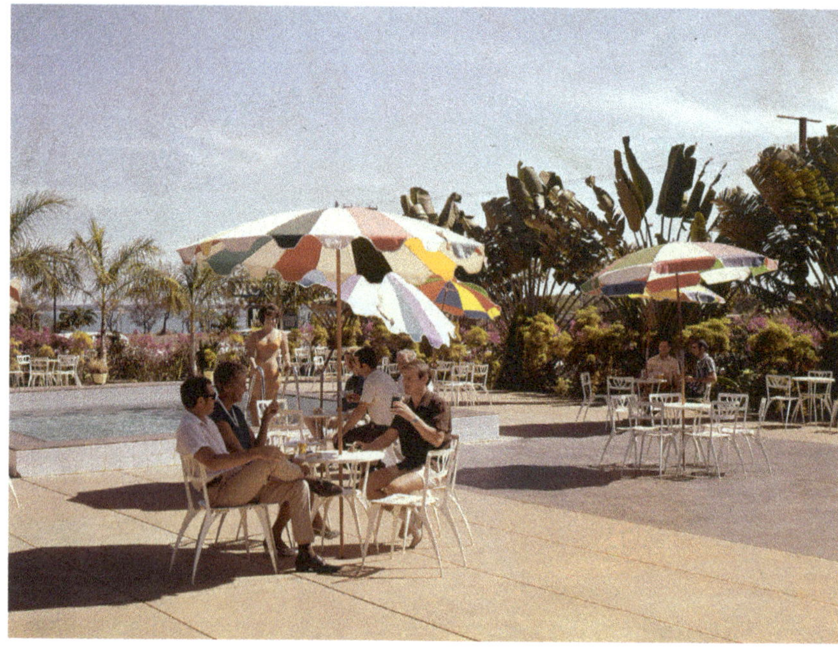

Fannie Bay Hotel, c1970s. (Unknown, NTAS, GPC, NTRS 3822-P2 Darwin Streets Buildings-Fannie Bay Hotel.)

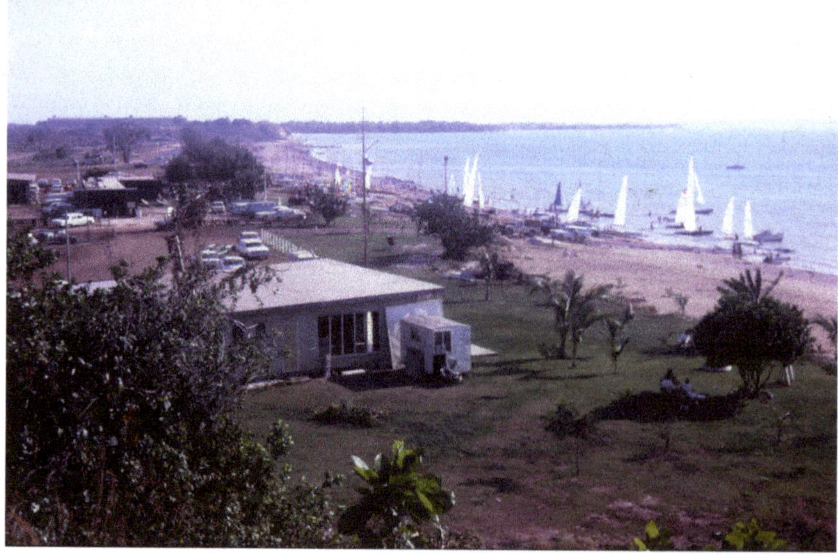

Darwin Sailing Club, 1970. (Cheater, F., NTL, Fay Cheater Collection, PH0049/0134.)

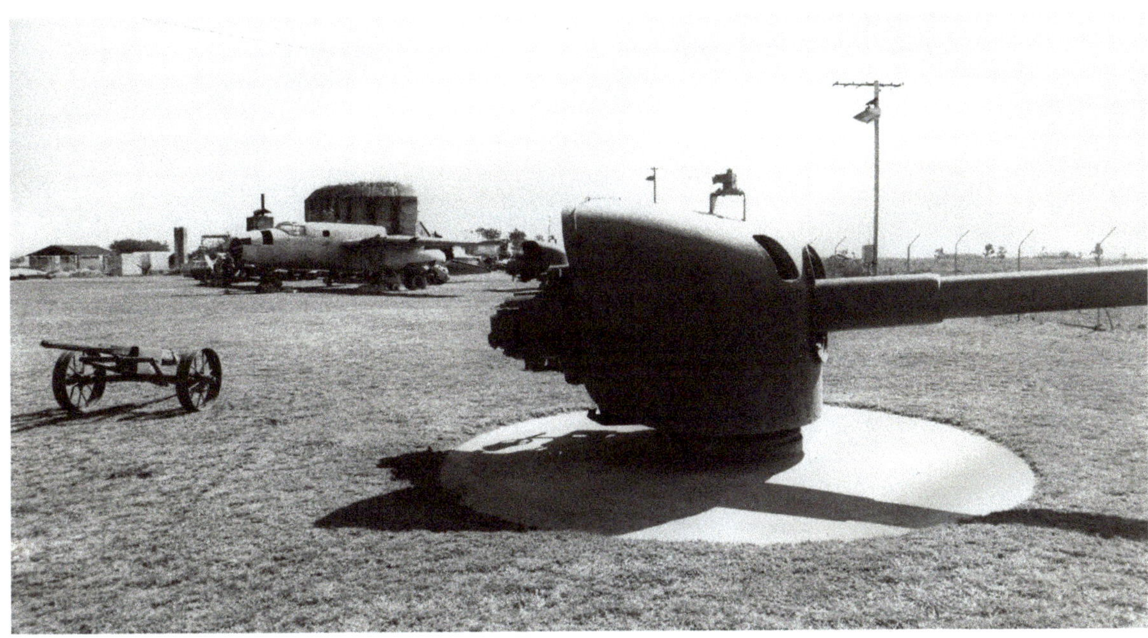

East Point Military Museum, c1970s. (Unknown, NTAS, GPC, NTRS 3822/P1/Bx7/GPC/Fldr 139, Museums.)

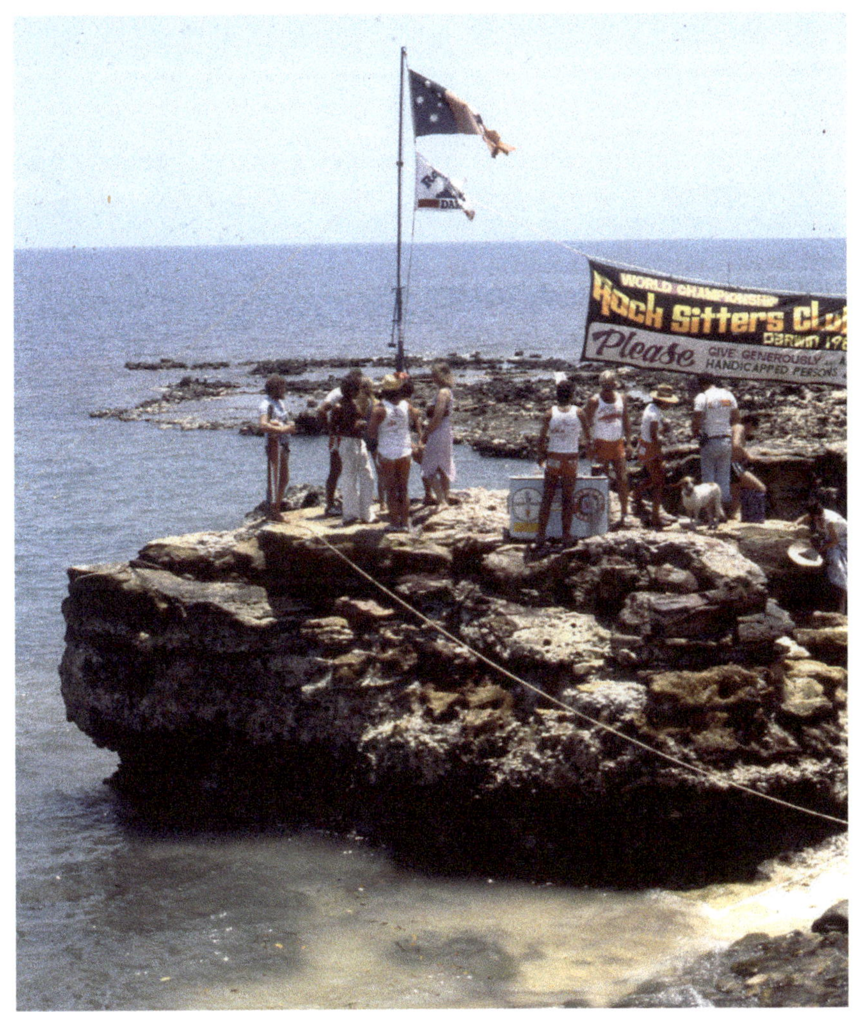

Darwin Rocksitters, East Point, c1980. (Skipsey, B., NTAS, GPC, NTRS 3822-P3 Rocksitters Slide 3.)

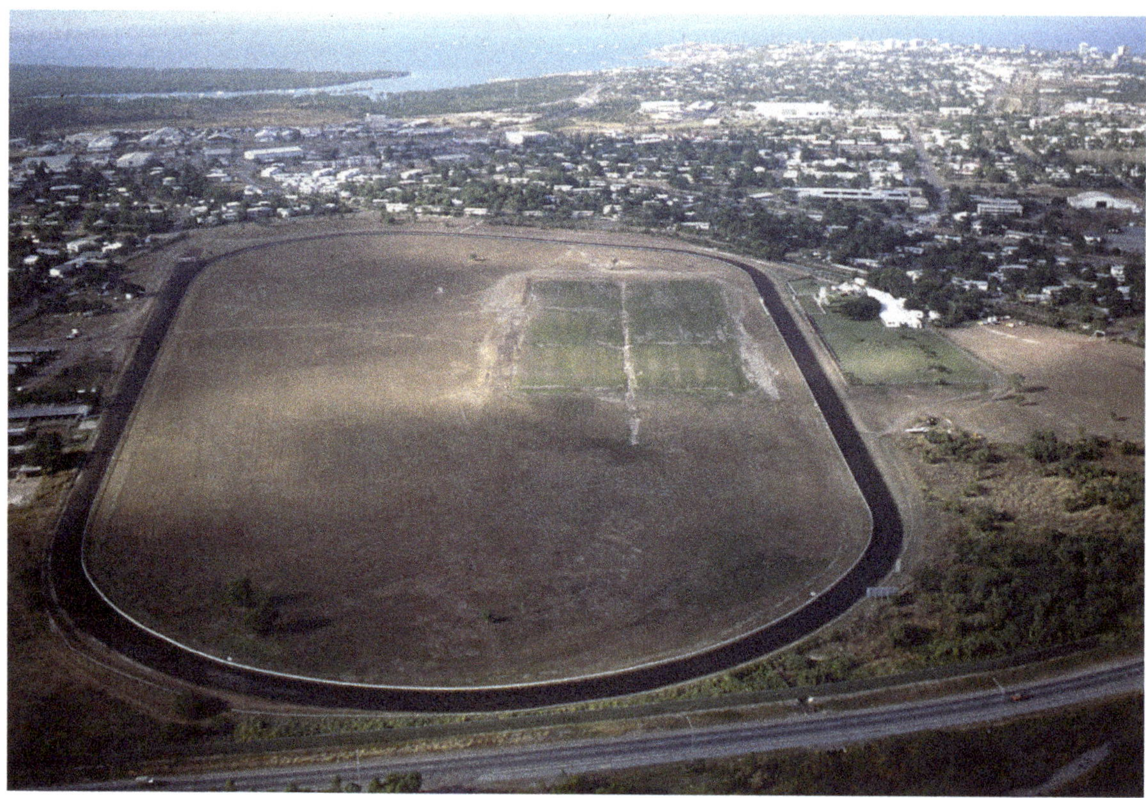

Darwin Turf Club, 1985. (Unknown, NTAS, GPC, NTRS 3822-P3 Horse Racing Slide 88.)

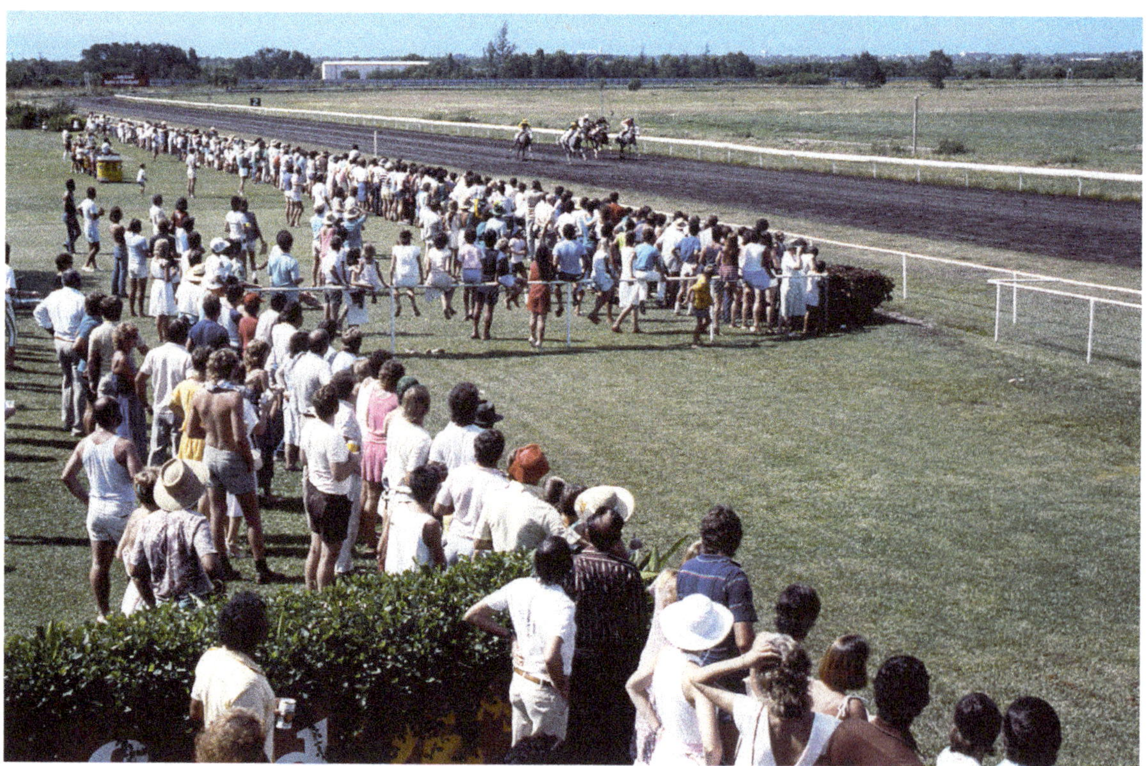

Darwin Turf Club, St Patricks Day races trackside, 1985. (Unknown, NTAS, GPC, NTRS 3822-P3 Horse Racing Slide 78.)

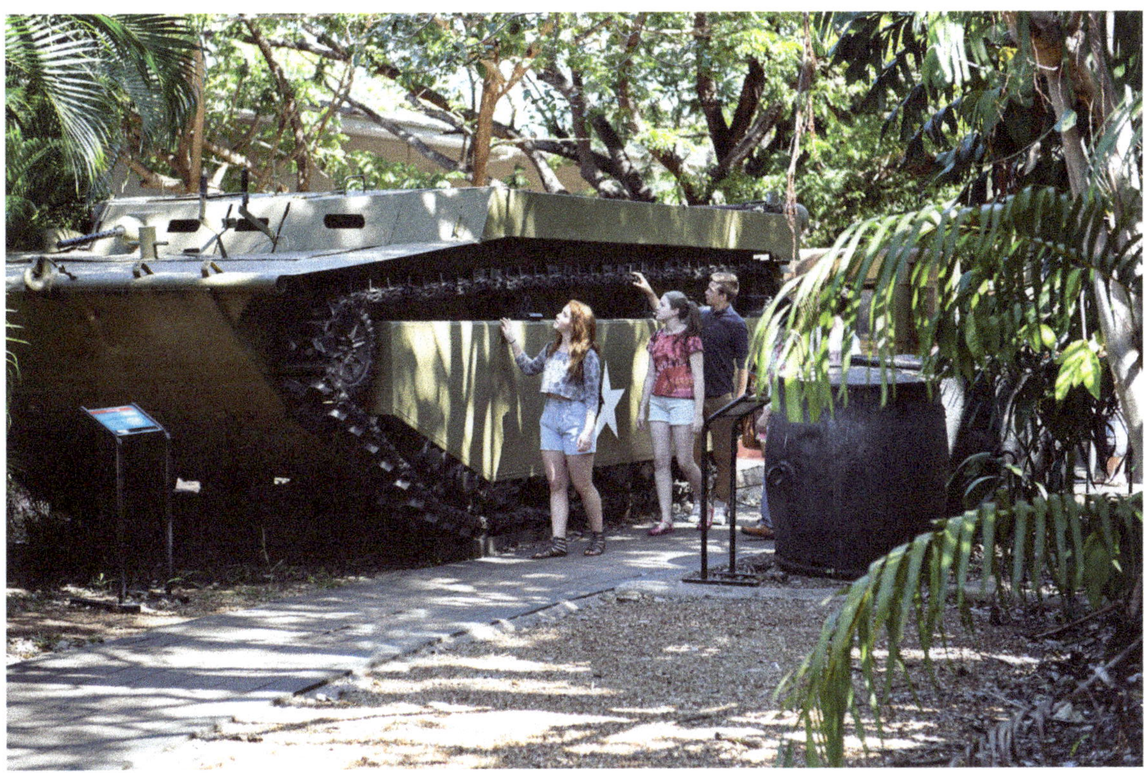

East Point Military Museum, c2010s. (McNaught, S., Tourism NT, Tourism NT Collection, 119224.)

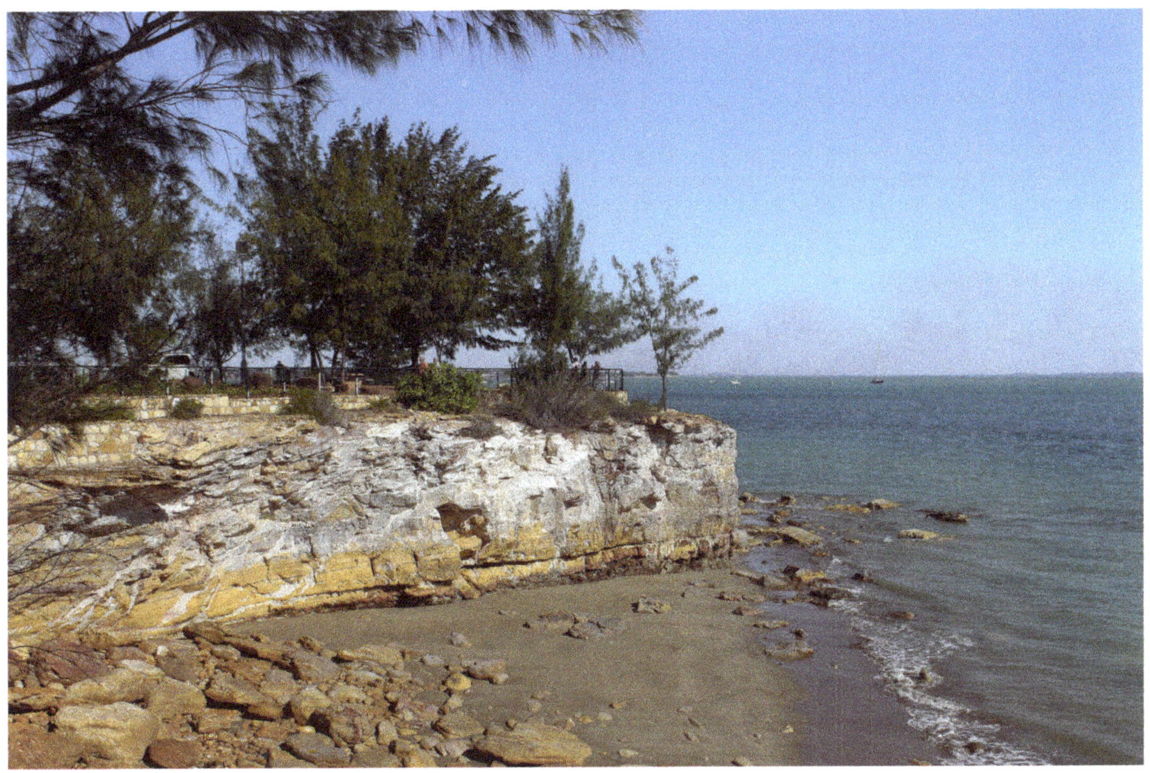

East Point, c2010s. (Mayans, A., Tourism NT, Tourism NT Collection, 120260-2.)

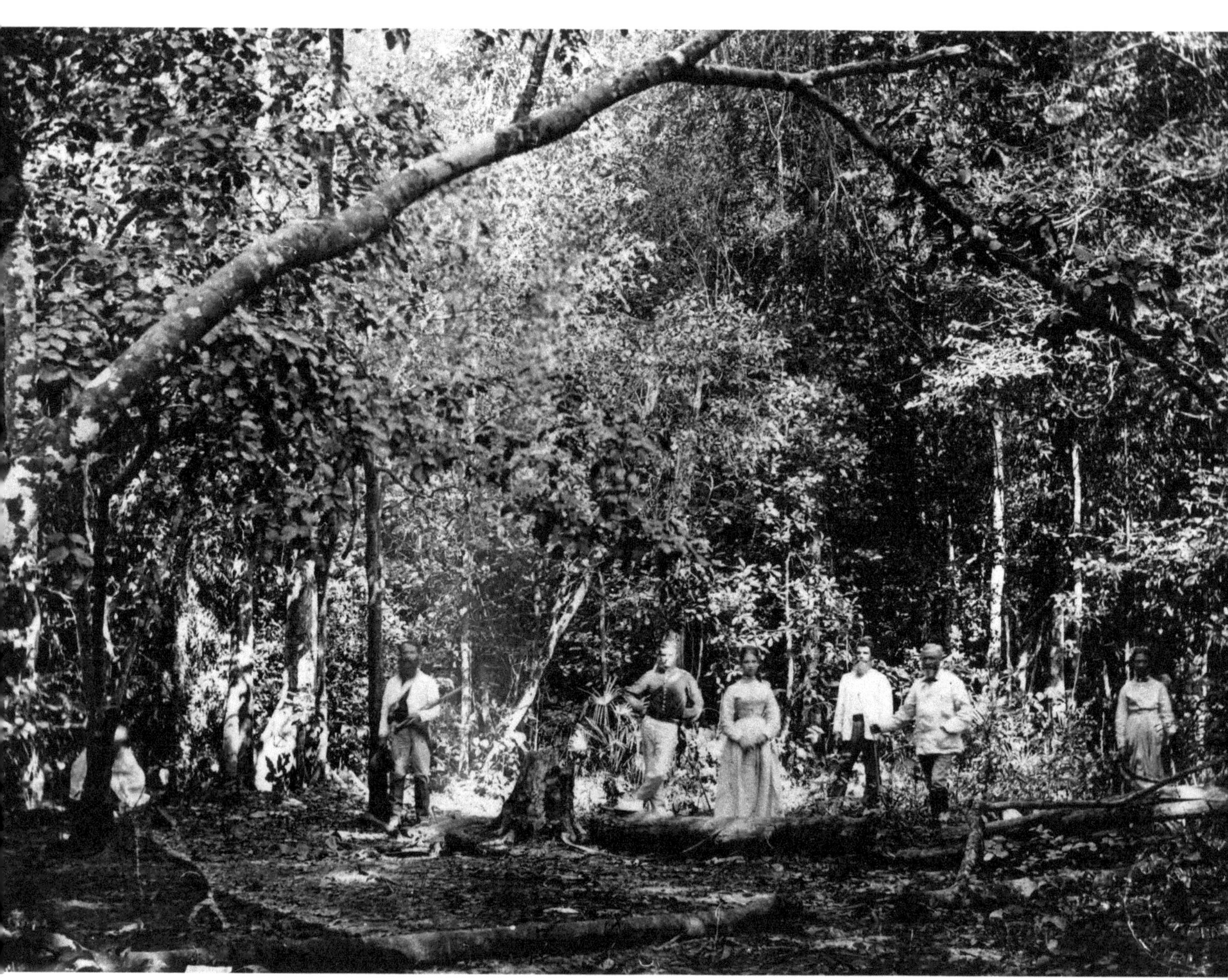

Port Darwin, Government Resident Douglas, picnic party in The Jungle, 1871. 'The Casuarinas' or 'The Jungle' was in the vicinity of Casuarina Beach. (Sweet, S.W., SLSA, Darwin Collection, B17389_1.)

Chapter 14

Darwin's Northern Beachside Suburbs:

Nightcliff ~ *Majamarraba*
Rapid Creek ~ *Gurrumbay*
Casuarina Beach ~ *Dariba Nungalinya*

Darwin's is blessed with beautiful harbour views and beaches but Australia's northern marine environment means our relationship with the coast is very different to that of southern Australia. Water sports can only be undertaken with precautions against dangers like crocodiles and 'stingers.'[1] Darwin's northern beaches of Nightcliff, Rapid Creek and Casuarina were largely undeveloped until World War II. Wartime infrastructure and Darwin's post war reconstruction saw the city grow to turn the northern beaches from distant picnic spots to beachside suburbs.

Nightcliff and Rapid Creek were named during Goyder's survey in 1869. Casuarina beach was referred to as 'The Casuarina's' for many years. All have Larrakia names. Nightcliff is *Majamarraba*.[2] Casuarina Beach, or more precisely the rocky reef visible at low tide from the beach, is *Dariba Nungalinya*, or Old Man Rock, which is the embodiment of a powerful ancestor who protects Larrakia land and people.[3] The Larrakia name for the shape of Rapid Creek near its mouth is *Gurrumbay* which is said to be the elbow of *Dariba Nungalinya*.[4]

In the early years of settlement the 10 Kilometres from Darwin city to the northern beaches made them places to visit for picnics or hunting expeditions and they were reached by boat as often as overland.

The first permanent settlement in the area was a Jesuit mission on Rapid Creek from 1882-1891. The mission was short lived but the missionaries did make a study of the Larrakia language and established a school to teach the Aboriginal children living there.[5] By the 1890s a number of agricultural leases were taken up in the Nightcliff, Rapid Creek area but the lack of available water and easily arable land made farming difficult.

1 The stinger season extends from October – May each year. This is due to the presence of venomus jellyfish, *Chironex fleckeri*, the world's most venomous marine creature, and the small Irukandji, *Carukia barnesi*.
2 NTL, *Origin of a City: How Darwin Was Named.*
3 Bauman, *Aboriginal Darwin*, 128.
4 Bauman, *Aboriginal Darwin*, 125.
5 Barter, *From Wartime Camp to Garden Suburb*, 5

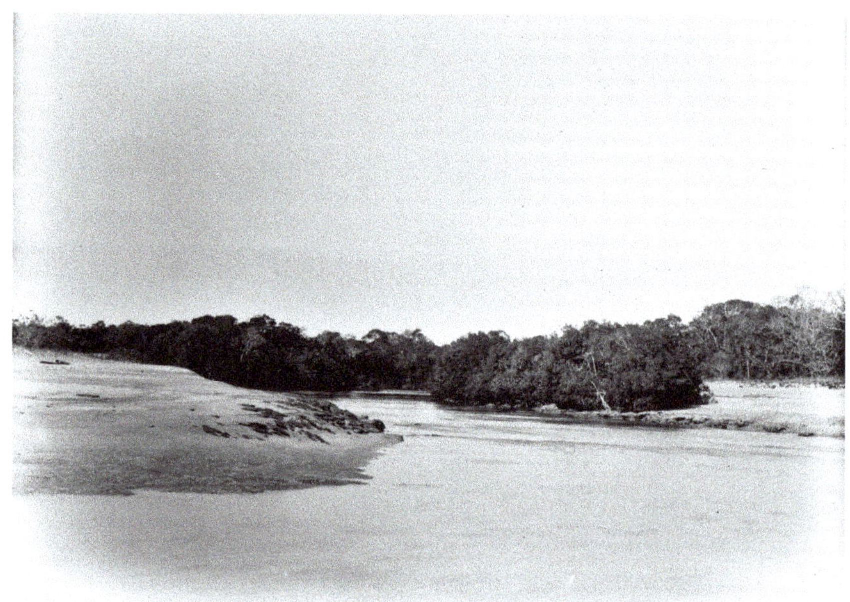

Rapid Creek, c1897. (Bleeser, F., NLA, Florenz Bleeser Collection, PIC/9981/28.)

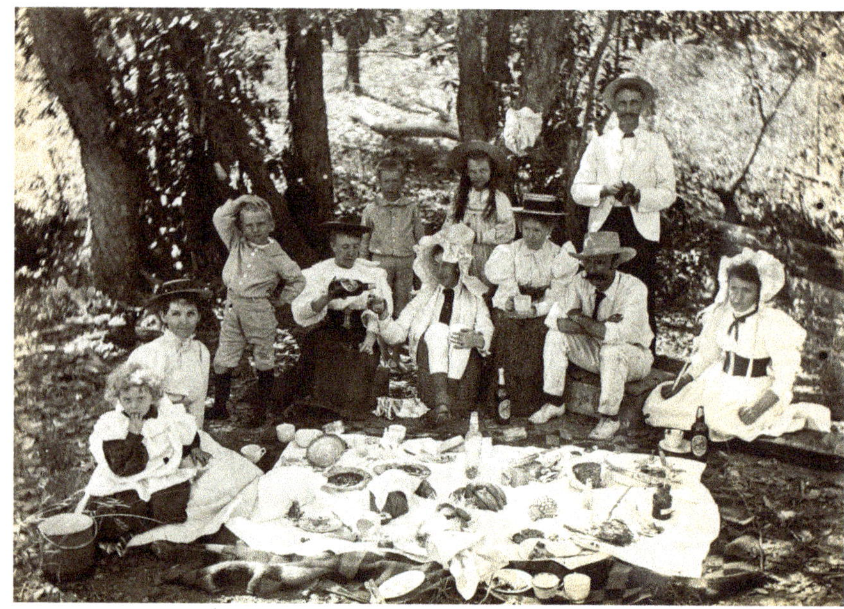

Rapid Creek picnic, 1899. (Unknown, NTL, Peter Spillett Collection, PH0238/2047.)

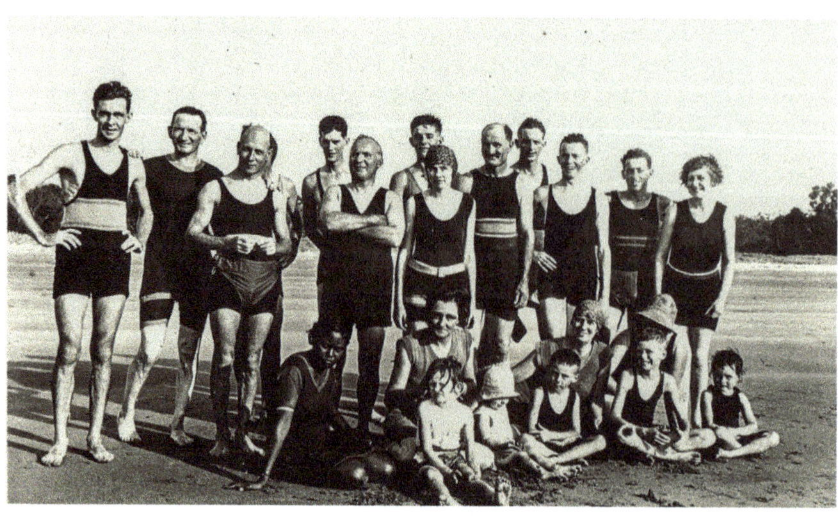

Beach party, Casuarina Beach, c1920s. (Unknown, NTL, M. Goodale Collection, PH0345/0152.)

Access to the northern beaches was greatly improved when Shirley Miles, the enterprising owner of Yellow Motor Bus Services, built his own road to Casuarina Beach via a bridge over Rapid Creek in 1926. The weekend service to this 'splendid swimming, fishing, shooting and picnic ground' could be extended to Dripstone Caves upon request.'[6] Despite the new road the northern beaches remained undeveloped until World War II.

Development of the northern beaches gained pace during the early years of World War II as defence infrastructure was developed in and around Darwin. Military installations built along the Nightcliff foreshore included a naval outpost with a high concrete artillery observation tower and a military camp to house elements of the 2/14 Field Regiment. Coastal defences including observation posts, machine gun pits, field gun sites, barbed wire entanglements and star pickets were constructed at strategic locations along the foreshore as far as Lee Point. Communications between the defences were improved by the construction of timber corduroy tracks through mangroves and over swampy ground. The defences were manned by units of the 2/4th Machine Gun Battalion.[7] On the 19th of February 1942 the camp at Nightcliff was strafed by Japanese Zeros while defenders attempted to bring them down with anti aircraft and machine gun fire. Fortunately the coastal defences on Casuarina beach were never put to the test.

As the war went on units based in the Nightcliff area included the RAF 54 Spitfire fighter squadron (1943-1944), the 65th and 86th American Camp and Station Hospitals (1944-1945). These military installations would form the basis of post war development in the area.

The town plan proposed for Darwin by R.A McInnes in 1940 recognised the recreational value of the Rapid Creek area when he recommended that sufficient land be reserved for a public picnic area while it was still possible.[8] In the immediate post war period the reconstruction of Darwin was controlled by the Commonwealth Government. In August 1945 it acquired all freehold land in and around Darwin through the *Darwin Lands Acquisition Act*. As a result residents had to lease land. Civilians began to return to Darwin after World War II after the *Emergency Control Regulations* in the region were lifted in late 1946.[9] Despite the government's desire to control development the extreme housing shortage in Darwin resulted in people squatting in accommodation wherever they could find it. By July 1946 accommodation at the former military hospital site, which had become the Nightcliff Community Centre, was full with 100 families living there. By Darwin standards the Nightcliff camp was well serviced with sewage and water tanks. By the end of the year a post office, store and bus service were in operation.[10]

A further sign of Nightcliff's growing popularity was the conversion of some of the former military buildings on the foreshore to the *Darwin Tourist Hostel* in 1947. Commander 'Chook' Fowler converted a Sidney Williams Hut in to a dining room and small huts were used for accommodation. Nightcliff was promoted as 'Darwin's Holiday Suburb' with its safe swimming beaches, attractive jungle walks and ever present cool breeze.[11] Granted a liquor license in 1950 the hostel was renamed the *Ludmilla Hotel*. By the mid 1950's the hotel was renamed *The Seabreeze*. *The Seabreeze* became famous for its Saturday night outdoor dances and would become a Darwin institution until its destruction in 1974 by Cyclone Tracy.

Development of Nightcliff accelerated after 1949 when waterfront land was made

---

6 *NS*, 6 July 1926.

7 Heritage Conservation Services, *WWII sites, Casuarina Coastal Reserve, Heritage Assessment Report*, 5.

8 Barter, *From Wartime Camp to Garden Suburb*, 9.

9 NAA, *Land of Opportunity: Australia's Post-war Reconstruction,* Research Guide, www.

10 Barter, *From Wartime Camp to Garden Suburb*, 27.

11 *NS*, 14 May 1948.

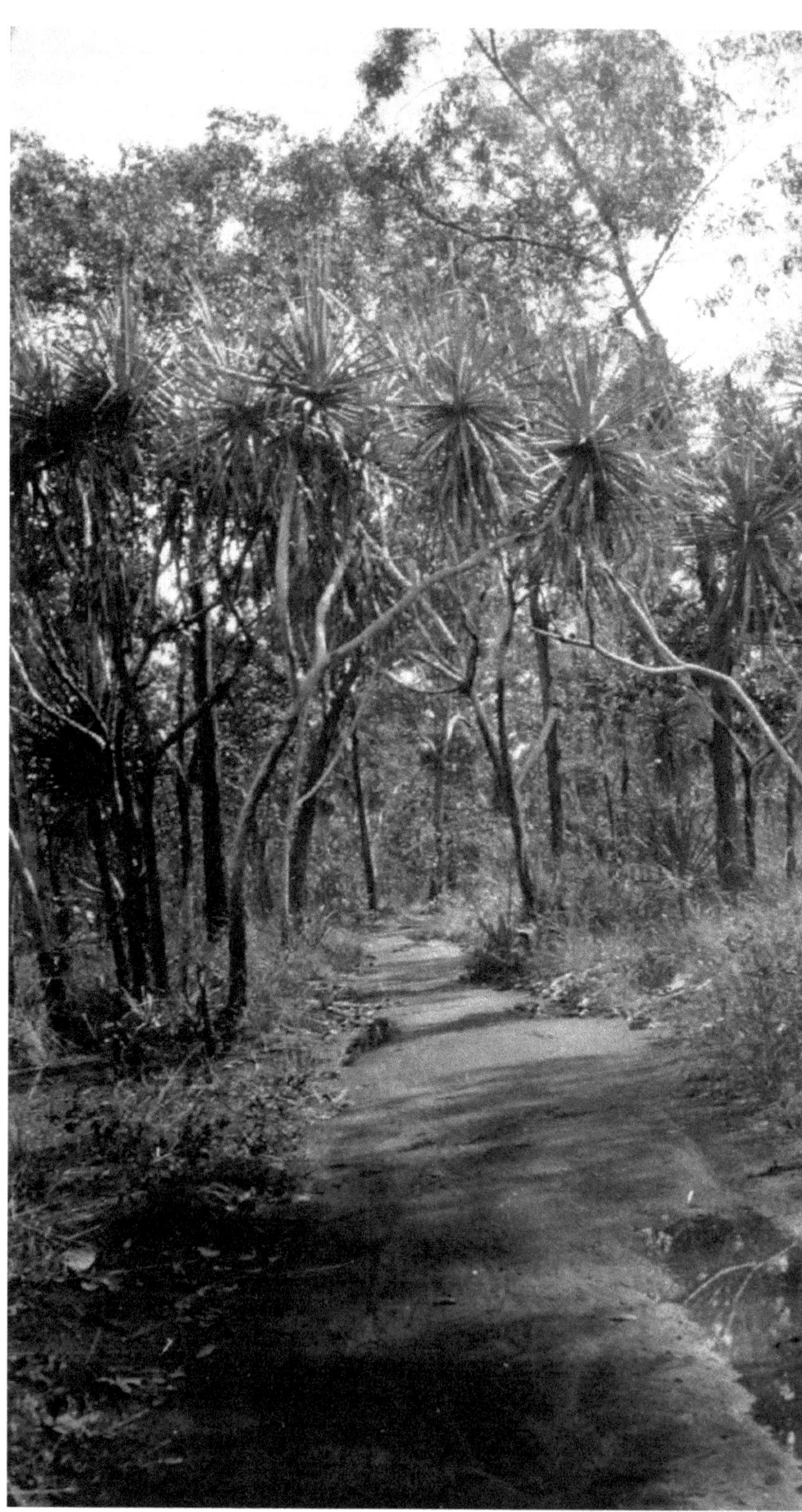

Rapid Creek road, c1930. (Unknown, NTAS, Charles Wilson Collection, NTRS 3335 Item 164.)

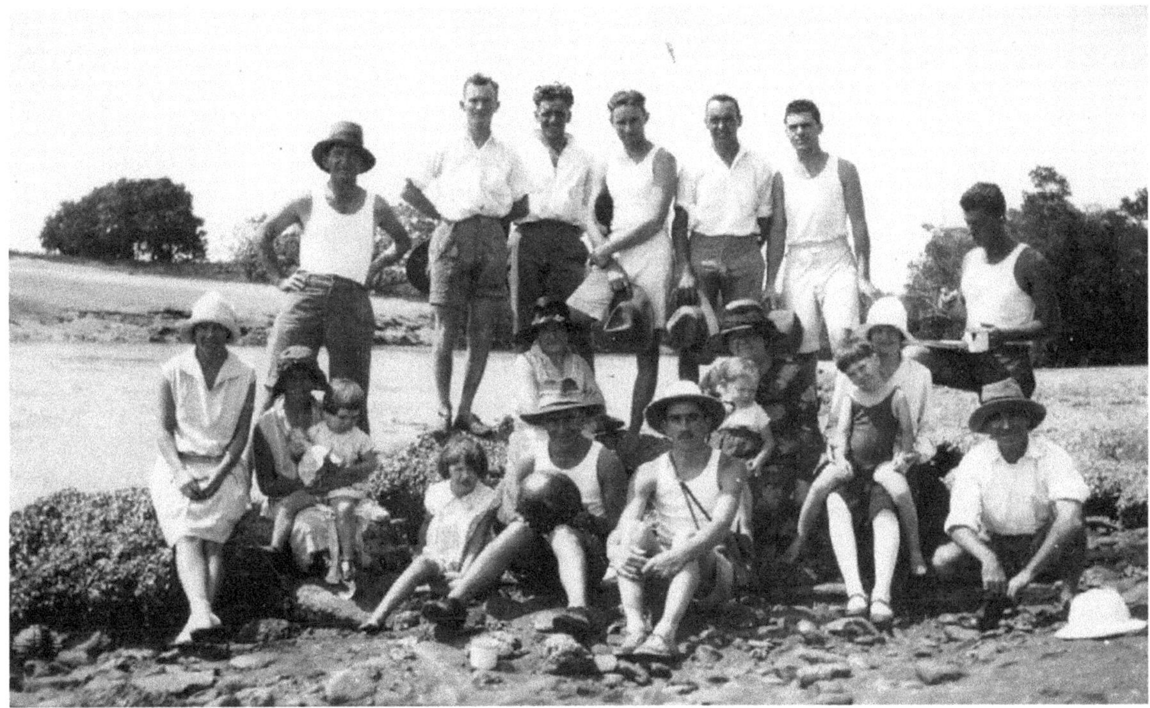

Rapid Creek picnic, c1930. (Unknown, NTAS, Charles Wilson Collection, NTRS 3335 Item 94.)

available for sale. Agricultural blocks were also sold on the western side of the peninsula. By the mid-1950s the Aralia Street shops were established and the Nightcliff shopping centre on Progress Drive followed soon after in 1958.

By 1960 the population of the Nightcliff and Rapid Creek area had grown to nearly 1,500. The Nightcliff camp, the centre of post war Nightcliff development, was removed during the 1960s and the land sold as residential blocks. The growth in the area resulted in the establishment of the Nightcliff Primary School (1961), the Rapid Creek Primary School in (1964) and Nightcliff High School (1970). The establishment of a drive-in theatre (1964), swimming pool (1967) and the Nightcliff Sports Club (1969) were further sign of the commercial and social development of the area.

A sign that the demographic and geographic centre of Darwin was gradually shifting towards the northern suburbs was the development of new institutions in the area. Construction of the Darwin Community College, the predecessor of the Northern Territory University and Charles Darwin University, began on its Casuarina Campus in 1972 and was opened in March 1974. The college was renamed the Darwin Institute of Technology in 1984. Nearby, Casuarina Square shopping centre, 14 Kilometres north of the CBD, opened in 1973. Casuarina High School also opened in 1973. Construction of Casuarina Hospital on Rocklands Drive, Tiwi, was also well under way in 1974 but Darwin's northern development was stopped in its tracks by Cyclone Tracy.

Cyclone Tracy hit the suburbs of Nightcliff and Rapid Creek particularly hard. A government audit found that out of 1,206 houses only 58 had survived the cyclone intact and 550 were totally destroyed.[12] Casuarina was also devastated by Tracy. Casuarina High School provided shelter for over 5000 displaced people in the days following the Cyclone.[13]

The reconstruction of Darwin post Cyclone Tracy gave the city its current character. The northern suburbs mushroomed around

12 Barter. *From Wartime Camp to Garden Suburb*, p.53.
13 De La Rue. *A Stubborn city: Darwin 1911-1978*, p.199

Darwin Airport. Casuarina Hospital became operational 20 May 1980. In 1982 the hospital was renamed Darwin Hospital and following Royal Assent, Royal Darwin Hospital on 10 January 1984.

In May 1990 the Federal Airports Corporation commenced construction of new airport terminal buildings on the northern side of Darwin Airport. Opened on 14 December 1991, the new terminal bought the airport closer to the majority of the population in the northern suburbs. It was also the end of an era with the closure of the old Darwin terminal with its links back to World War II.

Darwin's continues to grow along the coast with suburban development closing in on Lee Point. Darwin Airport is almost completely surrounded by residential and commercial suburbs. Casuarina shopping centre is the retail shopping centre of Darwin. The Charles Darwin University has continually developed its Casuarina Campus since its establishment and now has a Darwin Waterfront campus that may be augmented by an additional campus in the Darwin CBD. The Nightcliff foreshore and Casuarina Coastal Reserve are amongst Darwin's most used public parks. Few other capitals in the world can boast a turtle hatchery on a city beach. Few remnants remain of World War II when Darwin's beaches were covered in barbed wire and other entanglements awaiting a Japanese invasion. Retaining the balance of history and the environment while providing access to Darwin's growing population will be a continuing challenge for the city into the future.

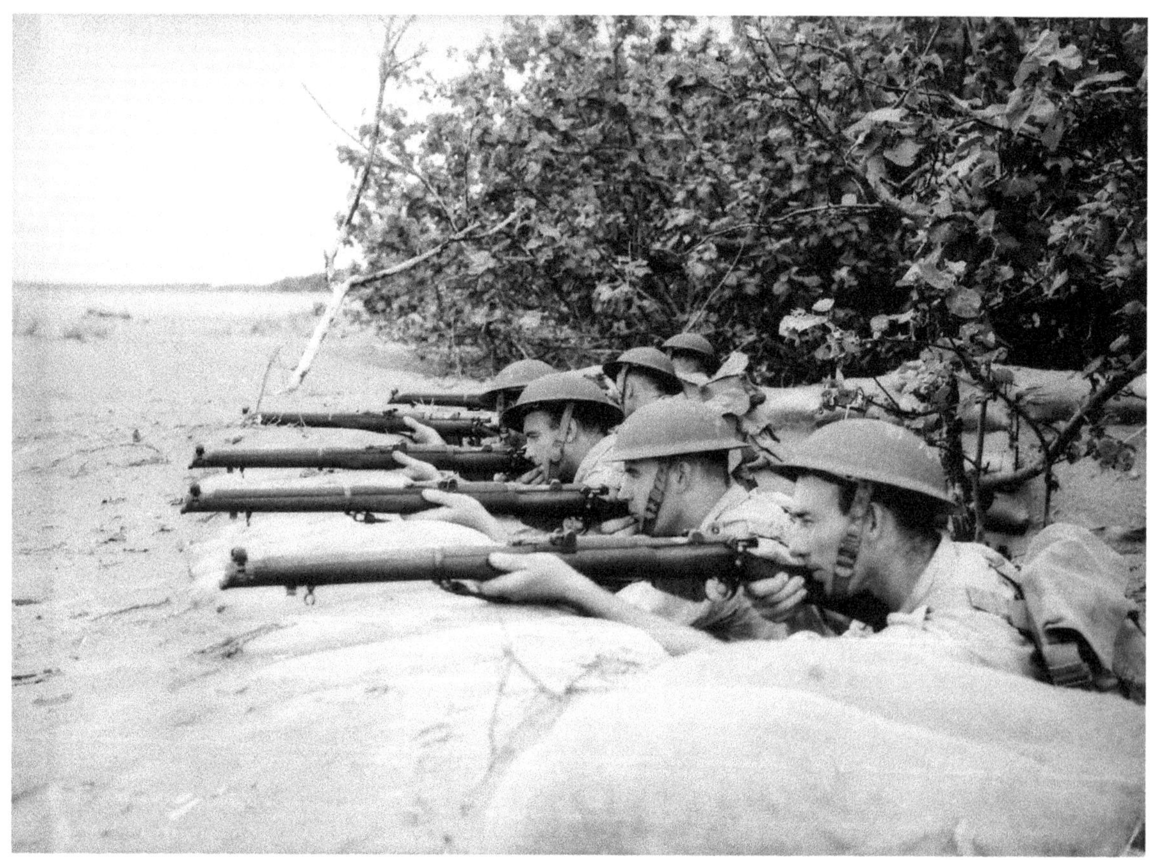

Darwin coastal defences, rifle trench, Lee Point, 25 January 1941. (Unknown, AWM, Photograph, 005352.)

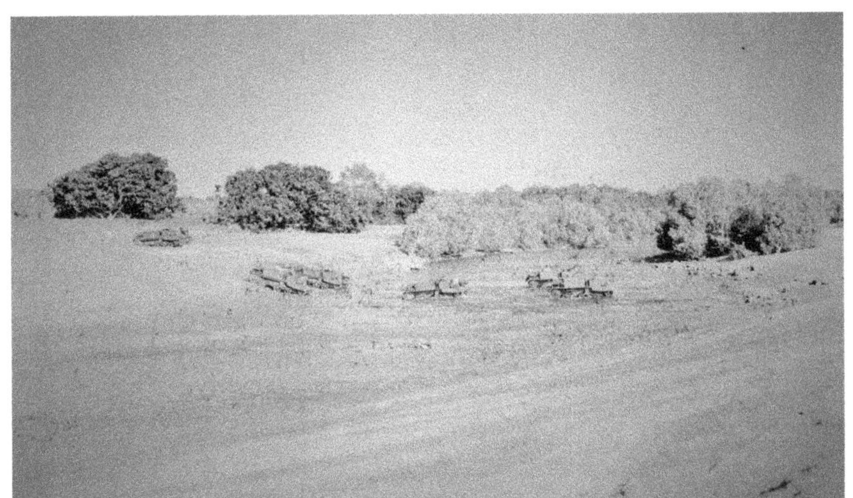

Two Bren gun carrier sections crossing Rapid Creek, 21 January 1941. (Pearse, R.G., AWM, Photograph, 005342.)

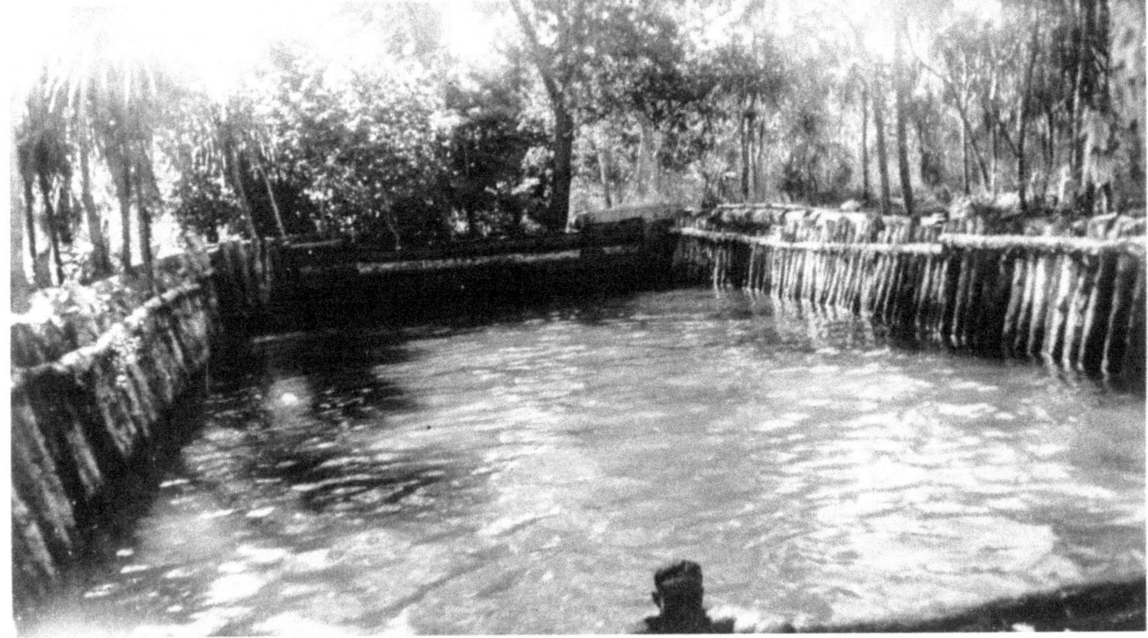

RAAF swimming pool on Rapid Creek, April 1942. (Unknown, NTL, A.F. Fleetwood Collection, PH0546/0008.)

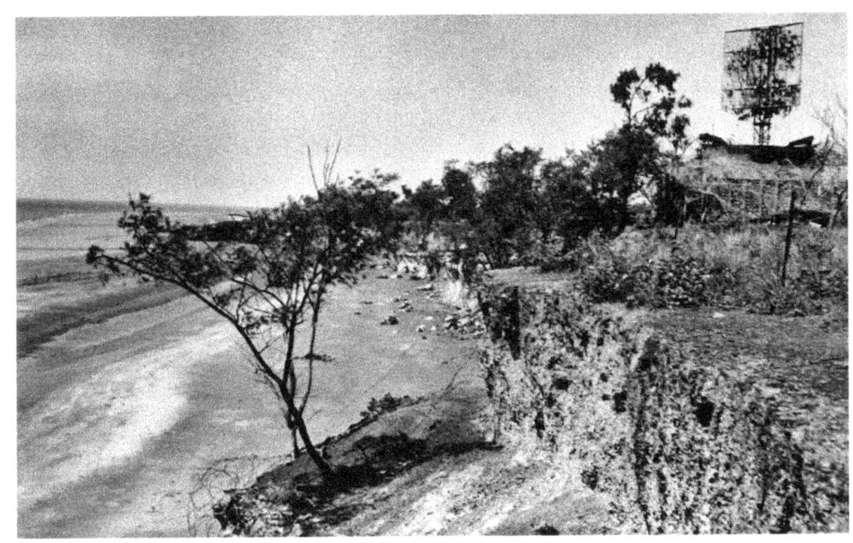

Darwin's first radar station on Dripstone Cliffs, 1942. Note the camouflage to resemble a tree. (Unknown, AWM, Photograph, NWA0979.)

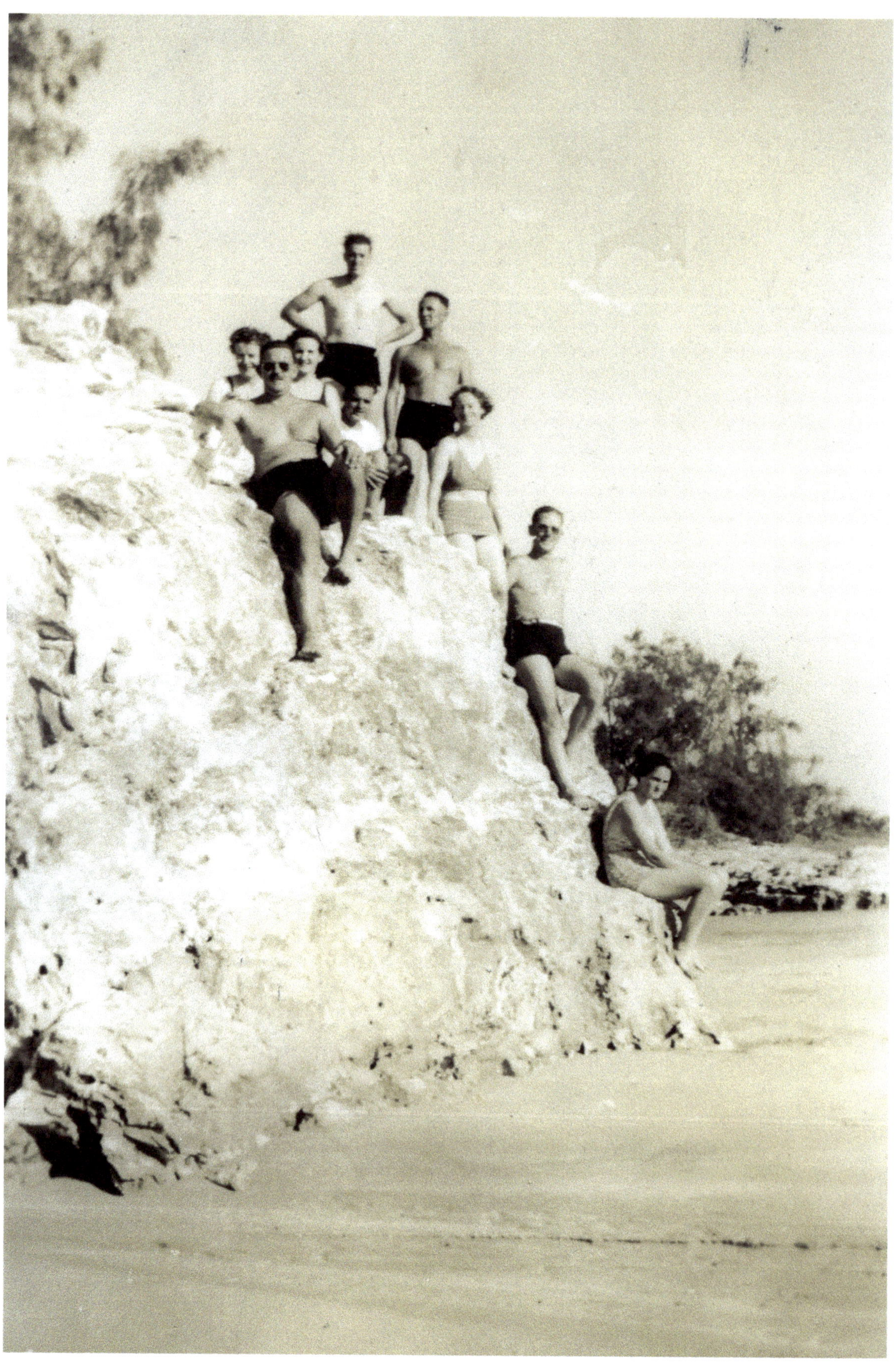

Casuarina Beach, 1 January 1944. Group from 107 Australian General Hospital. (Unknown, NTL, Tilson Collection, PH0779/0011.)

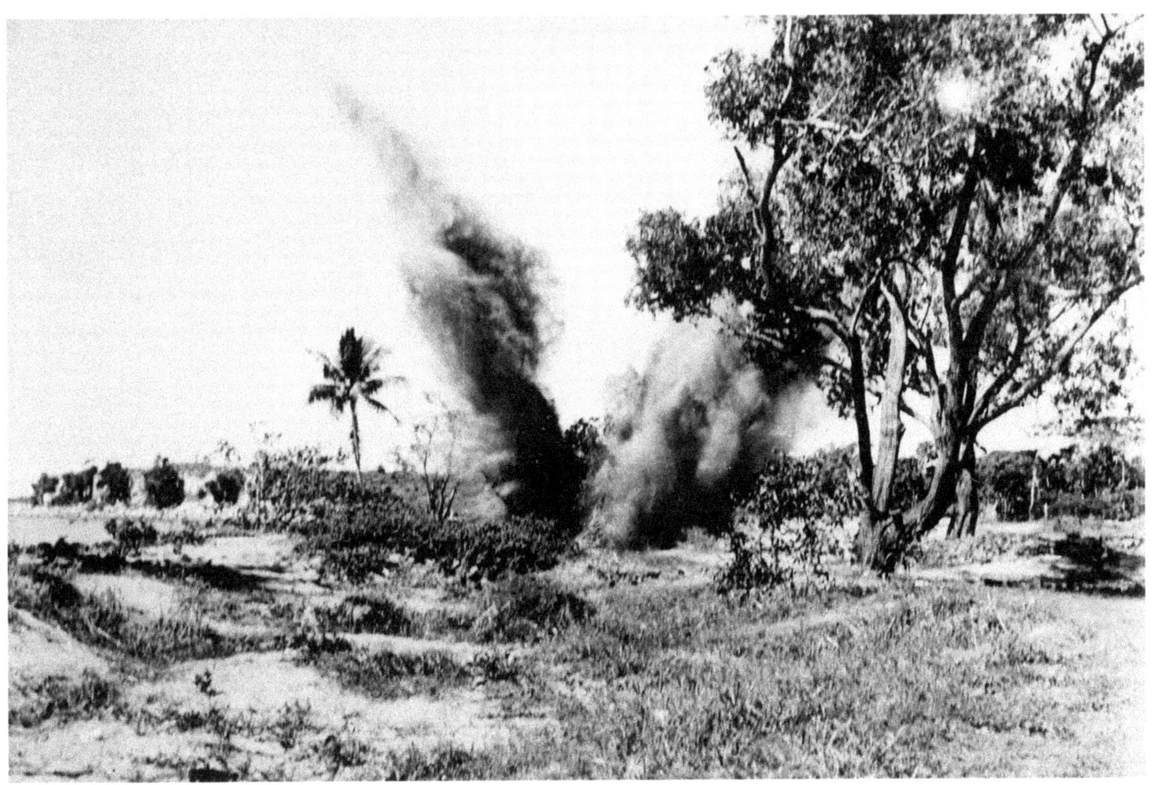

Military exercises, Casuarina Beach, 7 February 1944. (Unknown, AWM, Photograph, 016548.)

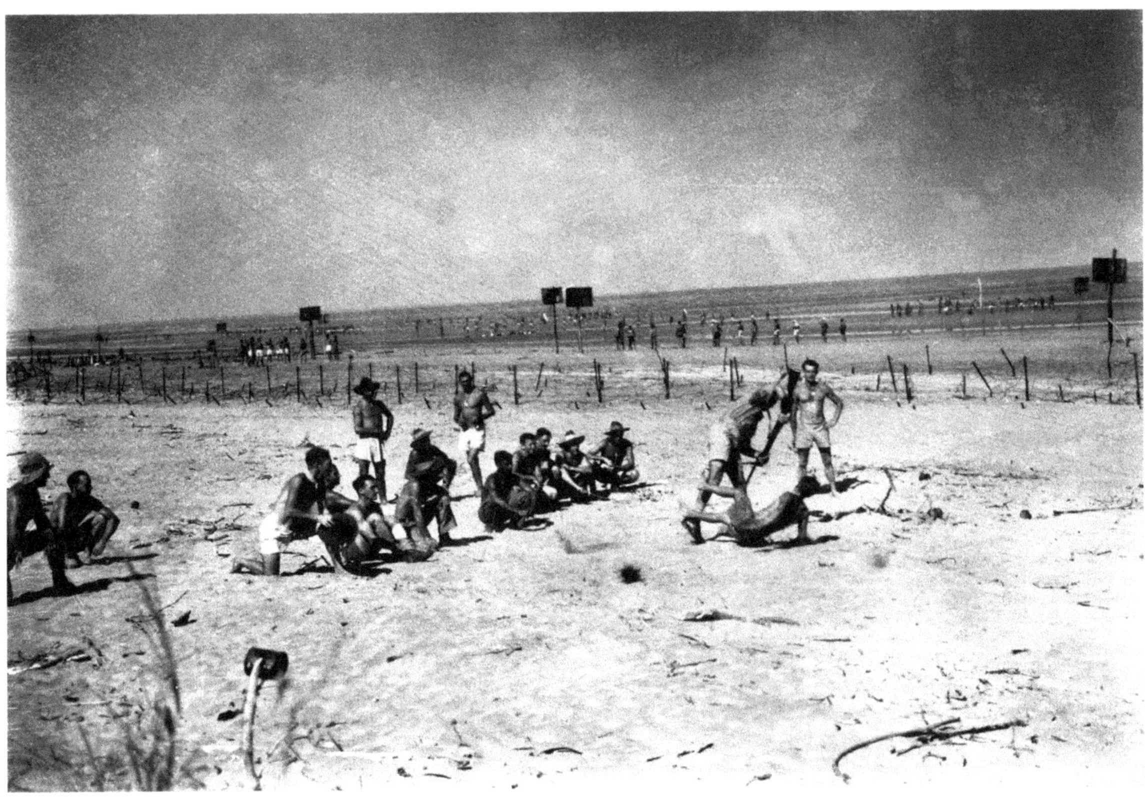

Military training & recreation, Lee Point, 13 October 1944. Note the basketball courts on the beach and the activities into the distance at low tide. (Unknown, AWM, Photograph, 081475.)

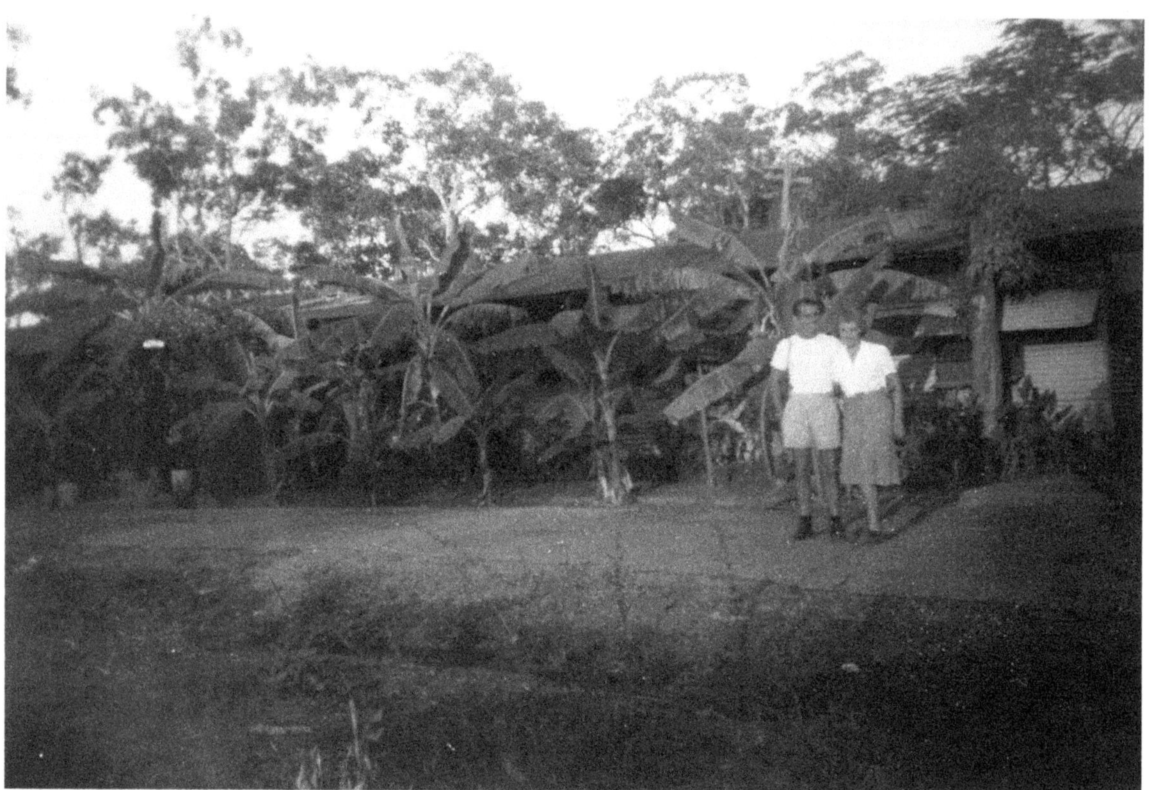

Ex army huts turned into flats, Nightcliff Camp, c1946. (Harford, B.P., NTAS, B.P. Harford Collection, NTRS 1299 Item 225.)

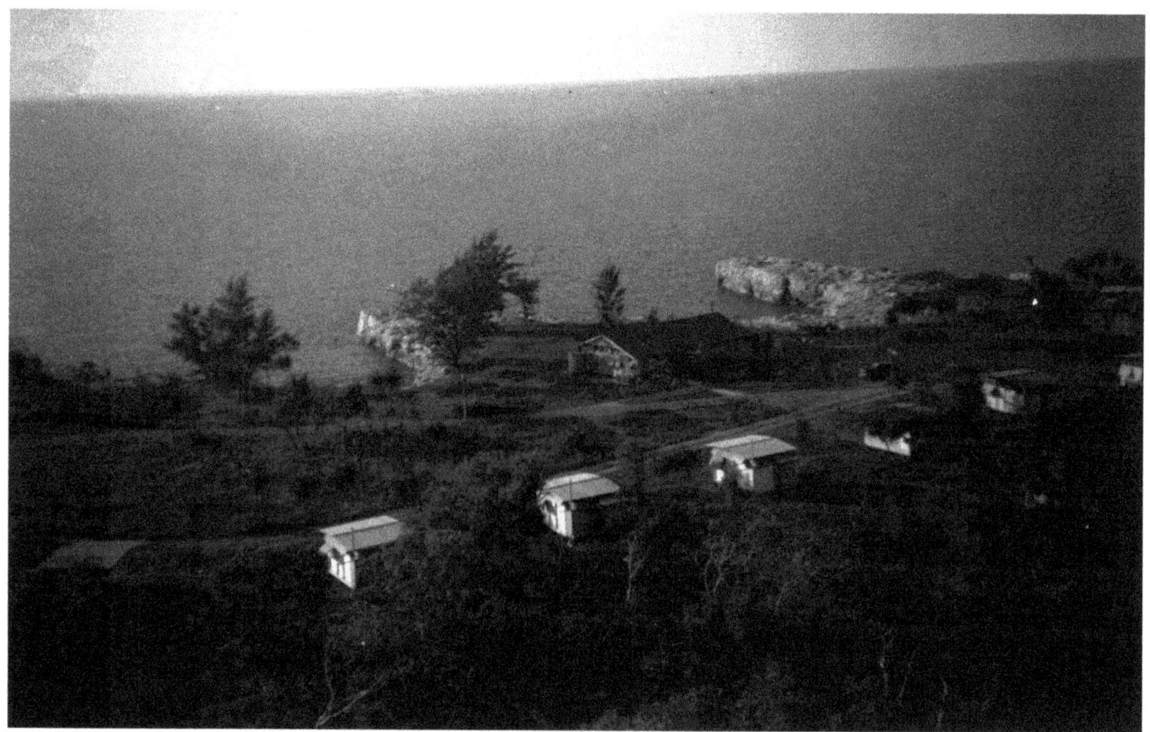

Ludmilla Guest House & Huts, Nightcliff, 1950. Photo taken from the RAAF radar tower. Later this would be known as the Sea Breeze Hotel. (Harford, B.P., NTAS, B.P. Harford Collection, NTRS 1299 Item 257.)

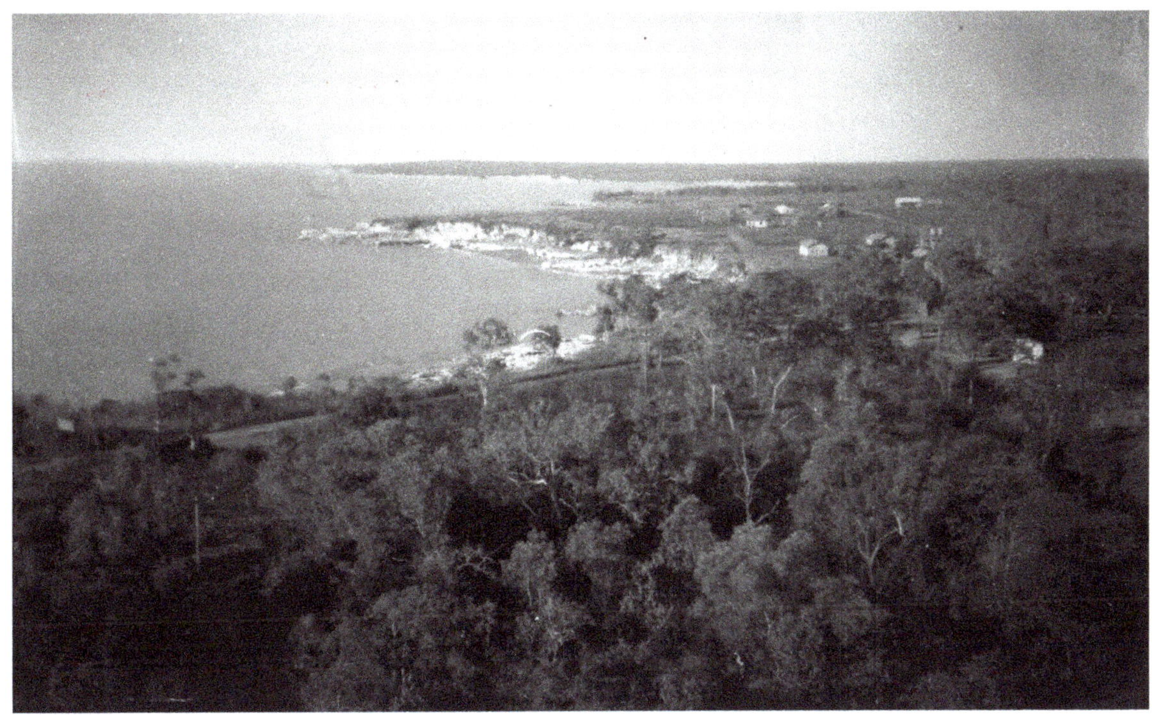

Nightcliff from the RAAF radar tower, c1950. (Harford, B.P., NTAS, B.P. Harford Collection, NTRS 1299 Item 226.)

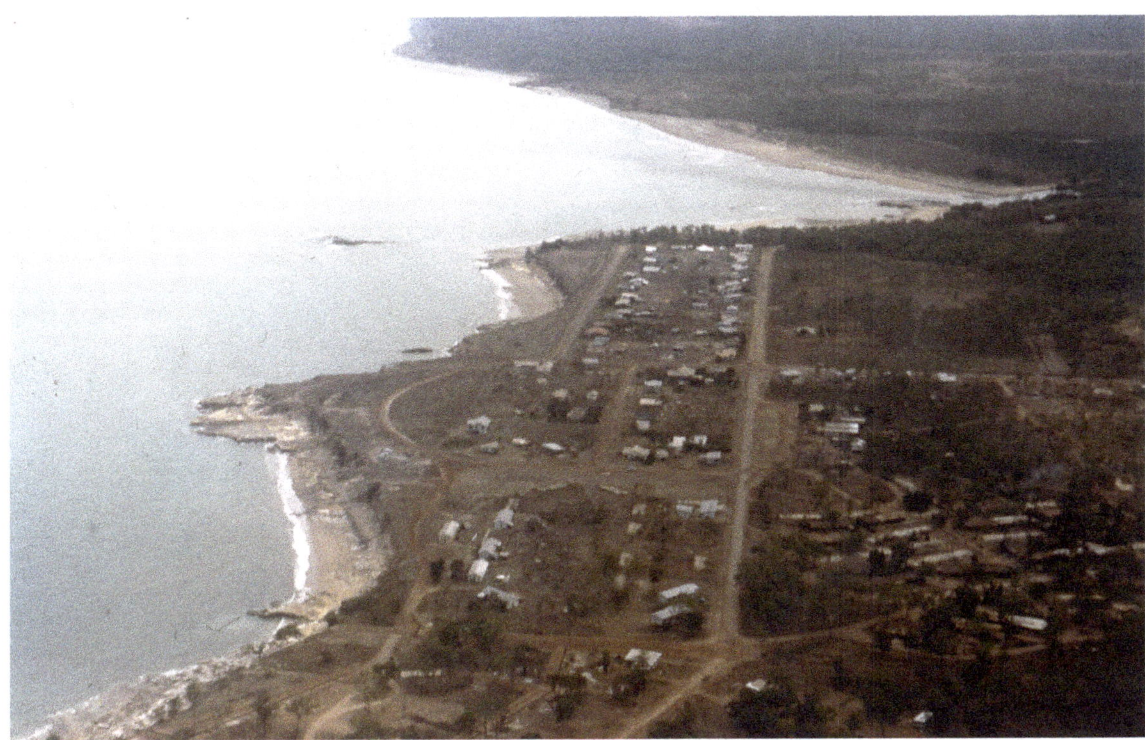

Nightcliff looking towards Rapid Creek on the right. Aralia Street in the centre, 1960. (Unknown, NTL, Howard Truran Collection, PH0406/0572.)

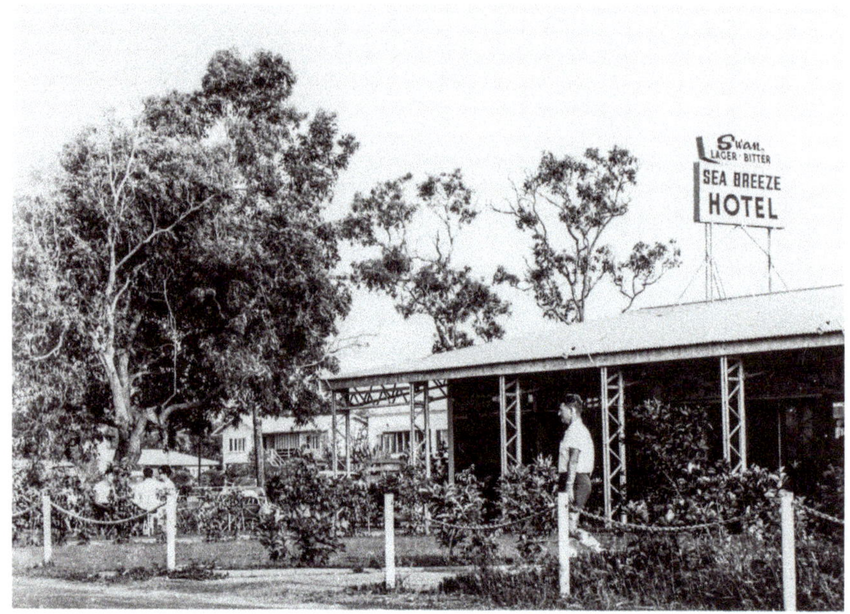

Sea Breeze Hotel, Nightcliff, c1965. (Unknown, NTL, Northern Territory Government Photographer Collection, PH0093/0079.)

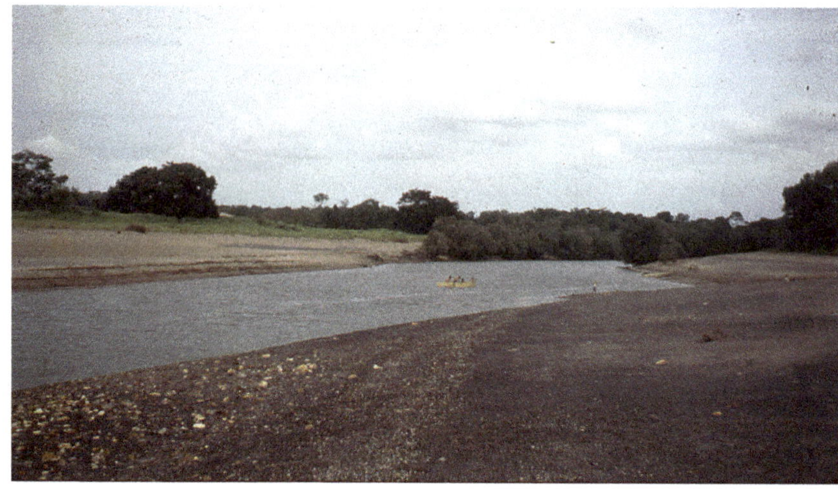

Rapid Creek, c1967. (Graham, H., NTAS, H. Graham, Collection, NTRS 3406/P1 Item 66.)

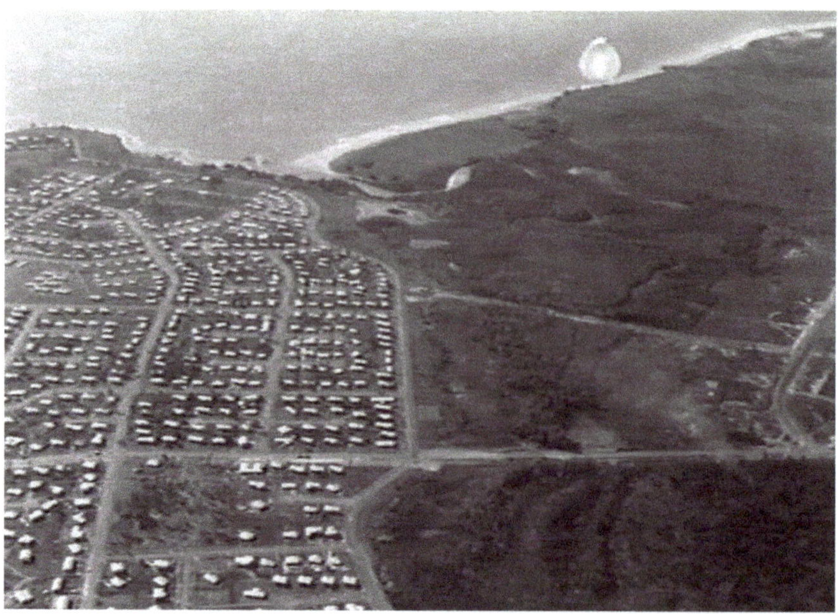

Rapid Creek, 1967. (Unknown, NTL, NTG Dpt of Lands Collection, PH0139/1842.)

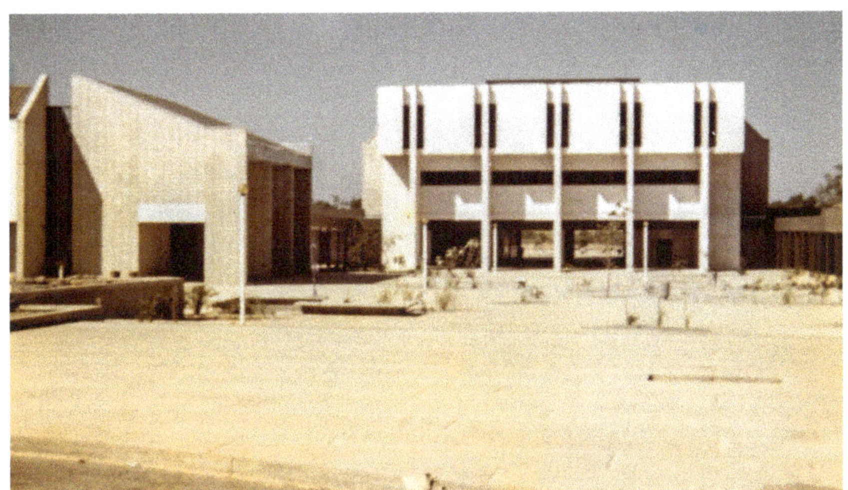

Darwin Community College, 1974. (Cheater, G., NTL, Darwin 1974-1975 Collection, PH0042/0029.)

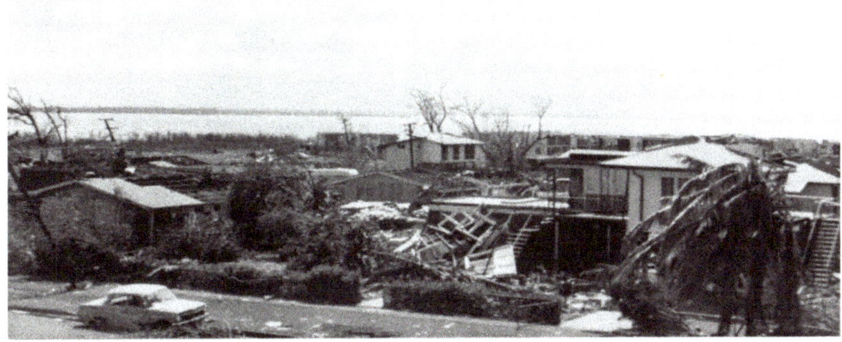

Nightcliff looking westward after Cyclone Tracy, 1974. (Unknown, NTL, B. Biddlecombe Collection, PH0610/0015.)

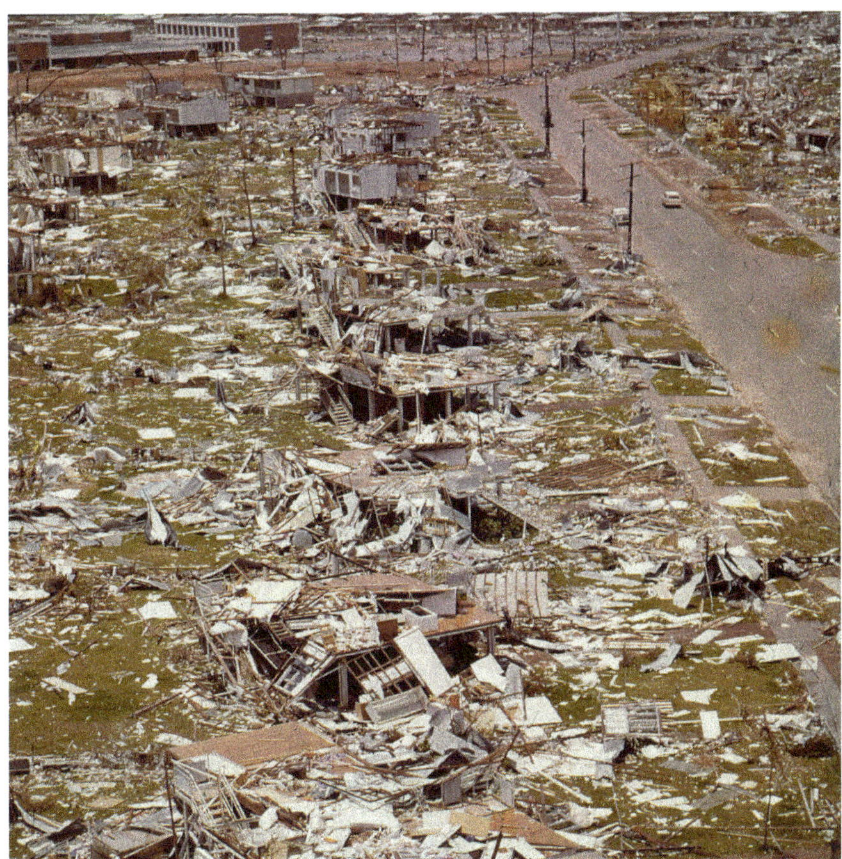

Parer Street looking towards Casuarina High School post Cyclone Tracy, 1975. Taken from Parer Street water tower. (Unknown, NTAS, GPC, NTRS 3822-P2 Cyclone slide 1.)

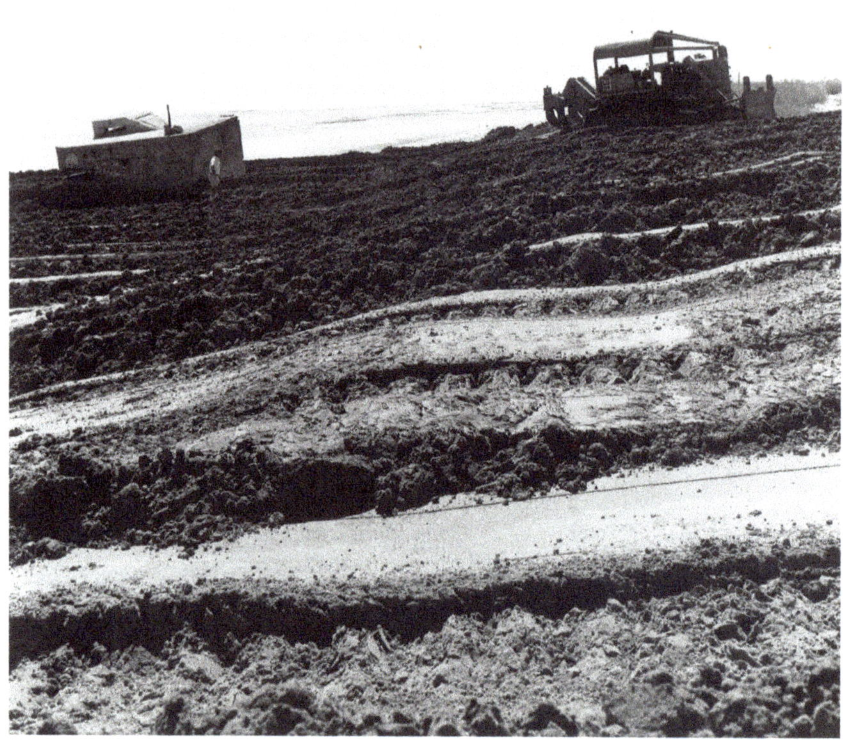

HD 16 Bulldozer undertaking reclamation works on the Casuarina Beach 'Free Beach Zone' near World War II machine gun emplacement, 1977. Sand erosion was experienced along the entire length of the Casuarina Coastal Reserve. (Unknown, NTAS, NTG Reserves Board, 024_NTRS 1234 Folder 9 Casuarina Coastal Reserve - HD16 bulldozer.)

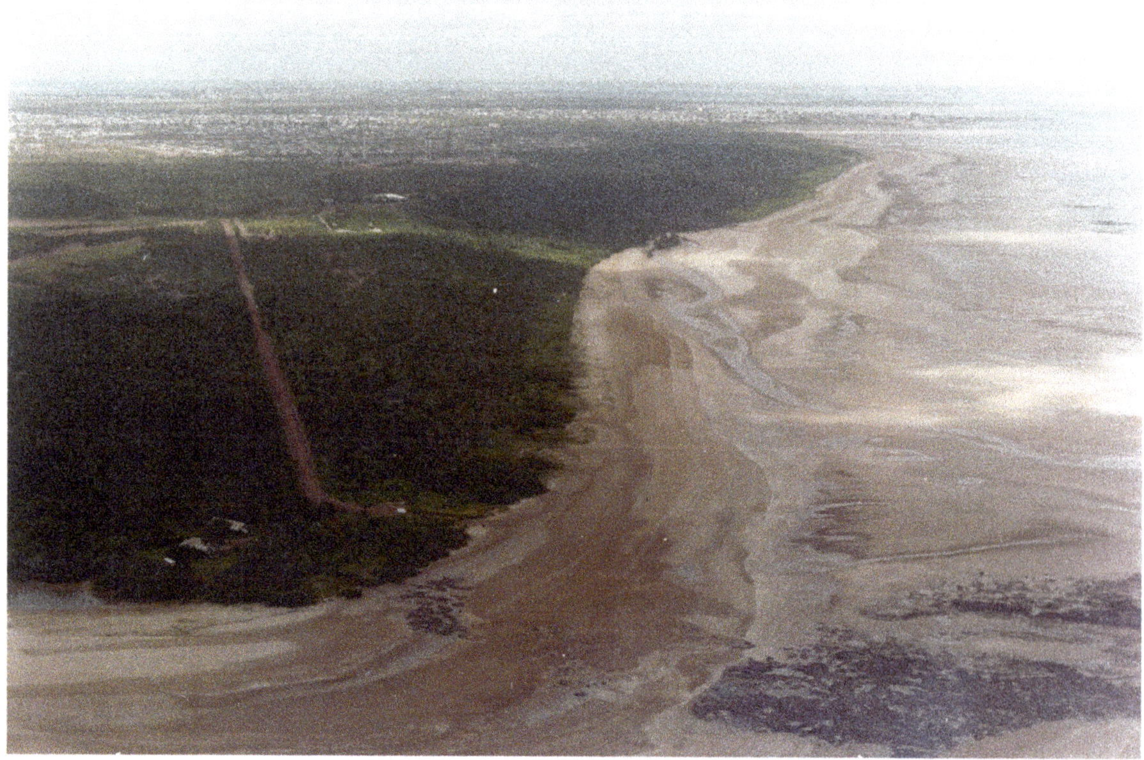

Lee Point, looking along Casuarina Beach towards Nightcliff, 1977. (Unknown, NTAS, NTG Reserves Board, NTRS 1234/NTG Reserves Brd/Folder 9/ Cas Coastal Res/Aerial/1977.)

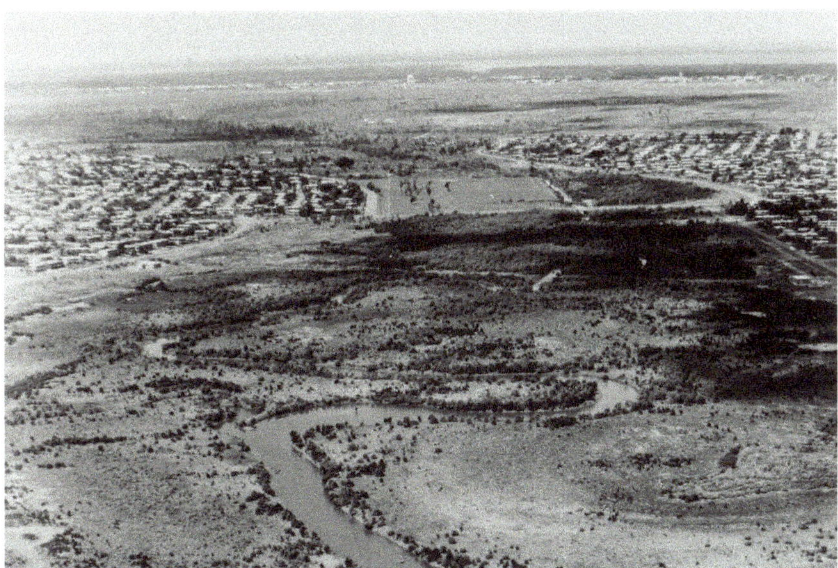

Rapid Creek, 1979. (Unknown, NTL, Northern Territory Government Photographer Collection, PH0095/0213.)

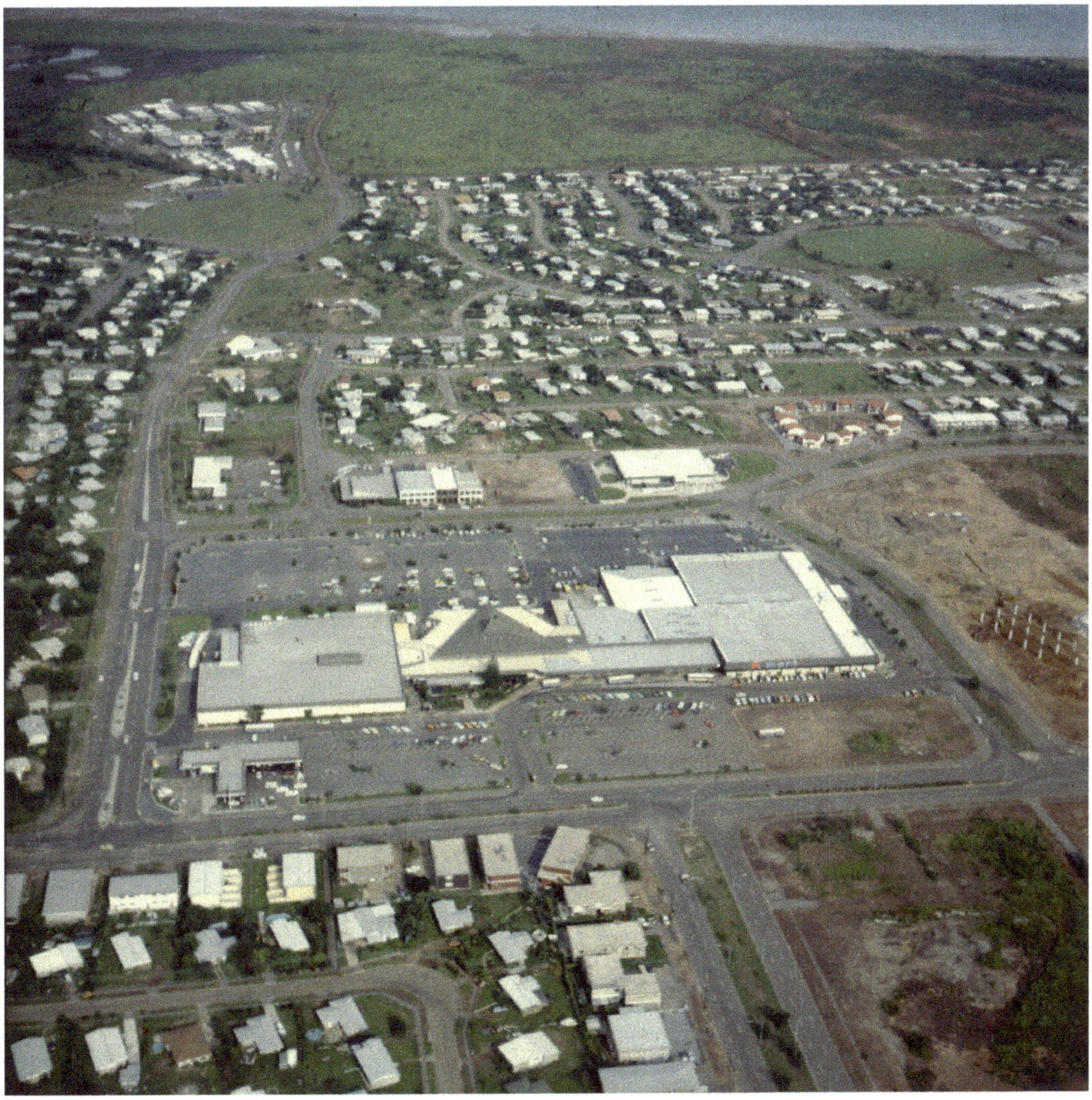

Casuarina Shopping Centre, 1980. (Unknown, NTAS, GPC, NTRS 3822-P3 Darwin Aerials Suburbs Slide 29.)

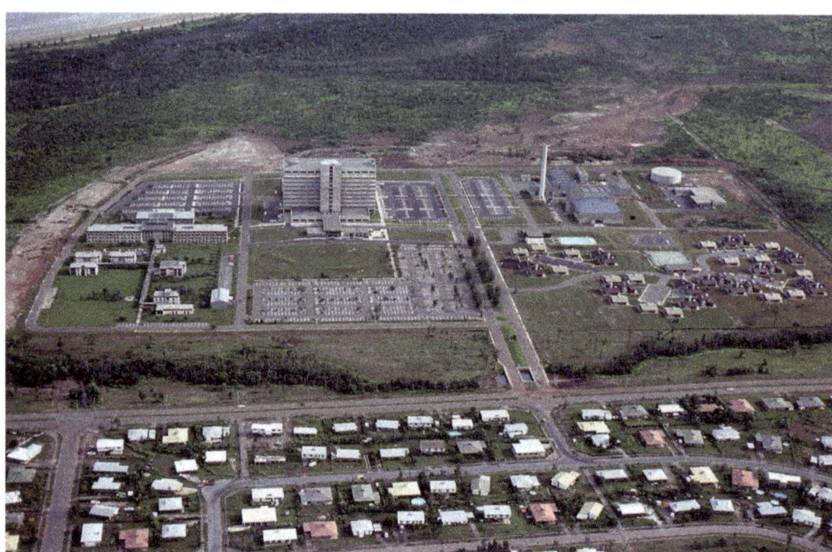

Casuarina Hospital, 1980. (Wiedemann, A., NTAS, GPC, NTRS 3822-P3 Hospital Slide 21.)

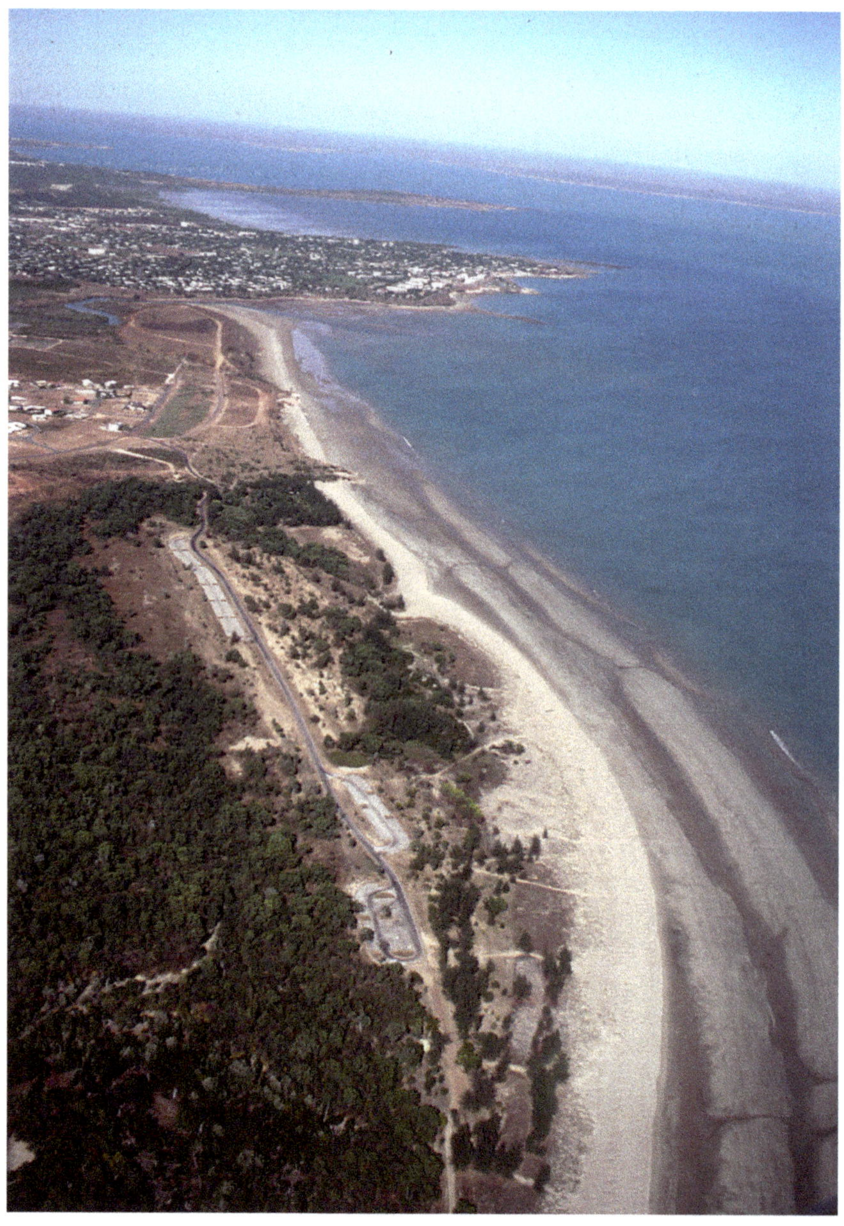

Casuarina Beach, 1985. (Wiedemann, A., NTAS, GPC, NTRS 3822-P3 Beaches & Coastlines Slide 39.)

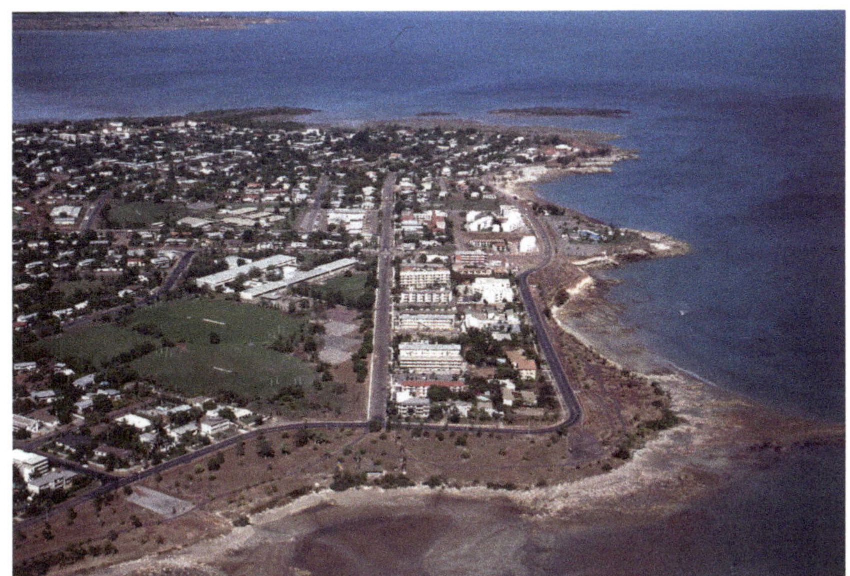

Nightcliff, 1985. (Wiedemann, A., NTAS, GPC, NTRS 3822-P3 Darwin Aerials Suburbs Slide 344.)

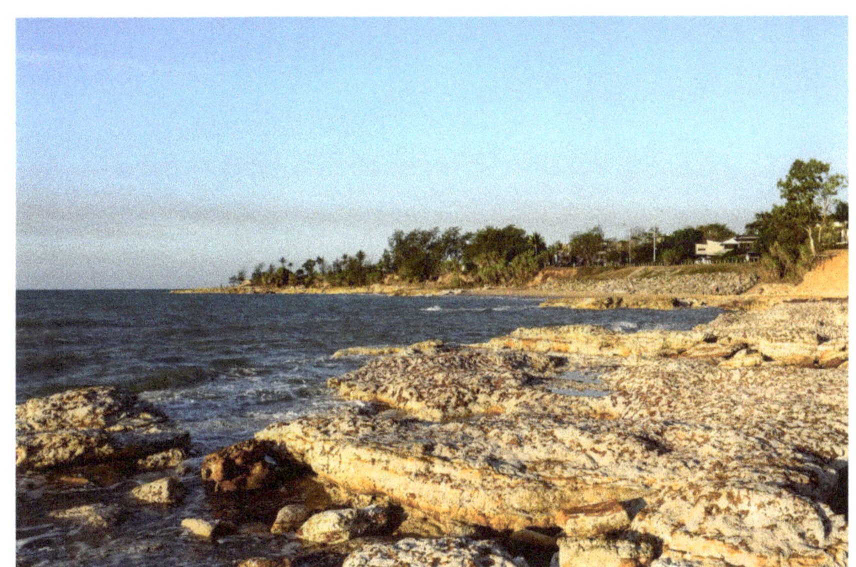

Nightcliff foreshore, 2017. (Martin, R., Matthew Stephen, Personal Collection, NightcliffForeshore_13.)

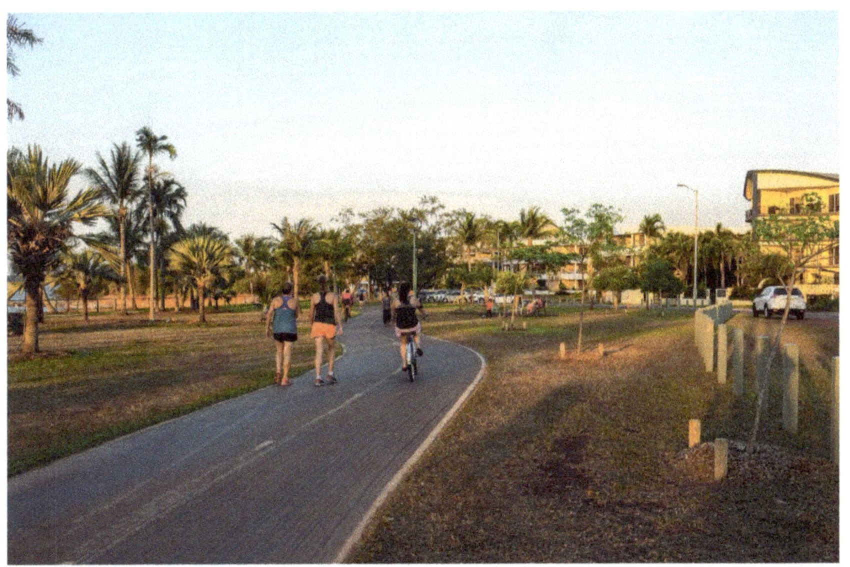

Nightcliff foreshore, 2017. (Martin, R., Matthew Stephen, Personal Collection, NightcliffForeshore_32.)

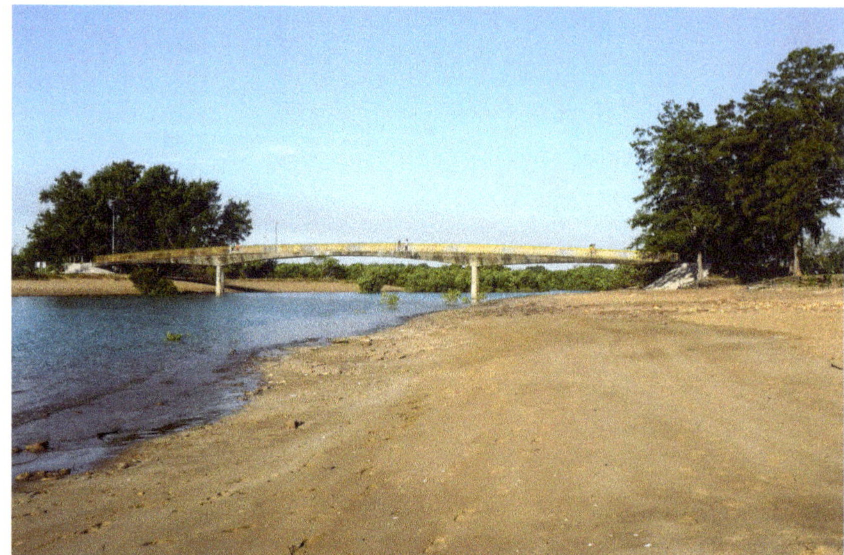

Rapid Creek bridge, 2016. (Martin, R., Matthew Stephen, Personal Collection, RapidCreek_07.)

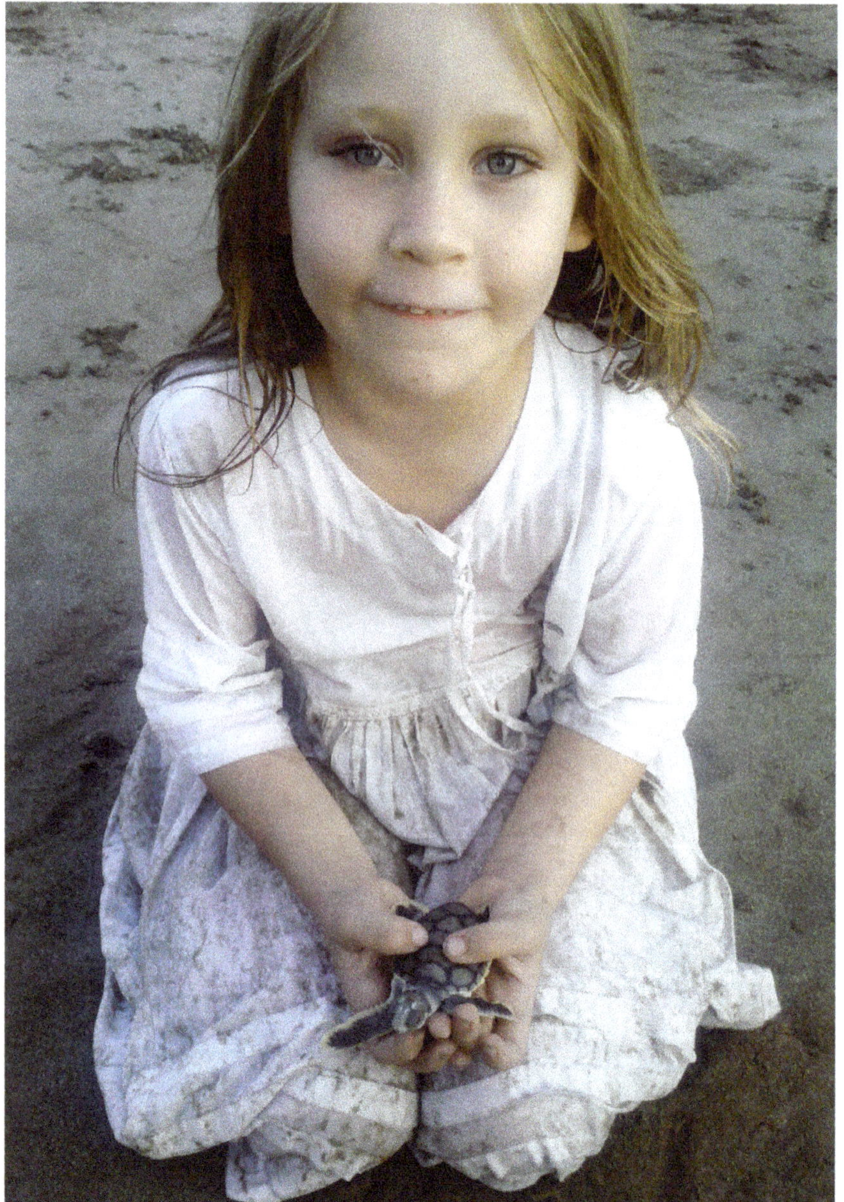

The photographer's daughter enjoying a turtle release on Casuarina Beach, 2017. Casuarina Beach is one of the few capital city beaches in the world where turtles still nest. NT Government Parks and Wildlife Rangers monitor and protect the nests to increase the survival rate of the hatchlings. The public release program raises conservation awareness. (Martin, R., Matthew Stephen, Personal Collection, Turtle Beach_01.)

Bibliography

Archival and Library Sources

National Archives of Australia (NAA)

F1, 1952/851.

Northern Territory Archives Service (NTAS)

NTRS 226, Oral History Interviews,

Caudle, Garnet Rex, Oral history interview by Dallas Cooper, TS 26, Adelaide, 1982.

Greentree, Geoffery, Oral history interview by Heather Chandler, TS 673, Darwin, 1992.

Richards, Joe, Oral history interview by Tresna Shorter, TS 602, Darwin, 1990.

Tilson Clyde, Oral history interview by Peter Thomas, TS 341, Melbourne, 1983.

State Library of the Northern Territory (NTL)

Catchlove, Edward Napoleon Buonaparte. 'Dairies 1870–73.' Volume 1 and 2. 1870.'

Parliamentary and Government Sources

Commonwealth

Bureau of Transport Economics, *Provision of General Cargo Facilities at the Port of Darwin*, Canberra: Commonwealth of Australia, 1976.

Department of Science, Bureau of Meterology, *Report on Cyclone Tracy December 1974*, Canberra: Australian Government Publishing Service, 1977.

Northern Territory Administrators' Reports

Northern Territory. Report of the Acting Administrator, Melbourne: Government Printer for Victoria, 1911.

Northern Territory, Report of the Administrator, 1918, Melbourne: Government Printer for Victoria, June, 1919.

Spencer, Baldwin. 'Preliminary Report on the Aboriginals of the Northern Territory.' In *Northern Territory of Australia, Report of the Administrator*, CPP, 45/1913, Melbourne: Government Printer of Victoria, 1913.

Northern Territory Government

Department of Natural Resources, Environment, The Arts and Sport, Heritage Branch, *Sue Wah Chin Building*, 2010.

Heritage Branch. *Brown's Mart, Fact Sheet*, 2011.

Heritage Branch, *George Brown Botanic Garden's Fact Sheet*, 2011.

Heritage Branch. *Kahlin Compound: Background Historical Information*, November, 2009.

Heritage Branch. *Town Hall Ruins, Fact Sheet*, 2011.

Heritage Branch, *Lyon' Cottage, Fact Sheet*, 2011.

Heritage Conservation Services, WWII *sites, Casuarina Coastal Reserve, Heritage Assessment Report*, 2011.

Pederson, Barbara-Mary. *Naval Oil Tanks The Esplanade Darwin*, Northern Territory Government, Heritage Branch, 2001.

Wells, Samantha. *Origin of a City: Garrmalang, Palmerston, Darwin*, Illustrated map produced for Northern Territory Library exhibition, Origin of a City, September 2014.

South Australia

Northern Territory Administrators' Reports

Northern Territory. Report of the Government Resident for the Year, March, 1881.

Northern Territory, Government Resident, Report on the State of the Northern Territory, August 1881,

Northern Territory. Report of the Government Resident for the Year, Quarterly Report, No.53B, 1884.

Northern Territory. Report of the Government Resident for the Year, Half-Yearly Report, No. 351/86, June & December, 1886.

Personal Communications

Austin, Maisie. Personal communication, email, 23 September 2018.

Chin, Darlene. Personal communication, email, 27 July 2018.

Cramp, Norm. Personal communication, email, 1 August 2018.

Crotty, David. Curator, QANTAS Heritage Collection, Personal communication, email 31 July 2018.

Elix, Bob. Personal communication, 12 January 2016.

Felsenthal, Ian. Personal communication, 17 November 2015.

Howison, Bernadett. DCC Records Administrator, Personal communication, email, 12 January 2018.

Howison, Bernadett. DCC Records Administrator, Personal communication, email, 9 May 2018.

Howison, Bernadett. DCC Records Administrator, Personal communication, email, 10 May 2018.

Parker, P. ABC Broadcaster, (Technical Specialist), Personal communication, email, 18 May 2018.

Unpublished Papers

Brian, Bernie. 'The Northern Territory's One Big Union. The Rise and Fall of the North Australian Workers' Union 1911–1972,' PhD Thesis, Charles Darwin University, 2001.

Phelts, Bev. 'Switching On: Darwin's History of Electricity Supply,' Honours Thesis, Northern Territory University, 1997.

5DR (8DR) Darwin at Blake Street, 1946-1965.

Public Photograph Collections

Citations; Title (Creator / Institution / Collection / Reference number)

AWM	Australian War Memorial
LNSW	Library of New South Wales
MAGNT	Museum and Art Gallery of the Northern Territory
NAA	National Archives of Australia
NLA	National Library of Australia
NTAS	Northern Territory Archives Service
NTAS	GPC Government Photographers Collection
NTDIPL	Northern Territory Department of Infrastructure Planning and Logistics
NTL	Northern Territory Library
QHC	QANTAS Heritage Centre
SLSA	State Library of South Australia
SLV	State Library of Victoria
SLWA	State Library of Western Australia
Tourism NT	Northern Territory Tourism

Published Work

Internet/Electronic Resources (www.)

Commonwealth

Australian Broadcast Corporation

Roussos, Eleni and Purtill, James. Cyclone Tracy: ABC reporter Bill Fletcher had the story but no way of telling the nation, 2014. http://www.abc.net.au/news/2014-12-23/reporter-recounts-struggle-in-studio-after-cyclone-tracy/5898004_accessed19052018.

National Archives of Australia, Research Guides.

Administration of the Northern Territory during the war.

http://guides.naa.gov.au/records-about-northern-territory/part1/chapter4/4.4.aspx_accessed05082017.

Civil Unrest & the Darwin Rebellion
http://guides.naa.gov.au/records-about-northern-territory/part1/chapter2/2.7.aspx_accessed18012018.

Electoral Franchise and Territorians
http://guides.naa.gov.au/records-about-northern-Territory/part1/chapter7/7.1.aspx_accessed26072018.

http://guides.naa.gov.au/records-about-northern-territory/part1/chapter7/7.1.aspx_accessed28042018.

Land of Opportunity: Australia's Post War Reconstruction.
http://guides.naa.gov.au/land-of-pportunity/chapter17/_accessed21022018.

Preparing for War
http://guides.naa.gov.au/records-about-northern-territory/part1/chapter4/4.1.aspx_accessed 05082017.

Navy: Serving Australia with Pride
Forster, Pat. Fixed Naval Defenses of Darwin Harbour 1939-1945. http://www.navy.gov.au/history/feature-histories/fixed-naval-defences-darwin-harbour-1939-1945_accessed03082017.

Thiem, David. Semaphore 75 Years After the Bombing of Darwin a Story Reconciliation Hope and Peace. http://www.navy.gov.au/media-room/publications/semaphore-semaphore-75-years-after-bombing-darwin-story-reconciliation-hope_accessed24092018.

Northern Territory Housing
http://guides.naa.gov.au/records-about-northern-territory/part2/chapter11/11.2.aspx_accessed10032018.

Northern Territory Government (NTG)

Heritage Register

Boab Tree, Cavenagh Street
http://www.ntlis.nt.gov.au/heritageregister/f?p=103:302:2537232805465703::NO::P302_SITE_ID:88.

Gardens Road Cemetery
http://www.ntlis.nt.gov.au/heritageregister/f?p=103:302:2398993336605962::NO::P302_SITE_ID:364_accessed08022018.

Peels Well
http://www.ntlis.nt.gov.au/heritageregister/f?p=103:302:992406632251484::NO::P302_SITE_ID:221_accessed19012018.

Ludmilla Salt Pans
http://www.ntlis.nt.gov.au/heritageregister/f?p=103:302:3603145453069543::NO::P302_SITE_ID:891_accessed26052017.

Old Admiralty House
http://www.ntlis.nt.gov.au/heritageregister/f?p=103:302:3423862410194865::NO::P302_SITE_ID:83_accessed11012018.

Place Names Register

Bullocky Point
http://www.ntlis.nt.gov.au/placenames/view.jsp?id=11365_accessed31012018.

Cavenagh Street
http://www.ntlis.nt.gov.au/placenames/view.jsp?id=5599_accessed26012018.

Fannie Bay
http://www.ntlis.nt.gov.au/placenames/view.jsp?id=12765_accessed02032018.

Mindil Beach
http://www.ntlis.nt.gov.au/placenames/view.jsp?id=15114_accessed26012018.

Myilly Point
http://www.ntlis.nt.gov.au/placenames/view.jsp?id = 16062_accessed25012018.

Parap
http://www.ntlis.nt.gov.au/placenames/view.jsp?id = 2074_accessed02032018.

Smith Street
http://www.ntlis.nt.gov.au/placenames/view.jsp?id = 7876_accessed 24012018.

Other

Austin, Maisie. *A Brief History of Basketball In Darwin*. http://websites.sportstg.com/assoc_page.cgi?c = 1-166-0-0-0&sID = 329248_accessed13092018.

Christ Church Cathedral
http://christchurchcathedral.org.au/about/history/

The Civil Aviation Historical Society & Airways Museum
http://www.airwaysmuseum.com/Australia%20&%20Back%20Cobham%20 1926.htm_accessed18042018.

Chung Wah Society
http://www.chungwahnt.asn.au/index.php?page = about-the-chung-wah-society_accessed11082017.

ConocoPhillips
http://www.conocophillips.com.au/who-we-are/our-history/_accessed06042018.

The Darwin Sailing Club
https://dwnsail.com.au/the-club/our-history/_accessed27042018.

Darwin Trailer Boat Club
https://dtbc.com.au/_accessed27042018.

Darwin Waterfront
Annual Report 2006-07.

https://www.waterfront.nt.gov.au/darwin-waterfront-corporation/publications/_accessed 03082017.

https://www.waterfront.nt.gov.au/darwin-waterfront-corporation/publications/

Barnes, Koolpinyah. *DarwinWaterfront: Heritage and Cultural Trail*

https://www.waterfront.nt.gov.au/.../DarwinWaterfront_Heritage_broA2_Feb12-web.pdf_accessed 08062017.

Bombing of Darwin: The Wharf
http://www.waterfront.nt.gov.au/darwin-waterfront-precinct/history/bombing-of-darwin-the-wharf/_accessed08062017.

Darwin Bowls and Social club
http://www.darwinbowlsclub.com.au/site/index.cfm?fuseaction = display_main&OrgID = 16135_accessed09052018.

Forster, Pat., Fixed Naval Defenses of Darwin Harbour 1939-1945. http://www.navy.gov.au/history/feature-histories/fixed-naval-defences-darwin-harbour-1939-1945_accessed16032018.

Inpex
http://www.inpex.com.au/our-projects/ichthys-lng-project/ichthys-in-detail/project-overview/_06042018.

Parap Village
http://parapvillagemarkets.com.au/2017/index.php/events-and-activities/historical-parap_accessed10032018.

Sydney Museums
Flying Boats: Sydney's Golden Age of Aviation.

https://sydneylivingmuseums.com.au/stories/flying-boats-sydneys-golden-age-aviation_accessed 03082018.

Newspapers

Army News, (AN) 1941-1946.

Canberra Times (CT) 1926-1995.

Centralian Advocate (CA) 1947 – Current.

The Cumberland Argus (TCA) 1950-1962.

The North Australian, (*NA*) 1883–1889.

The Northern Standard, (NS) 1921–1942, 1945–1954.

Northern Territory News, (NTN) 1952- Current.

Northern Territory Times and Gazette, (NTTG) 1873–1932.

South Australian Advertiser, (*SAA*) 1858-1889.

The South Australian Register (SAR) 1839-1990

Books and Journals

Books

Alcorta, Frank. *Darwin Rebellion 1911–1919*. Darwin: History Unit, Northern Territory University Planning Authority, 1984.

Austin, Maisie. *The Quality of Life: A Reflection of Life in Darwin during the Post-War Years*. Darwin: Colemans, 1992.

Barter, Leith. *From Wartime Camp to Garden Suburb*, Darwin: Historicial Society of the Northern Territory, 1994.

Bauman, Toni. *Aboriginal Darwin: A guide to Exploring Important Sites of the Past & Present*. Canberra: Aboriginal Studies Press, 2006.

Bisa, Debora. *Remember Me Kindly: A History of the Holtze Family in the Northern Territory*, Darwin: Historical Society of the Northern Territory, 2016.

Boldand, Judy. Fannie Bay History and Heritage Society. *Know Where You Stand: Fannie Bay and Surrounds Darwin's Industrial Heartland*. Darwin: Fannie Bay History and Heritage Society, 2016.

Carment, David. *Looking at Darwin's Past: Material Evidence of European Settlement in Tropical Australia*, Darwin: North Australia Research Unit, Australian National University, 1996.

Carment, David. *Australia's Northern Capital: A Short History of Darwin,* Darwin: Historical Society of the Northern Territory, 2005.

Carment, David. Christine Edward, Barbara James, Robyn Maynard, Alan Powell & Helen J Wilson. *Northern Territory Dictionary of Biography*. Revised Edition. Charles Darwin University Press, 2008.

Cramp, Norman, S. *The Silence of the Guns: A History of Fortress Darwin, East Point and The Darwin Military Museum*, Darwin: Darwin Military Museum, 2016.

Daly, Mrs Dominic D. *Digging, Squatting, and Pioneering Life in the Northern Territory of South Australia*. London: Samson Low, Marston, Searle & Rivington, 1887.

De La Rue, Kathy. *The Evolution of Darwin: A History of the Northern Territory's Capital City During the Years of South Australian Administration*. Darwin: Charles Darwin University Press, 2004.

De La Rue. *A Stubborn City: Darwin 1911-1978*. Darwin: Historical Society of the Northern Territory, 2017.

Donovan, P F. *At the Other End of Australia: The Commonwealth and the Northern Territory 1911–1978*. Brisbane: University of Queensland Press, 1984.

Donovan, P F. *A Land Full of Possibilities: A History of South Australia's Northern Territory*. Brisbane: University of Queensland Press, 1981.

Geddes, C.F. *Darwin Returned Services League (RSL), A Concise History of its Conception and Development*. Kent Town: Avonmore Books, 2013.

Gibson, Eve. *Beyond the Boundary – Fannie Bay 1869-2001*. Darwin: Historical Society of the Northern Territory, 2011.

Hall, Timothy. *Darwin 1942: Australia's Darkest Hour*. Melbourne: Mandarin, Australia, 1989.

Harvey, J.Y. *The Never Never Line: The Story of the North Australia Railway Line.* Melbourne: Hyland House, 1987.

Jones, Timothy. *The Chinese in the Northern Territory*. Darwin: Northern Territory University Press, 1997.

Masson, Elsie R. *An Untamed Territory: The Northern Territory of Australia*. London: Macmillian and Co, Ltd, 1915.

Powell, Alan. *Far Country: A Short History of the Northern Territory.* Melbourne: Melbourne University Press, 2000.

———. *The Shadow's Edge: Australia's Northern War*. Revised edition. Darwin: Charles Darwin University Press, 2007.

Raynor, Robert J. *Darwin Detachment: A Military and Social History*. Wollongong: Rudder Press, 2002.

Searcy, Alfred. *In Australian Tropics*. Facsimile edition, Adelaide: George Robertson, 1909, Carlisle: Hesperian Press, 1984.

Smith, I. & Nicholls, W. *Darwin Golf Club: 1930-2013, The First 83 Years*. Darwin: Smith, I. & Nicholls, W, 2013.

Yee, Glenice, *Through Chinese Eyes: The Chinese Experience in the Northern Territory, 1874-2004*. Parap: Glenice Yee, 2006.

Journals

Boland, Judy. 'Bullocky Point History.' *Darwin High School, Year Book*. Darwin: 2000, 131-136.

Dewar, Mickey. 'A Market for Memories: Understanding Public History at the Mindil Beach Site in Darwin.' http://www.nma.gov.au/audio/transcripts/NMA_Dewar_20080527.html_ accessed23032018.

Forrest, Yvonne. 'Memories of Frog Hollow: A School Ahead of its Time.' Darwin, Historical Society of the Northern Territory, Occasional Paper, 3/2007.

Mitchell, Thomas. 'Bullocky Point: From Market Garden to Museum and Art Gallery.' *Journal of Northern Territory History*, Historical Society of the Northern Territory, No. 12, 2001: 27-36. p.27.

Stanton, Sue., 'The Australian Half-Caste Progressive Association: The Fight For Freedom and Rights in the Northern Territory.' *Journal of Northern Territory History*, Historical Society of the Northern Territory, 1993, Vol 4, 37-46.

Tumarkin, Maria. 'First as a tragedy, second as a farce: traumascapes, memory and the curse of indifference' [online]. *Overland*, No. 175, Winter 2004: 22-26.

Woodrow, Brian. 'Opening Night at 5DR,' *The Broadcaster*, July, 1992, 18.

About the Author

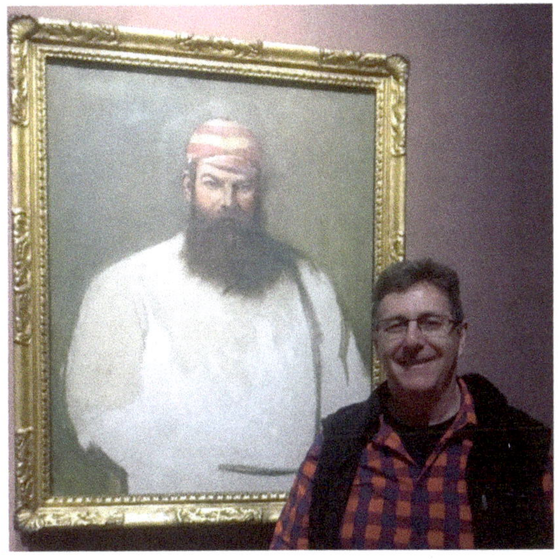

Matthew Stephen has lived in Australia's Northern Territory since 1987. Until 2001 he worked largely in the field of Aboriginal tertiary education. Since 2007 he has been the Manager of the Northern Territory Archives Service Oral History Unit. He completed his PhD at Darwin's Charles Darwin University in 2009. His thesis is entitled 'Contact Zones: Sport and Race in The Northern Territory, 1869–1953'. A revised version of his thesis with the same title was published by Charles Darwin University Press in 2010. In 2011 he undertook museum studies in the conservation of photographs and photographs in the museum environment at Edith Cowen University, Western Australia.

Since January 2015 Matthew has split his time between the Northern Territory Archives Service and working as a freelance historian. He has undertaken projects for the Darwin City Council and the Northern Territory Government Department of Sport and Recreation He has also contributed to numerous family history projects. He continues his research into Northern Territory history with a particular interest in oral history and photography and why some stories are 'often told' while others are 'forgotten'. These themes are explored in book 'Colour Bar: Remembering and Forgetting Northern Territory Football 1916 to 1955' published by the History Society of the Northern Territory in 2015. In 2018 *Wanderers Centenary History, 1917-2017* was released. Matthew has a passion for Northern Territory social history and has a number of projects in the pipeline that will be published in coming years. For more information see

https://www.nthistoryandmemory.com.au

www.ingramcontent.com/pod-product-compliance
Lightning Source LLC
LaVergne TN
LVHW060617110826
845154LV00003B/101
* 9 7 8 0 6 4 6 9 9 2 3 0 3 *